Biomechanics and Medicine in Swimming

Proceedings of the Fourth International Symposium
of Biomechanics in Swimming
and the Fifth International Congress
on Swimming Medicine
held in Amsterdam, The Netherlands
June 21-25, 1982

International Series on Sport Sciences

Volume 14

Series Editors:

Richard C. Nelson, Ph.D.
Chauncey A. Morehouse, Ph.D.

The Pennsylvania State University
University Park, Pennsylvania, USA

BIOMECHANICS AND MEDICINE IN SWIMMING

Scientific Editors:

A. Peter Hollander, Ph.D.

*University of Amsterdam
and Free University
Amsterdam, The Netherlands*

Peter A. Huijing, Ph.D.

*Free University
Amsterdam, The Netherlands*

Gert de Groot, Ph.D.

*University of Amsterdam
and Free University
Amsterdam, The Netherlands*

Human Kinetics Publishers, Inc.
Champaign, Illinois 61820

Production Directors
Margery Brandfon
Kathryn Gollin Marshak

Editorial Staff
Dana Finney
Peg Goyette

Typesetters
Sandra Meier
Carol McCarty

Text Layout
Lezli Harris

Cover Design
Jack Davis

Library of Congress Catalog Number
83-81474

ISBN
0-931250-50-1

Printed in the United States of America.

Human Kinetics Publishers, Inc.
Box 5076, Champaign, Illinois 61820

Contents

ELECTROMYOGRAPHY

PROPULSION, DRAG, AND EFFICIENCY

OXYGEN CONSUMPTION, METABOLISM, AND TRAINING EFFECTS

Congress Organization

The International Congress of Biomechanics and Medicine in Swimming was organized by the Royal Dutch Swimming Association, Faculty of Physical Education of the Free University of Amsterdam, and Netherlands Association of Sports Medicine.

Scientific Committee

J.P. Clarys
N.R. van Dam
G. de Groot
G.P.H. Hermans
A.P. Hollander
P.A. Huijing
J. Jiskoot
W.L. Mosterd

Organizing Committee

N.R. van Dam (chairman)
G. de Groot
G.P.H. Hermans
A.P. Hollander
W.L. Mosterd
R.H. Rozendal
H.M. Rozendal-Kraay
A. Vermeulen
C. de Vos

Sponsors

The sponsorship of this Congress was under the auspices of the Medical Committee of the Fédération Internationale de Natation Amateur (FINA), International Society of Biomechanics (ISB), and Working Group Biomechanics of Sport of the International Council of Sport and Physical Education (ICSPE-UNESCO).

Sponsors and Exhibitors

The congress has received financial support from the following organizations:

Amersfoortse Verzekeringen
Coca-Cola Company
Dutch Swimming Coaches Association
Faculty of Physical Education of the Free University
Free University at Amsterdam
International Business Machines (IBM)
Ministry of Cultural Affairs, Recreation and Social Welfare
Ministry of Education
Ministry of Health
Municipality of Amsterdam
Netherlands Association of Sports Medicine
Netherlands Heartfund
Royal Dutch Airlines (KLM)
Royal Dutch Swimming Association
Speedo Knitting Mills
Sportfondsen Nederland
Stichting Medisch Wetenschappelijk Onderzoek Zwemmen en
    Hartrevalidatie
Stichting Sporttotalisator

Exhibitors

BV Boekhandel H. de Vries
De Melkindustrie Veghel B.V.
Lode Instrumenten BV

Preface

Biomechanics and Medicine in Swimming contains a selection of papers presented at the International Congress of Biomechanics and Medicine in Swimming held in Amsterdam, The Netherlands, June 21 to 25, 1982. Since the organizers of this Congress succeeded for the first time in combining the International Congress on Swimming Medicine and the International Symposium of Biomechanics in Swimming into one congress, this volume should be considered as *Swimming Medicine V* and *Swimming IV* of the International Series on Sport Sciences.

We believe that work of high quality has been brought together in this volume and it has been the extraordinary interrelationship of several of the articles which has led us to write an editorial in an effort to increase the scientific and practical application of the information reported at this Congress. The editors wish to thank the contributors to this volume for their excellent cooperation in creating a high-standard work, as well as Chauncey A. Morehouse who, as Series Editor, supported our editorial efforts before, during and after the Congress and who, through very intensive cooperation, allowed us to take avantage of the resources of his enormous experience.

We expect that the work presented in this volume will have a considerable influence on the scientific and practical approach to swimming.

A. Peter Hollander
Peter A. Huijing
Gert de Groot

Biomechanics and Medicine in Swimming

Efficiency and Specificity of Training in Swimming: An Editorial

Peter A. Huijing, A. Peter Hollander, and Gert de Groot
Free University, Amsterdam, The Netherlands

Power Output and Efficiency

For years it has been generally accepted that total external power output of a swimmer can be calculated, assuming no velocity changes during the stroke and from stroke to stroke, according to the equation:

$$\dot{W} = \bar{D}_s \cdot \bar{v} \qquad (1)$$

where D_s (drag) is the resistive force exerted by water on the swimming body (diPrampero et al., 1974; Kemper et al., 1976; Holmér, 1978; Pendergast et al., 1977, 1978; Rennie et al., 1975). As the energy to overcome drag is one of the major expenditures in swimming, it is understandable why a great deal of attention has been given to this aspect. It has, however, been seldom recognized that not all of the external power the swimmer generates can be used for the swimmer's propulsion, as some power must flow to the water that is accelerated as the swimmer pushes against it (Holmér, 1974, 1975). This may be somewhat surprising because in the biological literature on the swimming of fish, it has been generally recognized that the power flow to the accelerated water should be included in the power bookkeeping (Alexander and Goldspink, 1977; Bone, 1974; Lighthill, 1969, 1970; Webb, 1971). Measurements in fish indicate that this fraction of total power may vary, depending on swimming speed, from 28% to more than 400% of the power invested in actual propulsion (Webb, 1971). This knowledge probably has not reached investigators of human swimming because of the relative inaccessibility of this literature to them.

One can estimate (according to Equations 2 and 3, which are shown later) that if the efficiency for converting chemical energy to total external mechanical energy is between 20-30% and the overall efficiency of swimming is 4% (diPrampero et al., 1974), the power flow to the water may be ca. 4-6 times as great as the power related to the swimming speed (Equation 1). The magnitude of this estimate indicates the importance of this concept. Van Ingen Schenau (1979, 1981; also, Toussaint et al., 1983, this volume) drew attention to this fact and also indicated that as a consequence, the calculations of human swimming efficiency were not good estimates for the efficiency of converting chemical energy into external power.

Theoretically, five levels of energy transfer (and thus efficiency) can be distinguished for swimming:

- the efficiency of the chemical reactions liberating the energy from the storage compounds (considering heat of activation, etc.)—metabolic efficiency;
- the efficiency of transducing this energy into mechanical energy (linking of cross bridges, etc.);
- the application of this mechanical energy toward the performance of internal work (stretching of tendons and other parts of the series elastic component);
- the delivery of external power; and
- the division of the external power into a propulsive part and a "loss" to the accelerated water.

For most physiological and biomechanical purposes, the first four levels cannot be identified separately, so that it is useful to combine them into one factor which we suggest should be called "muscular efficiency" (e_m). This muscular efficiency is equivalent to what is frequently called mechanical efficiency (e.g., Åstrand and Rodahl, 1977) of on-land activities such as cycling and running. Yet, it differs fundamentally from the efficiency of an isolated muscle doing external work, because it includes the energy expenditure of all the muscles performing isometric contractions. Remember that if oxygen consumption is used as an estimate of total energy liberated, the possibility exists that this variable will be underestimated because of anaerobic metabolism contributions. In such a case muscular efficiency will be overestimated.

The propulsion efficiency can be defined as:

$$e_p = \dot{W}_{swimmer} / (\dot{W}_{swimmer} + \dot{W}_{acc.\ water}), \qquad (2)$$

and thus equals the fraction of the total external power that is used for propulsion.

Total or overall efficiency can be defined as:

$$e_t = e_m \cdot e_p. \qquad (3)$$

For most on-land activities, the overall efficiency is equal to the muscular efficiency (i.e., $e_p = 1$) since the push-off is performed against the earth, which for all practical purposes is not accelerated, so that no power flows to it. In some on-land activities such as running in loose sand and cross-country skiing in powder snow, e_p will be smaller than 1. For rowing and flying the situation will be similar to swimming (e_p much smaller than 1).

Determining power flow to the water by studying the water movement is impractical if not impossible because of the very complicated hydrodynamics involved. However, if the force of propulsion is known and the velocity with which the propelling surface generating that force moves, the power transferred is by definition the scalar product of these two variables:

$$\dot{W} = \overline{F} \cdot \overline{v}. \qquad (4)$$

We must point out that the detailed kinematic analysis of Schleihauf et al. (1983, this volume) yields the necessary data for such calculations pertaining to the hand. Consultation with other contributors to this volume has led to the acceptance of these definitions and this nomenclature for the proceedings.

Specific Strength Training

From the literature one can compile indications that strength training is relatively specific, that is, improvement that may be gained is primarily connected with the function being trained. This means that static training, dynamic training, constant resistance training or variable resistance training increase predominantly static force (Berger, 1962; Dons et al., 1979; Petersen et al., 1961), dynamic force (Berger, 1962; Dons et al., 1979; Petersen et al., 1961) and force against constant or variable external loads (Pipes, 1978), respectively. There is also some evidence that training may be specific with respect to the speed of the movement (Lesmes et al., 1978), that is, "the effect of strength training may in part be limited to the speed used during training and/or at slower speeds." For that reason, apparatus design which would allow the simulation of the swimming movement while increasing the external load would be of great benefit to swimmers.

Several pieces of equipment have become commercially available, for which the specific nature of the training possibilities has been claimed more or less explicitly. Work presented in this volume indicates that the movements performed with such apparatus deviate substantially from the movements executed while swimming in the water. Two different types of techniques have been used to investigate this phenomenon: electromyography and a kinematic analysis of swimming movements. Olbrecht and Clarys (1983, this volume) showed that the EMG pattern of the muscles as well as the coordination is very much different in the two situations, whereas Schleihauf (1983, this volume) argues that, as some of the on-land apparatuses do not allow movement in more than one plane, they can never simulate the swimming motion, which, as he shows for the arm, occurs in several planes. Schleihauf (1983, this volume) also indicates that the speed of the movements performed on isokinetic equipment at the proper stroke frequency is too low with respect to the speed of the movements during swimming. This could be a serious drawback in view of the possible speed specificity of strength training.

This discussion should not be conceived as a recommendation to stop using these methods of training completely as some nonspecific effects are likely to occur, even though they should be expected to be much smaller than the specific effects (Berger, 1962). A discussion of the input-yield relationship of this type of training seems indicated.

Strength Training and Propulsion Efficiency

Gullstrand and Holmér (1983, this volume) argue that improvements by the Swedish National Teams of the last 5 years may be due to the swimmers' increased strength (as indicated by tethered swimming measurements), since oxygen consumption has not changed in this period. This hypothesis is attractive, but as the Gullstrand and Holmér data only allow conclusions of a correlative character, no unequivocal evidence is available. It seems quite likely, however, that the Swedish swimmers increased their propulsion efficiency in the period studied. This may be an effect of increased strength obtained through strength training, but may also be caused by a change in swimming technique unrelated to the increased strength. It seems that research into the relationship of these variables may be very informative, if not only average force (as in tethered swimming) but also peak forces and changes thereof are considered. Also in this context, application of work by Schleihauf et al. (1983, this volume) could be very productive.

References

ALEXANDER, R.M., and Goldspink, G. 1977. *Mechanics and Energetics of Animal Locomotion*, pp. 222-249. Chapman and Hall, London.

ÅSTRAND, P.-O., and Rodahl, K. 1977. *Textbook of Work Physiology*. McGraw-Hill, New York.

BERGER, R.A. 1962. Comparison of static and dynamic strength increases. *Res. Q.* (AAHPER) **33**:329-333.

BONE, Q. 1974. Muscular and energetic aspects of fish swimming. In: T.Y.T. Wu, C.J. Brokaw, and C. Brennen (eds.), *Swimming and Flying in Nature* (vol. 2), pp. 439-528. Plenum, New York.

diPRAMPERO, P.E., Pendergast, D.R., Wilson, D.W., and Rennie, D.W. 1974. Energetics of swimming in man. *J. Appl. Physiol.* **37**:1-5.

DONS, B., Bollerup, K., Bonde-Petersen, F., and Hancke, S. 1979. The effect of weight-lifting exercise related to muscle fiber composition and muscle cross sectional area in humans. *Eur. J. Appl. Physiol.* **40**:95-106.

GULLSTRAND, L., and Holmér, I. 1983. Physiological characteristics of champion swimmers during a five-year follow-up period. In: A.P. Hollander, P.A. Huijing, and G. de Groot (eds.), *Biomechanics and Medicine in Swimming*, pp. 258-262. Human Kinetics, Champaign, IL.

HOLMÉR, I. 1974. Propulsive efficiency of breaststroke and freestyle swimming. Eur. J. Appl. Physiol. **33**:95-103.

HOLMÉR, I. 1975. Efficiency of breaststroke and freestyle swimming. In: L. Lewillie and J.P. Clarys (eds.), *Swimming II*, pp. 130-136. University Park Press, Baltimore.

HOLMÉR, I. 1978. Time relations: Running, swimming and skating performances. In: B. Erikson and B. Furberg (eds.), *Swimming Medicine IV*, pp. 361-366. University Park Press, Baltimore.

KEMPER, H.G., Verschuur, R., Clarys, J.P., Jiskoot, J., and Rijken, H. 1976. Efficiency of swimming the front crawl. In: P.V. Komi (ed.), *Biomechanics V-B*, pp. 243-249. University Park Press, Baltimore.

LESMES, G.R., Costill, D.L., Coyle, E.F., and Fink, W.J. 1978. Muscle strength and power changes during maximal isokinetic training. *Med. Sci. Sports* **10**:266-269.

LIGHTHILL, M.J. (1969). Hydrodynamics of aquatic animal propulsion. *Ann. Rev. Fluid Mech.* **1**:413-446.

LIGHTHILL, M.J. 1970. Aquatic animal propulsion of high hydrodynamical efficiency. *J. Fluid Mech.* **44**:265-301.

OLBRECHT, J., and Clarys, J.P. 1983. EMG of specific strength training exercises for the front crawl. In: A.P. Hollander, P.A. Huijing, and G. de Groot (eds.), *Biomechanics and Medicine in Swimming*, pp. 136-141. Human Kinetics, Champaign, IL.

PENDERGAST, D.R., diPrampero, P.E., Craig, A.B., Wilson, D.R., and Rennie, D.W. 1977. Quantitative analysis of the front crawl in men and women. *J. Appl. Physiol.* **43**:475-479.

PENDERGAST, D.R., diPrampero, P.E., Craig, A.B., and Rennie, D.W. 1978. The influence of selected biomechanical factors on the energy cost of swimming. In: B. Erikson and B. Furberg (eds.), *Swimming Medicine IV*, pp. 367-378. University Park Press, Baltimore.

PETERSEN, F.B., Graudal, H., Hansen, J.W., and Hvid, N. 1961. The effect of varying the number of muscle contractions on dynamic muscle training. *Intern. Z. Angew. Physiol.* **18**:468-473.

PIPES, T.V. 1978. Variable resistance versus constant resistance strength training in adult males. *Eur. J. Appl. Physiol.* **39**:27-35.

RENNIE, D.W., Pendergast, D.R., and diPrampero, P.E. 1975. Energetics of swimming in man. In: L. Lewillie and J.P. Clarys (eds.), *Swimming II*, pp. 97-104. University Park Press, Baltimore.

SCHLEIHAUF, R.E. 1983a. Specificity of strength training in swimming: A biomechanical viewpoint. In: A.P. Hollander, P.A. Huijing, and G. de Groot (eds.), *Biomechanics and Medicine in Swimming*, pp. 184-191. Human Kinetics, Champaign, IL.

SCHLEIHAUF, R.E., Gray, L., and DeRose, J. 1983b. Three dimensional analysis of hand propulsion in sprint front crawl stroke. In: A.P. Hollander, P.A. Huijing, and G. de Groot (eds.), *Biomechanics and Medicine in Swimming*, pp. 173-183. Human Kinetics, Champaign, IL.

TOUSSAINT, H.M., van der Helm, F.C.T., Elzerman, J.R., Hollander, A.P., de Groot, G., and van Ingen Schenau, G.J. 1983. A power balance applied to swimming. In: A.P. Hollander, P.A. Huijing, and G. de Groot (eds.), *Biomechanics and Medicine in Swimming*, pp. 165-172. Human Kinetics, Champaign, IL.

van INGEN SCHENAU, G.J. 1979. Een biomechanisch onderzoek van het schaatsen. (A biomechanical investigation of speed skating.) *Geneesk. Sport* **12**:94-102 (Dutch).

van INGEN SCHENAU, G.J. 1981. *A Power Balance Applied to Speed Skating*. Doctoral dissertation, Free University, Amsterdam.

WEBB, P.W. 1971. Oxygen consumption and swimming efficiency. *J. Exp. Biol.* **55**:521-540.

Research in Swimming:
Historical and Scientific Aspects

Léon Lewillie
Université Libre de Bruxelles, Belgium

Our main interest is with swimming, but swimming as it is conceived today is a fairly new activity in the history of humankind; it is no older than one century. However, pictures of people in the water can be found in prehistory: among the rock paintings of Gilf Kebir dated at 5000 BC and later in Egyptian hieroglyphics (Figure 1).

In fact, swimming had little practical use. In many countries, water temperature is too low to make swimming pleasant, and besides, the density of the human body allows floating without effort if no load is carried. However, farmers and soldiers did not only wish to cross the river themselves, but also to transport their equipment to the other side. Humans have therefore always been more dependent on accessories such as rafts than on their ability to swim. Assyrian soldiers used inflated leather bottles to support their bodies and weapons and the Medieval knights stretched rope across rivers.

Figure 1 — Assyrian soldiers in flight, crossing a river. (coll. Seeman, T.A., Verlag)

Figure 2—The French game of "soule" often ended in the water. (Musée National des Arts et Traditions Populaires, Paris)

For centuries pictures showed only bathing, not swimming, as in the well known illustration from a book on the rules of hunting birds. The Frederic II "De Arte Venerandi cum Avibus" is dated 1220 and shows the hunter on a warm summer day, having given some prey as a reward to his hawk, putting his clothes on the branch of a tree and bathing in a pond. Other classic pictures show children playing in the mill course or jumping from a bridge as in the 16th Century German game: "Schwimmen vor einer Muhle." Those games were generally limited to children. In the "Allegory of Summer" that Villadornat painted around 1750, a scene describes pleasure as a function of age. The artist shows men fishing and children playing in the water. We know that during the same period, many ballgames were popular and competitions were organized worldwide.

But things are never so simple. Some adult games like the French "Soule," forefather of European football, sometimes ended in the water, (Figure 2) and in most of the older pictures, as in the case of the Assyrian soldiers (Figure 1), you can see that one of the men may be more skillful at swimming without help in a style similar to the front crawl, a technique rediscovered only in the 20th Century.

Borelli's "De Motu Animalium" is generally considered to be the first book on biomechanics. He looked only at divers, though, and some corrections must be applied to his proposals. At the end of the 18th Century,

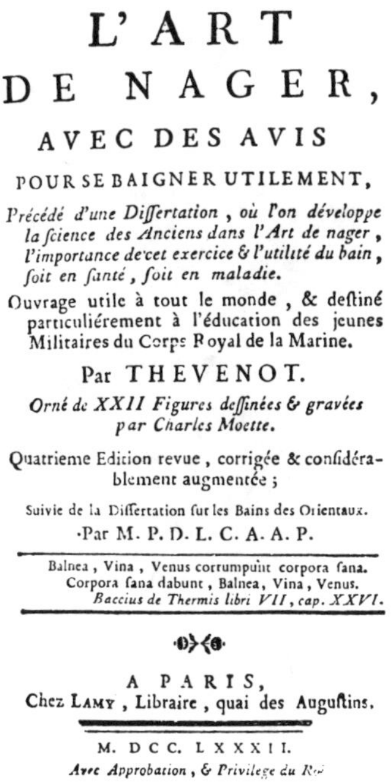

L' A R T
D E   N A G E R ,
A V E C   D E S   A V I S
POUR SE BAIGNER UTILEMENT,

Précédé d'une Differtation , où l'on développe la fcience des Anciens dans l'Art de nager , l'importance de'cet exercice & l'utilité du bain , foit en fanté , foit en maladie.

Ouvrage utile à tout le monde , & deftiné particuliérement à l'éducation des jeunes Militaires du Corps Royal de la Marine.

Par T H E V E N O T.

Orné de XXII Figures deffinées & gravées par Charles Moette.

Quatrieme Edition revue , corrigée & confidérablement augmentée ;

Suivie de la Differtation fur les Bains des Orientaux.

·Par M. P. D. L. C. A. A. P.

Balnea , Vina , Venus corrumpunt corpora fana.
Corpora fana dabunt , Balnea, Vina, Venus.
Baccius de Thermis libri VII , cap. XXVI.

·❂❂·

A   P A R I S,
Chez LAMY , Libraire , quai des Auguftins.

M. D C C. L X X X I I.
Avec Approbation , & Privilege du Ro·

Figure 3—Front page of a book describing the different methods used to move in the water. (Personal collection)

many books were published in various languages on the art of swimming (see Figure 3). Guts Muths and others described the different ways to float, to move on the front or on the back, and to turn around. However, the content of these books was far from providing satisfactory teaching methods, and anyway, the pedagogues of the time simply considered water a danger to be avoided.

Slowly, the idea that swimming was useful and important to learn was popularized and the engineers of the 19th Century built machines to help facilitate military group teaching—without water. But events moved fast: Modern sports developed and some rowers, finding it was more fun in than on the water, founded swimming clubs. Competition began at the Olympic Games as well as in long distance events such as swimming the English Channel. It seems that research in biomechanics actually followed two paths: modeling and field investigations. The first gives a global approach whereas the second provides the necessary measurements. This is not new, for the biomechanicians of the 19th Century had already established models very similar to our modern ones. In 1882 Marey introduced the basis for the scientific use of cameras and sensors (Figure 4). They lacked the speed of computers and the miniaturization of electronic components; however, their research was essentially directed toward locomotion of humans and animals and not to swimming.

In fact, research lagged behind the swimmers' experience. At the beginning of the 20th Century, Dubois-Reymond (1905) towed a swim-

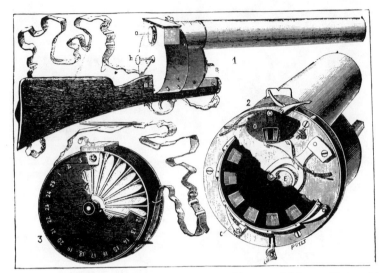

Figure 4—Mechanism of the chronophotographic gun of Marey. He used it to study man and animal movements, especially birds in flight. (From *La Nature*. 22 April 1882)

mer behind a boat and measured the forces using a dynamometer. A few years later, Houssay used tethered swimming to study the swimmer at zero speed. In the 1930s, Cureton and Karpovich launched the fundamental principles of research in swimming. Some papers were presented in seminars on biomechanics but not until 1970 was the first Symposium on Biomechanics in Swimming organized in Brussels. The most important progress was evident in *Swimming II* (Brussels, 1974), when the papers no longer tended to present one particular point with one technique, but attempted to solve problems using all the appropriate methods available.

The volume, *Swimming I*, had one integrated topic—biomechanics in swimming—but since the publication of *Swimming II*, important topics such as propulsion, drag and efficiency, and swimming starts have been grouped into chapters.

Several methods have become available such as tethered swimming, or zero speed, towing with different modifications of Karpovich's (1933) resistograph and the swimming mill, which are especially useful in studies of energy consumption. Tethered swimming is easy to use but presents limitations such as zero speed; with no drag, movements of the arms and legs through water differ from reality as light trace photography shows (Hoecke and Gruendler, 1975; Lewillie, 1971). A breast stroke swimmer's foot movement at zero speed is clearly different; the path of the hand in the front crawl is about half the diameter of the actual path during real swimming. However, tethered swimming opened the way for studies on speed and acceleration.

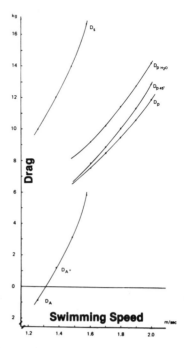

Figure 5—Comparison of mean passive drag results (Dp, DpH20, Dp 450) and active drag data [D$_A$ (−), D$_A$ (+), Ds]. (From Clarys, 1979)

Later, researchers tried towing active swimmers using a modified Resistograph (Alley, 1952; Counsilman, 1955) or a circular pool where the swimmer was followed by a platform moving at constant speed (di Prampero et al., 1974). Trying to keep the swimmer near the measuring devices, Åstrand and Englesson (1971) built an aquatic swim-mill. Even if the amount of energy lost in turbulence is unknown and the work performed by the propulsion forces is measured only in the direction of progression, this instrument allows measurement of energy consumption (Holmér, 1974; Holmér and Haglund, 1978). The ratio of propulsive power and total energy consumption provides a useful measure of efficiency which appears very low: 7% for the arms and 2% for the legs in a front crawl. This means that any improvement in technique may have important effects on economy and performance.

Miyashita and Tsunoda (1978) studied water resistance in relation to body size using another type of swimming flume. Clarys made dynamic measurements on towed swimmers using the Netherlands ship model basin described by van Manen and Rijken (1975). Clarys et al. conducted several more studies (1974, 1975, 1978). Clarys (1979) later was able to not only determine passive drag but also active drag, which is twice as high as passive drag (Figure 5). He showed that active drag is mainly influenced by changes in position and by movement of the body segments. That means a high resistance is created by faulty swimming technique, which can be corrected with training. Using the same technique, Jiskoot and Clarys (1975) showed that resistance is higher under water than at

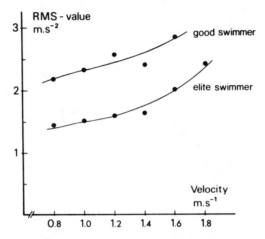

Figure 6—Root mean square (RMS) values of intracycle velocity fluctuations is used by Holmér to show the extra energy spent by less qualified swimmers due to accelerations and decelerations within the stroke cycle. (From Holmér, 1979)

the surface. Tethered swimming has shown periodical variations in the propeling forces, causing costly accelerations and decelerations. Miyashita (1971) used a system of cables and pulleys to find that even the Japanese record-holder who swam at a speed of 1.80 m/sec showed speed fluctuations of 0.6 m/sec. Holmér (1979), using a linear accelerometer, verified the Kornecki and Bober hypothesis (1978) stating that the deviation between extreme velocities and the mean velocity could give a useful measure of efficiency. The root mean square (RMS) values for two swimmers of different levels of qualification (Figure 6) give good, if indirect, evidence of the loss of energy due to those accelerations and decelerations.

The next logical step was to investigate propulsion and hand movements. Counsilman (1971) proposed a theory based on Bernouilli's principle. Stimulating much discussion, it opened the way for new studies: Barthels and Adrian, 1975; Dupuis et al., 1979; Miyashita, 1975; Bucher, 1975; Ungerechts, 1979; and Wood, 1979. Schleihauf (1979) investigated the various drag and lift forces on different plastic resin models of the human hand in an open-water channel, concluding that the hand may have various ways of creating the same propulsive force and that velocity could then be considered arbitrary to a certain extent. Schleihauf, like Adrian (1973), and others turned to high-speed cinematography to provide laboratory data for real swimming motion. The method is well known, and now apparatus has been built to follow the swimmer along the full length of the pool (Dal Monte, 1971). It is necessary to smooth the velocity and acceleration curves obtained by this method, but it is also important to keep in mind that swimmers' movements pass through two different media: water and air. MacIntyre and Hay (1975) have presented this problem for humans. Mathematical models like the one of Seireg and Baz (1971) now occupy a full session at the Congress. It may be important to underline how much these models contribute to practical conclusions, following the examples of Jensen and Blanksby (1975), Francis and Dean (1975), and Jensen and MacIlwain (1979).

In theory everything except muscular activity can be derived by calculation from cinematography. The electromyogram (EMG) can be recorded by surface electrodes (Lewillie, 1968) or fine-wire electrodes (Okamoto and Wolf, 1979). It can be transmitted by wire (Ikai, 1962; Oka et al., 1979; Tokuyama et al., 1976; Yoshizawa, 1976) or by telemetry (Lewillie, 1968, 1971, 1973, 1974, 1976). It is difficult to quantify, and generally has been done as a function of maximal isometric contraction. It has shown how much unnecessary activity can be developed during the nonpropulsive period (Lewillie, 1973). The evolution of research in this field is apparent in the works of Oka et al. (1979) who used EMG to understand how a child who could not swim without support first behaved in the water, then acquired the technique of the flutter kick similar to that seen in skilled adults.

Biomechanics research in swimming has now reached a level of knowledge where transfer to practitioners is possible. Craig et al. (1979) proposed a nomogram using stroke rate, distance per stroke and velocity relationship during training for competitive swimming, underlining the fact that swimmers' ability to improve their technique, that is, increase propulsion and decrease active body drag, is a better way to achieve success than to give them a 5-hour or longer workout each day.

It appears that biomechanics in swimming has followed the usual pattern: application of techniques, learning to solve a problem, transmission of results to the field, modeling and definition of general laws. But I choose to conclude using as an example the picture of a young blind man swimming because he alone followed the same pattern as the biomechanicians: He learned about weightlessness, which was for him a real problem for he had to forget all the references he used previously. He had to master an entirely new situation, but the influence of his new knowledge transformed his behavior outside of the water and his reward was a new freedom in his world.

References

ADRIAN, M. 1973. Cinematographic, electromyographic and electrogoniometric techniques for analyzing human movements. In: J.H. Wilmore (ed.), *Exercise and Sport Science Reviews*, Vol. I, pp. 339-364. Academic Press, New York.

ALLEY, L.E. 1952. An analysis of water resistance and propulsion in swimming the crawl stroke. *Res. Q.* 23:253-269.

ÅSTRAND, P.O., and Englesson, S. 1971. An aquatic swim-mill. In: L. Lewillie and J.P. Clarys (eds.), *First International Symposium on Biomechanics in Swimming*, pp. 197-198. Bruxelles, Université Libre de Bruxelles.

BARTHELS, K.M., and Adrian, M.J. 1975. Three-dimensional spatial hand patterns of skilled butterfly swimmers. In: L. Lewillie and J.P. Clarys (eds.), *Swimming II*, pp. 154-160. University Park Press, Baltimore.

BUCHER, W. 1975. The influence of the leg kick and the arm stroke on the total speed during the crawl stroke. In: L. Lewillie and J.P. Clarys (eds.), *Swimming II*, pp. 174-179. University Park Press, Baltimore.

CLARYS, J.P., Jiskoot, J., Rijken, H., and Brouwer, J.P. 1974. Total resistance in water and its relation to body form. In: R.C. Nelson and C.A. Morehouse (eds.), *Biomechanics IV*, pp. 187-196. University Park Press, Baltimore.

CLARYS, J.P., and Jiskoot, J. 1975. Total resistance of selected body positions in the front crawl. In: L. Lewillie and J.P. Clarys (eds.), *Swimming II*, pp. 110-117. University Park Press, Baltimore.

CLARYS, J.P. 1978. An experimental investigation of the application of fundamental hydrodynamics to the human body. In: B. Eriksson and B. Furberg (eds.), *Swimming Medicine IV*, pp. 386-394. University Park Press, Baltimore.

CLARYS, J.P. 1979. Human morphology and hydrodynamics. In: J. Terauds and E.W. Bedingfield (eds.), *Swimming III*, pp. 3-44. University Park Press, Baltimore.

COUNSILMAN, J.E. 1971. The application of Bernouilli's principle to human propulsion in water. In: L. Lewillie and J.P. Clarys (eds.), *First International Symposium on Biomechanics in Swimming*, pp. 59-72. Bruxelles, Université Libre de Bruxelles.

COUNSILMAN, J.E. 1955. Forces in swimming two types of crawl stroke. *Res. Q.* **26**:127-138.

CRAIG, A.B., Boomer, W.L., and Gibbons, J.F. 1979. Use of stroke rate, distance per stroke and velocity relationships during training for competitive swimming. In: J. Terauds and E.W. Bedingfield (eds.), *Swimming III*, pp. 265-274. University Park Press, Baltimore.

DAL MONTE, A. 1971. Presenting an apparatus for motion picture, television and scan shots of the movement of swimming. In: L. Lewillie and J.P. Clarys (eds.), *First International Symposium on Biomechanics in Swimming*, pp. 127-128. Bruxelles, Université Libre de Bruxelles.

DI PRAMPERO, P.E., Pendergast, D.R., Wilson, D.W., and Rennie, D.W. 1974. Energetics of swimming in man. *J. Appl. Physiol.* **37**:1-5.

DUBOIS-REYMOND, R. 1905. Zum physiologie des schwimmens. *Arch. Physiol.* **29**:252-279.

DUPUIS, R., Adrian, M., Yoneda, Y., and Jack, M. 1979. Forces acting on the hand during swimming and their relationship to muscular, spatial and temporal factors. In: J. Terauds and E.W. Bedingfield (eds.), *Swimming III*, pp. 110-117. University Park Press, Baltimore.

FRANCIS, P.R., and Dean, N. 1975. A biomechanical model for swimming performance. In: L. Lewillie and J.P. Clarys (eds.), *Swimming II*, pp. 118-124. University Park Press, Baltimore.

HOECKE, G., and Gruendler, G. 1975. Use of light trace photography in teaching swimming. In: L. Lewillie and J.P. Clarys (eds.), *Swimming II*, pp. 194-206. University Park Press, Baltimore.

HOLMÉR, I., and Haglund, S. 1978. The swimming flume: Experiences and applications. In: B. Eriksson and B. Furberg (eds.), *Swimming Medicine IV*, pp. 379-385. University Park Press, Baltimore.

HOLMÉR, I. 1974. Physiology of swimming man. *Acta Physiol. Scand.* suppl. 407.

HOLMÉR, I. 1979. Analysis of acceleration as a measure of swimming proficiency. In: J. Terauds and E.W. Bedingfield (eds.), *Swimming III*, pp. 118-126. University Park Press, Baltimore.

IKAI, M. 1962. Etude électromyographique de la natation. *Rev. Phys.* 2:124-126.

JENSEN, R.K., and Blanksby, B. 1975. A model for upper extremity forces during the underwater phase of the front crawl. In: L. Lewillie and J.P. Clarys (eds.), *Swimming II*, pp. 145-153. University Park Press, Baltimore.

JENSEN, R.K., and MacIlwain, J. 1979. Modeling of lower extremity forces in the dolphin kick. In: J. Terauds and E.W. Bedingfield (eds.), *Swimming III*, pp. 137-147. University Park Press, Baltimore.

JISKOOT, J., and Clarys, J.P. 1975. Body resistance on and under the water surface. In: L. Lewillie and J.P. Clarys (eds.), *Swimming II*, pp. 105-109. University Park Press, Baltimore.

KARPOVICH, P.V. 1933. Water resistance in swimming. *Res. Q.* 4:21-28.

KORNECKI, S., and Bober, T. 1978. External velocities of a swimming cycle as a technique criterion. In: B. Eriksson and B. Furberg (eds.), *Swimming Medicine IV*, pp. 402-407. University Park Press, Baltimore.

LEWILLIE, L. 1968. Telemetrical analysis of the electromyogram. In: J. Wartenweiler, E. Jokl, and M. Hebbelinck (eds.), *Biomechanics*, pp. 147-149. Karger, Basel.

LEWILLIE, L. 1971. Graphic and electromyographic analysis of various styles of swimming. In: J. Vredenbregt and J. Wartenweiler (eds.), *Biomechanics II*, pp. 253-259. S. Karger, Basel.

LEWILLIE, L.A. 1973. Muscular activity in swimming. In: S. Cerquilini, A. Venerando, and J. Wartenweiler (eds.), *Biomechanics III*, pp. 434-439. S. Karger, Basel.

LEWILLIE, L. 1974. Telemetry of electromyographic and electrogoniometric signals in swimming. In: R.C. Nelson and C.A. Morehouse (eds.), *Biomechanics IV*, pp. 203-207. University Park Press, Baltimore.

LEWILLIE, L.A. 1976. Variability of myoelectric signals during swimming. In: P.V. Komi (ed.), *Biomechanics V-B*, pp. 230-234. University Park Press, Baltimore.

MacINTYRE, D.R., and Hay, J.G. 1975. Dual media cinematography. In: L. Lewillie and J.P. Clarys (eds.), *Swimming II*, pp. 51-57. University Park Press, Baltimore.

MIYASHITA, M. 1975. Arm action in the crawl stroke. In: L. Lewillie and J.P. Clarys (eds.), *Swimming II*, pp. 167-173. University Park Press, Baltimore.

MIYASHITA, M. 1971. An analysis of fluctuations of swimming speed. In: L. Lewillie and J.P. Clarys (eds.), *First International Symposium on Biomechanics in Swimming*, pp. 53-56. Bruxelles, Université Libre de Bruxelles.

MIYASHITA, M., and Tsunoda, T. 1978. Water resistance in relation to body size. In: B. Eriksson and B. Furberg (eds.), *Swimming Medicine IV*, pp. 395-401. University Park Press, Baltimore.

OKA, H., Okamoto, T., Yoshizawa, M., Tokuyama, H., and Kumamoto, M. 1979. Electromyographic and cinematographic study of the flutter kick in infants and children. In: J. Terauds and E.W. Bedingfield (eds.), *Swimming III*, pp. 167-172. University Park Press, Baltimore.

OKAMOTO, T., and Wolf, S.L. 1979. Underwater recording of muscular activity using fine-wire electrodes. In: J. Terauds and E.W. Bedingfield (eds.), *Swimming III*, pp. 160-166. University Park Press, Baltimore.

PENDERGAST, D.R., di Prampero, P.E., Craig, A.B., Sr., and Rennie, D.W. 1978. The influence of selected biomechanical factors on the energy cost of swimming. In: B. Eriksson and B. Furberg (eds.), *Swimming Medicine IV*, pp. 367-378. University Park Press, Baltimore.

SCHLEIHAUF, R.E., Jr. 1979. A hydrodynamic analysis of swimming propulsion. In: J. Terauds and E.W. Bedingfield (eds.), *Swimming III*, pp. 70-109. University Park Press, Baltimore.

SEIREG, A., and Baz, A. 1971. A mathematical model for swimming mechanics. In: L. Lewillie and J.P. Clarys (eds.), *First International Symposium on Biomechanics in Swimming*, pp. 81-104. Bruxelles, Université Libre de Bruxelles.

TOKUYAMA, H., Okamoto, T., and Kumamoto, M. 1976. Electromyographic study of swimming in infants and children. In: P.V. Komi (ed.), *Biomechanics V-B*, pp. 215-221. University Park Press, Baltimore.

UNGERECHTS, B. 1979. Optimizing propulsion in swimming by rotation of the hands. In: J. Terauds and E.W. Bedingfield (eds.), *Swimming III*, pp. 55-61. University Park Press, Baltimore.

VAN MANEN, J.D., and Rijken, H. 1975. Dynamic measurement techniques on swimming bodies at The Netherlands ship model basin. In: L. Lewillie and J.P. Clarys (eds.), *Swimming II*, pp. 70-79. University Park Press, Baltimore.

WOOD, T.C. 1979. A fluid dynamics analysis of the propulsive potential of the hand and forearm in swimming. In: J. Terauds and E.W. Bedingfield (eds.), *Swimming III*, pp. 62-69. University Park Press, Baltimore.

YOSHIZAWA, M., Tokuyama, H., Okamoto, T., and Kumamoto, M. 1976. Electromyographic study of the breast stroke. In: P.V. Komi (ed.), *Biomechanics V-B*, pp. 222-229. University Park Press, Baltimore.

Value of Swimming in
Cardiac Rehabilitation and Internal Medicine

Ken De Meirleir
Free University of Brussels, Belgium

Our present society became conscious of the medical aspects of sports with the emerging emphasis on sports medicine and the whole area of adapted physical education. Surveys indicate that at least half of the population in most Western countries participate in one or more sports activities (Lambert et al., 1982). These primarily include walking, jogging, bicycling, swimming, tennis and team sports. Considerable publicity has been given to injuries and deaths of athletes, and discussions have centered on prevention and treatment of such accidents. Maintaining a good body form and functional capacity as well as concern for increasing the active lifespan have stimulated an interest in the role of endurance exercise for protecting the cardiovascular system. As a consequence of this increased enthusiasm at all levels of the population to become involved in some kind of physical activity, the internist is confronted with two main questions: (1) What is the role of physical activity in the prevention and therapy of medical illness? (2) How does one define contraindications to physical activity in certain instances?

These questions are not easily answered since most physicians have not learned how to prescribe exercise. To my knowledge sports medicine is not included in most medical school curricula. Most of this article will be devoted to the role and the problems of exercise in cardiac rehabilitation with special emphasis on swimming as an endurance sport. Swimming for prevention and treatment of some medical disorders is reviewed briefly.

Coronary Heart Disease and Cardiac Rehabilitation:
Scope of the Problem

Not long ago, patients with myocardial infarcts were usually declared invalids and no attempts were made to rehabilitate them. By the beginning of the 1960s patients with a history of myocardial infarction were being encouraged to lead productive, active lives (Cain et al., 1961; Torkelson, 1964). Major advances in the understanding and treatment of postmyocardial infarction patients have been made: cardiac rehabilitation programs are a consequence of this increased knowledge. We have learned a lot about the prognostic indexes which are based on the patient's condition before and after the MI. Among these indexes are age, risk factors such as hypertension and diabetes, previous and residual angina pectoris, and dangerous rhythm disturbances (Moss et al., 1974). Underlying these prognostic indicators are two important factors: the quantity of surviving myocardium and the risk that it may become necrotic as a consequence of further obstruction of narrowed coronary arteries. Other advances are the use of beta-blockers, drugs that inhibit platelet aggregation, new antiarhythmic drugs and the surgical treatment of coronary artery disease. Cardiac rehabilitation is defined as a comprehensive approach to helping individuals with cardiovascular disease. The purpose of cardiac rehabilitation is to prevent the progression of the disease, to avoid symptoms or complications, and to attain maximum allowable functional capabilities for such patients. In addition to careful prescription of exercise, cardiac rehabilitation includes education about risk factors and heart disease. As part of their rehabilitation, patients are encouraged to lose weight, maintain blood pressure control, and avoid cigarette smoking (Hellerstein, 1979).

Patients in physical activity programs following myocardial infarction have not demonstrated a significantly reduced morbidity or mortality when compared to control groups (Ilker, 1973; Shephard, 1979). Therefore, attempts are being made to study the impact of exercise on the progression of coronary heart disease.

Different types of exercise are offered in a cardiac rehabilitation program. Cardiovascular function and physical work capacity are best enhanced through dynamic aerobic activities (Fardy, 1977). These should be rhythmic movements of large muscle groups that do not exhaust the oxygen transport system. Resistance and isometric exercises are less beneficial and are more likely to place unnecessarily high oxygen demands on the myocardium (Rost et al., 1977). As a result of isometric training, dangerous Valsalva maneuvers, rhythmic alterations and pressor responses can be provoked (Flessas et al., 1976; Fox et al., 1971). The best dynamic aerobic activities for this purpose include: walking, jogging, bicycling and swimming. The basic prerequisite of physical training with cardiac patients is that this treatment should not shorten the patient's life. However, there are various reports of fatal cardiac incidents during rehabilitation training (Haskell, 1978; Wieser, 1980). This has raised several questions. One can ask if these incidents are really caused by physical exercise or if they are just statistical events which occur during sports, but are not caused by sports. The mortality rate in physically active groups generally is lower than in patients after myocardial infarction; but here we must keep in mind that they represent a select group, with better prognosis and less cardiac function impairment. For the "Hamburg Model" it must be concluded that if matched groups of patients are compared, both fulfilling the prerequisites of training, the mortality rate of the active group does not exceed the rate of the inactive group (Ilker, 1973).

Is There a Place for Swimming in a Cardiac Rehabilitation Program?

Swimming is frequently recommended for cardiac rehabilitation, but its application remains controversial. This controversy originates from the fact that cardiac arrhythmias seem to be more prevalent during swimming than during other exercise forms used in cardiac rehabilitation. One center reported that out of 13 patients who died while exercising, 10 fatal events occurred during swimming (Samek et al., 1977). However, no serious complications were encountered in more than 3,000 patient hours of swimming in another report (Haber et al., 1979). From these studies no prediction can be made of the risks as compared to other forms of physical exercise in patients after myocardial infarction.

Because swimming exercise differs in several important aspects from walking and running we should go over its physiology. Immersion of the body in water induces pronounced cardiorespiratory adjustments from a blood shift into the thoracic cavity and from the hydrostatic pressure on the chest wall. Central blood volume will increase by approximately 700 ml as a consequence of this blood shift. Gauer (1963) reported that the mean heart volume will increase in water from 770 to 920 ml. There are also respiratory changes. Due to hydrostatic pressure the diaphragm ascends and the ribcage compresses. Vital capacity is diminished by approximately 10% (Hollmann and Hettinger, 1976). Physiological changes in metabolism and movement as a consequence of water immersion include (Andersen, 1960; Åstrand and Rodahl, 1977; di Prampero et al., 1974; Keatinge et al., 1961): (a) considerably lower body weight; (b) greater energy cost for swimming a given distance which is about four times greater than running the same distance; (c) importance of swimming technique: good swimmers can swim a particular stroke at a given velocity with lower oxygen consumption than can relatively untrained swimmers; (d) increased heart rate and extensive vasodilatation from swimming in warm water (35-37°C); in contrast, a decrease in heart rate has been associated with immersion in water of an average swimming pool (27-31°C). The physiological response to immersion in cold water (15-20°C) has been shown to be a significant decrease in the partial pressure of carbon dioxide and higher ventricular irritability; and (e) use of all muscle groups.

The pathophysiology of swimming in patients with ischemic heart disease has been studied very little. Of particular concern in these patients with impaired cardiac function are the following parameters:

- As previously mentioned, immersion in water and a horizontal body position both increase the central blood volume, which could stress the limited reserves of patients with ischemic heart disease and lead to serious rhythm disturbances.
- Other factors could be responsible for an increase in left ventricular overload with a subsequent decrease in the patient's work level.
- A large part of the work is performed by the arms which results in higher peripheral vascular resistance than leg work at the same work load.
- Water has a compressive effect on the extremities.
- Skin blood flow decreases.

Regarding the work done as a result of swimming and its effects on patients with ischemic heart disease, the Heigenhauser, Fletcher and Magder studies are very important. Heigenhauser et al. (1977) found that maximal oxygen consumption during swimming was 21% lower than during cycling. Fletcher et al. (1979) concluded that swimming required a high $\dot{V}O_2$ compared to other exercises. The most recent of these three studies is the one by Magder et al. (1981) in which eight males were examined who had had a myocardial infarction months previously. The subjects were exercised to exhaustion or angina on a bicycle ergometer in sitting and supine positions. Oxygen uptake ($\dot{V}O_2$) was measured continuously to monitor the physiological power requirement. All eight patients took beta-blockers; four of them took digoxin. During cycling in a sitting position, angina occurred in four and ST-depression in five; during supine cycling, angina occurred in five and ST-depression in six. $\dot{V}O_2$ was then measured while they swam at their own comfortable speed in a swimming flume at water temperatures of 25.5 and 18°C. In six patients, the water speed was increased gradually until they were limited by symptoms. Comfortable swimming at 25.5°C was 87% and at 18°C, 89% of the sitting cycling peak $\dot{V}O_2$, whereas the heart rates were 92 and 91%, respectively. The mean peak $\dot{V}O_2$ and heart rate did not differ significantly between bicycle and swim tests. Only two patients reported angina while swimming in warm water and one in cold water, although ST-depression occurred in six patients during both swims.

What conclusions can be made from this study?

- In patients with a reduced exercise capacity due to ischemic heart disease swimming can require near-maximal effort. The maximal heart rate, ventilation and oxygen pulse did not differ significantly between cycling and swimming.
- In contrast to normal subjects, good as well as poor swimmers achieved the same $\dot{V}O_2$ peak during swimming as they did during cycling.

- There appeared to be a failure to identify ischemic symptoms during swimming.
- The heart rate at which ST-depressions occurred was similar during cycling and swimming; swimming at 18 and 25.5°C were subjectively (but not objectively) equally well tolerated.

A major issue in allowing cardiac patients to swim has to do with the diving reflex or oxygen consuming reflex. This has been a subject particularly well studied in diving animals (Andersen, 1966). Upon submergence, immediate cardiac slowing occurs. In these animals cardiac output diminishes because of decreased heart rate, but stroke volume is relatively constant. These cardiovascular adaptations also are present to a lesser degree in humans. Water temperatures of 22°C or less and apnea produce a slowing of the heart rate upon water immersion. Face immersion alone can produce bradycardia. Without water immersion breath-holding will produce a 10% drop in heart rate, augmented to a 14% decrease in heart rate by face immersion in water at 22°C (Irving, 1963; Olbridge et al., 1978). In *The Human Cardiovascular System* by Shepherd and Vanhoutte (1980) the mechanisms of this complex reflex are thoroughly explained. The afferent branch of the reflex which produces bradycardia in immersed humans appears to have multiple branches; these may include a specific facial receptor actuated by cool stimuli, thoracic stretch receptors and aortic and/or carotid sinus baroreceptors. In humans electrocardiographic changes with diving, simple facial immersion and/or breath-holding are cardioinhibitory—sinus bradycardia, sinus arrest with nodal or ventricular escape, AV block and AV nodal rhythm (Olsen et al., 1962). Brady-arrhythmias can cause sudden death in patients with coronary heart disease. The ventricular fibrillation threshold in this situation also is lowered (Wit and Bigger, 1975). So, until proven otherwise, one must regard this reflex as very dangerous in patients with coronary heart disease, particularly for those with higher risk of sudden death.

Finally, what must be concluded from these facts regarding swimming and cardiac rehabilitation? Swimming is useful for cardiac rehabilitation, but it should not be recommended universally for all patients. Because it has certain specific risks, more than other forms of endurance exercise, the patient's cardiac status should be carefully evaluated. The subjective comfort and large muscle groups involved make swimming a good exercise, but the relatively high energy cost and failure to identify ischemic symptoms indicate caution with cardiac patients. Patients should be informed of the fact that dyspnea might override the perception of angina. The temperature of the pool should optimally be between 26 and 30°C. The program requires careful collaboration of the physician and physical therapist, with emergency resuscitation equipment at the poolside. A telemetric system which enables one to follow ECG while a person is swimming is of particular value in a cardiac rehabilitation program. The necessity of having this equipment makes cost-effectiveness higher for swimming than for other exercise forms used in cardiac rehabilitation. When a fatal incident occurs, it is also more difficult, compared to other environments, to resuscitate patients immediately when they are in a swimming pool.

Lagerstrøm et al. (1980) state their experience has indicated that patients in cardiac rehabilitation who perform at least 75 W for 3 min without any problems can take part in a medically supervised swimming program. Personally, I do not agree with this statement. Because overloading of the left ventricle is more important in swimming, the following entrance criteria for postmyocardial infarction patients in a swimming program are probably more appropriate: at least 2 months after the infarction, swimming is allowed if they are without residual ischemic symptoms and can perform an exercise of at least 100 W for 2-3 min. Patients at risk for serious arrhythmias or latent cardiac failure as well as those with previous extensive myocardial infarctions and myocardial aneurysms should definitely be excluded from a swimming program. For the various physiopathological reasons mentioned, swimming cannot be permitted in the acute and subacute stages of myocardial infarction.

In addition to calisthenics, walking, jogging, cycling and volleyball, swimming can be included in the cardiac rehabilitation exercise program. A broad variety of activities in such an exercise program is beneficial to patient compliance with the program. Swimming is especially suited as exercise in cardiac patients who are obese or have ankle, knee, hip or lower-extremity muscular problems.

Application of Swimming in Other Medical Conditions

Among the many medical conditions other than ischemic heart disease in which swimming is used to restore or maintain fitness in patients are:
- pulmonary diseases—chronic obstructive lung disease, cystic fibrosis and asthma;
- neurological disorders—epilepsy, cerebral palsy, blindness, multiple sclerosis, poliomyelitis, mental retardation and hemiplegia as a result of stroke;
- rheumatological diseases—arthritis, spondylisthesis, and Scheuermann's disease;
- hematological disorders—hemophilia.

The value of swimming for patients with these disorders has been proven in the past. The two sport activities which are most beneficial for patients with hemophilia are skiing and swimming (Frederici et al., 1980). An increasing health consciousness has created a growing interest in various activities aimed at preventing degenerative diseases. Because the major causes of death are degenerative diseases, evidence for the beneficial effects of exercise, particularly in preventing diseases such as obesity, diabetes mellitus, hyperlipidemia, hypertension and atherosclerosis, must be discussed.

Regarding exercise and atherosclerosis, it is unclear at present whether physical activity can favorably influence the natural history of coronary heart disease in humans (Froelicher, 1978). In animals, results of studies on this subject also are conflicting (Link et al., 1972; Lofland et al., 1959; Prior et al., 1965; Weiss et al., 1966). Atherogenesis in dogs has even been reported to accelerate with exercise (McAllister et al., 1960).

Recently Kramsch et al. (1981) published the results of an investigation in which they studied the effect of moderate conditioning in monkeys with treadmill exercise and an atherogenic diet. Their physical training was demonstrated by slow heart rates. Postmortem examination revealed marked coronary atherosclerosis and stenoses in the nonconditioned monkeys only. Exercise was associated with substantially reduced overall atherosclerotic involvement and lesion size; it also produced much larger hearts and wider coronary arteries, further reducing the degree of luminal narrowing. This most convincing study suggests that exercise may prevent or retard coronary heart disease in primates, but it will be extremely difficult to obtain direct evidence that exercise may protect against coronary artery disease in humans.

Although obesity has not been established as an independent risk factor for coronary heart disease, it has long been associated with the development of vascular disease. Recent observations show that depressed left ventricular function is already present in relatively young obese people, even if they are free from signs of cardiopathy or associated diseases (De Divitis et al., 1981). Obesity is a major health problem of the Western population and its management often is unsuccessful. Relapse is frequent regardless of the weight-reducing method used.

Medical management of obesity includes one or more of the following: diet, exercise, behavior modification, medication, psychotherapy, or surgical intervention. The only way to lose weight is to create a negative energy balance. The effects of diet combined with exercise versus diet alone show that significantly more weight is lost by the group following both restricted calorie intake and regular exercise.

Swimming and various other exercises performed in water are considered among the best forms of exercise for the obese. Since the specific gravity of the body is not much different from that of water, the weight of the body submerged in water is reduced to a few kilograms, with obese individuals keeping afloat especially easily. However, it is clear that swimming ranks with jogging and cross-country skiing among the forms of exercise with the highest energy expenditure (McArdle et al., 1981).

For those same reasons, swimming should be included in exercise programs for diabetics. Obesity is a major and frequently occurring problem in the maturity-onset diabetic. Even modest weight reduction is often associated with marked improvement in carbohydrate metabolism. Exercise increases glucose utilization by a mechanism which does not depend upon increased secretion of insulin. The increased utilization is balanced by an increased liver glucose output in normal individuals. Blood glucose concentrations in patients with well controlled insulin-dependent diabetes will also decrease during exercise, diminishing the need for exogenous insulin (Vranic et al., 1979). In the insulin-dependent diabetic, increased blood flow to the subcutaneous tissues during exercise has been shown to increase circulating insulin levels by mobilization of the injected depot (Vranic et al., 1979). This is a situation that potentially can result in hypoglycemia, but the risk can be minimized by doing regular amounts of exercise at specific times. The risk of hypoglycemia also means insulin-treated diabetics should not be allowed to swim if they comply poorly with their insulin therapy or if they have impaired mental function and cannot understand the influence of exercise on their insulin requirements.

Chronic exercise has been shown to increase insulin sensitivity. Strong evidence exists that the muscles' increased insulin sensitivity is the primary factor producing an increase in the uptake of glucose by peripheral tissues (Harrison et al., 1976). Pederson et al. (1980) demonstrated that in patients with insulin-dependent diabetes, exercise significantly increases the insulin binding to erythrocytes and monocytes. It may be that the same changes occur in working muscles. If this hypothesis is true, it is another reason to choose swimming as exercise for diabetics because all muscle groups are used.

In diabetics and healthy persons, regular exercise is also associated with a decrease in very low density lipoprotein triglyceride concentration and with an increase in high density lipoprotein cholesterol levels, both of which tend to be associated with a decreased risk of artherosclerotic disease (Lopez et al., 1974; Ratcliff et al., 1978).

Swimming is thought to be a means of blood pressure control. The effect of endurance training in middle-aged, healthy persons and hypertensive patients is often a lowering of both systolic and diastolic arterial pressures (Clausen, 1976). The same effect has been demonstrated in a study by Cléroux in patients with labile hypertension (Cléroux et al., 1982), but the antihypertensive mechanism of training remains obscure. Exercise may reduce peripheral resistance immediately after exercise; however, there is no known physiological reason why this vasodilatation exists for several hours. It seems that relaxation and weight control from swimming can lower blood pressure. Hypertensive patients should avoid cold water because of the diving reflex but otherwise, swimming is a safe and good form of exercise for hypertensive patients. However, more research is needed to discover its true antihypertensive mechanisms; there is also a need to investigate whether antihypertensive vasodilator drugs cause adverse cardiocirculatory effects in hypertensive patients while they swim.

Conclusion

In my opinion, internists and cardiologists should be aware of the fact that they can advocate swimming as training for their patients. Assuming a proper recommendation and explanation of possible hazards, swimming can be a very valuable aid in restoring or maintaining patients' fitness. Nevertheless, each patient must be treated individually and the role of swimming in a rehabilitation program must be judged according to the degree and type of disease as well as the patient's skill and interest.

References

ANDERSEN, H.T. 1966. Physiological adaptation in diving vertebrates. *Physiol. Rev.* **46**:212-243.

ANDERSEN, K.L. 1960. Energy cost of swimming. *Acta Chirurg. Scand.* (suppl.): 253, 169.

ÅSTRAND, P.O., and Rodahl, K. 1977. *Textbook of Work Physiology*, pp. 586-589. McGraw-Hill, New York.

CAIN, H.D., Frasher, W.G., Jr., and Stivelman, R. 1961. Graded activity program for sage return to self-care after myocardial infarction. *J. Am. Med. Assoc.* **177**:111-115.

CLAUSEN, J.P. 1976. Circulatory adjustments to dynamic exercise and effect of physical training in normal subjects and patients with coronary disease. *Prog. Cardiovasc. Dis.* **18**:459.

CLÉROUX, J., Péronnet, F., and de Champlain, J. 1982. Training and labile hypertension: Blood pressure and plasma catecholamines. *Med. Sci. Sports Exercise* **14**(2):181.

DE DIVITIS, O., Fazio, S., and Petitto, M. 1981. Obesity and cardiac function. *Circulation* **64**:477-481.

DI PRAMPERO, P.E., Pendergast, D.R., Wilson, and Rennie, D.W. 1974. Energetics of swimming in man. *J. Appl. Physiol.* **37**:1-5.

FARDY, P.S. 1977. Training for aerobic power. In: E.J. Burke (ed.), *Toward an Understanding of Human Performance*, pp. 10-14. Movement, Ithaca.

FLESSAS, A.P., Connally, G.P., and Handa, S. 1976. Effects of isometric exercise on the end diastolic pressure, volumes and function of left ventricle. *Circulation* **53**:839-847.

FLETCHER, G.F., Cantwell, J.D., and Watt, E.W. 1979. Oxygen consumption and hemodynamic response of exercises used in training of patients with recent myocardial infarction. *Circulation* **60**:140.

FOX, S.M. III, Naughton, J.P., and Haskell, W.L. 1971. Physical activity and the prevention of coronary heart disease. *Ann. Clin. Res.* **3**:404-432.

FREDERICI, A.B., Lozej, E., and Mari, L. 1980. Sport education of hemophiliacs: Skiing. *Med. Sport Turini* **33**(1):19-26.

FROELICHER, V.F. 1978. Exercise and the prevention of coronary atherosclerotic heart disease. *Cardiovasc. Clin.* **9**:13-23.

GAUER, O.H., and Henry, J.P. 1963. Circulatory basis of fluid volume control. *Physiol. Rev.* **43**:423.

HABER, P., Niederberger, M., and Eder, H. 1979. A study of a swimming training program in the rehabilitation of patients following myocardial infarction. *Wien. klin. Wochenschr.* **91**:693-696.

HARRISON, L.C., Martin, F.I.R., and Melick, R.A. 1976. Correlation between insulin receptor binding in isolated fat cells and insulin sensitivity in obese human subjects. *J. Clin. Invest.* **58**:1435-1441.

HASKELL, W.L. 1978. Cardiovascular complications during exercise training of cardiac patients. *Circulation* **57**:920-924.

HEIGENHAUSER, G.F., Boulet, D., and Miller, B. 1977. Cardiac outputs of post-myocardial infarction patients during swimming and cycling. *Med. Sci. Sports* **9**:143-147.

HELLERSTEIN, H.K. 1979. Cardiac rehabilitation. A retrospective view-1979. In: M. Pollock and D. Schmidt (eds.), *Heart Disease and Rehabilitation*, pp. 509-520. Houghton Mifflin, New York.

HOLLMANN, W., and Hettinger, T. 1976. *Sportmedizin- Arbeits- und Trainingsgrundlage*, pp. 656-659. Schattauer Verlag, Stuttgart-New York.

ILKER, H. 1973. Einrichtung von Herzinfarkt-Sportgruppe am Wohnort. (Establishment of myocardial infarct sport group in dwelling places.) *Artztl. Praxis* **25**:3708.

IRVING, L. 1963. Bradycardia in human divers. *J. Appl. Physiol.* **18**:489.

KEATINGE, W.R., and Evans, M. 1961. The respiratory and cardiovascular response to immersion in cold and warm water. *Q. J. Exp. Physiol.* **66**:83.

KRAMSCH, D.M., Aspen, A.J., and Abramowitz, B.M. 1981. Reduction of coronary atherosclerosis by moderate conditioning exercise in monkeys on atherogenic diet. *New Eng. J. Med.* **305**:1484-1488.

LAGERSTRØM, D. 1980. Trainingsgrundlagen, Trainings- und Programmaufbau. (Fundamentals of Training, Training and Program Development.) In: O.A. Brusis and H. Weber (eds.), *Handbuch der Koronargruppenbetreuung*, p. 225. Peri Medisches Fachbuch.

LAMBERT, C.A., Netherton, D.R., et al. 1982. Risk factors and life style: A statewide health-interview survey. *New Engl. J. Med.* **306**:1048-1051.

LINK, R.P., Pedersoli, W.M., and Safanie, A.H. 1972. Effects of exercise on development of atherosclerosis in swine. *Atherosclerosis* **15**:107-122.

LOFLAND, H.B., Jr., and Clarkson, T.B. 1959. A biomechanical study of spontaneous atherosclerosis in pigeons. *Circ. Res.* **7**:234-237.

LOPEZ, S.A., Vial, R., and Balart, L. 1974. Effects of exercise and physical fitness on serum lipids and lipoproteins. *Atherosclerosis* **20**:1-9.

MAGDER, S., Linnarson, D., and Crullstrand, L. 1981. The effect of swimming on patients with ischaemic heart disease. *Circulation* **63**:979-986.

McALLISTER, F.F., Bertsch, R., and Jacobson, J. II. 1960. The accelerating effect of muscular exercise on experimental atherosclerosis. *Arch. Surg.* **80**:54-60.

McARDLE, W.D., Katch, F.I., and Katch, V.L. 1981. *Exercise Physiology*, p. 492. Lea & Febiger, Philadelphia.

MOSS, A.J., DeCamilla, J., and Engstrom, F. 1974. The post-hospital phase of myocardial infarction — Identification of patients with increased mortality risk. *Circulation* **49**:460-462.

OLBRIDGE, N.B., Heigenhauser, G.J.F., and Sutton, J.R. 1978. Resting and exercise heart rate with apnea and facial immersion in female swimmers. *J. Appl. Physiol.* **45**:875-879.

OLSEN, C.R., Fanestil, D.D., and Scholander, P.F. 1962. Some effects of breath holding and apneic underwater diving on the cardiac rhythm in man. *J. Appl. Physiol.* **17**:461.

PEDERSEN, O., Beck-Nielsen, H., and Hedwig, L. 1980. Increased insulin receptors after exercise in patients with insulin-dependent diabetes mellitus. *New Engl. J. Med.* **302**:886-892.

PRIOR, J.T., and Ziegler, D.D. 1965. Regression of experimental atherosclerosis: Observations in the rabbit. *Arch. Pathol.* **80**:50-57.

RATCLIFF, R., Elliott, K., and Rubenstein, C. 1978. Plasma lipid and lipoprotein changes with chronic training. *Med. Sci. Sports Exercise* **10**:55 (abstr.).

ROST, R., Hollmann, W., and Dreisbach, W. 1977. Hemodynamic reaction and adaptation during physical training considered from the viewpoint of cardiac rehabilitation. *Cardiology* **62**(2):137.

SAMEK, K., Kirste, B., and Roskamm, H. 1977. Herzrhythmusstörungen nach Herzinfarkt. (Heart arrythmias after myocardial infarcts.) *Herz Kreisl.* **9**:641.

SHEPHERD, J.T., and Vanhoutte, P.M. 1980. *The Human Cardiovascular System, Facts and Concepts*, pp. 165-166. Raven Press, New York.

SHEPHARD, R.J. 1979. Cardiac rehabilitation in prospect. In: M. Pollock and D. Schmidt (eds.), *Heart and Rehabilitation*, pp. 521-547. Houghton Mifflin, New York.

TORKELSON, L.O. 1964. Rehabilitation of the patient with acute myocardial infarct. *J. Chronic Dis.* **17**:685-704.

VRANIC, M., and Berger, M. 1979. Exercise and diabetes mellitus. *Diabetes* **28**:147-167.

WEISS, H.S., Braun, F.D., and Friminger, P. 1966. Physical activity and atherosclerosis in the adult chicken. *J. Atheroscler. Res.* **6**:407-414.

WIESER, H. 1980. Koronarkrankenrehabilitation: Zwischenfalle und Kontroversen bei der Bewegungstherapie. (Coronary rehabilitation: Incidents and controversies on movement therapy.) *Therapiewoche* **30**:5218.

WIT, A.L., and Bigger, J.T. 1975. Possible electrophysiologic mechanisms for lethal arrhythmias accompanying myocardial ischemia and infarction. *Circulation* **52**(suppl. III):96-115.

Stress Fracture of the Os Metatarsale I in a Swimmer

Jon Van Caspel and Leo P. Heere

Netherlands Sports Federation, Papendal, Arnhem, The Netherlands

Breithaupt (1855) first presented a clinical description of a stress fracture without fully understanding its exact etiology; Stechow (1897) was the first to establish its radiological aspects. In those years such fractures were mainly seen in army recruits, ca. 80% of the cases being localized in the metatarsal bones, usually the os metatarsale III (Doury et al., 1979). This type of fracture has also been referred to as a "march fracture" or a "fatigue fracture." Recently stress fractures have been described in various sites of the lower extremities in athletes, especially runners (Taunton et al., 1981).

The following case deals with a swimmer's stress fracture suffered in the course of an intensive training program in which extra large fins were used. Research of the literature has not revealed any previous presentations of cases with a similar etiology. This type of fracture, moreover, is seldom seen in this particular locus (MT I).

Case Report

A 14-year-old female swimmer with no previous history of foot trauma and good general condition was seen a few days after the onset of pain in her left foot and ankle. She felt this pain especially during swimming; it was relieved by rest. The patient had been a national selection of the Netherlands Underwater Sports Association for the 2 previous years and had been participating in four to five workouts a week of 1.5 hr each.

During competitive training, the swimmers wore extra large fins (Figure 1) to develop maximal speed. These fins were made of nylon, weighed 900 g each and were 85 cm long and 23 cm wide.

The patient denied having suffered any specific, acute injury. She stated, however, that , 1 week prior to her visit, she had participated in a

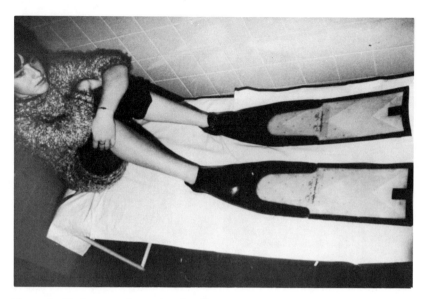

Figure 1 — Patient wearing swimming fins.

swimming contest wearing a pair of still heavier fins (made of rubber) because the sharp edges of her own fins were not protected with tape.

Examination of the left foot revealed a slightly swollen metatarsus showing tenderness with pressure upon the os metatarsale I and over the area of the talocrural joint. There was no impairment of ankle joint and foot movement. Forced passive dorsal/plantar flexion of the foot and straining the m. extensor digitorum communis against resistance were painful and so were all movements of the hallux. The x-ray (Figure 2) demonstrated the presence of a small fissure in the base of the os metatarsale I with no sign of dislocation.

The case was diagnosed as a stress fracture in the os metatarsale I of the left foot. The foot was immobilized using acrylastic bandage and tape, and the patient was prescribed crutches for 3 weeks with gradually increased loading of the foot. During that period, she was to abstain from any athletic activities.

Follow-up 5 weeks later showed the patient had no more complaint; upon examination, no clinical symptoms were found. Meanwhile, she had resumed training without suffering from foot trouble. In a follow-up x-ray of the left foot (Figure 3), the fracture line was no longer visible. Only a very small callus had formed.

Discussion

A great many theories have already been advanced to explain the cause of stress fracture. They have been compared, for instance, with fatigue

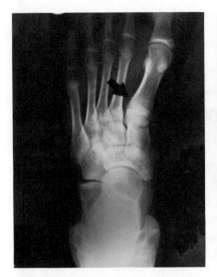

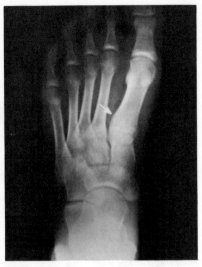

Figure 2 — X-ray of the fracture.   **Figure 3** — Healed fracture, 5 weeks later.

fractures within metals. This analogy, however, is only partly justified, for bone is a heterogeneous, anisotropic material; it requires stress for normal formation and remodeling (Stanitsky et al., 1977). On the histological level, the following processes are found to occur in bone tissue (Johnson et al., 1963): due to increased loading, microscopic changes develop which, combined with an increased blood flow resulting from enhanced muscle activity, give rise to piezo-electric potentials that stimulate the bone's remodeling process. However, a time lag occurs between the onset of bone destruction and the beginning of new bone formation. At a given moment, therefore, there is a weakened area within the bone in which fractures are likely to occur under the impact of external forces. A major etiological factor in this process is the rhythmic, repetitive muscle contraction causing slight mechanical lesions which summate beyond the stress-bearing capacity of the bone (Stanitsky et al., 1977).

As to the diagnostics of stress fractures, we emphasize the importance of an early diagnosis. The average time from the onset of symptoms to the request for medical help is 7.4 weeks (Taunton et al., 1981). The existence of a stress fracture should be suspected in any athlete complaining of pain in some part of the body which has been loaded during a period of intensive training. The pain develops during exercise and is relieved with rest but the athlete may not have suffered any acute injury. In most cases, physical findings will be limited to localized point tenderness over the bone and soft-tissue swelling. A stress fracture shows a characteristic picture in an x-ray — a "radiolucent hairline." In an early stage, however, this hairline crack is seldom visible in an ordinary x-ray. In some cases it may be detected in a tomogram which, with the help of a specialized radiographic technique, presents a kind of cross-section of an organ. X-ray examination, therefore, should be repeated after 2-3 weeks. If a stress fracture actually is present, a periosteal callus formation may be detected at the fracture site.

Another method now used frequently for early diagnosis is bone scanning with 99 m Tc polyphosphate-scintigraphy, in which a radiopharmacon formed by joining polyphosphates, tin and the radioactive element 99 m technetium is used. At the site of the fracture, an area of heightened radioactivity will become visible (so-called "hot spots") as the polyphosphates become involved in the increased bone turnover developing at the specific site as a result of the mechanism described above.

Stress fracture treatment should aim at minimizing the period during which the athlete will be unable to train. Usually, a combined treatment is applied including modified rest, ice massage, antiphlogistic medication, physiotherapy (especially for muscle training), maintaining cardiovascular fitness, and correcting, if necessary, static abnormalities (differences in leg length, forefoot varus). Not until the athlete has become asymptomatic can training resume and then only with a gradual build-up to the previous level. The physician should make sure that the training program will be well-balanced.

Comment

Returning to the patient, one can imagine the enormous forces acting upon the feet during swimming with these fins because of the huge masses of water they have to move. Both the m. tibialis anterior (dorsal flexion of the foot) and the m. peroneus longus (pronation, abduction and plantar flexion of the foot) insert partly on the os metatarsale I. The m. extensor hallucis longus and brevis pass across the os metatarsale I and insert on the bases of the two phalanges of the hallux. In swimming the front crawl, all of these muscles are used, meaning the os metatarsale I will be subjected to continuous forces.

Swimming without fins may cause an equal number of complaints, which has been described previously (Kennedy et al., 1978). Intensive training in front and back crawl strokes may give rise to surménage lesions of the extensor tendons along the dorsum of the foot. At the site of the retinaculum musculi extensorium inferius (cruciate-crural ligament) these tendons pass through a narrow sheath. With the movements the foot makes during these strokes ("flutter kick"), it is carried in extreme plantar flexion, causing these tendons to be stretched continuously. At the same time friction occurs within the sheath, giving rise to irritation of the tendons, resulting in edema, inflammation and adhesions.

This condition was also found in the patient we just described. The large fins (on one occasion even extra large and extra heavy) and the high training intensity were factors that may have contributed to the appearance of the stress fracture in this young girl. In this still little known branch of sport, more surménage lesions are likely to occur if the training intensity is not adapted to the swimmer's physical capabilities (e.g., muscle development, age group).

References

BREITHAUPT, M.D. 1855. Zur Pathologie des menschlichen Fusses. (The pathology of human feet.) *Med. Zeit.* **24**:169-171, 175-177.

DOURY, P., Delahaye, R.P., Pattin, S., Metges, P.J., and Mine, J. 1979. Fractures de fatigue. (Fatigue fractures.) In: L. Simon (ed.), *Le Pied du Sportif.* Masson, Paris.

JOHNSON, L.C., Stradford, H.T., and Geis, R.W. 1963. Histogenesis of stress fractures. Armed Forces Institute of Pathology Annual Lectures. *J. Bone Joint Surg.* **45**A:1542.

KENNEDY, J.C., Hawkins, R., and Kissof, W.B. 1978. Orthopedic manifestations of swimming. *Am. J. Sports Med.* **6**:309-322.

STANITSKY, C.L., McMaster, J.H., and Scranton, P.E. 1978. On the nature of stress fractures. *Am. J. Sports Med.* **6**:391-396.

STECHOW, A.W. 1897. Fussoedem und Roentgenstrahlen. (Foot edema and x-rays.) *Deuts. Milit. Aerzl. Zeit.* **26**:465-471.

TAUNTON, J.E., Clement, D.B., and Webber, D. 1981. Lower extremity stress fractures in athletes. *Physician Sports Med.* **9**:77-86.

Modulation of Hormone Levels
in Male Swimmers During Training

**Giancarlo Carli, Gilberto Martelli, Antonio Viti,
Lucia Baldi, Marco Bonifazi, and Concetta Lupo di Prisco**
University of Siena, Italy

Athletes in training are not given a constant workload since it is well known (Harre, 1972) that variations in intensity and duration are more efficient in reaching and maintaining good fitness levels. The type of schedule is usually homogeneous for groups of athletes performing similar competitions. During a competitive season, variations in training are related both to athlete response and to calendar of competition. Since physical exercise is known to modify hormone plasma levels, a regimen of repeated activity should be able to produce long-lasting modifications of hormones according to the intensity and the type of training. The purpose of this study was to investigate possible variations of some hormones in swimmers during two consecutive competitive seasons during which the amount of training differed.

Materials and Methods

Subjects

Eight males (ages 12-16 years) in the 1979-80 season and six males (five from the previous season) in the following year were studied. All subjects had 2-5 years of experience. Five prepubertal children (three males and two females) were also studied in the 1979-80 season. In Figures 2 and 3, results obtained with females are also reported by Carli et al. (1982).

Training Program

Training sessions (duration 90-120 min, six per week) varied according to the amount, intensity and duration of the swimming activity. Training

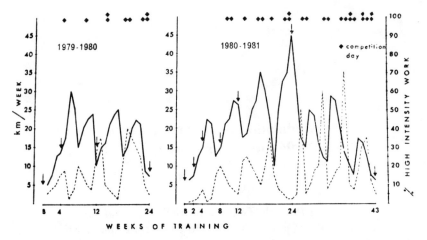

Figure 1 — Total distance swum (km/week) during training (continuous line) and percentage of high intensity work (dotted line) in the two seasons. The arrows indicate the occurrence of blood collection.

consisted of mixed types of techniques: fartlek, overdistance, interval, repetition, and sprint (Counsilman, 1968). The work performed at high intensity (over 90% of maximal speed capacity in short distances), with a recovery period sufficient to permit repetition at the same level of performance of the same distance was also analyzed as a percentage of the total distance swum in the week (Figure 1, dotted line). In 1979 training sessions and blood collection started on October 1 after 1 month of absolutely no training; in 1980 the beginning of activity in water (September 15) and the first blood samples were preceded by 1 month of rest followed by 2 weeks of moderate athletic exercises (jogging, joint mobility, etc.), which are not indicated in Figure 1. All athletes reached maximal performance in the competitions which were held at the end of the season.

Procedure

The blood was collected from the antecubital vein at about 8 a.m., more than 24 hours after an exercise session, and was placed in tubes containing EDTA (two drops of a 0.1 g/ml solution) and centrifuged. The plasma was stored at −20°C until analyzed within 7-10 days.

Hormonal Assay

ACTH was determined by radioimmunoassay (RIA) performed directly on plasma samples as reported by Vague et al. (1970) by adding ^{125}I-ACTH and antiserum anti-ACTH purchased from Sorin. Cortisol was determined by the competitive protein-binding method after extraction of the plasma with methylene chloride following the procedure of Nugent and Mayes (1966). Testosterone was extracted from the plasma with diethyl-ether and RIA was performed on the extracts using antigen and antibody, purchased from Sorin, according to the method of separation between free and bound steroid with charcoal-dextran described by Collins et al. (1972). Prolactin was determined by RIA according to a procedure described by Midgley (1966) in which plasma in buffer solution was added to ^{125}I-hPRL and to antiserum anti-hPRL purchased from Biodata; the antibody-bound hormone was precipitated by adding antigammaglobulin serum at the end of incubation time. Triiodothyronine (T_3) and thyroxine (T_4) were analyzed by RIA using antigen and antibodies purchased from Sorin and polyethylene glycol (PEG) to separate free and antibody-bound hormones as described by Creighton et al. (1973). Growth hormone (HGH), luteinizing hormone (LH) and follicle stimulating hormone (FSH) were analyzed by RIA using antigens and antibodies, purchased from Biodata, with PEG to precipitate the antigen-antibody complexes (Donini and Donini, 1969).

Statistical Methods

Analysis of variance and the least significant difference test were used for comparisons between samples collected at different times; a t-test for paired samples was used to compare hormone values of the same subjects in different competitive seasons. Linear regression (Pearson coefficient) was used to correlate variations of different hormones and the amount and type of training with hormonal values (Snedecor and Cochran, 1967).

Results

Figure 2 (top) indicates that ACTH and cortisol changed significantly during the 1980-81 competitive season, as shown by the analysis of variance. In particular ACTH reached a peak after 4 weeks of training, then gradually decreased below basal levels after 6 and 10 months. Cortisol levels, on the other hand, sharply increased at the beginning of training, reached a peak after 4 weeks and decreased after 8 weeks, adjusting to about initial levels afterward. However, no linear correlation (Pearson coefficient) between ACTH and cortisol values was found.

In 1979-80 ACTH was not modified by training whereas cortisol (Figure 2, bottom) showed a completely different pattern of variation: A sharp reduction was recorded after 4 weeks, followed by a recovery at about basal levels. During the same season (Figure 2, bottom) cortisol variations in girls (Carli et al., 1982) and in children who engaged in an identical training program displayed a similar pattern.

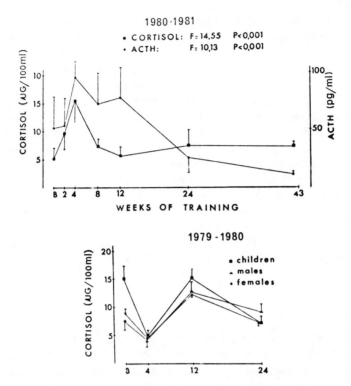

Figure 2—Changes in ACTH and cortisol during training. Means and standard errors (vertical lines). B = basal levels before training; 2, 4, 8, 12, 24, 43 = samples corresponding to weeks of training. Top: 1980-81 season. ACTH: B vs 4, B vs 43, 2 vs 4 $p < 0.005$; 4 vs 24, 4 vs 43 $p < 0.001$; B vs 24 $p < 0.05$. Cortisol: B vs 2 $p < 0.005$; 2 vs 4, 4 vs 8, 4 vs 12, 4 vs 24, 4 vs 43 $p < 0.001$. Bottom: 1979-80 season. Cortisol in males: analysis of variance ($df = 3/28$; $F = 4.36$) $p < 0.005$; B vs 4 $p < 0.025$; 4 vs 12 $p < 0.005$. Cortisol in females: 4 vs 12 $p < 0.01$; B vs 4, 12 vs 24 $p < 0.05$. Cortisol in children: B vs 4, B vs 24 $p < 0.02$; 4 vs 12 $p < 0.001$; 12 vs 24 $p < 0.01$.

A comparison of ACTH levels between the two seasons in the same five subjects showed higher values in 1980-81 than in 1979-80 (*t*-test for paired samples: B-I, basal values of the first year, vs B-II $p < 0.01$; 12-I vs 12-II $p < 0.001$). Initial and final cortisol levels did not differ between the two seasons but significant changes were recorded at 4 and 12 weeks (4-I vs 4-II $p < 0.01$; 12-I vs 12-II $p < 0.001$).

Testosterone levels in the 1980-81 season significantly increased after 8 weeks, reached the maximal value at 12 weeks, remained elevated at 24 weeks to decrease below initial levels at the end of the season (Figure 3, top). In the previous season, on the contrary, testosterone was unaffected by training in males; in females, however, a reduction between sample I and sample IV was recorded (Figure 3, top). The comparison

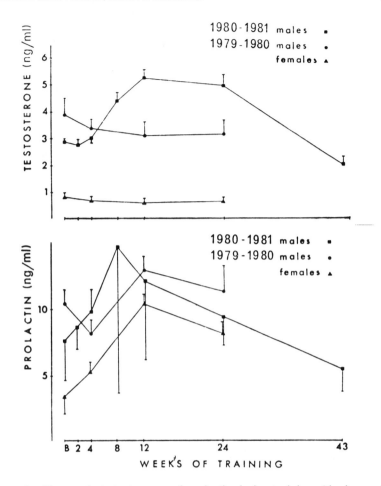

Figure 3 — Changes in testosterone and prolactin during training. Abscissa as in Figure 2. Top: analysis of variance for testosterone in males during the 1980-81 season ($df = 6/35$; $F = 29.70$) $p < 0.001$; B vs 8, B vs 12, B vs 24, 4 vs 8, (8, 12, 24) vs 43 $p < 0.001$; 8 vs 12, B vs 43 $p < 0.025$. Testosterone in the 1979-80 season: no significant changes in males and females. However, in females, by using the t-test for paired samples, a statistical significant difference ($p < 0.001$) between sample I and sample IV was recorded. Bottom: analysis of variance for prolactin in males during the 1980-81 season ($df = 6/35$; $F = 1.59$) not significant; in males during the 1979-80 season ($df = 3/28$; $F = 6.38$) $p < 0.001$; B vs 24 $p < 0.005$; 4 vs 12 $p < 0.001$; B vs 12 $p < 0.005$; in females during the season 1979-80 4 vs 12 $p < 0.05$.

between the two seasons performed on the five subjects from both showed no difference in initial and fourth-week values, whereas higher levels occurred in the second season at 12 and 24 weeks (12-I vs 12-II $p < 0.05$; 24-I vs 24-II $p < 0.01$).

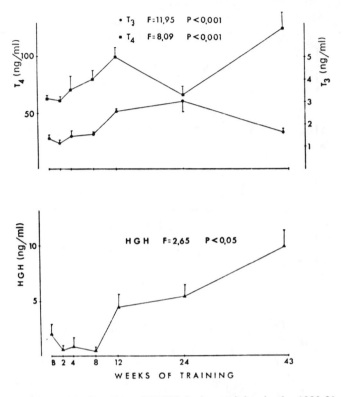

Figure 4—Changes in T_3, T_4 and HGH during training in the 1980-81 season. Abscissa as in Figure 2. Top: T_3—B vs 12, 4 vs 12 $p < 0.01$; (B, 2, 4, 8) vs 24 $p <$ 0.001; 8 vs 12 $p < 0.025$; 24 vs 43 $p < 0.005$. T_4—B vs 12, 2 vs 12 $p < 0.005$; 8 vs 12 $p < 0.025$; 12 vs 24 $p < 0.01$; (B, 2, 4, 8, 24) vs 43 $p < 0.001$. Bottom: HGH—(B, 2, 4, 8) vs 43 $p < 0.01$; 24 vs 43 $p < 0.05$.

Prolactin levels were affected by training in the 1979-80 season both in males and females with a peak in males at 12 weeks (Figure 3, bottom). In 1980-81 a similar trend was observed in males but without significant changes. However, initial and fourth-week levels were significantly lower in 1979-80 than in 1980-81 (B-I vs B-II $p < 0.02$; 4-I vs 4-II $p < 0.02$).

T_3 gradually increased with training, reaching its maximal value at 24 weeks and then returning to about initial levels at the end of the season (Figure 4, top). T_4 gradually increased during the first 12 weeks, then decreased at the 24th week to be found elevated again at the end of the season. No linear correlation between T_3 and T_4 changes was observed.

HGH levels were not significantly modified by training except for the last value (Figure 4, bottom), which was higher than the initial value and also greater than all the other samples. FSH and LH were unaffected by training, and no linear correlation was found between LH and testosterone values.

Testosterone and T_3 were found to be significantly correlated with the total distance (km) swum in the week before each blood collection (T: r = 0.81 p < 0.05; T_3: r = 0.92 p < 0.01), whereas prolactin was correlated with the percentage of high intensity work (Figure 1) of the week preceding the blood collection (r = 0.75, p < 0.05).

Discussion

The main results of this research are: (a) hormone basal levels were modified during training; (b) changes occurred either at the beginning of training and/or at later stages; (c) all variations were within the physiological range.

We believe this is the first longitudinal study on hormone basal levels in male swimmers during competitive seasons. Similar studies have been performed in male runners by Kuoppasalmi et al. (1981) but with different results. In particular, in their studies, testosterone and cortisol were unaffected by training, although a comparison with our results is rather difficult since the training program was not specified and blood was collected at different time intervals. According to Hartley et al. (1972) and Shephard and Sidney (1975), cortisol and HGH are not modified after 7-10 weeks of aerobic training.

In this research, it is likely that the amount and the type of training were responsible for the hormone variations and for the difference between the two seasons. During the second season, for instance, the first basal blood sample was collected after 2 weeks of moderate aerobic work and the maximal peak of load was reached only after 6 months, whereas in the preceding year training started suddenly and reached the highest peak at the sixth week. Moreover, the total workload was higher during the second season. As a consequence, some hormones such as ACTH and prolactin had different initial levels and others (ACTH, testosterone), unaffected during the first season, displayed gradual modifications during the second. Furthermore, the first season study lasted only 6 months and blood was collected at greater intervals. The intensity of training varied within a wide range: during the second season testosterone, T_3 and prolactin changes were correlated with the amount and type of training.

In general the decrease in training intensity occurring from the sixth to the tenth month was associated with a decrease in hormone basal levels. At the same time, the number and the importance of competitions increased. Increases in HGH and T_4 resulted at the end of the season. It cannot be excluded that hormones have been differentially affected by the interaction of a gradual decreasing intensity of training at a high level of fitness and the stress of exercise done at the limits of maximal performance.

Acknowledgments

We would like to thank the athletes of the Associazione Nuoto di Siena for their cooperation. This investigation was supported by a grant from the Dipartimento Cultura e Istruzione, Regione Toscana, Firenze.

References

CARLI, G., Martelli, G., Viti, A., Baldi, L., Bonifazi, M., and Lupo di Prisco, C. 1983. Effect of swimming training on hormone levels in girls. *J. Sports Med. Phys. Fitness* **23**:45-51.

COLLINS, W.P., Mansfield, M.D., Alladina, N.S., and Sommerville, I.S. 1972. Radioimmunoassay of plasma testosterone. *J. Steroid Biochem.* **3**:333-348.

COUNSILMAN, J.E. 1968. *The Science of Swimming.* Prentice-Hall, Englewood Cliffs, NJ.

CREIGHTON, W.D., Lampert, P.H., and Miesher, P.A. 1973. Detection of antibodies and soluble antigen-antibody complexes by precipitation with polyetylene glycol. *J. Immunol.* **111**:1219-1227.

DONINI, S., and Donini, P. 1969. Radioimmunoassay employing polymerized antisera. *Acta Endocrinol.* (suppl.):139-142.

HARRE, D. 1972. *Trainingslehre.* (Conditioning.) Sportverlag, Berlin.

HARTLEY, L.H., Mason, J.W., Hogan, R.P., Jones, L.G., Kotchen, T.A., Mougey, E.H., Werry, F.E., Pennington, L.L., and Ricketts, P.T. 1972. Multiple hormonal responses to prolonged exercise in relation to physical training. *J. Appl. Physiol.* **33**:607-610.

KUOPPASALMI, K., Naveri, H., Kosunen, K., Harkonen, M., and Adlercreuz, H. 1981. Plasma steroid levels in muscular exercise. In: J. Poortmans and G. Niset (eds.), *Biochemistry of Exercise IV-B.* University Park Press, Baltimore.

MIDGLEY, A.R. 1966. Radioimmunoassay: A method for human chorionic gonadotropin and human luteinizing hormone. *Endocrinology* **79**:10.

NUGENT, C.A., and Mayes, D.A. 1966. Plasma corticosteroids determined by use of corticosteroid-binding globulin and dextran coated charcoal. *J. Clin. Endocrinol. Metab.* **26**:1116-1120.

SHEPHARD, R.J., and Sidney, K.H. 1975. Effects of physical exercise on plasma, growth hormone and cortisol levels in human subjects. In: J.H. Wilmore and J.F. Keogh (eds.), *Exercise and Sport Sciences Reviews* **(Vol 3)**. Academic Press, New York.

SNEDECOR, G.W., and Cochran, W.G. 1967. *Statistical Methods.* Iowa State University Press, Ames, IA.

VAGUE, P., Olivier, C., Jaquet, P., and Vague, J. 1970. Le dosage radioimmunologique de l'ACTH plasmatique. *Ann. Endocrinol.* **31**:993-994.

Body Composition, Biological Maturation, and Socioeconomic Status of Young Talented Female Swimmers and Gymnasts

M.J.E. Bernink, W.B.M. Erich, A.L. Peltenburg, Maria L. Zonderland, and I.A. Huisveld
State University of Utrecht, The Netherlands

In recent years attention has been given to the effects of sport activities at younger ages on growth, body composition, and biological maturation. Female swimmers seem to be slightly taller than the average population but only after the age of 12 (Andrew et al., 1972). Eriksson et al. (1978) found in a longitudinal study that female swimmers grew only an average of 4 cm in height between ages 13 and 21 years. However, female gymnasts seem to be smaller and have less fat than control females (Erich, 1980; Parízková, 1977). Biological maturation seems to be delayed in female gymnasts but not in female swimmers (Märker, 1979; Malina et al., 1978).

Growth and biological maturation are influenced by genetic and environmental factors such as nutrition and socioeconomic status (Eveleth and Tanner, 1976). Children from parents with a high socioeconomic status are taller and mature earlier. This was also true in the Netherlands in 1965 (van Wieringen, 1972). However, in some highly developed countries (e.g., Sweden) the socioeconomic status no longer seems to be correlated with growth and biological maturation (Furu, 1976; Lindgren, 1976). The purpose of this study was to investigate whether differences in height, body composition, and biological maturation in young female athletes, swimmers and gymnasts can be explained by differences in socioeconomic status.

Procedures

Subjects

In a cross-sectional study during 1981 two groups of young female athletes served as subjects. Group S consisted of 52 talented female swimmers, mean age 134 ± 24 months, who were members of two top swimming clubs in The Netherlands. Group G included 78 highly talented female gymnasts, mean age 138 ± 18 months, who were members of the selection group of the Dutch Catholic Gymnastic Federation.

Anthropometric Measurements and Estimation of Biological Maturation

Height and weight were determined. In accordance with Durnin and Womersley (1974), four skinfolds were measured with a Harpenden skinfold caliper. Weight to height ratio (w/h) and the Quetelet index (w/h²) were calculated. Growth percentiles of the groups (using mean value for height) were determined using the data of Van Wieringen et al. (1968) for Dutch children. Biological maturation was estimated according to Tanner and Whitehouse (1975). Stages are numbered 1-5 for breast development (M) and 1-6 for pubic hair growth (P).

Data Obtained by Inquiry

The questionnaire requested the children's age of first menstruation (menarche), onset of participation in sport, and number of weekly hours of training. Based on an inquiry of the subjects' parents similar to that used by van Beem and Egger (1979), data on the following socioeconomic factors were obtained: occupation of both parents (scale 1 low-10 high level) and their function, the number of people receiving their guidance, education of both parents (1 low-7 high level), and the ages of both parents. The parents were assured that the data would be processed anonymously. Their response was 90%.

Estimation of Socioeconomic Status

For socioeconomic status five classifications were used, based on the statistics of Attwood (1979), appropriate for the Dutch society; Class 1 reflected high and Class 5 low socioeconomic states. The estimate of socioeconomic status was made using the following objective criteria: (a) occupation and function of the breadwinner, (b) educational level of the breadwinner, (c) age of the breadwinner, and (d) the number of persons under the breadwinner's guidance.

Statistical Procedures

To identify significant differences between the groups a Student t-test for unpaired data was used. Level of significance $p \leq 0.05$. A percentage distribution was made for P, M, and for P and M per age category, menarche, and socioeconomic status to identify percentage differences within and between the groups.

Results

Age, Anthropometric Results and Biological Maturation

All means, standard deviations, and significant differences of both groups for age, anthropometry, weight-to-height ratio and Quetelet index are presented in Table 1. The swimming group had the same chronological age as the gymnastic group. The female swimmers were taller and heavier and had more fat than the female gymnasts. Height, expressed in percentiles, indicated the female swimmers and female gymnasts were in the 85th and 37th percentiles, respectively. The weight-to-height ratio was higher for the swimmers than for the gymnasts, but the Quetelet index was not different. Data for biological maturation are shown in Table 2. The swimmers were more mature as indicated by pubic hair growth and breast development. Already 19.2% of the girl swimmers were menstruating in contrast to 8.2% of the female gymnasts of the same chronological age. In Figure 1a & b, a percentile distribution of P and M for both groups is presented. The swimmers had lower percentages of P_1 and M_1 and higher percentages of P_{4-6} and M_{3-5}. These results indicate that the swimming group was taller, had more fat, and was biologically more mature than gymnasts. In Figure 2a-c a subdivision by chronological age is presented for height, weight, and the sum of the skinfolds. A percentile distribution per age category for P and M is shown in Figure 3a & b. The same phenomena as for the total groups can be seen.

Table 1

**Age and Anthropometric Results
of Girl Swimmers (S) and Female Gymnasts (G)**

Groups		S		G
Number		52		78
Age (months)	M[a]	134		138
	SD	24		18
Height (cm)	M	151.0	—[b]	144.2
	SD	13.7		9.4
Growth percentile	M	85		37
Weight (kg)	M	39.9	—[b]	34.7
	SD	10.1		7.6
Sum of four skinfolds (mm)	M	37.2	—[b]	26.1
	SD	11.9		6.1
Weight to height ratio (w/h)	M	0.26	—[b]	0.24
	SD	0.05		0.04
Quetelet index (w/h²)	M	0.17		0.16
	SD	0.02		0.02

[a]Mean (M) ± standard deviation (SD).
[b]$p < 0.05$.

Table 2

Biological Maturation of the Girl Swimmer (S) and Female Gymnasts (G)

Groups		S		G
Number		52		78
Pubic hair growth (1-6)	M^a	2.2	$-^b$	1.6
	SD	1.4		1.0
Breast development (1-5)	M	2.0	$-^b$	1.6
	SD	1.2		1.0
Menarche	N	10		5
	%	19.2		8.2

aMean (M) ± standard deviation (SD).
b$p < 0.05$.

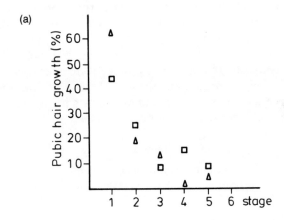

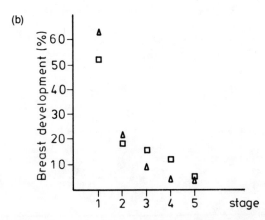

Figure 1a & b — Percentile distribution of pubic hair growth (P) and breast development (M) for female swimmers (□) and female gymnasts (△).

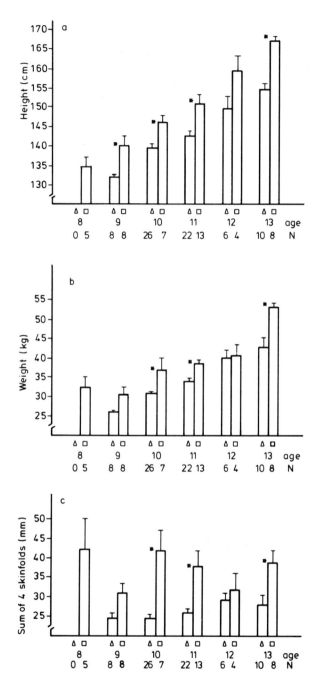

Figure 2a-c — Height, weight, and sum of four skinfolds per age category for female swimmers (□) and female gymnasts (△). Mean (*M*) and standard error of the mean (*SEM*); $p \leq 0.05$.

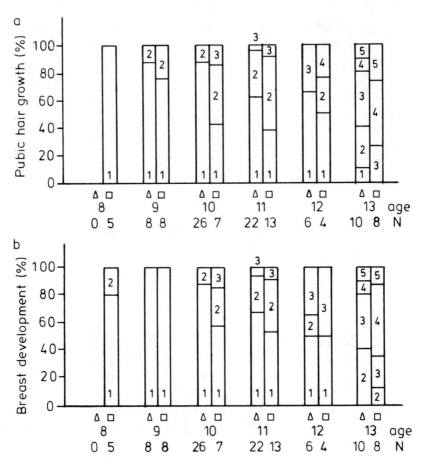

Figure 3a & b—Percentile distribution for pubic hair growth (P) and breast development (M) per age category for female swimmers (□) and female gymnasts (△).

Data from the Questionnaire

The results of the questionnaire concerning duration of training expressed in months and weekly hours of training are presented in Table 3. A significant difference existed in the duration of training expressed in months between the swimmers and the gymnasts. The swimmers started their sport activities later than the gymnasts; however, the number of hours of weekly training was the same for both groups.

Socioeconomic Status and Factors

The results of the questionnaire on the socioeconomic status and the socioeconomic factors are depicted in Table 4. The socioeconomic status

Table 3

Data from the Inquiry with Girl Swimmers (S) and Female Gymnasts (G)

Groups		S		G
N		52		78
Duration of training (months)	M[a]	49.7	$-$[b]	72.0
	SD	21.0		23.4
Weekly training time (hr)	M	6.35		6.45
	SD	3.68		1.87

Girl Swimmers (S) and Female Gymnasts (G).
[a]Mean (M) ± standard deviation (SD).
[b]$p < 0.05$.

Table 4

**Socioeconomic Status and Socioeconomic Factors
of the Swimming Group (S) and Gymnastic Group (G)**

Groups		S		G
N		52		78
Socioeconomic status (5-1)	M[a]	3.4		3.0
	SD	0.9		1.2
Occupation of father (1-10)	M	5.0	$-$[b]	6.4
	SD	1.8		2.4
Education of father (1-7)	M	2.5	$-$[b]	3.3
	SD	1.1		1.8
Education of mother (1-7)	M	2.0	$-$[b]	2.5
	SD	1.0		1.4

[a]Mean (M) ± standard deviation (SD).
[b]$p < 0.05$.

was the same for the swimming and the gymnast groups. A percentile distribution of the socioeconomic status of the groups revealed that in the swimming group the highest socioeconomic status was not represented (Figure 4). The occupation of the father and educational levels of the parents were lower in the swimming group compared to the parents of the gymnasts.

Discussion

The purpose of this study was to investigate whether differences in body composition and biological maturation between the groups were related to differences in socioeconomic status and socioeconomic fac-

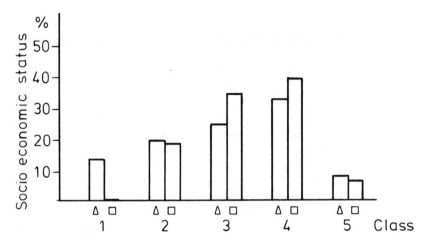

Figure 4 — Percentile distribution of socioeconomic status for girl swimmers (□) and female gymnasts (△).

tors. It was found in agreement with the literature that female swimmers were taller, had more fat, and were biologically more mature compared to female gymnasts (Andrew, 1972; Eriksson, 1978). However, no difference in socioeconomic status was found; therefore, the difference in height could not be explained by socioeconomic status. This finding was in agreement with the investigation of Lindgren (1976) in Sweden, who found that socioeconomic status was no longer an important factor influencing the height of a child because differences in living conditions between different socioeconomic classes were diminishing. This may be true for all highly developed countries. However, van Wieringen (Note 1) still found a positive relationship in The Netherlands, as he did in 1965 (van Wieringen, 1972). For biological maturation, the same result occurred: A delayed biological maturation was not accompanied by a low socioeconomic status in the investigated groups. This was in agreement with the data of Furu (1976) in Sweden. She found that although there were differences in socioeconomic status, the biological maturation was the same, presumably because of good social conditions. In contrast, Eveleth and Tanner (1976) found that poor girls reached menarche later than wealthier girls.

The difference in biological maturation could not be explained by the number of hours of weekly training, because female swimmers and gymnasts were training equally long, although the onset of training in female gymnasts was earlier. So the energy drain as postulated by Warren (1980) did not seem to be the cause of the delayed biological maturation. To obtain more insight into the cause of the differences in height, body composition, and biological maturation, a longitudinal study concerning genetic factors, fat metabolism, and hormonal regulations was designed with an investigation of nutrition included. In a cross-sectional pilot study (Note 2) on sex hormone profiles in female swimmers and gymnasts, our expectation that female gymnasts do show a delayed biological maturation was confirmed.

In conclusion, the differences in height, body composition, and biological maturation between talented female swimmers and highly talented female gymnasts cannot be explained by differences in socioeconomic status. Therefore, other factors must be responsible for the differences between the investigated groups.

Acknowledgment

The writers are most grateful for the helpful comments of Dr. J.C. van Wieringen.

Reference Notes

1. Wieringen, J.C. van. Personal communication, March 1982.
2. Peltenburg, A.L., et al. Sex hormone profiles and biological maturation of (pre)pubertal female athletes – swimmers and gymnasts. In preparation.

References

ANDREW, G.M., Becklahe, M.R., Guleria, J.S., and Bates, D.V. 1972. Heart and lung functions in swimmers and nonathletes during growth. *J. Appl. Physiol.* **32**:245-251.

ATTWOOD, B.V. 1979. *Attwood Statistics, Division into Socioeconomic Status.* Attwood Panels, Dongen, The Netherlands.

BEEM, A. van, and Egger, R.J. 1979. *Onderzoek naar de voedingstoestand van 15-16 jarige scholieren in Nederland.* (Nutritional Status of Dutch School Children Age 15-16 Years.) Report n. 6564 C.I.V.O.T.N.O., Zeist, The Netherlands.

DURNIN, J.V.G.A., and Womersley, J. 1974. Body fat assessed from total body density and its estimation from skinfold thickness: Measurements on 481 men and women aged from 16 to 72 years. *Br. J. Nutr.* **32**:77-97.

ERICH, W.B.M. 1980. *Over motorische grondeigenschappen bij jonge turnsters van 8 tot en met 11 jaar. In het bijzonder de lenigheid.* (Motor Abilities in Young Gymnasts Age 8-11 Years, Especially Flexibility.) Thesis, University of Utrecht.

ERIKSSON, B.O., Engstrom, I., Karlberg, P., Lundin, A., Saltin, B., and Thoren, C. 1978. Long term effect of previous swim training in girls, a 10 year follow up of the "girl swimmers." *Acta Paediatr. Scand.* **67**:285-292.

EVELETH, P.B., and Tanner, J.M. 1976. *World Wide Variation in Human Growth.* Cambridge University Press, Cambridge.

FURU, M. 1976. Menarcheal age in Stockholm girls. 1967. *Ann. Human Biol.* **3**:587-590.

LINDGREN, G. 1976. Height, weight and menarche in Swedish urban schoolchildren in relation to socioeconomic and regional factors. *Ann. Human Biol.* **3**:501-528.

MÄRKER, K. 1979. Zur Menarche von Sportlerinnen nach mehrjahrigen Trainung im Kindesalter. *Med. Sport* **19**:329-332.

MALINA, R.M., Spirduso, W.W., Tate, C., and Baylor, A.M. 1978. Age at menarche and selected menstrual characteristics in athletes at different competitive levels and in different sports. *Med. Sci. Sports* **10**:218-222.

PAŘÍZKOVÁ, J. 1977. Body build and body composition in girl gymnasts and in non-training girls. In: J. Pařízková (ed.), *Body Fat and Physical Fitness*, pp. 152-156. Nijhoff, Den Haag.

TANNER, J.M., and Whitehouse, R.H. 1975. Clinical longitudinal standards for height, weight, height velocity, weight velocity and the stages of puberty. *Arch. Dis. Child.* **51**:170-179.

WARREN, M.P. 1980. The effects of exercise on pubertal progression and reproductive function in girls. *J. Clin. Endocrinol. Metab.* **51**:1150-1157.

WIERINGEN, J.C. van, Wafelbakker, F., Verbrugge, H.P., and Haas, J.H. 1968. *Groeidiagrammen Nederland 1965.* (Growth Diagrams 1965, The Netherlands.) Wolters & Noordhoff, Groningen.

WIERINGEN, J.C. van. 1972. *Seculaire groeiverschuiving, lengte en gewicht surveys 1964-1966 in Nederland in historisch perspectief.* (Secular Trend, Height and Weight Surveys 1964-1966 in The Netherlands in Historical Perspective.) Thesis, University of Leiden.

Plasma Lipids and Apolipoproteins
in Young Female Swimmers and Gymnasts

**Maria L. Zonderland, W.B.M. Erich, M.J.E. Bernink,
A.L. Peltenburg, and P. Wilms**
State University of Utrecht, The Netherlands

L. Havekes
Gaubius Institute, Leiden, The Netherlands

Regular physical activity affects the lipid metabolism and lipid profile and is also associated with decreased mass of body fat. Trained subjects have higher high density lipoprotein-cholesterol (HDL-C) and often lower low density lipoprotein-cholesterol (LDL-C) and triglyceride (TG) levels than sedentary persons (Wood and Haskell, 1979). Fat mass also seems to affect lipid metabolism. Obese persons often have elevated serum cholesterol and TG levels compared to leaner subjects. In obese groups, the fat mass correlates with the serum lipids, especially with TG, but in nonobese groups these correlations are very low (Ylitalo, 1981). Therefore, the effect of training on lipid metabolism and lipid profile seems to be mainly due to activity itself with a very small part due to the decrease in body fat mass. These observations were made on adults, but there were indications that they are true for children, too (Gilliam and Burke, 1979; Laskarzewski et al., 1980). Erich (1980) reported that female gymnasts were leaner than control females of the same age. Female swimmers were found to have the same amount of body fat as control females (Åstrand et al., 1963). Therefore, the lipid profiles and apolipoproteins in a group of female swimmers and gymnasts were investigated and it was proposed that differences in lipid profile and apolipoprotein levels would not be related to differences in body composition. The levels of total cholesterol (TC), HDL-C, free cholesterol (FC), TG, and total lipids (TL), and the concentrations of the apolipoproteins A-I, A-II, and B (apo A-I, apo A-II, apo B) were measured. LDL-C was calculated and the following ratios were computed: HDL-C/TC, HDL-C/LDL-C, HDL-C/apo A-I, LDL-C/apo B, and apo A-I/apo B.

Methods

Prepubertal female gymnasts ($n = 14$) and prepubertal female swimmers ($n = 14$) participated in this study. Informed consent was obtained from the parents. Blood samples were taken on the same day as the anthropometric data and the estimation of sexual maturation. In order to try to exclude the effects of sex hormones on the lipid metabolism, the groups were matched according to sexual maturation and age. Table 1 summarizes some characteristics of the groups.

Sexual maturation was determined according to Tanner (1962) by breast development (M = 1-5) and pubic hair growth (P = 1-6). Height was recorded to the nearest 0.1 cm and weight to the nearest 0.5 kg with a standardized anthropometer and balance. Skinfold thickness was measured according to Durnin and Rahaman (1976) with a Harpenden skinfold caliper. The percentage of body fat was calculated on the basis of the density method (Dauncey et al., 1977; Durnin et al., 1976; Siri, 1956).

Blood was sampled from the vena cubiti in EDTA-tubes after an overnight fast. The plasma was distributed in Eppendorf cups, frozen in liquid nitrogen and transported on carbon dioxide ice. Until analysis, plasma was stored at $-20°C$. TC, HDL-C, FC, TG, and TL were measured using colorimetric methods. LDL-C was calculated (Boehringer, 1979). Quantification of apo A-I and apo A-II was performed using a radial immunodiffusion procedure by the workers of the Gaubius Institute in Leiden, The Netherlands (Cheung and Albers, 1977). Apo B was measured as described by Havekes et al. (1981). HDL-C/TC, HDL-C/LDL-C, HDL-C/apo A-I, LDL-C/apo B, and apo A-I/apo B ratios were computed.

Differences between the groups were tested using the two-tailed Student t-test ($p < 0.05$). Pearson correlation coefficients were calculated between lipids, apolipoproteins and body composition. The square of the correlation coefficient may be interpreted as the proportion of variance in variable B attributable to variations in variable A. It was assumed that a correlation coefficient must be at least 0.70, otherwise it was not considered to be an important relationship. The level of significance was $p < 0.001$.

Table 1

Group Characteristics (mean $\pm$ SEM)

Variable	Gymnasts	Swimmers
Number	14	14
Age (months)	134 ± 2	134 ± 1
Breast development	1.2 ± 0.1	1.5 ± 0.2
Pubic hair growth	1.3 ± 0.1	1.5 ± 0.2
Hours training per week	6.1 ± 0.6	5.5 ± 0.7

Results

The data, shown in Table 2, indicate that the swimming group females were taller, heavier, and had a higher percentage of body fat than gymnastic group females. Figures 1 and 2 depict the levels of blood lipids and apolipoproteins. In the gymnastic group, FC and apo B levels were higher than in the swimming group, and the LDL-C level also tended to be higher. TC, HDL-C, TG, TL, apo A-I, and apo A-II levels were similar in the two groups. Table 2 summarizes the ratios. The apo A-I/apo B ratio was higher in the swimming group. The correlations of lipids and apolipoproteins with body composition are shown in Table 3. There were no correlations higher than 0.70.

Table 2

**Anthropometric Data and Ratios (mean ± *SEM*)
of Gymnastic and Swimming Groups**

Variable	Gymnasts	Swimmers	
Number	14	14	
Height (cm)	140.0 ± 1.8	149.5 ± 2.4	—[a]
Weight (kg)	31.2 ± 1.0	36.6 ± 1.2	—[a]
Sum of skinfolds (mm)	26.2 ± 1.9	38.6 ± 4.2	—[a]
Percentage of body fat	16.7 ± 1.5	22.8 ± 1.6	—[a]
Fat mass (kg)	5.3 ± 0.5	8.4 ± 0.7	—[a]
Lean body mass (kg)	25.9 ± 0.7	28.2 ± 0.9	
Ratios			
HDL-C/TC	0.32 ± 0.06	0.34 ± 0.07	
HDL-C/LDL-C	0.54 ± 0.17	0.59 ± 0.16	
apo A-I/apo B	2.4 ± 0.5	3.2 ± 0.8	—[a]
HDL-C/apo A-I	0.92 ± 0.11	0.84 ± 0.14	
LDL-C/apo B	0.42 ± 0.06	0.46 ± 0.05	

[a]$p < 0.05$.

Table 3

**Pearson Correlations of Lipids and Apolipoproteins
with Parameters of Body Composition**

	TC	HDL-C	LDL-C	TG	TL	apo A-I	apo A-II	apo B
Weight	−.22	−.02	−.28	.22	.18	.23	−.10	−.42
Skinfolds	.13	−.33	.16	.52	.27	−.03	−.05	.04
Fat mass	−.11	−.24	−.10	.42	.18	.06	−.13	−.21
Lean body mass	−.25	−.17	−.34	−.03	.12	.29	−.03	−.45

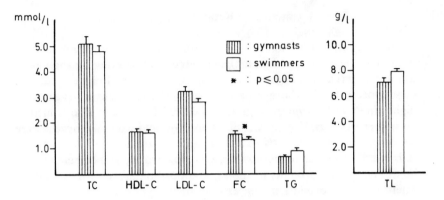

Figure 1—Plasma cholesterol, TG and TL levels of (pre)pubertal girl swimmers and gymnasts (mean ± *SEM*); *t*-test.

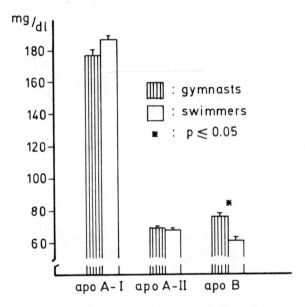

Figure 2—The levels of some apolipoproteins in the swimmer and gymnast groups (mean ± *SEM*); *t*-test.

Discussion

In this study, the influence of the fat mass on the lipid profile and levels of apolipoproteins in young female athletes was investigated. Because the groups differed in body composition while undergoing an equal number of training hours per week, it was proposed that the differences in lipid profile and levels of apolipoproteins could not be associated with differences in body composition. The correlations found between body composition and lipid profile were too low to represent an important relationship, so the hypothesis of no relationship was retained.

In the literature, only correlations between the triceps skinfold or obesity indices and lipid levels were reported and these correlations were even lower than .30 (Frerichs et al., 1978). The correlations obtained in this study were higher. The observation of TG correlating with body composition better than cholesterol was in agreement with what was found in the literature (Frerichs et al., 1978).

As suggested in the introduction, physical activity alone could change the lipid profile. From the literature, it is known that endurance training especially affects lipid and the apolipoprotein levels as noted by Nikkilä et al. (1978). Swim training is a more aerobic endurance sport as opposed to gymnastics, so the difference in type of sport can be an explanation for the difference in lipid profile and levels of apolipoproteins. In addition, there may have been a difference in the subjects' prolonged dietary habits. This factor needs further investigation.

Something should be said about the values of the calculated ratios. The HDL-C/LDL-C and HDL-C/TC ratios give some information about the distribution of cholesterol over the lipoproteins in blood. These ratios are considered predictive in coronary heart disease, with high ratios indicating lower risk (Brussaard, 1981). In this study these ratios are interesting because there are indications that the levels of TC and HDL-C (and consequently the values of ratios mentioned) at younger age are predictive for those at older age (Laskarzewski et al., 1979). However, all ratio values in both groups were normal or slightly increased (Brussaard, 1981; Frerichs et al., 1978).

In conclusion, it was found that differences in lipid profile and apolipoprotein level between female swimmers and gymnasts are not well correlated with differences in body composition, and an explanation for the difference in apo B can only be speculative. In our opinion, this phenomenon may be caused by differences in diet and/or type of sport.

References

ÅSTRAND, P.-O., Engstrom, L., Erikson, B.O., Karlberg, P., Nylander, I., Saltin, B., and Thoren, C. 1963. Girl swimmers. *Acta Paediatr.* (suppl.):147.

BOEHRINGER. 1979. *Manual for Test Combination Cholesterol, CHOD-PAP method; Manual for Test Combination HDL-Cholesterol, precipitation; Manual for Free Cholesterol, CHOD-PAP method; Manual for Triglycerids, fully enzymatical; Manual for Total Lipids.* Boehringer: Mannheim, GmbH Diagnostica.

BRUSSAARD, J.H. 1981. *A Comparison of Various Cholesterol Lowering Diets in Young Healthy Volunteers: Effects on Serum Lipoproteins and Other Risk Indicators for Cardiovascular Disease.* Thesis, Agricultural University Wageningen, The Netherlands.

CHEUNG, M., and Albers, J. 1977. The measurement of apolipoprotein A-I and A-II levels in men and women by immunoassay. *J. Clin. Invest.* **60**:43-50.

DAUNCEY, M., Gandy, G., and Gairdner, D. 1977. Assessment of total body fat in infancy from skinfold thickness measurement. *Arch. Dis. Child.* **52**:223-227.

DURNIN, J., and Rahaman, M. 1967. The assessment of the amount of body fat in the human body from measurements on skinfold thickness. *Br. J. Nutr.* **21**:681-687.

ERICH, W.B.M. 1980. *About Motor Abilities of Young Female Gymnasts, Aged 8-11 Years, with Special Reference to the Flexibility.* Thesis, State University of Utrecht, The Netherlands.

FRERICHS, R., Webber, L., Srinivasan, S., and Berenson, G. 1978. Relation of serum lipids and lipoproteins to obesity and sexual maturity in white and black children. *Am. J. Epidemiol.* **108**:486-496.

GILLIAM, T., and Burke, M. 1978. Effects of exercise on serum lipids and lipoproteins in girls, ages 8-10 years. *Artery* **4**:203-213.

HAVEKES, L., Hemmink, J., and de Wit, E. 1981. Low-density-lipoprotein apoprotein B in plasma as measured by radial immunodiffusion and rocket immunoelectrophoresis. *Clin. Chem.* **27**:1829-1833.

LASKARZEWSKI, P., Morrison, J., Mellies, M., Kelly, K., Gartside, P., Khoury, P., and Glueck, C. 1980. Relationship of measurement of body mass to plasma lipoproteins in schoolchildren and adults. *Am. J. Epidemiol.* **111**:395-405.

LASKARZEWSKI, P., Morrison, J.A., de Groot, I., Kelly, K., Mellies, M., Khoury, P., and Glueck, C.J. 1979. Lipid and lipoprotein tracking in 108 children over a four year period. *Pediatrics* **64**:584-591.

NIKKILÄ, E.A., Taskinen, M.R., Rehunen, S., and Härkönen, M. 1978. Lipoprotein lipase activity in adipose tissue and skeletal muscle of runners: Relation to serum lipoproteins. *Metabolism* **27**:1661-1667.

SIRI, W.E. 1956. Gross composition of the body. *Adv. Biol. Med. Physics* **4**:239-280.

TANNER, J.M. 1962. *Growth at Adolescence* (2nd Ed.), p. 325. Blackwell, Oxford.

WOOD, P., and Haskell, W. 1979. The effect of exercise on plasma high density lipoproteins. *Lipids* **14**:417-427.

YLITALO, V. 1981. Treatment of obese schoolchildren *Acta Paediatr.* (suppl.):290.

The Effects of Refit® on Elite Swimmers

I. Drăgan, C.A. Vasiliu, and E. Georgescu
Sports Medicine Center, Bucharest, Rumania

Interest is becoming great in a food ration for elite sports competitors as well as in the sports medicine field, both for the biological preparation of elite athletes and for the recovery after training and competition (Åstrand, 1973; Drăgan et al., 1974; Gontea, 1971; Mincu, 1974; Strauzenberg, 1969). Some protein concentrates have proven their efficiency in the biological preparation of elite athletes. Such pharmacological products are composed of animal proteins, vitamins, and/or mineral salts (Drăgan, 1977; Schwarz and Teich, 1975).

The product Refit®, a powder[1] consisting mainly of proteins extracted from fresh milk and containing 86.5% protein, 2% fat, lactose and 3.9% minerals (calcium 1.35%, phosphorus 0.63% and sodium 0.04%) was administered to a group of elite swimmers who prepared daily for high-level competition (Universiade, 1981). The purpose of this study was to determine the biological effects (biophysical, biochemical, functional and behavioral) of this product on selected variables involved in exercise metabolism and thus in sports performance.

Materials and Methods

Twenty-six swimmers (17 boys and 9 girls) ranging in age from 16 to 21 years with mean body weight of 78 kg participated in this study. The subjects were randomly divided into two groups: The experimental group included 16 swimmers (10 boys and 6 girls) whereas the control group included 10 swimmers (7 boys and 3 girls).

A prospective double-blind, placebo controlled trial of Refit was carried out with these swimmers. All subjects had been under medical supervision for 60 days during hard daily training (4 hr daily), and had similar programs and diets (60-65 calories/kg and 1.8-2.3 g of proteins/kg daily). A supplement of 43.25 g proteins (50 g Refit) was given to the experimental group (n = 16) incorporated into 500 ml of cocoa-milk and 250 g of yoghurt, whereas the control group (n = 10) received 500 g cocoa-milk and 250 g of yoghurt without Refit.

No other drugs were given during the study. The following variables were recorded on the first day and on the last day of the study (60 days later), except for behavior parameters which were recorded every 15 days: (a) subjective symptoms (behavior, fatigue after swimming, appetite and the personal feelings of well-being at the time of the training session). These subjective opinions were obtained by a short questionnaire every 2 weeks at the time of a training session. Statistical analyses for subjective symptoms were carried out using an arbitrary scale from 1 to 4 (unsatisfactory, satisfactory, good and very good); (b) body composition (Faulkner modified, see Drăgan et al., 1974), percentage fat and percentage (body) mass; (c) strength of right and left forearm flexion by dynamometry; (d) working capacity—aerobic power described by Åstrand method, $\dot{V}O_2$ max (Drăgan et al., 1974); anaerobic power by original method on cycloergometer 20" and 60" (kgm/kg); (e) blood sample factors as described by Manta et al. (1976) and Richterich (1969) including HB (g%, Drabkin method); serum proteins (g%, Weichselbaum method); lipids (mg%, Zöllner-Kitsch method); cholesterol (mg%, Zlatkis-Zak method); serum urea (mg%, Berthelot method); serum Ca (meq/L, flame photometry method); serum K (meq/L, flame photometry method); serum phosphorus (mg%, Briggs method); urinary mucoproteins (mg/24 hr, Biserte-Montreuil method); and serum magnesium (meq/L Mann Joe method).

The mean differences of the changes in these parameters for both groups were analyzed statistically using Student's t-test.

Results and Discussion

In order to interpret the effects induced by Refit, a method commonly used in clinical pharmacological research was followed. This involves an analysis of the differences between the difference in mean experimental and control groups, as shown in Table 1.

Statistically significant effects were found for right hand strength ($p < 0.05$); lean body mass ($p < 0.05$); $\dot{V}O_2$ max ($p < 0.05$); Hb ($p < 0.05$); serum proteins ($p < 0.025$); potassium ($p < 0.05$); calcium ($p < 0.05$); phosphorus ($p < 0.05$) and urinary mucoproteins ($p < 0.02$). The other blood sample factors were not statistically significant between the groups.

Effects of the protein supplement on the treated group seemed to benefit the feelings of well-being on the treated group as well as appetite and fatigue after training; however, these effects were not evaluated statistically.

Table 1
Experimental Study on Refit® in Top Swimmers

Parameter	Treated group ($n=16$)			Control group ($n=10$)			Difference between treated and control groups $\bar{X}_D - \bar{Y}_D$	Significance (p)
	$\bar{X}_1$ (before)	$\bar{X}_2$ (after)	$(\bar{X}_2 - \bar{X}_1) =$ $\bar{X}_D$; $\pm SD$	$\bar{Y}_1$ (before)	$\bar{Y}_2$ (after)	$(\bar{Y}_2 - \bar{Y}_1) =$ $\bar{Y}_D$; $\pm SD$		
Weight (kg)	77.63	75.27	-2.36 ± 2.06	79.26	76.68	-2.57 ± 2.43	$+0.21$	NS[a]
Fat body mass (%)	17.01	15.67	-1.34 ± 1.23	18.67	17.13	-1.54 ± 1.33	$+0.20$	NS
Right flexor strength (kg)	43.56	44.93	$+1.37 \pm 3.69$	45.19	43.59	-1.60 ± 2.62	$+2.97$	< 0.05
Left flexor strength (kg)	42.00	43.29	$+1.29 \pm 4.23$	43.00	44.50	$+1.50 \pm 6.00$	-0.21	NS
Lean body mass (%)	83.18	84.25	$+1.06 \pm 0.53$	81.33	82.00	$+0.66 \pm 0.38$	$+0.40$	< 0.05
$\dot{V}O_2$ max ml/min STPD	3770.48	4145.85	$+375.28 \pm 2.96$	354.9	3636	$+87.67 \pm 104.3$	$+287.71$	< 0.05
TTR/kg 60"	30.27	32.28	$+2.01 \pm 3.43$	29.42	32.99	$+3.57 \pm 4.71$	-1.56	NS
TTR/kg 20"	11.22	12.38	$+1.16 \pm 1.64$	11.63	13.24	$+1.60 \pm 2.30$	-0.44	NS
Hemoglobin (g%)	13.92	14.28	$+0.35 \pm 0.532$	14.33	14.18	-0.14 ± 0.63	$+0.49$	< 0.05
Proteins (g%)	6.79	6.94	$+0.15 \pm 0.275$	7.27	7.12	-0.15 ± 0.25	$+0.30$	< 0.025
Lipids (mg%)	738.06	708.68	-29.00 ± 86.76	759.00	746.00	-43.00 ± 52.80	-16	NS
Cholesterol (mg%)	167.93	167.18	-0.75 ± 20.68	168.00	170.00	-2.00 ± 18.06	-2.75	NS
Urea (mg%)	26.62	25.00	-1.62 ± 6.24	27.59	23.00	-4.59 ± 6.60	$+2.97$	NS
Sodium (meq/L)	140.31	139.3	-1.01 ± 2.50	138.09	140.69	$+2.60 \pm 2.92$	-3.61	NS
Potassium (meq/L)	4.43	4.59	$+0.16 \pm 0.24$	4.45	4.39	-0.06 ± 0.20	$+0.22$	< 0.05
Calcium (meq/L)	4.76	4.85	$+0.09 \pm 0.29$	4.82	4.64	-0.18 ± 0.38	$+0.27$	< 0.05
Magnesium (meq/L)	1.82	1.89	$+0.07 \pm 0.32$	2.10	2.13	$+0.03 \pm 0.14$	$+0.04$	NS
Mucoproteins (mg/24 hr)	170.93	146.25	-24.68 ± 40.22	135.00	151.00	$+16.00 \pm 21.17$	-40.68	< 0.02
Phosphorus (mg%)	2.42	2.51	$+0.09 \pm 0.05$	3.17	3.22	$+0.05 \pm 0.02$	$+0.04$	< 0.05

[a]NS = not significant.

59

No side-effects were noted and Refit was tolerated well by all swimmers. The majority of the treated swimmers obtained high performances (+1.6 to +3.8%) at the Universiade 1981, greater than those obtained by the control group (+0.6 to +2.4%).

The favorable changes were statistically significant and could be explained as a result of this high quality milk protein supplement which seemed to be very useful both during hard training in elite swimmers and during the recovery period (Drăgan et al., 1979).

Conclusion

Based on these data (subjective symptoms, biological data and sports performances) beneficial effects of Refit were noted in elite swimmers. Therefore, it is suggested that a daily supplement of these high-quality proteins be administered during hard training for elite competitive swimmers.

Acknowledgment

This research was supported in part by De Melkindustrie, Veghel, The Netherlands.

Notes

1. Refit® powder is produced by De Melkindustrie Veghel, The Netherlands.

References

ÅSTRAND, P.O. 1973. Nutrition and physical performance. *Med. Sport* **26**(6):140-152.

DRĂGAN, I. 1977. Recovery after exercise and biological preparation for competition. *Rev. Educ. Fiz. Sport* **10**:8-12.

DRĂGAN, I., et al. 1974. *Sports Medicine*. Ed. Stadion, Bucharest.

DRĂGAN, I., Vasiliu, A., Georgescu, E., and Lazar, N. 1979. Recovery after sports efforts. *Sports Medicine Center of Bucharest* **7**:113-117.

GONTEA, I. 1971. *Rational Diet of Man*. Ed. didactica si pedagogica, Bucharest.

MANTA, I., et al. 1976. *Biochemical Methods in Clinical Laboratory*. Ed. Dacia, Cluj-Nopoca.

MINCU, I. 1974. *Diet and Exercise.* Ed. Medicala, Bucuresti.

RICHTERICH, R. 1969. *Clinical Chemistry, Theory and Practice.* S. Karger, Basel (Switzerland), New York; Academic Press, New York and London.

SCHWARZ, V., and Teich, V. 1975. Der Einfluss einer zusätzlichen Eiweissernährung auf den Muskel und Kraftzuwachs während eines dreiwöchigen isometrischen Muskeltrainings. (The influence of a nutritional protein supplement on muscle and strength improvement during a three weeks of isometric muscle training.) *Sport. Sportmed.* **5**:96-99.

STRAUZENBERG, S.E. 1969. Beitrag zu Ernährungsfragen im Sport. (Contribution to the Question of Nutrition in Sport.) *Med. Sport* **10**(1):307-312.

Medical Advice for Baby Swimmers

M. O'Brien, J. Smith, and M. Bolger
Irish Amateur Swimming Association, Dublin, Ireland

Hydrotherapy has been used for many years to improve muscle tone and coordination in babies and adults (Davis, 1967; Duffield, 1976; Newman, 1975). Babies exposed to graded exercise in warm swimming pools improve in coordination and gain physical, mental and social skills exceeding those observed in their peers (Quinn, 1981). Children born and brought up in the tropics often swim before they can walk and learn this skill before they have acquired a fear of water.

In Ireland baby swimming has been pioneered by international swimming coach Jack Smith, who started baby swimming classes in a private school 3 years ago. In September 1980 other baby swimming classes were started, one in Dublin and one in Belfast. In 1982 the public pools set aside hours for mother and baby swimming but had no organized teaching. Because of the great interest that has arisen, the Northern Ireland Sports Council and its equivalent body, Cospoir, in the Republic, in association with the Education Committee of the Irish Amateur Swimming Association, currently are providing guidelines to be used by leisure centers and swimming pools wishing to provide facilities for baby swimming.

Methods

Sessions for babies should be held weekly and should last no longer than 2 hr. The actual time in the water varies and depends on the age of the child, varying from 10 min to 1 hr, with an average of 30 min. The ideal class consists of 10-15 mother and baby swimming pairs, supervised by a minimum of two teachers, preferably one male and one female. It is important to establish a good relationship between teachers, mothers and babies. The atmosphere in the pool should be pleasant and confident, with the teachers present all the time.

The mother acts as a swimming teacher (Timmerman, 1970). She enters the water first and the baby is handed to her. Older babies may require arm bands which should be in position when a child is handed to the mother. When the baby is relaxed, mother and baby should immerse together to shoulder level in the water. The mother faces the baby at all times, holding the infant with both hands in the water. She walks backwards, talking to the baby. The child is placed in a vertical position for a short time and then on its back again. The baby should be completely immersed during the first lesson with water splashed over its head from behind (Carlisle, personal communication, 1982). The mother relinquishes her hold on the baby as soon as it is happy or as soon as the mother has confidence in letting go.

Although there are large individual variations of response in any age group with some babies more advanced than others, certain basic patterns can be recognized. An 8-week-old baby has no fear of the water and instinctively holds its breath when submerged. Reflex alternate movements of arms and legs produce a paddling action. The reflexes are lost when the baby is about 4-8 months old. After 4 months of age the rhythmic paddling action tends to become disorganized and if swimming is initiated at this age the babies tend to swim on their backs. Some babies are unable to control their heads and need support. After 8 months of age movement in the water is more deliberate, but in the absence of arm band support, some babies have difficulty in lifting their heads to breathe.

The mother initiates training by holding the baby's legs straight and moving them up and down, close together. This action must be repeated many times in either the prone or supine position. The baby should practice swimming each day at home in the bathtub.

Over 400 babies have attended these classes, approximately 70% of whom were 6 months or older; 25% were younger, and the youngest baby was only 10 weeks old. Ninety percent learned to swim though not with conventional strokes. There was a marked variation in the time that it took for the babies to learn. The mother's role is vital and if she was confident, the child learned to "swim" in a few lessons. A large number of the babies progressed to the toddlers classes when they were 2 years old.

Mothers wishing to join classes are advised to have prior consultation with their pediatricians, as only healthy babies should be allowed to enroll in the class. Ideally, the babies should have completed their first two combined triple and polio inoculations before they join the class unless they are being breast-fed. At least 3 weeks should elapse between the second inoculation and the commencement of classes. The polio vaccine is a live, attenuated virus with excretion from the bowel peaking within 3 weeks of administration. Mothers not previously inoculated against polio are also advised to seek immunization (Aickin, personal communication, 1982).

The pool area and changing rooms should be clean and warm. Adequate facilities for diaper changing must be provided. Pool water temperature should be higher than normal, a minimum of 86°F or 27°C. The pH and free chlorine concentration should be checked regularly to achieve the bacteriological satisfactory free-chlorine level of 0.8-1 mg/L. Regular bacterial counts should also be performed (Cabelli, 1978; Galbraith, 1980; Humphrey, 1978; Wyatt and Wilson, 1979).

On swimming days, babies should be given only a light breakfast. During the session, they should wear toweling or trainer pants, as napkins or plastic pants fill up with water and create drag. The wearing of double-chamber, all-around arm bands is recommended for older children. In comparison to single-chambered, flat-bottomed bands these stay on well even if one chamber is deflated. Colorful swimming aids, such as multicolored floating toys and rubber balls are useful for attracting the babies' attention.

The time spent in the water should be carefully monitored as the babies' thermoregulatory mechanisms are not as well developed as those of adults. At the completion of the session they should be wrapped in a towel as soon as they are taken from the water and should be dressed before the mother gets dressed.

Most mothers agreed that the training sessions were well worth the trouble involved. The babies ate and slept better on the session days; they also passed more urine. An increased incidence of colds or of sore eyes was a rare finding. The therapeutic value of the classes was emphasized, particularly in the case of an initially apathetic Down's syndrome child who became considerably more alert and coordinated as the sessions progressed. The baby learns to swim before it develops a fear of water. The quality of life perhaps improves both for the mother and baby.

References

CABELLI. June 1978. Swimming Associated Disease Outbreaks, *Journal WPCF* 1347-77.

DAVIS, C.B. 1967. A technique of re-education in the treatment pool. *Physiotherapy* **53**:257.

DUFFIELD, M.H. 1976. *Exercises in Water*, Balluee,

GALBRAITH, N.S. Feb. 1980. Infections associated with swimming pools. *Environ. Health* 31-32.

HUMPHREY, W.H. 1978. Public swimming pool water disinfection. *Royal Soc. Health J.* **98**:22-24.

NEWMAN, J. 1975. *Swimming for Children with Physical and Sensory Impairment*. C.C. Thomas, Springfield, IL.

QUINN, S. 1981. *Water Babies*. Report from Northern Ireland Sports Council.

TIMMERAN, C. *How to Teach Your Baby to Swim*. Heinemann, London.

WYATT, T.D., and Wilson, T.S. 1979. A bacteriological investigation of two leisure centre swimming pools, disinfected with ozone. *J. Hyg. Cambridge* **83**:425-441.

Descriptions of the Leg Movements of Infants in an Aquatic Environment

Czeslaw Wielki and Marielle Houben
Catholic University of Louvain, Louvain-La-Neuve, Belgium

The majority of research concerning the mechanics of swimming has been confined to competitive swimming strokes of males and females over the age of 10 yr. With the increased emphasis on teaching children to swim during infancy, there is a need to investigate infants' swimming patterns. The purpose of this study, therefore, was to describe the movement patterns for the lower limbs of infants aged 3-20 months as they propelled themselves in the water under different support conditions. It was felt that this might provide a greater understanding of the natural evolution of aquatic movement patterns and help in developing guidelines for manipulation of the learning environment (Wielki, 1980).

Procedures

The study took place over a period of 4 yr, with 40 infants as subjects. These infants participated in aquatic activities in a specially conditioned pool at Universite Catholique de Louvain at Louvain-La-Neuve, Belgium.

Observations were made in weekly classes grouped by age, each session lasting 30 min in the water at a temperature of 32°C. All infants required support of some type: a parent or a floating appliance. The infants' behavior was studied using two methods: (a) *Direct observation* of each infant's movements were recorded on an observation form; and (b) *indirect observations* were made through underwater videotaping or by using a 16-mm camera. Each infant passed in front of the camera during these aquatic activities.

In general, these two methods recorded the infants in three positions: vertical, prone and supine. These methods of analysis permitted a study of the infants' behavior, an analysis of the lower limb gestures and even an attempted classification of the motor actions. These observations were specifically designed to be carried out in a natural context rather than in a laboratory situation. Patterns of similar action by the lower limbs were identified and placed into classification types and stages. Tracings were made from stop-action viewings in order to depict each pattern.

Results of Observations

Taking into consideration both the direct and indirect observations, some general remarks on the evolution of infants' motor actions in this study are given initially. First, development of the infants' movements in the water was very diversified; each infant progressed at its own rate, just as in other normal physical activities. Development of the infants' behaviors in different aquatic situations was influenced by many factors. Among these, the most influential seems to be the age at which the infant began the aquatic experience. Each age group had a characteristic level of aquatic motor skills, but individual variations were quite evident. After having analyzed the lower limb motor actions of 40 infants, it was possible to distinguish two stages of development. These stages will be discussed in the remainder of this article.

First Stage: Movements of Infants Aged 3-11 Months

These were considered reflex-bound movements since they occurred immediately upon the presentation of the stimulus (e.g., placement in a new position or presentation of a toy). These movements were "violent" and random in nature. In this first stage, it was possible to classify the lower limb motor actions into four types. *Movement similar to a "cigarette lighter"* (Figure 1) was observed in infants aged 3, 4 and 5 months. In an action that alternates, the toes of one foot rub against the opposite leg. This behavior appears to be innate and manifests itself mostly in the vertical position; however, it has been observed in the prone and supine positions as well.

Alternating flexion and extension of the leg (Figure 2) was seen at a constant speed or with a certain tempo. This seems to be an innate, coordinated reflex; no forward efforts could be observed. As in the "cigarette lighter" type, this behavior was noted in infants up to the age of 5 months and most often in the vertical and prone positions. These two types of motor action observed as a part of the aquatic activities of infants aged 3-5 months were considered archaic reflexes, made in response to the outside environment such as water pressure, temperature, etc.

Figure 1—"Cigarette lighter" movement.

Figure 2—Alternating reflex leg movements.

Figure 3—Simultaneous kicking movements of the legs.

Figure 4—Alternating kicking movements of the legs.

Simultaneous flexions and extensions of the leg (Figure 3) were shown in the behavior of infants 5-10 months old. This motor activity consisted of 2-4 repetitions of flexion and extension movement. Between each series of movements, there was a brief interlude of inactivity. In some infants, one can observe an undulating movement of the body accompanying this series of movements.

The fourth type of action observed was *alternating flexions and extensions of the leg* (Figure 4). This motor activity can be characterized the same way as the previous type: a series of rapid and rhythmic flexions and extensions of the legs, with the added distinction that one leg extends with more force or speed than the other.

For these last two actions, involving simultaneous and alternating kicking, it was postulated that the infant expresses its affective state toward its mother or its emotional state toward the aquatic environment, a toy, etc. These reactions were observed in more than 80% of the infants near the age of 5 months and often in both prone and vertical positions. Since these reactions disappear toward the age of 10 months, it is likely that these reactions also are reflex-bound.

Figure 5—Movement of the legs: The knee flexes forward.

Figure 6—Movement of the legs with the lower leg behind.

Figure 7—"Bicycle" movement.

Second Stage: Appearance of Alternating Leg Movements

This stage was seen in infants aged 11-20 months, and was considered voluntary. In the second stage, "voluntary" alternating movements of the legs appear. We distinguished three types of propulsive movements which progressively developed into a bicycle movement.

Alternating movements of the legs: lifting of the leg and extension of the foot (Figure 5). The infant, in a vertical position, carries the leg forward and flexes the knee at the same time. Then he or she pushes the leg downward, maintaining an extended foot. The extension of one leg, coordinated with the flexion of the other, permits the infant to move slowly forward. It is the first appearance of forward propulsion and manifests itself near the age of 11-12 months.

Alternating movements of the legs: The knee flexes but remains in place as the lower leg goes backwards (Figure 6). The infant, in a vertical position, obtains propulsion by alternately flexing the knees. After flexion, the leg is brought back to a vertical position. This rhythmic and coordinated movement permits the infant to progress forward more rapidly than the previous action because the sole of the foot is used. This type of propulsion was observed in infants near the age of 12-13 months.

Alternating movements of the entire lower limbs (Figure 7). Using a combination of the first two movements in this group, the infant begins to simulate a "bicycle" motion with the legs. Being in a vertical position, the infant gradually demonstrates a more efficient means of propulsion

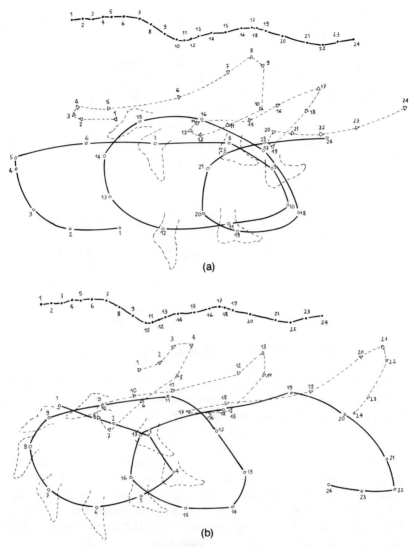

Figure 8—Positions of (a) right and (b) left lower limbs in the bicycle movement.
——o——, progressive motion of the ankle joint; – – –▲– – – , the knee joint;
—— • —— , the hip joint.

by flexing the leg in front of the body, then reaching forward to increase the "hold" on the water in front of the body. He or she then pushes the water backward, executing a "bicycle" movement.

In this type of movement, the infant has included movement of the foot, resulting in a more rapid and constant progression forward through the use of the ankle joint. This movement is more coordinated and the alternate leg movements become more symmetrical. To illustrate this type of movement, a trace is shown in Figure 8. The infant is in the vertical position supported by the mother and facing her.

Conclusion

Infants' lower limb actions in an aquatic environment may be divided into two stages and seven types. Since the younger children exhibited patterns of a reflex-bound nature (McGraw, 1943), these may be considered to be stage 1 types. Stage 2 types seemed to be of a voluntary character (McGraw, 1943).

These stages and types occur in a variety of supportive situations. The influence of the manner in which support is provided to the infant has not been analyzed. The relationship of manner of support to type of lower limb movement patterns needs to be determined. In our opinion, an infant after passing these two stages of development is able to cope with the aquatic environment and to develop skills within the confines of the situation introduced in the aquatic activity.

References

McGRAW, M.D. 1943. *The Neuromuscular Maturation of the Human Infant.* Columbia University, New York.

WIELKI, C. 1980. Approche d'une éducation acquatique des enfants. *Sport* **23**:136-149.

Selected Methodology in Biomechanics with Respect to Swimming

Benno M. Nigg
University of Calgary, Canada

Research methodology can be discussed from several different viewpoints. One may emphasize the instrumentation, describing the different possibilities of data collection and analysis, one may discuss the research design of studies in a certain field or one may also consider the basic concepts as very important aspects of methodology. Discussions of all these aspects may contribute to the improvement of knowledge in a discipline and it would be erroneous to argue about the importance of one aspect compared to another, because all of them are important. From a historical perspective one would expect an emphasis initially on the publication of basic concepts, followed by the development of research design, leading finally to the development of instruments for measuring the relevant parameters. However, this is not the usual development (Nigg, 1982) and quite often instruments for data collection and analysis are available before the basic concepts are worked out.

The purpose of this paper is to describe the three methodological aspects for the biomechanics of swimming: (a) basic concepts, (b) research design, and (c) instrumentation.

Basic Concepts of an Analysis of Swimming

The ultimate objective of research in biomechanics (of swimming) is to increase the understanding of human movement (in the water medium). This is usually, if not always, concerned with an attempt to optimize or maximize the movement in order to achieve the "best" results (Nigg, 1982). It is therefore necessary to know the factors limiting performance in swimming.

Since biomechanics is the science that examines the internal and external forces acting on a human body and the effects produced by these

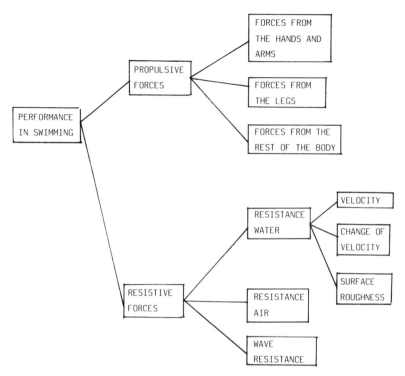

Figure 1—Basic concept of the factors limiting performance (velocity) in swimming (without start and turns).

forces (Hay, 1978), it is essential to know the acting forces. If performance is described as a race time, for example, the limiting factors for performance are various forms of propulsive and resistance forces (Figure 1).

This basic concept, in this case a model, is applicable for many movements in water and can be used for other aquatic sports (e.g., rowing). A systematic analysis of swimming therefore should include each of these factors. Considering all the confounding factors, Clarys (1979) mentioned that "the problems seem endless." However, this model may be the starting point for a systematic analysis.

Propulsive Forces

The basic concept of propulsive forces seems to be simple and the effects can be recorded easily. Schleihauf (1979) describes the basic concept of force production in swimming using a model which includes lift and drag for the hand. This part of the theory seems to be well understood. However, a basic concept (or a model) to understand the contributions for propulsion of the hand, arm, leg, etc. doesn't seem to exist. Efforts have been made to show the percentage contribution of the arms and legs but with little success (Bucher, 1975; Karpovich and Pestrecov, 1939).

Resistance

Basic considerations about resistance in swimming are reported by Jaeger (1937), Counsilman (1968), Francis and Dean (1975), Miller (1975) and Clarys (1979). The three types of resistance are from air, water and waves (Figure 1). Since the water resistance makes the greatest contribution to the total resistance, many studies report on that type. Clarys (1979) cites about 100 publications in the field of passive drag (resistance). However, he reports that "the active drag has never been measured directly."

With active drag, Clarys describes the resistance produced by the movement of various body parts (arms, legs) relative to the "total body" (perhaps the center of mass). Clarys bases these comments on the publications of Alley (1949, 1952) and Safarian (1968). Since the basic concept for this aspect is missing, an attempt should be made to solve this problem.

Basics about the Influence of Velocity and Velocity Change on the Work in Swimming

The following ideas are the result of several discussions between Busch (ETH, Zurich) and the author. There are three basic assumptions on which these ideas are based:

- The purpose of swimming (in competition) is to reach maximal velocity over a distance, $v = v(max)$.
- Velocity is determined by the propulsive force and the resistance.
- Water resistance is proportional to the square of the velocity:

$$R \text{ (water)} = a \cdot v^2,$$

where a is a constant (Miller, 1975).

Since the work a swimmer must produce is a limiting factor for performance, the following estimations will use this variable. The symbols are: R = water resistance (resultant horizontal force exerted by water on swimmers); W = work/stroke; v = velocity; x = displacement; s = length of a stroke; t = time; and τ = integration constant (= duration of one stroke). By definition:

$$W = \int_0^s R \, dx, \text{ where } dx = v \cdot dt$$

$$W = \int_0^\tau R \cdot v \, dt, \text{ with the third assumption } R = a \cdot v^2$$

$$W = \int_0^\tau a \cdot v^3 \, dt.$$

This means that the work one has to do to overcome water resistance is proportional to the cube of the velocity, $W \sim v^3$, and performance, $P \sim v^3$!

Difference between Constant and Variable Velocity

$$v = v_0 = \text{constant}$$

$$W = \int_0^T a \cdot v_0^3 \, dt$$

$$W = a \cdot v_0^3 \cdot \tau = W_{const}.$$

$v = v_0 + \Delta v(t) \neq \text{constant, where } v_0 = \bar{v} = \text{average velocity/stroke}$

$$W = \int_0^T a \, [v_0 + \Delta v(t)]^3 \, dt$$

$$W = a \left\{ v_0^3 \cdot \tau + 3 \cdot v_0^2 \cdot \int_0^T [\Delta v(t)] \, dt \right.$$

$$+ 3 \cdot v_0 \cdot \int_0^T [\Delta v(t)]^2 \, dt$$

$$\left. + \int_0^T [\Delta v(t)]^3 \, dt \right\}$$

A comparison between the work done while swimming with constant velocity and while swimming with fluctuating velocity is described by the following equation:

$$\frac{W}{W_{const}} = 1 + \frac{3}{\tau} \underbrace{\int_0^T \left[\frac{\Delta v(t)}{v_0} \right] dt}_{\substack{= 0 \\ \text{by definition}}} + \frac{3}{\tau} \underbrace{\int_0^T \left[\frac{\Delta v(t)}{v_0} \right]^2 dt}_{> 0} + \frac{1}{\tau} \underbrace{\int_0^T \left[\frac{\Delta v(t)}{v_0} \right]^3 dt}_{\substack{= 0 \\ \text{by definition}}}$$

The result shows that every change in velocity results in an increase in the amount of work the swimmer must do. The optimal solution for a given work capacity, therefore, would be to swim at a constant velocity. Changes in velocity of 10% (for one stroke) result in an additional work demand of about 3%! In reality, however, constant velocity in swimming may be difficult to achieve.

The body does not move at a constant velocity and the arms and legs, acting as motors, are in a constantly changing movement. Therefore, they are responsible for the additional work term in our equation which means a reduction of the average speed. This (among other influences) may illustrate the difference in average speed between the front crawl stroke and breast stroke. (The total body movement as well as the arm movement is less constant in the breast stroke than in the front crawl.) Of course, this is not the only limiting factor in swimming, but an important aspect in an athlete's training process may be in learning to control the steady pace of the total body as well as of the arms and legs.

Research Design in Swimming Studies

Research can be categorized as analytical or descriptive. Early studies in the biomechanics of sports were most frequently descriptive and it is only recently that analytical studies with the application of modeling theories have become more common. Biomechanical studies in swimming seem to be an exception in this respect. Several studies in swimming have examined the effect of fundamental hydrodynamics on the human body. DuBois-Reymond (1927) published a study concerning the water resistance of human bodies. Cureton (1930) reported on the mechanics and kinesiology of swimming. Gadd (1963) described the hydrodynamics in swimming. Seireg and Baz (1971) published a mathematical model for swimming mechanics. Gallenstein (1973) presented an analysis of swimming motion using a mathematical model of the human body including both viscous and inertial forces.

These examples illustrate the current work in this field, but the list is incomplete and should mention many other authors. These researchers have attempted to apply the theories of hydromechanics and especially hydrodynamics to the swimming movement. Several ideas and findings used in ship construction could easily be transferred and applied to swimming analysis. The studies in the ship industry may have helped in the development of basic concepts and models for swimming. However, no publication is known by this writer that applies an organizational framework (as illustrated in Figure 1) in order to develop a model for swimming. This may be because too many complicated influences are still unknown and must be studied in detail.

Instrumentation

Some of the conventional measuring devices currently are being used in studies of the biomechanics of swimming. The available techniques will be discussed in this section. Since several papers have been published on this topic (e.g., Cavanagh et al., 1975; Clarys et al., 1973) this section will be condensed.

Force Platforms and Force Measuring Devices

Special force platforms have been developed to measure the forces exerted by the hands and/or feet on the starting blocks (Cavanagh et al.,

1975; Zatsiorsky et al., 1979). Cavanagh's device was used by Bowers and Cavanagh (1975) and Stevenson and Morehouse (1979). Since the forces of interest are "active forces" (Nigg, 1980), the use of strain gauge techniques is adequate in terms of the frequency response. Force platforms may also be applied for measurement of forces during turning. Other force measuring devices which have been used to gather information on drag and/or propulsive forces on the human body in water are summarized by Clarys (1979). The different methods used are not without problems, especially if the body is moving in one location (at zero velocity). The force measuring devices are not only related to problems for the start and turns but also are critical to the study of swimming movement.

Force Distribution Measuring Devices

In the last 5 years different transducers have been developed to measure force distribution. Nicol (1977) developed a capacitive system for force distribution measurements and used it for the measurements of impulses exerted in performing several kinds of swimming turns (Nicol and Krueger, 1979). Hennig et al. (1983) developed a force distribution measuring device based on piezoelectric ceramic force transducers. It would be interesting to develop such devices for the arms and hands to further our understanding of propulsion. However, such pressure distribution measuring devices for arms and hands in swimming have yet to be developed, and it may well be that they would change the surface of the body and lead to erroneous results. A waterproof sensory-bonded strain gauge pressure transducer taped to a rubber glove (placed between the first and second fingers), as developed by Dupuis et al. (1979), may serve as an example for both the techniques and the problems of such a pressure distribution measuring device.

Film and Other Photo-optical Methods

Clarys et al. (1973) and Reischle (1978) developed and applied the lightstreak method for data collection in swimming. Cinefilm has been one of the major research tools in the biomechanical analysis of swimming. It is applied to relatively simple frequency and stroke length analysis as well as to highly sophisticated, three-dimensional analyses of propulsive force and resistance (Schleihauf, 1979). Waterproof equipment is available and the data analysis techniques of general two- or three-dimensional film analysis can thus be used.

Other Instrumentation

The list of equipment and instrumentation could be extended by describing EMG equipment, on-line velocity transducers, electronic goniometers, accelerometers and other sophisticated measuring devices which have been developed and applied in swim studies. The volumes *Swimming I, II* and *III* of the International Series of Sport Sciences offer descriptions and/or applications of a large number of different devices. A comparison of all the possible measuring techniques leads this writer to the conclusion that probably the most valid findings are based on results from film studies.

Concluding Remarks

Methodological aspects on biomechanics of swimming have been discussed from three different viewpoints — basic concepts, research design and instrumentation. It is obvious that fairly sophisticated instrumentation is available. (This is also true for many other areas of biomechanics — not just swimming.)

However, a general, basic concept does not seem to exist, which has resulted in a body of knowledge, which "lacks uniformity, completeness, and depth" (Miller, 1975). This may be because a large percentage of the literature in this area consists of research conducted as a master's thesis or a doctoral dissertation as Miller (1975) has suggested. But this situation has changed dramatically in the late 1970s and early '80s. Now the greatest contributions to research come from well established laboratories world-wide. It may also be due to the complexity of the topic, as mentioned by Clarys (1979). Future progress in understanding the biomechanics of swimming depends on the development of a basic theory describing the limiting factors of swimming in a general way followed by a more detailed analysis of specific aspects.

References

ALLEY, L.E. 1949. An analysis of resistance and propulsion in swimming the crawl stroke. Ph.D. Thesis, State University of Iowa, Iowa City, cited in Clarys, J.P. 1979. Human morphology and hydrodynamics. In: J. Terauds and E.W. Bedingfield (eds.), *Swimming III*, pp. 3-41. University Park Press, Baltimore.

ALLEY, L.E. 1952. An analysis of water resistance and propulsion in swimming the crawl stroke. *Res. Q.* **223**:253-270; cited in Clarys, J.P. 1979. Human morphology and hydrodynamics. In: J. Terauds and E.W. Bedingfield (eds.), *Swimming III*, pp. 3-41. University Park Press, Baltimore.

BOWERS, J.E., and Cavanagh, P.R. 1975. A biomechanical comparison of the grab and conventional sprint starts in competitive swimming. In: L. Lewillie and J.P. Clarys (eds.), *Swimming II*, pp. 225-232. University Park Press, Baltimore.

BUCHER, W. 1975. The influence of the leg kick and the arm stroke on the total speed during the crawl stroke. In: L. Lewillie and J.P. Clarys (eds.), *Swimming II*, pp. 180-187. University Park Press, Baltimore.

CAVANAGH, P.E., Palmgren, J.V., and Kerr, B.A. 1975. A device to measure forces at the hands during grab start. In: L. Lewillie and J.P. Clarys (eds.), *Swimming II*, pp. 43-50. University Park Press, Baltimore.

CLARYS, J.P. 1979. Human morphology and hydrodynamics. In: J. Terauds and E.W. Bedingfield (eds.), *Swimming III*, pp. 3-41. University Park Press, Baltimore.

CLARYS, J., Jiskoot, J., and Lewillie, L. 1973. L'emploi de traces lumineuses dans l'analyse biomecanique de differents styles de natation. (Use of the light-streak method in the biomechanical analyses of different swimming styles.) *Kinanthropologie* **5**:127.

COUNSILMAN, J.E. 1968. *The Science of Swimming*. Prentice-Hall, Englewood Cliffs, NJ.

CURETON, T.K. 1930. Mechanics and kinesiology of swimming. *Res. Q.* **1**:87-121.

DUBOIS-REYMOND, R. 1927. Der Wasserwiderstand des menschlischen Koerpers. (The water resistance of human bodies.) *Pfluegers Arch.* **216**:770-773.

DUPUIS, R., Adrian, M., Yoneda, Y., and Jade, M. 1979. Forces acting on the hand during swimming and their relationship to muscular spatial and temporal factors. In: J. Terauds and E.W. Bedingfield (eds.), *Swimming III*, pp. 110-117. University Park Press, Baltimore.

FRANCIS, P., and Dean, N. 1975. A biomechanical model for swimming performance. In: L. Lewillie and J.P. Clarys (eds.), *Swimming II*, pp. 118-124. University Park Press, Baltimore.

GADD, G.F. 1963. The hydrodynamics of swimming. *New Sci.* **355**:483-485.

GALLENSTEIN, J. 1973. Analysis of swimming motions. *Human Factors* **15**:91-98.

HAY, J.G. 1978. *The Biomechanics of Sports Techniques*. Prentice Hall, Englewood Cliffs, NJ.

HENNIG, E.M., Cavanagh, P.R., and Macmillan, N.W. 1983. Pressure distribution measurements by high precision piezoelectric force transducers. In: H. Matsui and K. Kobayashi (eds.), *Biomechanics VIIIB*, pp. 1081-1088. Human Kinetics, Champaign, IL.

JAEGER, L.D. 1937. Resistance of water as a limiting factor of speed in swimming. Master's thesis, State University of Iowa, Iowa City.

KARPOVICH, P.V., and Pestrecov, K. 1939. Mechanical work and efficiency in swimming crawl and back strokes. *Arbeits. Physiol.* **10**:504-515.

LAP, A.J.W. 1954. Fundamentals of ship resistance and propulsion. *National Shipbuilding Progress* (Publ. 129a; N.S.M.B.), Rotterdam.

MILLER, D.I. 1975. Biomechanics of swimming. In: J.H. Wilmore and J.F. Keogh (eds.), *Exercise and Sport Sciences Reviews*, pp. 219-248. Academic Press, New York.

NICOL, K. 1977. Druckverteilung unter dem Fuss bei sportlichen Abspruengen und Landungen im Hinblick auf eine Reduzierung von Sportverletzungen. (Pressure distribution on the foot on take-off and landing in respect to a reduction of sport injuries.) *Leistungssport* **3**:22-227.

NICOL, K., and Krueger, F. 1979. Impulses exerted in performing several kinds of swimming turns. In: J. Terauds and E.W. Bedingfield (eds.), *Swimming III*, pp. 222-232. University Park Press, Baltimore.

NIGG, B.M. 1980. Biomechanische Ueberlegungen zur Belastung des Bewegungsapparates. (Biomechanical aspects on the loading of the human body.) In: H. Cotta, H. Krahl and K. Steinbrueck (eds.), *Die Belastungstoleranz des Bewegungsapparates*, pp. 44-54. George Thieme Verlag, Stuttgart.

NIGG, B.M. 1982. Perspectives in biomechanics applied to sport and physical education. In: *Proceedings of the Third Meeting of the European Society of Biomechanics*, Jan. 1982, Nijmegen, Holland (in press).

REISCHLE, K. 1978. Lightstreak photography: A simple method for recording movement patterns. In: B. Eriksson and B. Furberg (eds.), *Swimming Medicine IV*, pp. 408-414. University Park Press, Baltimore.

SAFARIAN, I.G. 1968. Hydrodynamic characteristics of the crawl (trans. from Russian). *Theoret. Pract. Phys. Educ.* USSR **11**:18-21; cited in Clarys, J.P. 1979. Human morphology and hydrodynamics. In: J. Terauds and E.W. Bedingfield (eds.), *Swimming III*, pp. 3-41. University Park Press, Baltimore.

SCHLEIHAUF, R.E. 1979. A hydrodynamic analysis of swimming propulsion. In: J. Terauds and E.W. Bedingfield (eds.), *Swimming III*, pp. 70-109. University Park Press, Baltimore.

SEIREG, A., and Baz, A. 1971. A mathematical model for swimming mechanics. In: L. Lewillie and J.P. Clarys (eds.), *Proceedings of the First International Symposium on Biomechanics in Swimming*, pp. 81-104. Presse Universitaire de Bruxelles, Brussels.

STEVENSON, J.L., and Morehouse, C.A. 1979. Influence of starting block angle on the grab start in competitive swimming. In: J. Terauds and E.W. Bedingfield (eds.), *Swimming III*, pp. 207-214. University Park Press, Baltimore.

ZATSIORSKY, V.M., Bulgakova, N.Z., and Chaplinsky, N.M. 1979. Biomechanical analysis of stating technique in swimming. In: J. Terauds and E.W. Bedingfield (eds.), *Swimming III*, pp. 199-206. University Park Press, Baltimore.

The Validity of the Reynolds Number for Swimming Bodies Which Change Form Periodically

Bodo E. Ungerechts
Universität Bielefeld, West Germany

The knowledge of forces a swimmer has to overcome is important in calculating the energy consumption or the stress for people who swim in rehabilitation programs. The task of determining drag or propulsive forces on competitive swimmers has been frustrating because measurements of drag under field conditions is practically impossible, especially in a competitive race.

Therefore, calculations of drag and propulsive forces must be based on well established hydrodynamic equations which take into account the fact that a submerged body moving in water has to deal with different forces: drag, hydrodynamic lift and inertia.

Background

Drag forces are a combination of viscous drag and pressure drag, respectively, acting on the total body. In the science of hydrodynamics, the calculation of the total drag force of a rigid body is based on the equation:

$$D = 1/2 \; \varrho v^2 \; AC_d, \qquad (1)$$

where: ϱ = density of water; A = cross sectional area; v = swimming speed; and C_d = drag coefficient. Density of water, surface area and swimming velocity can be measured directly. The drag coefficient, a critical parameter as Schleihauf (1979) mentioned, must be determined experimentally. It depends on the shape of the body, the roughness of the surface and the state of the flow, whether laminar or turbulent. One problem here is that the state of the flow is also difficult to measure, so it must be estimated on the basis of the Reynolds number (Re), a "characteristic number" in fluid dynamics:

$$Re = \frac{vl}{\nu}, \tag{2}$$

where: v = swimming speed; l = characteristic length; and ν = kinematic viscosity of water.

The nondimensional Reynolds number is a mathematical representation of the ratio of inertial to viscous forces on rigid bodies and characterizes the state of the flow, which can be laminar or turbulent. According to Clarys (1979), in competitive swimming this number is in the range of $2 \times 10^5 < Re < 2 \times 10^6$, without mentioning the chosen characteristic length. The choice of this length is a crucial one, a point which will be discussed later in this article. At these high Reynolds numbers, the inertial forces dominate which means that the boundary layer along a rigid body is expected to be turbulent. In contrast to laminar flow the resistance is increased considerably. A number of experiments with rigid bodies of different shapes over a wide range of Re values have shown that the drag coefficient (C_d) is a function of Re. From appropriate diagrams C_d can be estimated on the basis of Re and incorporated into Equation 1. From experiments with towed swimmers, Clarys (1979) was able to determine the dependence of C_d from Re for a rigid human body. He stated that the flow around a rigid human body is totally turbulent and the total drag remains high.

Clarys (1979) also examined the drag of self-propelling bodies and found significantly higher values than those recorded for passively towed bodies. He concluded "that a hydrodynamically fundamental error is made when the total propulsive force of a moving body is derived from the resistance data from a passively towed body." Moreover, he expressed doubts as to whether the shape of the body has any influence on drag during active swimming. In his opinion, "the active drag is mainly, but not solely influenced by changes in shape."

The determination of drag when a body propels itself and changes its form—a subject that has received little attention in fluid dynamics—is also of general interest for biologists working on Gray's Paradoxon. The results presented here are parts of a dissertation (Ungerechts, 1980) dealing with the fluid dynamics of fast-swimming vertebrates. The tail motion of dolphins and the dolphin kick of the butterfly stroke in competitive swimming are nearly identical in the following respect: Both actions simultaneously provide the propulsive forces and active body drag in one unified motion. It is therefore conceivable that findings could be transferred. The extension to the study of hand and arm motion by Schleihauf (1979) or Wood (1979) cannot be made easily because it is unknown whether the situations are similar. As fluid flow basically determines drag, the flow around bodies which change their form periodically was examined. The purpose was to determine if there is a correlation between the state of flow and the Reynolds number as it exists for rigid bodies.

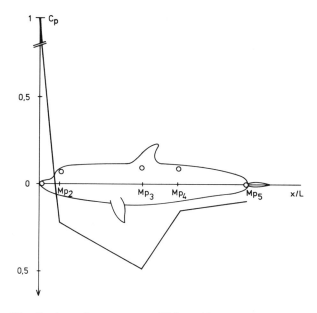

Figure 1 — Distribution of pressure coefficient (C_p) along a streamlined rigid dolphin model in relation to the relative body length (X/L). The points of measurements are indicated (M_{p_1}-M_{p_5}).

Procedure

The model was prepared according to measurements taken from a dolphin (*Tursiops truncatus*), on a scale of 6:1 (Figure 1). It was modeled of silicone rubber to make it flexible; the model was then fixed by a string in the test section of a water tunnel. The swimming movements of the model were generated by a module as described by Ungerechts (1981). In order to perform a dolphin-like movement, kinematic analyses of underwater films of swimming dolphins were conducted. The results of this analysis are presented elsewhere in this volume (Ungerechts, 1983).

Higher swimming velocities demand a higher frequency by the propelling parts of the body in dolphins' tails and flukes. The same is true for humans in competitive swimming: Swimming velocity increases when the extremities are moving faster. Different Reynold numbers were achieved at different velocities of water tunnel flow. Consequently, the frequency of the movements of the model had to be adjusted. This could be done on the basis of the nondimensional "reduced frequency" (Σ):

$$\Sigma = \frac{\omega \cdot l}{v}, \tag{3}$$

where ω = frequency; l = characteristic length; and v = swimming (or flow) velocity.

The reduced frequency, derivable from the Laws of Similitude for hydrodynamics, is used when the flow around an oscillating model will be similar to that around a geometrical similar body. It relates the steady inertial forces to the inertial forces due to the body form's periodical change. The choice of the appropriate "characteristic length" is the same crucial point as it is for Re. As a convention in these experiments, the length of the body (L) was taken as the characteristic length. This makes sense because nearly the whole body influences the flow. In accordance with the scope of this experiment—to examine whether there is a correlation between the flow around an oscillating body and the Reynolds number—different combinations of flow velocities (v) and reduced frequencies (Σ) were used (Table 1). Some of these combinations are unlikely to occur in practice, but for the first time a more comprehensive approach was necessary. The flow conditions were controlled by measuring the hydrodynamic pressure (p). This is a well established method of obtaining information about the dynamics of the flow. The hydrodynamic pressure depends on the local flow velocity (u) and the shape of the body. The local velocity is different from the flow velocity (v) of the free stream, which corresponds to the free stream pressure (p_0). The difference between the hydrodynamic pressure and the free stream pressure gives information about how the body shape influences the flow.

Moreover, the distribution of the hydrodynamic pressure influences the state of the flow, and therefore, is highly correlated with the behavior of the flow: As long as the hydrodynamic pressure along a streamlined body decreases, the flow may be expected to stay laminar. A quantity of interest is the pressure acting directly on the surface of the body, which is easy to measure. Small tubes were embedded in the model normal to the surface. Figure 1 illustrates how the openings were located on the dorsal side of the body. The free end of the tube was connected to a strain gauge manometer, which was situated outside the water tunnel. The free stream

Table 1

**The Relationship of Flow Velocities (v) and Reduced Frequencies (Σ)
to Calculate the Appropriate Frequency (Hz)
by Which the Model Was Oscillating**

Reduced frequency (Σ)	v(msec^{-1})			
	1.5	2.0	2.5	3.0
0.2	1 Hz	1.3 Hz	1.6 Hz	2.0 Hz
0.3	1.5 Hz	2.0 Hz	2.5 Hz	3.0 Hz
0.5	2.5 Hz	3.3 Hz	4.1 Hz	5.0 Hz
0.7	3.5 Hz	4.6 Hz	5.8 Hz	7.0 Hz

pressure was measured in front of the dolphin and acted as the reference pressure. The difference $p - p_0$ was recorded. Then the pressure coefficient (C_p), a nondimensional parameter, was defined:

$$C_p = \frac{2(p - p_0)}{pv^2},\tag{4}$$

where: p = hydrodynamic pressure; p_0 = pressure of the free stream; ϱ = density of water; and v = swimming velocity. The pressure coefficient is in the range of $-\infty < C_p \leq 1$ and makes the comparison of the results easier, because the influence of the given velocity (v) is excluded. Theoretically, at the rostrum the velocity of the stream is almost zero and all of the energy is converted into hydrodynamic pressure: $C_p = 1$.

Findings

The accompanying figures describe the distribution of the hydro-dynamic pressure, expressed as pressure coefficients (C_p) along a model scaled to the shape of a dolphin. Figure 1 represents the findings of a rigid model. The hydrodynamic pressure was measured at five points, ($M_{p_{1-5}}$), with locations related to body length. For the velocities, mentioned in Table 1, the same curves were obtained.

In Figure 2 the pressure distributions along the body which change its form periodically are presented for all combinations of flow velocity (v) versus reduced frequency (Σ) from Table 1. In each single diagram the distribution of the pressure along the body is represented at four different times during one cycle. Here the pressure is also highest at the rostrum as it is for a rigid body. The values at this point of measurement (M_{p_1}) cluster around 0.9 and are not included in these diagrams because of the scale of the reference. At point M_{p_2} the pressure coefficient is also equal to C_p of the rigid model. Over the following points the distribution of the pressure differs drastically from the findings of the rigid body. Large fluctuations occur, especially at M_{p_5} lying between the two lobes of the fluke. Regarding the pressure distribution at different times during one period, it is notable that the pressure drops again after having already increased and can be called "intermediate maximum." This especially occurs when the body is convex relative to the location of the points of measurements. Whereas under stationary flow conditions the location of the lowest pressure coincides with the maximal diameter of the body, it is not the case here; on the contrary, it sometimes shifts.

Discussion

These experiments were conducted to examine whether the flow conditions are different for nonstationary flow, that is, when the body changes

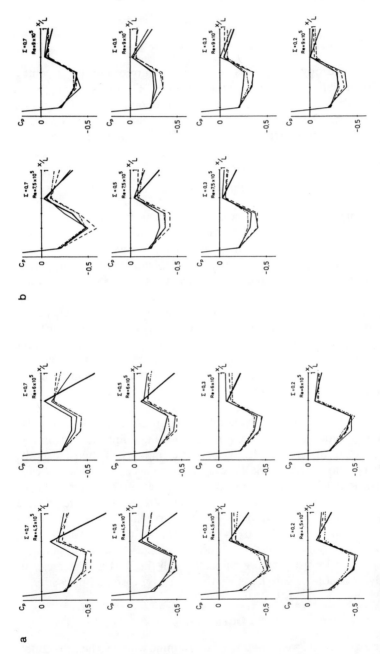

Figure 2 – Distribution of pressure coefficient (C_p) along the relative body length (X/L) of an oscillating dolphin model at different Reynolds numbers (Re) and reduced frequencies (ς). In each plot C_p is given at four different times during one cycle. In relation to Figure 1, an added point of observation between M_{p2} and M_{p3} is given.

its form periodically. The distribution of the pressure, an indicator of the flow conditions, is totally different compared to the stationary conditions. First, in nonstationary conditions the pressure fluctuates with the change of the body form during one cycle. Second, the existence of an "intermediate maximum" indicates that the flow is accelerated again. DuBois et al. (1974) also reported the existence of another decrease in pressure toward the end of the body, measured along an actively swimming fish, referring to the average pressure during one cycle. But taking only the average may delay conclusions about the effect of fluctuating pressure on the state of the flow.

As mentioned previously, an accelerated hydrodynamic pressure field is one way to prevent transition to turbulence. In the stationary condition, the pressure increases and at an appropriate Reynolds number it becomes turbulent and stays turbulent because the inertial forces prevail. But as far as we know from fluid dynamics it takes a brief period for turbulence to develop, and is dependent on constant flow conditions. The periodic change in pressure field may retard the development of turbulence by altering the conditions.

If this is so, it can be proven only by observing the boundary layer flow. First experiments in this context have indicated that the transition zone from laminar to turbulent flow was shifted backward, toward the end of the body, when the body was convex. This coincides with the position when the slope of the newly decreasing pressure was largest. In this context the use of the Reynolds number needs to be qualified. At the present state of knowledge, this characteristic of fluid dynamics number represents the stationary world. Its mathematical derivation does not take into account the frequency by which the body is changing its form.

Figure 2 shows that the pressure fluctuation varies from row to row where the flow velocity is different, as well as from column to column where the flow velocity is constant. These observations indicate there is no correlation with the Reynolds number; instead, they support the idea that reduced frequency, perhaps in combination with the Reynolds number, seems to be the more appropriate characteristic number to represent the flow along bodies changing form periodically.

Conclusion

The preceding results are presented as a contribution to the collaboration between the sport and hydrodynamics sciences. Further studies are necessary to find the exact mathematical formula to describe the flow under nonstationary conditions as valid for the Reynolds number in stationary flow. Meanwhile, it is suggested that detailed information be given when referring to hydrodynamic parameters based on Reynolds numbers.

References

CLARYS, J. 1979. Human morphology and hydrodynamics. In: J. Terauds and E.W. Bedingfield (eds.), *Swimming III*, pp. 3-41. University Park Press, Baltimore.

DuBOIS, A.B., Cavagna, G.A., and Fox, R.S. 1974. Pressure distribution on the body surface of swimming fish. *J. Exp. Biol.* **60**:581-591.

SCHLEIHAUF, R.E. Jr. 1979. A hydrodynamic analysis of swimming propulsion. In: J. Terauds and E.W. Bedingfield (eds.), *Swimming III*, pp. 70-109. University Park Press, Baltimore.

UNGERECHTS, B. 1980. *Ober die Hydrodynamik schnell schwimmender Wirbeltiere.* (On the hydrodynamics of fast swimming vertebrates.) Unpublished doctoral dissertation, Ruhr-Universität-Bochum.

UNGERECHTS, B. 1981. A device for the estimation of forces in a flexible shark model at high Reynolds-numbers. In: A. Morecki, K. Fidelus, K. Kedzior, and A. Wit (eds.), *Biomechanics VII-A*, pp. 230-235. Polish Scientific, Warsaw and University Park Press, Baltimore.

UNGERECHTS, B. 1983. A comparison of the movement of the rear parts of dolphins and butterfly-swimmers. In: A.P. Hollander, P. Huijing and G. de Groot (eds.), *Biomechanics and Medicine in Swimming*, pp. 215-221. Human Kinetics, Champaign, IL.

WOOD, T.C. 1979. A fluid dynamic analysis of the propulsive potential of the hand and forearm in swimming. In: J. Terauds and E.W. Bedingfield (eds.), *Swimming III*, pp. 62-69. University Park Press, Baltimore.

A Criterion Measure for the Swimming Start[1]

Rod Havriluk
Indiana University, Bloomington, USA

In 1971 Elliott and Sinclair questioned the appropriate criterion measure for the swimming start: "should it be evaluated from the sound of the gun to encompass the whole race, or a few strokes, or perhaps one length of the pool, or what?" They reasoned that starting ability "should be directly linked with the horizontal component of . . . velocity after leaving the block." Groves and Roberts (1972) demonstrated agreement with the Elliott and Sinclair opinion by using horizontal take-off velocity as a dependent measure for the start in an attempt to determine the optimal angle of projection.

Most often, however, starts have been measured by the time to a set distance. Starting performances have been assessed by time intervals between the starting stimulus and the instant a given distance is reached such as 10 ft (3.05 m; Disch et al., 1979), 12 ft (3.66 m; Roffer and Nelson, 1972), 5 m (Ayalon et al., 1975), 20 ft (6.10 m; Lowell, 1975), 25 ft (7.62 m; Gibson and Holt, 1976), 8 m (Lewis, 1980), 10 yd (9.14 m; Bowers and Cavanagh, 1975), and 25 yd (22.86 m; Stevenson and Morehouse, 1979).

The impulse-momentum equation ($F\Delta t = m\Delta v$, where F = force, Δt = time of application of force, m = mass, and Δv = change in velocity) can be rearranged ($\Delta v = F\Delta t/m$) and used to explain the trade-off in measuring starting performance by only horizontal take-off velocity or only time to a set distance. The quantity ($v_f - v_o$) can be substituted for Δv, where v_f = final velocity and v_o = initial velocity. Since $v_o = 0$ at the beginning of the start, from the equation $v_f = F\Delta t/m$ it can be predicted that a swimmer who applies force over a short time could leave the block with a low take-off velocity (v_f), but achieve a fast response time to a short distance. Conversely, the same swimmer exerting the same force over a relatively long time would produce a high take-off velocity and possibly a fast response time to a long distance. Conflicting evaluations of starting techniques could therefore result from utilization of different criterion measures. To eliminate invalid measurement due to the take-off velocity/measurement distance trade-off, the start can be measured to some point where additional propulsive forces are generated with swimming movements.

Since the effects of the start may extend beyond a designated reference, arbitrary selection of a criterion measure is unacceptable. Subsequent determination of factors associated with success, in terms of an unjustified criterion measure, does not necessarily concurrently identify the factors important in "starting."

A starting motion supplies the unbalanced force required for positive acceleration. Applying Newton's Second Law, the termination of positive acceleration would indicate the starting movements can no longer be supplying an unbalanced force. Therefore, a defensible measure of a swimming start would include only the distance over which positive acceleration exists.

The criterion measure for the start can then be defined as the distance from the starting end of the pool at which positive acceleration has terminated. If the swimmer is no longer accelerating, a constant velocity has been achieved. The constant velocity phase can be identified when no significant difference in time to traverse successive, equal distances is apparent. In addition to including the final, positive acceleration phase, any succeeding movement is excluded by the definition. The objective of this study therefore was to determine the criterion distance for the swimming start.

Establishment of a justifiable criterion measure for the swimming start will allow: (a) definition of a swimming start based on the extent of the starting movements, (b) evaluation of the validity of previous studies on the basis of the distance over which the start was tested, (c) determination of the percentage variance accounted for by the start in the times of different swimming events, (d) future identification of predictor variables related to performance in the start, and (e) future comparison of starting techniques over a distance that is representative of the starting phase of a swimming event.

Method

Standard deviations as small as .06 sec were found in pilot work for movement time measurements of swimming starts. Since minimal variability of the dependent measure was expected for the present experiment, .06 sec was used as the within-population standard deviation for the calculation of effect size (f, "the degree of departure from no effect"; Cohen, 1977, p. 274). A .05-sec difference between means was designated as an important difference, and it converted to a velocity change that was smaller than intracycle velocity fluctuations reported by Holmer

(1979) and Schleihauf (1979). Effect size was calculated according to Cohen's (1977, p. 277) formula as $f = .34$. To detect the nontrivial effect size at $\alpha = .05$ with statistical power greater than .80, a sample size of 30 was deemed necessary (Cohen, 1977, p. 384).

Male high school and college swimmers ($n = 30$) involved in a competitive training program at the time of testing volunteered to participate in the study. Prior to participation in the study, informed consent was obtained from each subject. Subjects were attired in nylon racing suits and were permitted to warm-up until they felt prepared to participate.

Each subject was asked to perform one practice and two filmed trials of his normal grab start with a swim to 25 yd (22.86 m) at maximal speed. All trials were started according to NCAA rules by an experienced starter. Subjects were provided a minimum of 2 minutes rest between trials.

Subjects were filmed perpendicular to the principal plane of motion with a 16-mm Locam camera operated at 100 frames/sec. The camera was positioned 11 m from the starting end of the pool at a distance of 19 m from the center of the lane used for filming. The filming was conducted outdoors with Ektachrome (7239) film. The camera was started before the subject broke the surface, and stopped as the subject passed the 14-m point.

The lane lines that bordered the lane used in the filming were narrowed and the colored buoys were aligned to allow determination of three consecutive, 1-m, horizontal distances beginning at 8.7 m from the starting end of the pool. The time interval for the swimmer's crown to traverse each distance was determined by a frame count.

Only one subject had not surfaced by the 8.7 m mark, and he was eliminated from further analyses. For the 29 subjects included in the statistical analysis, the mean age was 17.8 yrs ($SD = 2.6$), the height was 172.6 cm ($SD = 9.4$), and the weight was 68.9 kg ($SD = 11.4$). The mean career best time for the 50-yd (45.72-m) freestyle swim was 23.9 sec ($SD = 1.9$).

Results

The investigator's reliability of evaluation of the dependent variable was ascertained by intraclass correlation coefficients (Atwater et al., 1976, p. 32) to be greater than $R = .90$ for all three 1-m distances ($R = .915$, $R = .905$, and $R = .908$ for the first, second, and third intervals, respectively). The subjects' reliability was also calculated with intraclass correlation coefficients and exceeded $R = .77$ for each 1-m distance ($R = .777$, $R = .815$, and $R = .858$).

The mean times for the sample to traverse the first, second, and third 1-m distances were: .568 ($SD = .057$), .564 ($SD = .060$), and .562 sec

(*SD* = .056), respectively. The data were analyzed as a randomized block factorial design (RBF-23; Kirk, 1968, p. 237) with subjects as blocks, and trials and distances as factors. An ANOVA was performed on the data with an SPSS computer program (Nie et al., 1975). See Table 1 for experimental design and group results. No significant trial × distance interaction was revealed. Inspection of the *F* ratios for the main effects manifested that both the trial and distance factors were nonsignificant. Since the trial factor was not significant, the scores were collapsed across trials for further analyses.

Since the nonsignificant *F* value for the distance factor could be the result of a negative bias from a block × treatment interaction, Tukey's test for nonadditivity of the subject and distance effects as described by Kirk (1968) was applied. The subject × distance interaction was found to be significant, $F(1,55) = 10.55$, $p < .25$ (a liberal *F* test was used to avoid the possibility of a negative bias in the test for the distance effect) and a transformation was sought that would remove the interaction. Using the procedure outlined by Kirk (1968), pp. 66-67), a logarithmic transformation ($\log_{10}$) was selected as most appropriate. The transformed data were evaluated with the test for nonadditivity, and it was determined that the block × distance interaction had been removed. However, the ANOVA performed on the transformed data still revealed a nonsignificant distance effect.

Discussion

The failure to find a significant trial × distance interaction, or a significant distance effect led to the conclusion that immediately after

Table 1

Experimental Design with Representative Data
for the First Two Subjects[a]

		D_1	D_2	D_3
S_1	T_1	.50	.51	.49
	T_2	.50	.52	.55
S_2	T_1	.65	.68	.73
	T_2	.67	.66	.70
↓				
S_{29}				
M		.568	.564	.562
SD		.057	.060	.056

[a]S = subject; T = trial; D = distance; time in sec; *M* = mean; *SD* = standard deviation.

surfacing, no significant differences existed among the subjects' times to traverse each of three consecutive 1-m distances. Subjects' attainment of a constant velocity over the interval 8.7-11.7 m from the starting end of the pool was indicated by the results. Termination of positive acceleration, and therefore the starting motion, must have occurred by the point between the first and second test distances. Although positive acceleration might have terminated as swimming movements were initiated, methodological limitations prohibited the determination of that precise instance. The defensible criterion measure for the swimming start in the tested sample is a distance of 9.7 m from the starting end of the pool. The swimming start can then be defined as the movement sequence between the starting signal and the criterion measure.

Naturally the appropriate criterion measure will vary slightly for other samples. Based on the results of the present study, it is expected that a distance of 1 m past the point where all members of a homogeneous sample have surfaced will serve as an adequate criterion measure for that sample.

In the majority of the studies reviewed, starting techniques were measured to a point prior to surfacing and therefore were not evaluations of the entire starting motion. In only three studies (Bowers and Cavanagh, 1975; Gibson and Holt, 1976; Lewis, 1980) were starts measured to a point that required a minimal amount of swimming after surfacing.

For competitive swimmers Gibson and Holt (1976) found no significant differences among the conventional, grab, and variation of the grab starting techniques to a distance of 25 ft (7.62 m). For untrained subjects Lewis (1980) found no significant differences among three arm-swing and two grab starting techniques to a distance of 8 m. Bowers and Cavanagh (1975), however, determined the grab start to be faster than the conventional start to a distance of 10 yd (9.14 m) for female swimmers.

When the validity of the criterion measure is considered, there appears to be little evidence to support the well established belief of the grab start as superior to the conventional start. The reported advantage of the grab start to distances prior to surfacing (Disch et al., 1979; Lowell, 1975; Roffer and Nelson, 1972) might actually be diminished or completely eliminated when evaluated to a more valid criterion. A significant advantage in quickness off the block with the grab start might be retained for a short distance, but could be equalized by another starting technique using a longer time on the block. As predicted from the impulse-momentum equation, a longer block time could result in a higher take-off velocity and ultimately a shorter time to a distance that represented an adequate criterion measure.

The study in which starts were measured using a distance greater than 11.7 m from the starting end of the pool (Stevenson and Morehouse,

1979) could have allowed other variables to influence measurement of the dependent variable. Once the starting motion was completed, factors related to swimming velocity could have affected the assessed performance.

In conclusion, based on the present establishment of a defensible criterion measure for the swimming start, the validity of most previous research on the start is questioned. The previously reported superiority of the grab start has not been conclusively demonstrated to a valid criterion. Future research can be directed at determination of the percentage variance accounted for by the start in different swimming events. If the start accounts for a significant proportion of the variance in performance for an event, then research can be aimed at comparisons of starting techniques and identification of factors related to performance using a valid criterion measure.

Note

1. This research was conducted in the Department of Physical Education, Indiana University, Bloomington, IN.

References

ATWATER, A.E., Baumgartner, T.A., and West, C. 1976. *Reliability Theory.* American Alliance for Health, Physical Education, and Recreation, Washington, DC.

AYALON, A., Van Gheluwe, B., and Kanitz, M. 1975. A comparison of four styles of racing start in swimming. In: J.P. Clarys and L. Lewillie (eds.), *Swimming II.* University Park Press, Baltimore.

BOWERS, J.E., and Cavanagh, P.R. 1975. A biomechanical comparison of the grab and conventional sprint starts in competitive swimming. In: J.P. Clarys and L. Lewillie (eds.), *Swimming II.* University Park Press, Baltimore.

COHEN, J. 1977. *Statistical Power Analysis for the Behavioral Sciences.* Academic Press, New York.

DISCH, J.G., Hosler, W.W., and Bloom, J.A. 1979. Effects of weight, height, and reach on the performance of the conventional and grab starts in swimming. In: J. Terauds and E.W. Bedingfield (eds.), *Swimming III.* University Park Press, Baltimore.

ELLIOTT, G.M., and Sinclair, H. 1971. The influence of the block angle on swimming sprint starts. In: L. Lewillie and J.P. Clarys (eds.), *Proceedings of the First International Symposium on Biomechanics in Swimming, Waterpolo and Diving.* Universite Libre de Bruxelles, Brussels.

GIBSON, G., and Holt, L.E. 1976. A cinema-computer analysis of selected starting techniques. *Swim. Tech.* **13**:75-76, 79.

GROVES, R., and Roberts, J.A. 1972. A further investigation of the optimum angle of projection for the racing start in swimming. *Res. Q.* **35**:81-82.

HOLMER, I. 1979. Analysis of acceleration as a measure of swimming proficiency. In: J. Terauds and E.W. Bedingfield (eds.), *Swimming III*. University Park Press, Baltimore.

KIRK, R.E. 1968. *Experimental Design: Procedures for the Behavioral Sciences.* Brooks/Cole, Belmont, CA.

LEWIS, S. 1980. Comparison of five swimming starting techniques. *Swim. Tech.* **16**:124-128.

LOWELL, J.C. 1975. Analysis of the grab start and the conventional start. *Swim. Tech.* **12**:66-69.

NIE, N.H., Hull, C.H., Jenkins, J.G., Steinbrenner, K., and Bent, D.H. 1975. *Statistical Package for the Social Sciences.* McGraw-Hill, New York.

ROFFER, B.J., and Nelson, R.C. 1972. The grab start is faster. *Swim. Tech.* **9**:101-102.

SCHLEIHAUF, R.E., Jr. 1979. A hydrodynamic analysis of swimming propulsion. In: J. Terauds and E.W. Bedingfield (eds.), *Swimming III*. University Park Press, Baltimore.

STEVENSON, J.R., and Morehouse, C.A. 1979. Influence of starting-block angle on the grab start in competitive swimming. In: J. Terauds and E.W. Bedingfield (eds.), *Swimming III*. University Park Press, Baltimore.

A General Computing Method
for Obtaining Biomechanical Data in Swimming

Marc Bourgeois
Université Libre de Bruxelles, Belgium

This study provides a description of a general computing method for obtaining kinematic and dynamic parameters pertinent to crawl swimming. In addition, the influences of these parameters on the fundamental understanding of human movement are included.

The tridimensional analysis of kinematic parameters of different bodies of swimmers can be done with information provided by one camera (under restricted conditions) by a solution of discrete Fourier Transform (DFT) and by an optimization function when using a Direct Linear Transformation (DLT). The dynamic model for this method includes an optimized algorithm by matrix calculation of generalized torques in Lagrangian mechanics using a mathematical model with 18 degrees of freedom.

Various researchers have studied the dynamics of the swimmer by using mathematical simulations (Belokovsky and Kuznetsov, 1976; Bourgeois and Lewillie, 1981; Huston and Passerello, 1971; Seireg and Baz, 1971; Seireg et al., 1971). Many other researchers have analyzed the dynamics of swimmers using experimental data as a basis. Among the most recent research is that of Martin et al. (1981). Most of these dynamics models are based on Newtonian mechanics. This type of investigation requires the knowledge of several parameters of dynamics, such as the forces acting between human bodies. Lagrangian dynamics applied to the human movement therefore seems to be more appropriate (Hatze, 1977).

In this study a computing method is described which allows synthesis of both types of investigation by inputting experimental kinematic data into a theoretical mathematical model. The value in this technique is in being able to determine the energy transfers between the different human bodies and to evaluate the levels of synchronization in the swimmers by a spectral analysis of the movement studies.

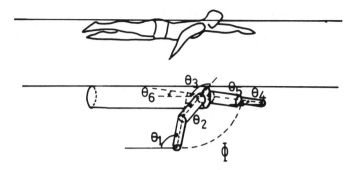

Figure 1—Geometric representation in the sagittal plane of the mathematical model with five cylinders and six degrees of freedom in each plane.

Mathematical Model

The proposed algorithm represents an "Inverse Dynamic Problem" in which it is possible to determine the torques applied about the different articulations of the human body from kinematic data derived from films (16 mm/64 fps). The geometric representation of the model of the swimmer in the sagittal plan is shown in Figure 1. This model has 6 degrees of freedom in each plane, or a total of 18 degrees of freedom in the three dimensions. Each body is represented by a cylinder of which the dimensions, weight, moment of inertia, etc., are established on the basis of the anthropometric data of the specific swimmer being studied. Figure 2 provides a schematic diagram of the mathematical model.

2D/3D Conversion

The 2D/3D conversion of the biomechanical data extracted from films is accomplished by a "Direct Linear Transformation" (DLT) method developed by Abdel-Aziz and Karara (1971). The developed algorithm allows the use of only one camera. The X, Y and Z coordinates of each anatomical landmark of the swimmer are obtained through operation research and a simplex procedure by optimizing a function based on 11 DLT parameters. This technique allows a 3-dimensional representation of the location of the anatomical landmarks.

However, this method is only valid if at least the X, Y, and Z coordinates of one landmark are known in an inertial coordinate system. In the 2D/3D conversion it is assumed that the shoulder moves in a vertical plane, parallel to the long side of the swimming pool. This approximation allows one to obtain a good projection of the anatomical landmarks in the sagittal plane and corrects for the perspective errors in this plane. In the other two planes, the DLT technique provides a good estimation of the displacement of the human body parts but does not allow one to derive data for velocities and accelerations because of its imprecision.

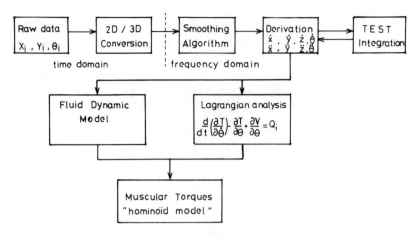

Figure 2—Schematic of the computed mathematical model.

Kinematic and Smoothing Algorithm

For the smoothing and the derivation of the biomechanical data obtained by the DLT, a transformation in the frequency domain is done by the Fast Fourier Transform, with "detrended" data after an odd extension with 2 N points (linearly transformed data, as described by Anderssen and Bloomfield, 1974). The complex Fourier coefficients are:

$$G_i = \frac{1}{2N} \sum_{i=1}^{N-1} g_i \cdot e^{-jiw_i}, \tag{1}$$

where g_i is the detrended data; $j = \sqrt{-1}$; N = number of observations; and $w_i = 2\pi i/2N$.

For the derivations of degrees (0), (1) and (2) of the experimental biomechanical data, the Complex Fourier Coefficients are smoothed by Collum's regularization theory (Anderssen and Bloomfield, 1974). This theory consists of minimizing a logarithmic function to optimize a regularization parameter (α):

$$\frac{(N+1)}{2} \text{Log} \left[\sum_{i=1}^{N} I(w_i) \right] / \left[1 + 1 / \sum_{j=1}^{m+1} \alpha (w_i/\Delta)^{2 \cdot j} \right]$$

$$+ \frac{1}{2} \sum \text{Log} \left[1 + 1 / \sum_{j=1}^{m+1} \alpha (w_i/\Delta)^{2 \cdot j} \right] = \text{Min} \tag{2}$$

with $\Delta = \frac{1}{N}$, $w_i = 2\pi i/2N$, designs to the slope of the theoretical spectrum, and the periodogram:

$$I(w_i) = \frac{1}{2\pi} (N + 1) \mid \sum_{i=1}^{N} g_i e^{-ijw} \mid^2 \qquad (3)$$

This function represents the best statistical approach which eliminates noise in the data when α is used in the transfer function (λ), defined as (Anderssen and Bloomfield, 1974):

$$\lambda_\alpha^{(n,m)} (w_i) = 1/1 + \alpha (w_i N)^{2N} \cdot \sum_{j=0}^{m} (w_i N)^{2 \cdot j}, \qquad (4)$$

where n = derivative ($n = 0, 1, 2$).

The Complex Fourier coefficients are filtered by the use of this transfer function (λ). Then the smoothed Complex Fourier coefficients become:

$$C_i^{(n)} = G_i \cdot \lambda_\alpha^{(n,m)} (i). \qquad (5)$$

By this method a spectral analysis ($m = 2$) of displacement, velocity and acceleration of human body parts during swimming is possible.

Dynamics

In order to determine the variation in the muscular torques applied about each articulation in swimming, the kinematic data of the swimmer are input into the Lagrangian dynamic model within which the general equation is:

$$\frac{d}{dt} (\frac{\delta T}{\delta \theta}) - \frac{\delta T}{\delta \theta_i} + \frac{\delta V}{\delta \theta_i} = Q_i, \qquad (6)$$

where T and V are the kinetic energy and potential energy of the system, respectively; and Q_i is the generalized torque applied about each articulation (i). In fact, this consists of the sum of the moments of all forces applied about the joint (i.e., hydrodynamic forces, muscular forces, gravity, etc.).

The hydrodynamic forces are determined on the basis of the Reynolds numbers corresponding to each body segment in swimming. The drag coefficients are defined for cylinders from the experimental results published by Welsh (1953). The muscular torques applied about the shoulders are transformed in this mathematical model into the frequency domain by Fast Fourier Transform (FFT) and are represented by Equation 1. This representation of muscular torques in the frequency domain also permits the use of the Collum's regularization theory calculated by Equation 2.

This regularization function is indeed based on the resulting spectrum *periodogram*. The value of the α regularized coefficient shows the "quality" of the periodicity for the analyzed spectral function in theory. Under these conditions, the value of the α coefficient is to show the synchronization level of the transfer of energy from the arms to the trunk.

The mathematical simulation permits the modification of the differences in phase angle (Φ) between the arms in the water in order to optimize the value of the α coefficient in Equation 2. The objective of this calculation is to determine the difference in phase angle Φ between both arms, which is best for a given set of experimental kinematics. This mathematical simulation model of swimming is called a "hominoid model" (Figure 2). Some recent studies, not yet published, show that high dynamic frequencies of the trunk create more random movements and induce an increased drag into the water.

Results and Discussion

The results gathered in the present investigation are based on 10 different movements including a complete cycle of the arms in one swimmer with an average performance of 58 sec for the 100-m freestyle (film speed by frames/sec). The analysis of these movements by the method described enables one to estimate the swimmer's potential and technical errors, not only from a kinematic standpoint but also from a dynamic point of view.

Figure 3 shows the evolution of the generalized torques applied about the general axis of the shoulders for one complete cycle of the arms. The average swimming velocity in this case was 1.81 m/sec. For the difference in phase of the two arms, ϕ_1 is equal to 98° when the right arm is entering the water and ϕ_2 is equal to 142° when the left arm is entering the water.

These results show the lack of synchronization in energy transfer from the arms to the trunk. Furthermore, the same representation of torques applied on the trunk, but in the frequency domain (Figure 4), shows that the trunk is submitted to these torques at frequencies between 1.5 and 2.5 Hz for one complete cycle of arms.

In this case, the α regularization coefficient, calculated for these torque variations applied to the trunk, was equal to 2.6×10^{-3}. In other words, the trunk was submitted to a high dynamic "noise." On the basis of the same kinematic data, the best difference of phase angle has been

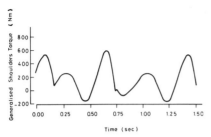

Figure 3—Experimental results of the generalized shoulder torques with ϕ_1 = 98° and ϕ_2 = 142°.

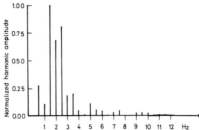

Figure 4—Representation in the frequency domain of the general shoulder torques calculated on the basis of experimental data.

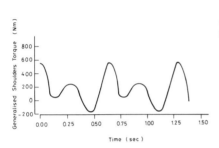

Figure 5—Optimal computed shoulder torques simulated with the α regularization coefficient of 1.024×10^{-11}. The difference in phase angles ϕ_1 are equal to 115°.

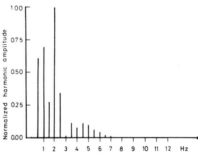

Figure 6—Optimal shoulder torques computed which are represented in the frequency domain.

calculated from the mathematic model by optimizing the α regularization coefficient. Figures 5 and 6 show the results of the optimization for a minimal α value equal to 1.024×10^{-11}. Figure 5 shows a much smoother dynamic function applied to the trunk. In this case, the difference in the phase angle ϕ is equal to 115°. This difference in phase angle between the arms in the example shows that as the forearm comes out of the water, it describes an angle of 148° with the horizontal.

Figure 6 shows that in the frequency domain, the swimmer's trunk would be submitted to dynamic torques at frequencies between 0.5 and 2 Hz for ϕ = 115°. The estimated average velocity gain would be more than 4% based on the results of this mathematical model. Furthermore, the low dynamic frequencies applied to the trunk in this model show the value of a two-beat kick, with a propulsive and powerful up-beat, in reducing the positive spikes and the dynamic torques applied to the trunk as shown in Figure 5.

Conclusions

A general computing method for obtaining spatial kinematic and dynamic parameters of biomechanical systems from cinematographic data in swimming was developed. This algorithm provides an estimation of the torques coming from the musculoskeletal system as well as the hydrodynamic torques calculated on the basis of Reynolds numbers corresponding to each segment of the swimmer during the crawl stroke. This general method also provides an evaluation of energy transfer and consequently, the synchronization of the movements in the different segments of the body. This mathematical model shows the value of the "two-beat" kick with propulsive up-beat based on a spectral analysis of crawl swimming.

References

ABDEL-AZIZ, Y.I., and Karara, H.M. 1971. Direct linear transformation from comparator coordinates into object-space coordinates. *Proc. ASP/UI Symps. on Close-range Photogrammetry*, pp. 1-18. American Society of Photogrammetry, Falls Church, VA.

ANDERSSEN, R.S., and Bloomfield, P. 1974. Numerical differentiation procedures for non-exact data. *Numer. Math.* **22**:157-182.

BELOKOVSKY, V.V., and Kuzenetsov, V.V. 1976. Analysis of dynamic forces in crawl stroke swimming. In: P.V. Komi (ed.), *Biomechanics V-B*, pp. 235-242. University Park Press, Baltimore.

BOURGEOIS, M.A., and Lewillie, L.A. 1983. Mathematical model and Lagrangian analysis for the dynamics of the human bodies in crawl stroke. In: H. Matsui and K. Kobayashi (eds.), *Biomechanics VIIIB*, pp. 978-985. Human Kinetics, Champaign, IL.

HATZE, H. 1977. A complete set of control equations for the human musculoskeletal system. *J. Biomech.* **10**:799-805.

HUSTON, R.L., and Passerello, C.E. 1971. On the dynamics of a human body model. *J. Biomech.* **4**:369-378.

MARTIN, R.B., Yeather, R.A., and White, M.K. 1981. A simple analytical model for the crawl stroke. *J. Biomech.* **14, 8**:539-548.

SEIREG, A., and Baz, A. 1971. A mathematical model for swimming mechanics. In: L. Lewillie and J.P. Clarys (eds.), *Biomechanics in Swimming*. Universite Libre de Bruxelles, Brussells.

SEIREG, A., Baz, A., and Pattel, D. 1971. Supportive forces on the human body during underwater activities. *J. Biomech.* **4**:23-30.

WELSH, C.J. 1953. *The Drag of Finite-Length Cylinders Determined from Flight Tests at High Reynolds Numbers for a Mach Number Range from 0.5 to 1.3, Nacatn 2941*. Langley Aeronautical Laboratory, Washington, DC.

Measurement of the Waves Caused by Swimmers

Hitoshi Ohmichi, Miwako Takamoto,
and Mitsumasa Miyashita
University of Tokyo, Japan

Water resistance is a primary problem in the biomechanics of swimming. However, it is extremely difficult to identify the frictional, wave-making and/or eddy resistance, because the swimmer's propulsion along the water's surface is regarded as a collection of a large number of traveling pressure points (Lap, 1954). Therefore, many researchers have tried to measure the resultant water resistance by towing the swimmer in relation to velocity, body position and body size, as reviewed by Clarys (1978). In other words, most previous studies have not been focused on the water surrounding the swimmer.

A swimmer's performance may be affected by the waves caused by other swimmers and/or themselves, especially in competitive swimming. On the other hand, the resultant waves caused by a swimmer may reflect water resistance. Hence, the present study was designed to measure wave-height in relation to swimming velocity and stroke.

Methods

The resultant waves caused by a subject swimming in lane 2 were recorded in a 25-m swimming pool. A Capacity Wave Height Meter (C-500, Kenek Inc., Tokyo) was located at point L_1 (experiments 1 and 3) which was 0.3 m from the subject's swimming course, or at point L_2 (experiment 2) which was 5 m from the subject's swimming course as shown in Figure 1. The Wave Height Meter, which was equipped with a capacity sensor and an amplifier system, could detect electrically the level of water surface. The output signals from the meter were recorded on a magnetic tape recorder (cassette data recorder, SONY Inc., Tokyo). Three top male Japanese swimmers, A, B and C, volunteered as subjects in experiments 1, 2 and 3.

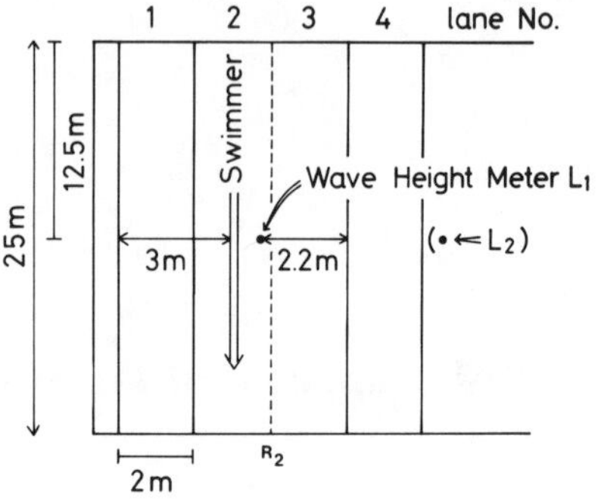

Figure 1—Location of the Wave Height Meter.

Experiment 1

All floating lane lines except for the second one, R_2, were set in the swimming pool (Figure 1). Subject A performed a 25-m swim 15 times at various constant velocities ranging from 1.4 to 2.0 m/sec using the front crawl stroke.

Experiment 2

All floating lane lines were removed from the pool and subject B also swam using the crawl stroke, 17 times at various constant velocities ranging from 1.2 to 2.1 m/sec.

Experiment 3

With the same floating lane lines as experiment 1, subject C swam with four different strokes—crawl, back, breast and butterfly—at the same velocity of 1.5 m/sec. The subject performed three trials using each swimming stroke.

In all experiments, it took ca. 15 min for the water surface to recover to the resting level in terms of wave height. The change in wave height was recorded 3 min after the 25-m swim. The output signals were stored in a minicomputer system (Atac 2300, Nippon Kohden Inc., Tokyo) which included A-D conversion (sampling rate 0.1 sec) for the spectral analysis (through FFT program) and other numerical calculations of the wave height analysis.

Results and Discussion

The mean swimming velocity was calculated from the times for the 25-m swims, that is, $12.3 \sim 17.5$ sec/25 m for A, $12.0 \sim 20.2$ sec/25 m for B, and $16.7 \sim 16.9$ sec/25 m for C. A typical record of the wave height related to time h(t) in experiment 1 is shown in Figure 2a and b. The

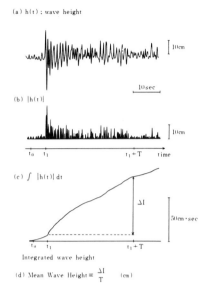

Figure 2—Change of the wave height and calculation of the mean wave height.

lower figure (b) was obtained from rectifying the upper one (a), where the zero level was regarded as the resting level of the water surface. The subject took off at time t_0 and passed in front of the Wave Height Meter at time t_1, when a maximal amplitude of 25 cm was recorded. The amplitude of wave fluctuation gradually decreased after t_1.

In order to average the wave height, the rectified wave $|h(t)|$ was integrated numerically using the following equation:

$$\Delta I = \int_{t_1}^{t_1 + T} |h(t)| \, dt. \tag{1}$$

The results are shown in Figure 2c.

The mean wave height, H (cm), during T (sec) was given as $\Delta I / T$, that is:

$$H = \frac{1}{T} \int_{t_1}^{t_1 + T} |h(t)| \, dt. \tag{2}$$

In the present study, 10 and 90 sec were used as values of T, with two kinds of mean wave height, H_{10} and H_{90}, calculated for each trial.

In experiment 1, the values of H_{10} ranged from 2.7 to 5.8 cm and the values of H_{90} from 2.0 to 3.2 cm, as shown in Figure 3. In experiment 2, the H_{10} values ranged from 2.3 to 3.5 cm and the H_{90} values ranged from 2.3 to 3.4 cm (Figure 4). The H_{10} values in experiment 1 were definitely higher than in experiment 2, which suggested that the wave amplitude attenuated as it traveled to the point L_2 in experiment 2.

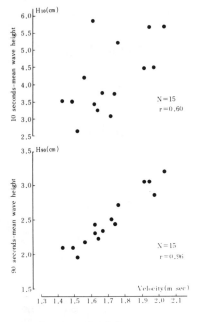

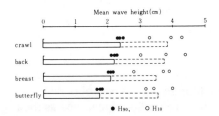

Figure 4—Correlations between the swimming velocity and the mean wave height H_{10} and H_{90} (in experiment 2 for subject B).

Figure 3—Correlations between the swimming velocity and the mean wave height H_{10} and H_{90} (in experiment 1 for subject A).

Figure 5—Mean wave height in four different strokes (in experiment 3 for subject C; —, mean of three H_{90} values; ---, mean of three H_{10} values).

The H_{90}/H_{10} ratio was considered as the rate of attenuation in the wave height. These ratios were 0.60 ± 0.10 (mean $\pm$ SD) for experiment 1 and 0.90 ± 0.12 for experiment 2. In both experiments 1 and 2, there were highly linear correlations between the swimming velocity and the H_{90} value (correlation coefficient $r = 0.96$ in experiment 1, and $r = 0.90$ in experiment 2). On the other hand, the H_{10} values were not so highly dependent upon the swimming velocity ($r = 0.60$ in experiment 1, $r = 0.42$ in experiment 2).

The results obtained from experiment 3 are shown in Figure 5. The values of H_{10} were higher than the H_{90} in all strokes. Though Swimmer C was asked to swim at a constant velocity, the H_{10} scattered widely in three trials. On the other hand, the H_{90} showed almost similar values. It is difficult to explain why the H_{90} value of butterfly stroke was lower than that of the crawl stroke.

Power spectra of the wave height h(t) are shown in Figure 6. In both experiments 1 and 2, the frequencies above 3 Hz contribute little to the total power, and the spectra showed similar patterns. (The spectral analysis was conducted for 30 sec after the 25-m swim.) The higher the mean wave height (i.e., swimming velocity), the more the total power. In

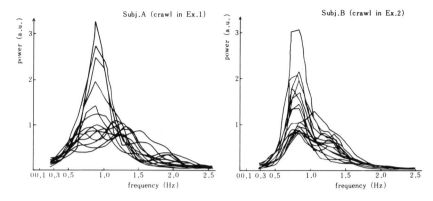

Figure 6 — Power spectra of waves caused by the subject swimming at different velocities.

detail, however, the shape of the spectrum changed with the swimming velocity; it had a peak at 1.3 Hz for relatively low velocities, whereas the peak occurred at 0.8 Hz for higher velocities. The reasons for the different types of spectra are unclear within the limitations of the present study.

In this pilot study, the researchers tried to measure directly the resultant wave height caused by a swimmer, with limitations such as: (a) the effect of the floating lane lines; (b) the locations of the Wave Height Meter; and (c) the sampling duration of the mean wave height H_T. From the viewpoint of hydrodynamics, however, the wave energy might be estimated from the wave height. If the total energy maintained in the swimming pool was known, the mechanical energy output of the swimmer could be determined.

References

LAP, A.J.W. 1954. *Fundamentals of Ship Resistance and Propulsion*. National shipbuilding progress (Publ. 129a; N.S.M.B.), Rotterdam.

CLARYS, J.P. 1978. Human morphology and hydrodynamics. In: J. Terauds and E.W. Bedingfield (eds.), *Swimming III*, pp. 3-41. University Park Press, Baltimore.

Multifunctional Modular Ergometer for Simulating the Specific Dynamics in Swimming

Vladimir Schor
The Research Centre for Physical Education and Sport
Bucharest, Rumania

An ergometer involves a system for transforming a more complex movement into a simple movement (rotation or translation) and another system for making a simple movement more difficult. In most types of ergometers for swimming, the system for transforming the movement is based on the same principle (use of flexible elements). Differences are in the ways of rendering the movement more difficult (e.g., inertial, gravitational, elastic and friction directly proportional to velocity, isokinetics).

Since the capacity for developing useful energy depends on both the type and size of the loading (Kume and Ishii, 1981; Ueya, 1981), load selection is important when measuring work output. The strong relationship between performance and the displacement of the weight center of mass in swimming suggests the idea of resorting to a loading which would simulate the dynamic equilibrium of the interaction forces between athlete and environment, produced at the athlete's center of mass. This would also allow for the instantaneous recording of certain movement parameters, measurement of which is difficult because of poor access in the swimming pool (propulsive force, displacement, velocity of displacement), and it would permit experimental study with a view toward optimization of the relationship between propulsive force and displacement velocity throughout the race.

It seems that, at present, loadings on ergometers try to utilize the two aspects of the dynamics of the weight center of mass: *inertial* (gravitational, inertial loadings) and *resistive* (elastic, isokinetic loadings with friction being dependent on velocity). The apparatus loads specific movements of the arms in swimming according to simplified dynamics for the interaction of forces determining the weight center of mass displacement.

108

The writer's opinion is that a modularized, constructive solution will allow for adequate selection of the moduli, reestablishing the usual types of loadings and creating the possibility of using combinations of them, with the percentages of each depending on the requirements of the situation.

Methods

The model for dynamic equilibrium of the forces determining weight center of mass displacement in swimming may be represented by the equation:

$$M \frac{d^2S}{dt^2} + R \left(\frac{dS}{dt}\right) = F(t), \tag{1}$$

where M = the athlete's body mass; $R\left(\frac{dS}{dt}\right)$ = resistance to movement depending on velocity; $F(t)$ = propulsive force depending on time; and $S(t)$ = variation of the position of the center of gravity, which is a simplified version neglecting changes in the water and coincides with active arm movement.

Trying to maintain the structure of the left member (one inertial term, $M\frac{d^2S}{dt^2}$ = accumulation of energy and one resistive term, $R\left(\frac{dS}{dt}\right)$ = dissipation of energy), an approximation was worked out between $R\left(\frac{dS}{dt}\right)$ and the linear variation of $K\frac{dS}{dt}$, resulting in the following equation:

$$M\frac{d^2S}{dt^2} + K \frac{dS}{dt} = F(t). \tag{2}$$

Equation 2 was simulated using a rotational movement with the transformation:

$$F = \frac{U}{r}; \ M = \frac{J}{r^2}; \ S = r\theta; \ K = \frac{K_1}{r^2},$$

where: r = radius of rotational movement; U = torque couple; J = moment of inertia; θ = angular displacement; and K_1 = drag coefficient in rotational movement, which leads to:

$$J\frac{d^2\theta}{dt^2} + K_1 \frac{d\theta}{dt} = U(t). \tag{3}$$

Technically, the term $J\frac{d^2\theta}{dt^2}$ is best expressed by a flywheel (Figure 1), whereas the term $K_1\frac{d\theta}{dt}$ resulted in a linear electromagnetic brake (Figure

Figure 1—Module for simulating the inertial loading $J\dfrac{d^2S}{dt^2}$.

Figure 2—Module for simulating loadings proportional to velocity.

Figure 3—Module for simulating the elastic loading.

Figure 4—General front view of the ergometer.

2). To insure the return movement, a plane spiral spring was added inside the drum (Figure 3) to develop a traction force, P, given by the formula:

$$P = P_0 + K_2\theta, \qquad (4)$$

where P_0 is the pretension force and K_2 is the elasticity coefficient.

The parallel assembling of the three moduli (Figure 4) resulted in a dynamic equation:

$$J\frac{d^2\theta}{dt^2} + K_1\frac{d\theta}{dt} + K_2\theta + P_0 = U(t). \qquad (5)$$

Through adjustments in the strength of the spring we may obtain $P_0 = 0$. By selecting a spring with $K_2 = 0.3$ N/radian allows one to consider

Figure 5 — Module for transforming a certain movement into a rotational movement.

that Equation 5 does not differ significantly from Equation 3, when $K_2\theta$ is overlooked.

In order to utilize the dynamics of Equation 3 in a specific movement in swimming, a module was established for transforming certain linear movements into rotational movements (Figure 5). A one-way coupling was attached to it so that the movement could be transmitted in one direction only, from athlete to apparatus.

Modeling the dynamics, Equation 3 allows an analogy of the model parameters with the real ones. If conditions are created for the continuous, instantaneous measurement of the parameters of the model, an image will be obtained (under the specified approximation) of the evolution of the real parameters. These can be measured as follows:

- the propulsion force by the tension in the wire, resulting from the arm action;
- the position of the center of pressure in the palm, approximated through the length variation of the position vector from a given point;
- the position of the weight center of mass by the angular displacement of the flywheel;
- the velocity of the weight center of mass by the angular velocity of the flywheel.

Results

Though simplified (several specific aspects were not modeled such as the body shape, buoyancy and possibility for water dislocation), the modeling of the dynamics in Equation 2, due to the term $M\dfrac{d^2S}{dt^2}$, offered the possibility of maintaining an average speed on which fluctuations are modeled, because of the propulsion force F(t) and the advancing resistance K $\frac{dS}{dt}$. For M = 60 kg and K = 29.5 N•sec/m, average speeds in freestyle and backstroke were around 1.5 m/sec whereas for the butterfly they were ca. 1.4 m/sec. Fluctuations around the average were in freestyle and backstroke where V_{max} = 1.73 m/sec and V_{min} = 1.34 m/sec whereas for the butterfly V_{max} = 1.70 m/sec and V_{min} = 0.96 m/sec.

Both average speeds and the fluctuations of the instantaneous speed around the average agree somewhat with those reported by Persyn et al. (1981) and Reischle et al. (1981), obtained by filming in the swimming pool and confirming the exactness of the simulation for these parameters as well as the closeness of the force-velocity relationship to the actual one.

The modularized building of the system also allows for developing dynamics other than the specific ones. The module for simulating dissipating resistance (Figure 1), the one for simulating inertial resistance (Figure 2) or that for simulating elastic resistance may be used separately or in combinations, according to the requirements of the situation.

The simplicity of the modeled differential equation together with the possibility of controlling, through propulsion force and pacing of the movement, the achievement and maintenance of a certain mean velocity as well as the fluctuations of the instantaneous speed around the average, allow the theoretical and experimental study of optimal controls.

References

KUME, S., & Ishii, K. 1981. Biomechanical analysis of isokinetic exercise. In: A. Morecki, K. Fidelius, & A. Wit (eds.), *Biomechanics VII-B*, pp. 404-410. PWN-Polish Scientific, Warsaw, and University Park Press, Baltimore.

PERSYN, U., Vervaecke, H., & Hoeven, R. 1981. Hydromechanical information obtained from artificially changed swimming styles and motor and anthropometric factors. In: A. Morecki, K. Fidelius, & A. Wit (eds.), *Biomechanics VII-B*, pp. 447-454. PWN-Polish Scientific, Warsaw, and University Park Press, Baltimore.

REISCHLE, K., Gaisser, G., & Vollers, B. 1981. A kinematic analysis of intracycle speed fluctuations and movement patterns in swimming using cronocyclographic LED drivers. In: A. Morecki, K. Fidelius, & A. Wit (eds.), *Biomechanics VII-B*, pp. 460-464. PWN-Polish Scientific, Warsaw, and University Park Press, Baltimore.

UEYA, K. 1981. Using an inertial wheel and power meter to measure muscular power and energy with an application to biomechanics. In: A. Morecki, K. Fidelius, & A. Wit (eds.), *Biomechanics VII-B*, pp. 370-378. PWN-Polish Scientific, Warsaw, and University Park Press, Baltimore.

Measurement of Power Delivered to an External Weight

Robert T. Hopper
Health Management Associates, Pasadena, California, USA

Carol Hadley, Mark Piva, and Ben Bambauer
Occidental College, Los Angeles, California, USA

The importance of strength and power in swimming is evidenced by the rapid improvement of swimming times with the advent of weight training. Measurements of strength and power for swimmers have been made using dryland techniques (Sharp et al., 1982). However, the swimming stroke is a complex series of sculls and diagonal movements which cannot be duplicated with dryland testing techniques. Although power developed by a swimmer is very difficult to quantify, the power delivered to an external weight can be measured. The purpose of this article is threefold: first, to describe an inexpensive, commercially available,[1] and practical test to measure power delivered to an external weight by a swimmer in the water; second, to report results from the testing of elite swimmers at the United States Olympic Testing Center; and third, to report case studies on how athletes have been trained successfully using only this type of apparatus for tethering.

External Weight Power Test

This test measures the velocity with which an external weight can be moved vertically by a swimmer in the water. Swimmers are tethered to an apparatus which allows them to swim forward a given distance while lifting a weight plate supported on a pole. Measurements of distance swum, weight lifted, time to lift the weight, and number of strokes to lift the weight are used to compute a power-like value called "the power/stroke" value (work/time/strokes). This is not the true power developed by the swimmer, but rather power delivered to an external weight by the swimmer. Hereafter this value is referred to as power/stroke.

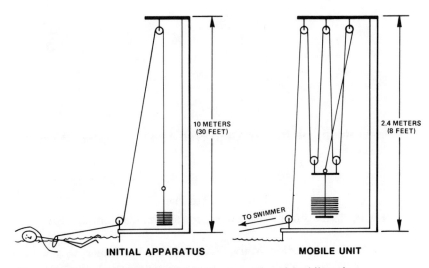

Figure 1—Schematic drawing of initial apparatus and mobile unit.

The original apparatus was a 10-m pole cemented into the ground. The subject swam 9 m forward while lifting the weight plate to the top of the pole (Figure 1). The swimmer wore a canvas belt around the waist, with one end of a rope clipped to the belt and the other end to the weight plate.

A second version of this testing apparatus was developed to provide a convenient, mobile unit that could be used for mass testing and training. The 10-m pole was made into a compact unit through the use of a pulley system. The pole height was reduced to 2.4 m (8 ft) and mounted on a metal base. The unit is balanced and does not need to be bolted to the pool deck. A triple pulley is attached to the top of the pole and a double pulley to the weight plate (Figures 1 and 2). This pulley system provides a 5:1 mechanical advantage.

The pulley at the bottom of the apparatus which changes the direction of the rope from vertical to horizontal is ca. 22.5 cm (9 in.) above the pool deck. This allows a slight rise in the rope to prevent interference with the kicking action. Swimmers have not been affected by either the rope or the slight angle of upward pull.

The calculation of power/stroke is based on four measurements: force, distance swum, swim time, and number of strokes. With a mechanical advantage of 5:1, 45 kg (100 lb) of weight provides 9 kg (20 lb) of resistance to the swimmer. For example, if the swimmer swims 8.70 m (30 ft) in 10 sec, and uses 15 strokes (or arm pulls), the power/stroke is computed using the following formula:

$$P/S = force \times distance/time/number\ of\ strokes$$
$$P/S = 9\ kg \times 8.7\ m/10\ sec/15\ strokes$$
$$P/S = .52\ kg\text{-}m/sec/stroke$$

Figure 2–Photograph of mobile unit with subject.

or

$$P/S = 20 \text{ lb} \times 30 \text{ ft}/10 \text{ sec}/15 \text{ strokes}$$
$$P/S = 4 \text{ ft-lb/sec/stroke}$$

Test Protocol

The swimmer is allowed three practice swims with the beginning load of 13.5 kg (30 lb on the weight plate, or ca. 6 lb of effective resistance). The exact values are determined by calibration before the testing begins. The pretest instructions to the swimmer are as follows: First, use your best swimming form; second, swim as fast as possible to the end of the rope. Swimmers always begin each swim with an underwater pushoff. Swimmers are allowed ca. 3-10 maximal-effort swims, with a 1-min rest between trials. Each swim lasts an average of 10 sec. After each swim, a 4.5-kg (10-lb) weight is added.

Two persons can record the necessary information; one records the swim time (first movement of weight plate until plate touches upper pulley), and the other person counts the number of strokes during that same time period. However, one person can easily do both tasks. Each arm pull counts as one stroke and is counted when the hand enters the water in front of the head. The distance swum can be measured before the test using a tape measure.

The criteria for stopping the test are: failure to lift the weight to the top of the pole; a marked increase in the number of strokes required to lift the weight (more than five strokes per increment of weight); and a marked increase in time to lift the weight (more than 3 sec increase per increment of weight).

After the test, the power/stroke is computed for each workload. With increasing workloads the power/stroke values first rise to a maximal value and then fall. The highest value or maximal power/stroke value is selected as the criterion variable.

Procedures

Subjects for this project were elite and developmental men and women swimmers participating in a special training program at the US Olympic Training Center in Colorado Springs, CO. Elite athletes were either Olympic potential or previous Olympic athletes, and developmental athletes were in a slightly lower classification group. During the course of one of the two daily workouts, each swimmer was taken to an outside lane, rested for 10 min, and then tested for power and speed in their dominant stroke. The test for swimming speed was a 50-m time trial. The time trial and the power test were administered within a 30-min segment of the workout. The 50-m swim time was correlated with the maximal power/stroke to demonstrate the relationship between swimming speed and power/stroke.

Results

The results are presented graphically in Figure 3 and illustrate the negative relationship between power/stroke and 50-m time. This relationship is observable in all strokes. When the data for men and women, elite and developmental swimmers were combined, the Pearson correlation coefficients showed a negative correlation between power/stroke and 50-m time (butterfly, $r = -0.89$; backstroke, $r = -0.84$; breaststroke, $r = -0.90$; and freestyle, $r = -0.80$). The means and standard

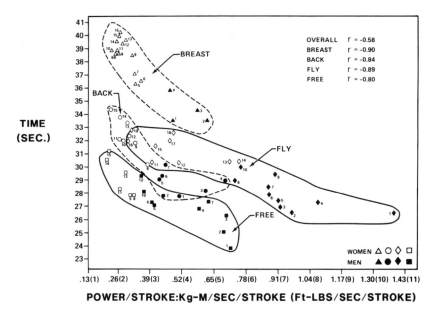

Figure 3 — Relationship between power/stroke and 50-m time-trial time, including correlation coefficients.

deviations for the developmental and elite groups for both men and women are presented in Table 1.

Discussion

Results of this study demonstrated the relationship between swimming speed and power, verifying preliminary studies. The freestyle correlation coefficient was slightly lower than previous tests (-0.87), and could be attributed to sampling fluctuation.

It was unfortunate that all testing of this apparatus has taken place under nonlaboratory conditions. It is the writer's opinion that the correlation coefficients would approach .95 under laboratory conditions. On the other hand, the testing conditons reflect the actual conditions under which most coaches may be using this test, and the mean values will have greater meaning.

Some interesting observations were made when swimmers were grouped into sprinters and distance swimmers (Hopper, 1981). The top three male sprinters had power values 1.5-2 times the value of the distance men (mean values: 0.7 kg-m/sec/stroke versus 0.37 kg-m/sec/stroke [5.4 ft lb/sec/stroke versus 2.9 ft-lb/sec/stroke]). The distance men in turn had power values which approached values for women sprinters: 0.31 kg-m/sec/stroke (2.4 ft-lb/sec/stroke), yet were always

Table 1

Mean and Standard Deviation Power/Stroke Values for Men and Women in Developmental and Elite Groups for the Four Competitive Strokes

		Developmental group				
	Men				Women	
		Mean power/stroke kg-m/sec/stroke				Mean power/stroke kg-m/sec/stroke	
	n	(ft-lb/sec/stroke)	SD	*n*	(ft-lb/sec/stroke)	SD
Fly	3	0.84 (6.53)	0.07	5	0.46 (3.54)	0.11
Back	3	0.44 (3.40)	0.01	5	0.27 (2.14)	0.03
Breast	2	0.53 (4.10)	0.08	7	0.27 (2.09)	0.02
Free*	—	—	—	—	—	—
		Elite Group				
Fly	10	0.93 (7.22)	0.17	9	0.49 (3.79)	0.15
Back	7	0.51 (3.95)	0.10	8	0.29 (2.25)	0.04
Breast	4	0.54 (4.19)	0.07	13	0.28 (2.18)	0.03
Free	9	0.54 (4.17)	0.15	6	0.27 (2.12)	0.04

slightly higher than the women. Similar, less dramatic trends were seen for women sprinters and distance swimmers. This test may have some value in evaluating potential for distance and sprint swimming.

The choice of the power/stroke value over the power value alone was based upon preliminary studies in which the coefficient of determination for power/stroke was 11% higher than the power alone. A considerable shortening of the swimming stroke was noticed in short time trials of 10-25 m; therefore, the 50-m time trials, which represented more accurately the stroke used in the 100- and 200-m swimming events, were used in this project.

The problem of angle of inclination from the swimmers waist to the apparatus was accepted as a compromise between some loss of accuracy for an appreciable gain in efficiency of administration for a large number of subjects in a limited space. This is especially true for training, where eight swimmers using four apparatuses can train effectively in one lane of a 25-m pool. While other tethering attachments to the swimmers may be possible, this present method seems to be best for testing and training large numbers of swimmers.

Three Case Studies

This apparatus was developed initially as a training apparatus and later as a test instrument. The training protocol involved repeated all-out swims (20) against heavy resistance. One swimmer was trained for one summer, three times per week in a 10-m pool using only this apparatus, and was a national AAU finalist in the 100-m backstroke. Thirteen years later, a swimmer at a local college repeated that training protocol and recorded the second fastest time in the 100-yd butterfly at the NCAA Division III championships. An article in *Sports Illustrated* (1981) reported a University of Florida swimmer who stopped swimming entirely between April and June, and then was coaxed back into the sport by his coach who suggested he do all his workouts using "bands, belts, and baskets," an assortment of tethering-type training. He won the 1981 AAU outdoor nationals in the 200-m freestyle (time: 1:50.86, a personal best by .93 sec).

This apparatus has wide application in the training and testing of swimmers, and a research project has been used successfully by one team to monitor power changes during the course of season (Kirkendall, 1981, personal communication). It has also been used by numerous universities in the United States as a tool for speed and power development. It appears that swimmers with already highly developed aerobic capacities (high school and college swimmers) can train well on a fraction of a normal workout yardage. However, further research will be necessary to clarify the benefits of this type of tethered training. The authors conclude that this apparatus is an inexpensive, commercially available, and effective tool for investigator, coach, and swimmer.

Notes

1. Seabreeze Enterprises, 99 S. Raymond Ave., Suite 605, Pasadena, CA 91105.

References

HOPPER, R.T. 1981. Power values for sprint and distance swimmers. *Med. Sci. Sports Exercise* **13**:115.

SHARP, R.L., Troup, J.P., and Costill, D.L. 1982. Relationship between power and sprint freestyle swimming. *Med. Sci. Sports Exercise* **14**:53-56.

SPORTS Illustrated, August 1981.

A Simple System for Underwater Video Filming

Luc Vertommen, Hans Fauvart, and Jan Pieter Clarys
Vrije Universiteit Brussel, Belgium

The most important part of a swimming stroke occurs underwater where propulsion is accomplished. This means that the coach or teacher concerned with evaluating the stroke mechanics of swimmers must have a clear picture of the underwater action. Therefore, a watertight plexiglass box was developed which allows video recording of stroke technique below the surface of the water. Conventional filming through an underwater camera is expensive and one must wait for the film to be developed in order to see the result. It also requires trained photographers, which most coaches and teachers are not.

Dal Monte (1971) described a sophisticated apparatus allowing cinematographic recordings perpendicular at all times to the swimmers' movements and at a speed identical to that of the swimmers' displacements in the water. McIntyre and Hay (1975) solved the observation problem with the development of an inverse periscope. Although we don't want to criticize this method, we think the method described by Hoffman (1976), which was used as the basis for the development of our watertight plexiglass box, is a more economical and less time-consuming approach to observing and evaluating underwater movements.

It is the purpose of this article to provide a description of a device that is easy to build in a technical laboratory at low cost. In addition, it is portable and therefore can be used in any pool. Furthermore, trained individuals are not needed to obtain clear and usable video pictures.

Equipment and Design

The box is made of 1.2-cm plexiglass and stands 100 cm high with 45-cm length and 15-cm width. It can be attached to the side of the swimming pool with screws. An aluminum joint permits 180° rotation and 90° tilt. This box can also be lowered into the water to a depth of 80 cm

Figure 1—Overall view of the video-plexi-box.

Figure 2—Overhead view of the video-plexi-box.

Figure 3—Attachment and counterweight.

(camera level). A grip on top of the box allows one to operate it with one hand (Figures 1-3). The camera is held in position by two U-shaped plexiglass standards fixed at the bottom of the box. A counterweight of 24 kg is necessary to compensate for the buoyancy of the water.

The videocamera was an Akai model VC 115, with a portable videotape recording device. It has an image and sound recording system, enabling the coach to comment on the swimmer's stroke during the recording. The filming can be viewed and therefore controlled through a monitoring screen on the recorder.

Applications

Pictures can be taken from nearly every angle due to the relatively large ranges of rotation and tilt of the device. However, there is a restriction in filming. After the camera is lowered in the box, further focusing is impossible. Therefore, one is able to use only full-zoom focus. A problem arises when the swimmer moves toward or away from the camera, for then the range of a clearly focused picture is restricted. A solution can be achieved by maintaining the swimmer at an equal distance from the camera, for example, in tethered swimming. But this situation creates new problems since less-skilled swimmers are affected by the tethering device, whereas good swimmers do not seem to be disturbed by this type of training.

Conclusions

For coaches or teachers who wish to observe their swimmers underwater, this device offers the following advantages:
- Video recording affords greater clarity than filming through an underwater viewing window.
- Communication is simplified. During playback, swimmers can immediately observe their stroke technique on the monitor and be corrected by the coach.
- The device can be built by a technical laboratory at low cost.
- It can be easily operated by an inexperienced photographer.
- It is portable and can be used in any pool.
- The device described is an improved version of the Hoffman (1976) apparatus and should facilitate coaches' work and help to improve the swimmers' techniques and motivation.

References

DAL MONTE, A. 1971. Presenting an apparatus for motion picture, television and scan shots of the movement of swimming. In: L. Lewillie and J.P. Clarys (eds.), *Swimming I*, pp. 127-128. Université Libre de Bruxelles, Belgium.

HOFFMAN, C. 1976. Underwater video tape box. *Swim. Tech.* **12**:4.

McINTYRE, D.R., and Hay, J.G. 1975. Dual media cinematography. In: J.P. Clarys and L. Lewillie (eds.), *Swimming II*, pp. 51-57. University Park Press, Baltimore.

A Review of EMG in Swimming:
Explanation of Facts and/or Feedback Information

Jan Pieter Clarys
Vrije Universiteit Brussel, Belgium

Reading between the lines of the earlier publications by Cureton (1930) and Karpovich (1935), one can assume that ± 44 different muscles are active in swimming the front crawl. Weineck (1981) listed 30 active muscles. Between 1930 and today many authors, coaches and physical education teachers have made attempts to describe anatomical function and muscle participation in swimming the front crawl.

Using a combination of elementary anatomical knowledge and functional reasoning, within the front crawl technique all statements are acceptable. If one concludes the concentric-, the eccentric-, the agonist-, the antagonist-, the spurt- and the shunt-muscle action over the different joints of a swimming body, it probably would be very close to reality to assume that *all* skeletal muscles of the body are active in swimming the front crawl, in other words ± 170 single muscles — we are not sure about the m. cremaster.

Muscle participation is only one element. The muscle pattern with a complex rhythmical swimming movement is another far more important element, and this information cannot be obtained by functional anatomical deductions. The first study of myoelectric signals during swimming was published by Ikai et al. (1961 in Japanese and 1964 in English; Note 1) and described 15 muscle patterns in 14 subjects, comparing the EMG results of university and Olympic swimmers and stressing the importance of the m. triceps brachii, m. biceps brachii, m. latissimus dorsi, m. deltoideus and m. teres major in top-level swimming. The results of Ikai et al. (1964) have been used widely and have provided a better interpretation of swimming movements (e.g., in Counsilman's *Science of Swimming* [1968]).

Despite the limitations of this first EMG study, such as a lack of calibration and lack of pattern normalization necessary for comparison, it offered information to trainers and coaches that was never available previously. At the same time, the Ikai et al. (1961-1964; Note 1) studies initiated EMG investigations in new directions.

In East Germany during 1966 Kipke (1966, p. 116) stated "in order to improve performance, a swimmer needs power, which cannot be developed in water alone." If the swimmer wants to reach the top level, he or she must strengthen the arm musculature by working with specific dryland exercises.

Since the coordination and economic use of muscles in swimming movement is regulated by the nervous system (Counsilman, 1962), Kipke and many others have accepted the idea that the actual swimming movement had to be reproduced on dry land. Kipke (1966) used the findings of Ikai (1962) for selecting the muscles. He took 507 EMGs on 17 subjects during dryland crawl movements against the resistance of a rubber rope and compared his results with those of Ikai (1962) without calibration and without normalization of the data.

Drawing conclusions out of such a comparison obviously is very difficult. Nevertheless, Kipke (1966) had initiated controversy and, at the same time, presented a problem for further investigation. In his discussion he stated that by using a rubber rope, the EMG patterns were totally different from the patterns in water, but Kipke concluded that if the dryland exercise is executed correctly at 50-60 pulls/min, the relationship between the tension and the relaxation of the muscle is optimal and thus will improve the muscular strength and endurance of the swimmer.

Ikai et al. (1961-1964) initiated methodological research on the electromyographic analysis of different swimming techniques using conventional wire electrodes with the EMG apparatus mounted on a trolley which moved along with the swimmer. Lewillie (1968a, 1968b) attempted to determine the possibilities of telemetry in EMG choosing the swimmer as his major subject. Lewillie's experiments were conducted in a community swimming pool. The dimensions of the transmitter, amplifier antennae and recorder he used have been described elsewhere (Lewillie, 1968a). The entire telemetric system as developed by Lewillie (1968a, 1968b) and his collaborators avoid the cumbersome work with conventional wire EMG apparatuses and allows the swimmer complete freedom of movement in space.

With Ikai et al. (1961-1964) and Lewillie (1968a, 1968b) as methodological founders of EMG research in swimming, different researchers have attempted to investigate the myoelectric signals for the four major swimming strokes.

Front Crawl

Already mentioned were Ikai et al. (1961-1964) and Ikai (1962) with the study of 15 muscles, Kipke (1966) with six muscles and dryland movements, and Lewillie (1968a, 1968b, 1973) with three muscles. Vaday and Nemessuri (1971) studied 20 muscles using the conventional wire apparatus and stressing the importance of the pull-and-push phase in the crawl movement. Clarys et al. (1973) compared the water polo and competitive front crawl measuring telemetrically, four arm muscles. Maes et al. (1975) studied six muscles with the same device in an attempt to evaluate the movements of handicapped swimmers. Belokovsky (1971) was the first to work with a reasonably large group of 57 subjects, investigating the dynamic elements and fundamental deviation of these elements within the front crawl arm movement.

Renner (1980) used three muscles to analyze the various components of the front crawl underwater arm stroke, combining the wire apparatus EMG technique with the use of maximal isometric contraction as introduced by Lewillie (1971). Front crawl EMG research by Clarys et al. (1983, this volume) presented standardized myoelectric integrated EMG patterns of 25 muscles.

Using the methodological investigations of Lewillie (1967; 1968b; 1971) and based on previously published preliminary research (Clarys et al., 1973; Maes et al., 1975; Piette and Clarys, 1979) this writer has attempted to produce a total experimental image of all superficial body muscles presumed to be electrically active during the front crawl movement (excluding the smaller hand, feet and head musculature).

In order to allow practical use and a possibility for comparison of these data, the results are presented as normalized pattern diagrams based on the nondimensional expression of integrated EMG patterns. These results are the subject of further discussion in this article.

Breaststroke

Electromyography of the breaststroke has been studied by Ikai et al. (1964, 14 muscles); Lewillie (1971, three muscles; 1974, two muscles); Tokuyama et al. (1976, 14 muscles) and Yoshizawa et al. (1978, 16 muscles).

Backstroke and Dolphin

Compared to the front crawl and breaststroke, very little work has been done to gather information and/or to explain the myoelectric patterns in the backstroke (Lewillie, 1974, two muscles) and the dolphin (Barthels and Adrian, 1971, six muscles; Lewillie, 1974, two muscles). From these studies, interesting feedback information was obtained concerning the high variability and thus differences observed in the kicking patterns of top dolphin swimmers.

EMG in Infants and Children

In completing the review of EMG swimming research, one must mention the work of Tokuyama et al. (1976), Oka et al. (1979) and Okamoto and Wolf (1979) for two distinct reasons:

- These studies show the importance of EMG feedback information in the process of learning to swim.
- New possibilities arise since the experiments used fine wire electrodes instead of the more typical surface electrodes.

As an example of the first case, Oka et al. (1979) trained a 6-year-old boy with appropriate instruction based on the electromyographic observations obtained from skilled adults. After some time his flutter kick movement was much improved and the discharge patterns approached those of the skilled adult.

The other possibilities were introduced when Okamoto and Wolf (1979) used nylon-karma alloy fine-wire electrodes. Movement artifacts can now be avoided and recording sessions can last for several hours without interruption. Since percutaneous recordings from muscles have the advantage of enabling the investigator to assume that the pickup is from a specific muscle, this technique will enable one to explain more precisely the myoelectric behavior during various aquatic activities.

Considering all these studies over the last 20 years, they have not solved the problem of both quantitative and qualitative comparison of EMG data. We investigated 25 muscles (Clarys et al., 1983) covering the overall surface area of the human body; the selection criteria have been described previously (Piette and Clarys, 1979).

Subjects ($n = 60$) were studied (30 competitive swimmers and 30 swimmers with good technical skills). Swimming speed was standardized for all subjects using a series of successive lights, fixed 1 m below the water surface. Before fixation of the electrodes, the "motor point" of each muscle was defined. Unfortunately, the localization of these high-potential points was not always technically adequate for efficient recordings in all muscles. Therefore, the electrodes were cutaneously fixed in the topographical midpoint of the muscle surface area, independent of the motor point position and according to the recommendations of Basmajian (1967) and Goodgold (1974).

Before the actual data collection, the amplification apparatus was adjusted to the signal intensity of each subject, while the actual EMG recording consisted of the integrated recording of: (a) the dynamic swimming contraction at a known speed of 1.7 m $\cdot$ sec^{-1} (DC); (b) the (relative) isometric maximal contraction (IC), and (c) a constant calibration value (CV).

The surface area of the integrated patterns was also measured (Piette and Clarys, 1979). Expressing microvoltage results in terms of surface area simplifies further calculation and allows for a normalized dynamic

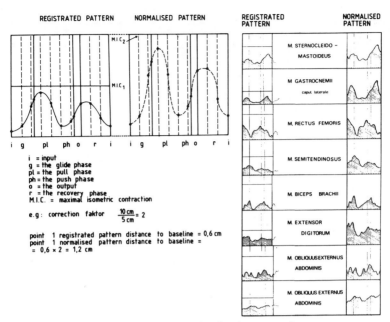

Figure 1—Pattern normalization or standardization procedures.

contraction index:

$$NDC = DC \ (cm^2 \cdot sec)/CV \ (cm^2 \cdot sec),$$

and a normalized (relative) isometric maximum index:

$$NIC = IC \ (cm^2 \cdot sec)/CV \ (cm^2 \cdot sec),$$

through which muscle activity can be presented as a percentage of the isometric maximum:

$$\frac{NDC}{NIC} \times 100.$$

This nondimensional expression of integrated EMG patterns allows for a comparison of muscle activity between subjects of totally different swimming capabilities, enabling one to establish an overall image of muscle contraction for the front crawl movement (Figure 1).

For each part of the investigation the m. biceps brachii was used as a reference muscle in order to clarify the chronological order of the contractions within the different phases of the crawl movement. One arm cycle was derived according to the distribution of the movement pattern as described by Vaday and Nemessuri (1971). As it is not the purpose of this review article to give detailed qualitative and quantitative analysis of muscle activity, an overall and average review of 25 normalized contraction pattern diagrams are presented in Figures 2 through 9.

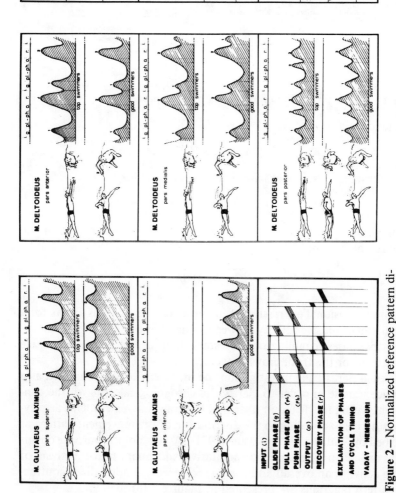

Figure 2 – Normalized reference pattern diagram of the m. gluteus maximus and explanation of phases and cycle timing.

Figure 3 – Normalized reference pattern diagram of the m. deltoideus.

Figure 4 – Normalized reference pattern diagram of the m. biceps and triceps brachia.

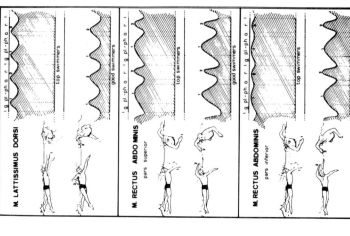

Figure 5 – Normalized reference pattern diagram of the m. ext. digitorum and trapezius.

Figure 6 – Normalized reference pattern diagram of the m. sternocleidomastoideus and obliquus externus.

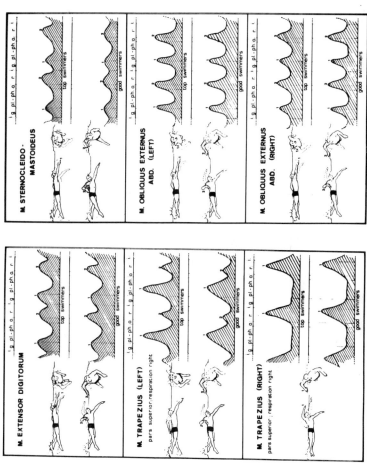

Figure 7 – Normalized reference pattern diagram of the m. latissimus dorsi and rectus abdominis.

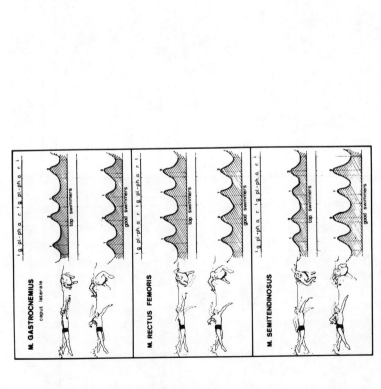

Figure 8—Normalized reference pattern diagram of the m. gastrocnemius, rectus femoris and semitendinosus.

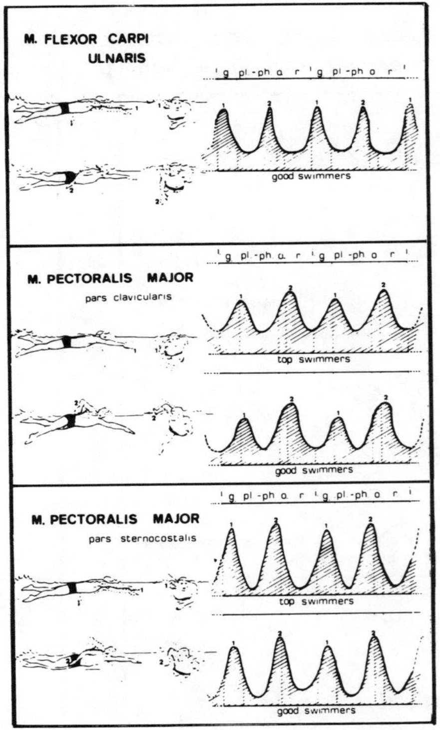

Figure 9—Normalized reference pattern diagram of the m. flexor carpi ulnaris and pectoralis major.

In reference to the different levels of muscle participation during total body movement, the normalized pattern diagrams presented in this article should allow for a better selection of specific "dryland power training" exercises and should provide the necessary information to the coach and swimmer in order to establish an efficient training program. In order to consider dryland strength training exercises as a "specific training" one should take into account the following principles:

- The difference in activity of the various heads of the same muscle indicates that the nonspecific development of a swimmer's training should be undertaken (Lewillie, 1971).
- The utilization of a swimming movement as it is performed in water for dryland exercises does not guarantee an exact reproduction of time, acceleration and joint angulation phenomena, although this is often the assumption (Counsilman, 1962; Kipke, 1966; Ratow, 1977; Kalganow, 1979; Absaljamow et al., 1979).
- Although Kipke (1966) investigated dryland exercises using EMG, there currently is no actual or direct comparison of data between swimming EMG with corresponding specific dryland exercises.

Since more information is needed, Olbrecht and Clarys (1983) have investigated a series of specific dryland exercises using different strength training devices, including callcraft, roller-board, isokinetics, expander and latissimus apparatus. Using the "normalized reference pattern diagrams" as a basis for analyses, a combination of "dry and wet" EMG patterns was established as shown in Figure 10. These analyses included a comparison of: (a) amplitude — differential curve; (b) slope and direction coefficient; and (c) discrepancies in the slope and direction coefficient data and the influence of amplitude and time shift on both dry and wet muscle activities.

Methods and Procedures

Ten muscles were selected that were presumed to be important for a competitive front crawl swimmer. As propulsion muscles, the m. extensor digitorum, the m. flexor carpi ulnaris, the m. triceps (caput laterale and longum), the m. latissimus dorsi and the m. pectoralis major were chosen. As recovery muscles, the m. deltoideus (pars anterior and posterior), and as the equilibrium muscle the m. abdominus obliquus externus were selected. The m. biceps brachii was added as an overall control muscle.

The recordings were carried out according to the method and following the same criteria as described by Clarys et al. (1983), except that no telemetric device was needed in this situation. Before and after a series of movement executions, the relative maximal isometric contraction (*RMIC*) was measured as described by Jonsson et al. (1972), Daniels and

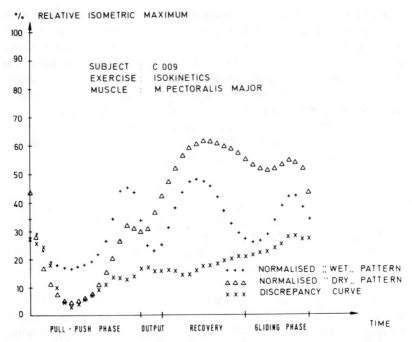

Figure 10—Normalized "wet" and "dry" muscle activity patterns including a discrepancy curve.

Worthingham (1972), Stijns (1973) and Clarys et al. (1983). During dry-land exercise, EMG recordings and integration were synchronized with video film.

All movement patterns were selected based on their correct execution. After the cycle time and the amplitude of the total cycle time were determined, a standard dry curve was made by selecting 15 points from the rest of the total cycle. These standard dry curves (*SDC*) contained a time sequence as described by Vaday and Nemessuri (1971) and were presented as "normalized pattern diagrams" (Clarys et al., 1983). In this manner, the standard dry curves of 10 muscles per subject and per exercise were plotted against the normalized pattern diagrams for the standard wet curves of the same muscles. For these procedures, a Hewlett-Packard Digitizer 9874 and a desk-top computer 9825A with the Model 17601 plotter were used.

It is expected that the comparison of both the normalized "wet" and "dry" myoelectric recordings will provide practical information and direct feedback for training. Detailed results are reported by Olbrechts and Clarys (1983) elsewhere in this volume.

Note

1. Similar results were published by Ikai in 1962 in French.

References

ABSALJAMOW, T.M., Bashanow, W.W., Danilotschking, W.A., and Melkonow, A.A. 1979. Krafttrainingsapparate in der Vorbereitung von Spitzenschwimmern (vol. 1). Translation of Plavanje, Moskow.

BARTHELS, K.M., and Adrian, M.J. 1971. Variability in the dolphin kick under four conditions. In: L. Lewillie and J.P. Clarys (eds.), *Swimming I*, pp. 105-118. Université Libre de Bruxelles, Brussels.

BASMAJIAN, J.V. 1967. *Muscles Alive: Their Functions Revealed by Electromyography*. Williams & Wilkins, Baltimore.

BELOKOVSKY, V.V. 1971. An analysis of pulling motions in the crawl arm stroke. In: L. Lewillie and J.P. Clarys (eds.), *Swimming I*, pp. 217-221. Université Libre de Bruxelles, Brussels.

CLARYS, J.P., Jiskoot, J., and Lewillie, L. 1973. A kinematographical, electromyographical and resistance study of water polo and competition frontcrawl. In: S. Cerquiglini, A. Verano and J. Wartenweiler (eds.), *Biomechanics III*, pp. 446-452. S. Karger Verlag, Basel.

CLARYS, J.P., Massez, C., Van Den Broeck, M., Piette, G., and Robeaux, R. 1983. Total telemetric surface EMG of the front crawl. In: H. Matsui and K. Kobayashi (eds.), *Biomechanics VIIIB*, pp. 951-958. Human Kinetics, Champaign, IL.

COUNSILMAN, I.E. 1962. Isometrische und isotonische Übungen für Schwimmer. *Swimming Times Croydon* **39**:52-55.

COUNSILMAN, I.E. 1968. *Science of Swimming*. Pelham, London.

CURETON, T.K. 1930. Mechanics and kinesiology of swimming. *Res. Q.* **1**:87-121.

DANIELS, L., and Worthingham, C. 1972. *Muscle Testing*. W.B. Saunders, Philadelphia.

GOODGOLD, J. 1974. *Anatomical Correlations of Clinical Electromyography*. Williams & Wilkins, Baltimore.

IKAI, M. 1962. Etude électromyographique de la natation. *Rev. Educ. Physique* **2**:124-126.

IKAI, M., Ishii, K., and Miyashita, M. 1964. An electromyographic study of swimming. *Res. J. Physical Educ.* **7**:47-54.

JONSSON, B., Olofsson, B.M., and Stefner, L.C. 1972. Function of the ters major latissimus dorsi and the pectoralis major muscles. *Acta Morphol. Neer. Scand.* **9**:275-280.

KARPOVICH, P.V. 1935. Analysis of propelling force in the crawlstroke. *Res. Q.* **6**:49-58.

KIPKE, L. 1966. Das elektromyographische Bild des am Trainingsgerät imitierten Armzuges der Freistilschwimmer. *Med. Sport* **6**:116-121.

LEWILLIE, L. 1968a. Analyse télémétrique de l'electromyogramme du nageur. *Trav. Soc. Méd. Belge Educ. Physique Sport* **20**:174-177.

LEWILLIE, L. 1968b. Telemetrical analysis of the electromyograph. In: J. Wartenweiler, E. Jokl and M. Hebbelinck (eds.), *Biomechanics I*, pp. 147-149. S. Karger Verlag, Basel.

LEWILLIE, L. 1971. Quantitative comparison of the electromyograph of the swimmer. In: L. Lewillie and J.P. Clarys (eds.), *Swimming I*, pp. 155-159. Université Libre de Bruxelles, Brussels.

LEWILLIE, L. 1973. Muscular activity in swimming. In: S. Cerquiglini, A. Venerando and J. Wartenweiler (eds.), *Biomechanics III*, pp. 440-445. S. Karger Verlag, Basel.

LEWILLIE, L. 1974. Telemetry of electromyographic and electrogoniometric signals in swimming. In: R.C. Nelson and C.A. Morehouse (eds.), *Biomechanics IV*, pp. 203-207. University Park Press, Baltimore.

MAES, L., Clarys, J.P., and Brouwer, P.J. 1975. Electromyography for the evaluation of handicapped swimmers. In: J.P. Clarys and L. Lewillie (eds.), *Swimming II*, pp. 268-275. University Park Press, Baltimore.

OKA, H., Okamoto, T., Yoshizawa, M., Tokuyama, H., and Kumamoto, M. 1979. Electromyographic and cinematographic study of the flutter kick in infants and children. In: J. Terauds and W. Bedingfield (eds.), *Swimming III*, pp. 167-172. University Park Press, Baltimore.

OKAMOTO, T., and Wolf, S.L. 1979. Underwater recording of electromyographic activity using fine-wire electrodes. In: J. Terauds and W. Bedingfield (eds.), *Swimming III*, pp. 160-166. University Park Press, Baltimore.

OLBRECHT, J., and Clarys, J.P. 1983. EMG of specific strength training exercises for the front crawl. In: A.P. Hollander, P. Huijing and G. de Groot (eds.), *Biomechanics and Medicine in Swimming*, pp. 136-141. Human Kinetics, Champaign, IL.

PIETTE, G., and Clarys, J.P. 1979. Telemetric EMG of the front crawl movement. In: J. Terauds and W. Bedingfield (eds.), *Swimming III*, pp. 153-159. University Park Press, Baltimore.

RATOW, I.P. 1977. Zur Veränderung des Trainingssystems durch technische Mittel und Trainingsapparate. *Leistungssport* **7**:129-135.

RENNER, I. 1980. *A Cinematographical and Electromyographical Analysis of the Underwater Arm Stroke of the Front Crawl.* Masters thesis, University of Oregon. (Eugene Microfilm Publ., College of Health Physics, Education and Recreation, Eugene, OR.)

STIJNS, H.J. 1973. *Klinisch Onderzoek van de Spierfunctie.* (Clinical analysis of the muscle function.) Acco, Leuven.

TOKUYAMA, H., Okamoto, T., and Kumamoto, M. 1976. Electromyographic study of swimming in infants and children. In: P.V. Komi (ed.), *Biomechanics V-B*, pp. 215-221. University Park Press, Baltimore.

VADAY, M., and Nemessuri, N. 1971. Motor pattern of free style swimming. In: L. Lewillie and J.P. Clarys (eds.), *Swimming I*, pp. 167-173. Université Libre de Bruxelles, Brussels.

WEINECK, J. 1981. Sportanatomie Beitrage zur Sportmedizin. Perimed Fachbuch Verlaggesellschaft, Erlangen.

YOSHIZAWA, M., Okamoto, T., Kumamoto, M., Tokuyama, H., and Oka, H. 1978. Electromyographic study of two styles in the breaststroke as performed by top swimmers. In: E. Asmussen and K. Jørgensen (eds.), *Biomechanics VI-B*, pp. 126-131. University Park Press, Baltimore.

EMG of Specific Strength Training Exercises
for the Front Crawl

Jan Olbrecht and Jan Pieter Clarys
Vrije Universiteit Brussel, Belgium

Many swimming coaches stress the advantage of specific dryland training (Brunner et al., 1976; Cambrill, 1971; Carlile, 1964; Clark, 1967; Connellan, 1971, 1972; Costill and Sharp, 1980; Counsilman, 1969, 1971, 1978; Easterling, 1972, 1973; Glenn, 1977; Hessburg, 1972, 1973; Hogg, 1972; Hopper, 1980; Jiskoot, 1971; Kruger, 1971; Lender, 1971; Miller, 1977). A general definition for this type of training was given by Leeuwenhoek (1977). In order to test this theory in a practical strength or power training program for front crawl swimmers, there were many empirical conditions which determined the nature and execution of the exercises. The principles of such a conditioning program were extracted from the literature (mentioned previously) as follows:

- The exercise was intended for the development of the propulsion muscles only.
- Dryland exercises must have movement patterns identical to those in water with respect to: (a) the drag encountered, (b) the overall coordination and specifically pelvis-shoulder coordination, (c) the assumed muscle contraction, and (d) rhythm analogous to the accelerations and decelerations involved.

In this study, a simulation of the crawl movement with an expander (EX), a call-craft (CC), a latissimus apparatus (LA), an isokinetic swim bench (ISOK), and a roller board (RB) were examined by EMG analysis.

A correctly executed simulation of a swimming stroke was assumed to comply with the empirical and theoretical descriptions as outlined previously.

Methods and Procedures

Recording technique, transformation of the data into normalized pattern diagrams, muscle selection, approach to the analysis of both wet and dry data curves and overall procedures are described in Clarys (1983, this volume).

Results

The original (unpublished and more extensive) study (Olbrecht, 1980) considered four different characteristics of the dryland EMG traces. Since space is limited, only some of the results have been selected for presentation.

This article deals with the "dry and wet" myoelectric pattern comparison of the total arm cycle. Using the front crawl, the total arm cycle was divided into a "pull-phase" (PP), including glide, pull and push and in a "rest-phase" (RP), including exit and recovery. These phases were compared for all five dryland devices and 10 muscles (Figures 1 and 2).

Variability and Reproducibility

Among individuals, all myoelectric signals were extremely reproducible and negligible variability was observed between individuals. However, a common pattern was always present. This variability was nonexistent in the standard wet curves.

Arm Cycle Time

The average total arm cycle time on land was significantly ($p \leq 0.001$) longer than in water. The mean dryland arm cycle time ranged from 1.75 ± 0.35 sec using the expander device to 4.17 ± 0.47 sec using the roller-board. The mean arm cycle in water was 1.98 ± 0.26 sec (Table 1).

Amplitude

In order to compare the amplitudes of the myoelectric signals for the dryland exercises with the signals measured in water, the areas under the respective integrated curves which did not overlap were measured. Contrary to what one might expect, a substantially smaller amplitude was expressed by the greater fraction of the area, which was located under the wet curve especially for the roller-board and the latissimus apparatus.

Isokinetics appeared to give the best results but they were still unsatisfactory, since 39% of the nonoverlapped portions of the "dryland" recording was of a greater amplitude than the recordings made while swimming. The best comparison was found between the "dry" and "wet" normalized amplitudes per functional muscle group, but again these yielded far from satisfactory results. In the case of the equilibrium and propulsive muscles, 33 and 13%, respectively, of the nonoverlapping area under the dryland curve had a higher amplitude than the curve recorded during swimming.

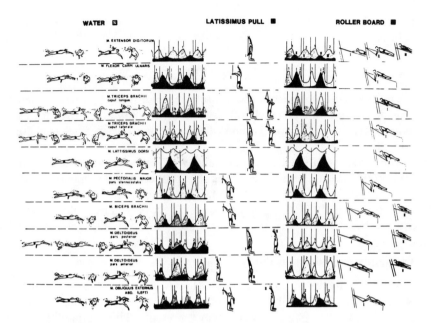

Figure 1—Dry and wet normalized diagrams for 10 muscles on nonresistance accommodating devices.

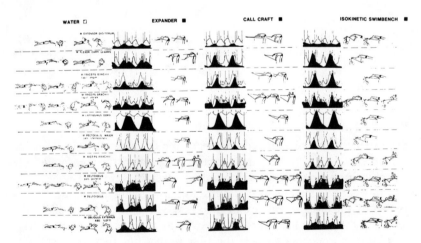

Figure 2—Dry and wet normalized diagrams for 10 muscles on resistance accommodating devices.

Pattern Analysis

The pattern analysis between both the normalized "dry and wet" pattern diagrams is one of the major criteria for acceptance or rejection of comparative muscle movements on dry land and in water. Therefore, the

Table 1

**Means and Standard Deviations of Arm Cycle Times (sec)
for Five Dryland Exercise Devices (n = 7)**

Expander	Call-craft	Lattisimus apparatus	Isokinetics	Roller board
1.746 ± 0.345	2.307 ± 0.330	2.857 ± 0.494	2.862 ± 0.867	4.166 ± 0.470
493[a]	354	330	312	317

[a]This row indicates the number of cycles measured for calculation of the mean.

contraction peak frequencies were compared. Generally speaking, there was a tendency for either an equal number or a lesser number of contraction peaks in the land exercises as compared to swimming. Considering all the muscles together, the best reproduction of the number of peaks existed while using isokinetics, where 6 out of 10 muscles showed a number of peaks identical to swimming. Considering the propulsion and equilibrium muscle groups separately, it was found that they were best reproduced using isokinetics.

Coordination

Apart from the m. triceps and m. biceps, most of the myoelectric contractions appeared earlier during the dryland cycles than during swimming. Dryland exercises created different antagonist and synergist activity and in some, no contraction at all was shown at times when activity was found during swimming. The dryland exercises were characterized by a more marked alternation of contraction and relaxation within a cycle with the exception of the m. deltoideus pars posterior and m. triceps caput lateralis in the expander, call-craft and isokinetics, respectively.

Discussion and Conclusions

With respect to the mechanical aspects of dryland equipment and to the biomechanical differences in the execution of the front crawl on dry land and in water, the best results based on EMG comparison for the propulsion muscles were found when using devices with accommodating resistance. Recovery muscles were best imitated using isokinetics, but despite the greater effort on land, lower EMG activity was recorded than in water. It was generally observed that whenever the swimmer acted against a mechanical resistance an important pattern deviation was noted. Therefore, it must be concluded that specific training, as described by Leeuwenhoek (1977), cannot be accomplished with dryland devices because of mechanical and environmental differences.

   This conclusion agrees with some authors who have criticized the use of training on land. Their rejections are based on sensomotoric and/or physical and also empirical considerations. They claim that the senso-motoric patterns developed on dry land interfere with the sensomotoric patterns that are used in water competition. Boicev (1978) found no similarity between force/time and time to maximal force occurrence in and out of the water using isokinetics, roller-board and call craft. He proposed using these dryland devices in the preparatory phase of training only and not during the competitive phase.

   It can be stated that there is little electromyographic similarity between swimming movements on dry land and the front crawl movement under normal conditions since this investigation indicated that: (a) overall time differences occurred between dry and wet arm cycle executions; (b) the muscle potential amplitudes were different in all five devices studied; (c) most muscles showed fewer EMG peaks on dry land; and (d) the dryland coordination created a different pattern of movement.

   The idea of "specific dryland training" cannot be supported on the bases of these results. Suggestions can be made for adaptations of some of the better devices, but coaches should not try to convince their swimmers that training is the same as in a swimming situation.

References

BOICEV, K., Damjanova, R., and Doksinov, H. 1978. *Vaproci na Fysiceskata kultura, Bulgaria*, 1:672-679.

BRUNNER, Knebel, and Wirth. 1976. *Das Konditionstraining des Schwimmers-Teil I: Trockentraining*. (Conditioning Training of Swimmers-Part I: Dryland Training.) Verlag Bartels & Wernitz, Berlin.

CAMBRILL, F. 1971. *Krafttraining, Sportschwimmen, Technik Training*. (Strength Training, Competitive Swimmers, Training Technique.) B.L.V. Verlagsgesellschaft, Munich.

CARLILE, F. 1963. *Forbes Carlile on Swimming*. Pelham Books, London.

CLARK, S. 1976. *Competitive Swimming as I See It*. Swimming World, North Hollywood, CA.

CLARYS, J.P. 1983. A review of EMG in swimming: Explanation of facts and/or feedback information. In: A.P. Hollander, P.A. Huijing, and G. de Groot (eds.), *Biomechanics and Medicine in Swimming*, pp. 123-135. Human Kinetics, Champaign, IL.

CONNELLAN, D.M. 1971-72. Early season weight training for swimmers. *Swim. Tech.* 8:78-79.

COSTILL, D., and Sharp, R. 1980. Muscle strength contribution to sprint swimming. *Swim. World* 21:29.

COUNSILMAN, J.E. 1969. Isokinetic exercises: A new concept in strength building. *Swim. World* **10**:4-15.

COUNSILMAN, J.E. 1971. Dry land exercises. *Zwemkroniek* **41**:937-939.

COUNSILMAN, J.E., Fahneman, A., Meisel, M.J., and Wachholder, F. 1978. *Des Prinzipes des Isokinetischen Training für Schwimmer und Trainingsanleiten für das Trainen von Kraft, Kraftausdauer und Schwimmtechnik an der Schwimmbank record—Trainingsanleitung.* (The Principles of Isokinetic Training for Swimmers and Training Regimen for the Training of Strength, Endurance and Swimming Technique on Dry Land Record—Training Regimen.) Nieders Zentral—institut für Sporterziehung, Hannover.

EASTERLING. 1972-73. Put a little sex in your program. *Swim. Tech.* **9**.

GLENN, G. 1977. Program dry land exercises. *Swim. World* **18**:14-27.

HESSBURG, F.C. 1972-73. A new system of dry land training for swimmers. *Swim. Tech.* **9**:74-77.

HOGG, J.M. 1972. *Land Conditioning for Competitive Swimming.* The E.P. Group of Companies, Wakefield.

HOPPER, B. 1980. Getting a grip on strength, scientists talk about strength training. *Swim. Tech.* **17**: 10-43.

JISKOOT, J. 1971. Krachttraining. *Zwemkroniek* **48**:13.

KRUGER, A. 1971. Isokinetische Krafttraining. (Isokinetic strength training.) *Leistungssport* **1**:22.

LEEUWENHOEK, A.A. 1977. *Trainingsbouwstenen.* (Training.) Uitgeverij De Vriesborch, Haarlem.

LENDER, A.D. 1971. Weight training and exercise training. *Swim. World* **12**:7-13.

MILLER, B. 1977. Dry land exercises for ages group swimmers. *Swim. World* **18**:33.

OLBRECHT, J. 1980. *Specifieke Krachttrainingsoefeningen Voor de Borstcrawl: Concept of Realiteit?* (Specific Strength Training for the Front Crawl: Concept or Reality?) Unpublished dissertation, Vrije Universiteit Brussels.

Biomechanics and Mathematical Modeling

Marlene J. Adrian
University of Illinois at Urbana-Champaign, USA

The difference between analysis of swimming and activities conducted in the air (such as diving or racing starts) and on the land can be summarized in one word — "environment." The environment (that is, water) is of paramount importance to the analysis and the performance whereas the effect of air may be considered negligible for all practical purposes (Eaves, 1968). Therefore, although the general analyses may be similar in all activities, swimming analysis, because it is unique, will be considered in this article. Diving and swimming starts will not be discussed.

Biomechanical analysis includes three considerations: environmental, mechanical, and anatomical (Cooper et al., 1982). These are interrelated and are necessary in the goal of the analyst in biomechanics to improve a competitor's performance. This goal may be fulfilled by (a) determining what exists; (b) constructing a model to predict performance; and (c) using simulation techniques to predict improvements or potential performance.

Determining what exists was the focus of the body of research which was completed during the 1930s to the end of the 1960s. The development of the computer and its use, together with models of the human body, and subsequent simulation during the 1950s and 1960s as a result of the aerospace program provided the foundation for modeling in sports.

Modeling in swimming may have lagged behind land sports modeling because so little was known about swimming activities compared to land activities. As Plagenhoef has stated, "swimming presents two special problems for analysis: there is no fixed point, and the external forces due to movement through water are very difficult to measure" (p. 121, 1971). Prior to a description of the use of modeling and simulation, the three categorical considerations for biomechanical analyses will be presented as each affects modeling.

Environment

The nature of the fluid (water) and its effect on the swimmer was the topic of early research and continues to be a subject of immense interest today. Although DuBois-Reymond was purported to have towed a person behind a rowboat and measured resistance with a dynamometer in 1905, Karpovich (1933) provided the "classic" research concerning differences in resistance of the total body in various positions relevant to swimming while being towed through the water. Jiskoot and Clarys (1975) determined that resistance was lower at the surface than underwater at 1.5-1.9 m-sec^{-1}.

In order to determine the effect of body shape (form) on resistance, three persons having ectomorphic component values, based on Sheldon's somatotypes (1940), of 1 and at least a 7 in either the endo- or mesomorphic component, and three swimmers having an endomorphic component of 1 and at least a 5 on the ectomorphic component were towed at the surface and below the water in a glide position (Clarys et al., 1974). The total resistance was greater in the more corpulent subjects at all speeds except the initial starting speeds.

di Prampero et al. (1974) recorded resistance and oxygen consumption during swimming. Mean resistances were 64 N at .94 m-sec^{-1} for 10 male subjects. Passive resistance values also were determined and were found to be approximately half that of the active resistance. Rennie et al. (1975) found values to be significantly less for women than the men tested by di Prampero et al.

Nelson (1976) determined the effect of wearing a resistance device, a belt with an attached cup-like extension which, when worn around the swimmer's waist, creates drag. Female swimmers were towed in the prone position and resistances were measured by means of a strain gauge proving ring and oscillograph. An average increase of 90% in resistance was calculated when swimmers wore the resistance device compared to when they did not.

Thus, resistance is a variable factor to be considered in swimming. It may be the most illusive of the factors utilized in modeling and simulation techniques. The resistance changes because of complex wave formation, turbulence, changes in body position due to movement of limbs, and changes in buoyancy due to breathing. Surface area, buoyancy, anthropometric profiles, training devices used, and specific swimming techniques influence the magnitude of resistance. The most comprehensive review of research in this area (human morphology and hydrodynamics) was compiled by Clarys (1979) and is recommended to the swimming analysts who consider modeling techniques in research, especially an understanding of active and passive resistance.

Anatomy

Since the size, shape, and weight of the human body is of paramount importance with respect to the resistance bodies will encounter or produce in the water, the study of kinanthropometry is as vital as fluid mechanics in the understanding of swimming performance and the subsequent modeling and simulation thereof. Kinanthropometry refers to the measurement of the human body with respect to movement. Therefore, the size, shape, proportion, composition, maturation, and gross function are measured and related to growth, exercise, and performance (Carter, 1966; Hebbelinck and Ross, 1978). Some relationships have been determined to be meaningful for swimming and are summarized in the following paragraphs.

The best swimmers (medal winners) at the Mexico Olympiad tended to be taller and heavier than their peers. Female swimmers showed a central somatotype (DeGaray et al., 1974; Hebbelinck et al., 1974). Freestyle swimmers showed higher ectomorphy than breaststroke, backstroke, and medley swimmers. The body size variables showed no differences among groups. Male swimmers had greater mesomorphic somatotypes, with the second highest group being an ectomesomorphic body type and the third being a central somatotype. The freestylers were taller, had wider hips, and greater leg length than the breaststrokers. Backstrokers also showed this greater leg length.

Ross suggests that a profile be constructed with respect to a metaphoric phantom to assess performance differences among athletes (Ross, 1978), with respect to anthropometry. This approach, the profiling of each swimmer by means of composite factors, has been utilized at the Evaluation Center of Competitive Swimmers (Persyn et al., 1979). The profile card consists of ranking anthropometric, flexibility, strength, and speed parameters. The relationships of motor, time-space, and hydromechanic factors to these parameters also have been investigated. Altogether, 30 time-space, 44 anthropometric, 22 flexibility, 7 strength, 24 swim tests, and 117 derived indices have been used. Limited results have been reported suggesting that some significant correlations have been found, that the profile has been instrumental in improving some swimmers' performances, and that additional dynamometric data regarding drag, propulsion and buoyancy are needed.

Phantoms for 15-year-old Belgian average and elite swimmers, and DDR elite swimmers were identified by Vervaecke and Persyn (1979). The phantom of the average swimmer was different than the elite. Women and men showed the same somatotypes as that of Mexico Olympians. Women had 6% lower hand surface values and had lower surface values for the foot (7%), arm and leg lengths (5%), and vital capacity (8%). Women have better floating ability and flexibility, except for shoulder flexibility. Men have higher strength values (11%). When corrected to body weight, this strength difference is 1%. One of the major differences noted from the film data of time-space relationships for four strokes was that men had greater slippage of the hand (11%) than did the women.

A better understanding of the effect of anthropological characteristics on stroke mechanics might be obtained by reviewing selected studies concerning the use of fins, wrist weights, and hand paddles. A more acute angle of entry and exit occurred with wrist weights; the hand paddle had greater underwater and greater recovery time, and had a lesser backward component than the other conditions (Welch, 1981). The width of pull at the narrowest point was significantly greater with paddles than with no paddles (Stoner and Luedtke, 1979). It appeared that the hand paddles tended to reduce asymmetry.

Individuality of responses was noted by Persyn et al. (1975) with respect to two subjects using hand paddles. The subject with shorter and stronger arms, for example, showed less slippage than the other subject. Thus, when modeling the swimmer, anthropometric data from each subject must be utilized if greatest accuracy is to be achieved. An alternate approach is to subclassify swimmers into groups, such as by phantom or profile scores.

Mechanics

Observations and study of movie films of competitive swimmers comprise the majority of investigations into the mechanics of swimming strokes. Cinematography and light trace photography are being used to determine qualitative patterns and quantitative data. Champion swimmers' styles have been analyzed and compared to each other and to lesser skilled swimmers. Division of strokes into phases, comparison of the contributions of arm and leg actions to propulsion of total body speed, and intracycle variations of speed have provided other parameters for modeling techniques.

Karpovich and Alteveer (1940) examined intracycle velocity variations of several strokes by means of a natograph. They found 0.3-m $\cdot$ sec^{-1} fluctuations in the crawl strokes and three times that for the breast stroke and side stroke. deVries (1959) was among the first to quantitatively investigate the intracycle speed variations in the dolphin stroke. His data showed that the peak velocities were approximately twice that of the lowest velocities for two expert swimmers filmed at 128 frames $\cdot$ sec^{-1}.

A newer device (Kent and Atha, 1975), the swim speed recorder (SSR), was used to determine intracycle speed variations during the breaststroke of a top class swimmer. Accelerations (negative and positive) were 8-9 m $\cdot$ sec^{-2}.

A different approach to the study of intracycle speed variations was used by Holmer (1979). An accelerometer was attached to three swimmers: one recreational, one middle class, one elite. The elite swimmer showed less variation in acceleration and in velocity than did the recreational swimmer. The root mean square (RMS) was found to be 30-40% lower for the elite than the middle class swimmer, confirming the better economy of movement.

In general, these data suggest that the relative contributions to propulsion from arm and leg action and the fluctuation in intracycle velocity represent fundamental data for modeling and simulation and prediction of biomechanically sound techniques of swimming.

Yet one question has not been answered. Since the body changes its position and thus changes its coefficient of drag, some speed variation within a cycle would be expected and, in fact, cannot be avoided. Application of muscle force at certain angles of muscle function may be less economical than to apply more force at a better angle. Likewise, preparation and recovery phases require time. In addition, relaxation of muscle groups is required in order to delay fatigue. The question is how much fluctuation may be tolerated. This may be another example in which the human body must be modeled as a biological system and not simplified to an inanimate rigid object.

What happens as a swimmer changes the speed of swim? Czabanski and Koszczyc (1979) showed that asymmetry tended to increase as speed increased during breast stroke swimming and that asymmetry of leg action existed for all subjects tested. Other researchers also have noted such asymmetry (Dupuis et al. 1979; Plagenhoef, 1971). It may be speculated that the anthropometric asymmetry normally found in human beings and the brain dominance and utilization of each brain hemisphere accounts for normal asymmetry in swimming.

With respect to modeling and simulation, both arms and both legs need to be included in the model. Simulations might produce different responses to the contralateral limbs as one or more variables are manipulated.

The effect of variations in speed and stroke on the kinematics and kinetics for the dolphin kick when swimming with the legs alone, whole stroke and at pace and sprint speeds (Barthels and Adrian, 1975) was found to be individual and significant. These results confirm the interrelationships between anthropometric, strength, and flexibility characteristics of swimmers.

Three-dimensional photography has not been used as extensively in swimming as in other sports. Again, the problems of filming underwater have not been easily overcome. Barthels (1974) and Schleihauf (1979) have quantified three-dimensional data and quantitatively depicted patterns of motion. These data are required for most swimming strokes. More recent research has been centered on the assessment of forces produced by the swimmer: muscle action by means of electromyography, and forces acting on the hand by means of dynamography. The research in this area is fragmented and incomplete. Forces on the hand provide direct input into mathematical models. With respect to electromyography, no major contribution to modeling has been made. However, electromyography can provide data to substantiate the role of muscles at the joint and, therefore, isolate moments and forces at these joints. The work of Higgs and Gallagher (1979) provides information for modeling the muscles and their contributions. The strength of the muscles were determined with respect to the position of body parts and the angles at the joints as would exist in swimming.

Thus, data with respect to the category of mechanics are incomplete. Partial data, however, exist for all competitive strokes with limited subjects. More research is needed comprising multiple instrumentation systems in order to provide the necessary data for modeling.

Modeling and Simulation

The first reported mathematical model using anthropometric, mechanical, and environmental considerations was that by Seireg and Baz (1970). They used a simplified mathematical model with the arms and legs consisting of one link each and the head-trunk as one link (five-link system). The body is considered to be a system of geometric links — as many as are needed to represent the motion to be modeled. Experimental data, such as swimming speeds and excursion and synchronization of limbs, were used to formulate the model. General equations of motion were written to determine forces and moments acting at the different body parts. Drag forces and buoyancy force were determined based on the hydrodynamic literature discussed previously in this article. Propulsive forces produced from kicking were generated and compared with data obtained experimentally by Christianson et al. (1965). Although the two sets of data showed the same sinusoidal pattern of thrust per kick cycle, the maximal and minimal forces did not agree (errors were 30-100%). A major reason for the error in the mathematical model was not including the contribution of the foot. Propulsive and vertical forces for the arm were calculated as 10 times that of the legs. Time phases, power and speed of swimming were calculated. Optimal power and efficiency were determined through simulation based on oxygen data reported in the literature. Except for the model itself being nonrepresentative of any swimming technique, this study presents the capsule of the benefits of mathematical modeling and simulation techniques: (a) prediction of main body motions and rotations through the identification of main influential factors; (b) determination of optimal speeds at different power levels; and (c) prediction of propulsive power, drag power, mechanical efficiency, and overall efficiency.

A similar model of the arms was that of Martin et al. (1981) who used a two-link system depicting a paddlewheel action of the arm on the torso. Existing data were again the basis for the modeling of the motion. Reaction forces and moments were determined and propulsive drag was calculated. The mathematical model showed greater drag than that measured experimentally.

Jensen and Blanksby (1975) could be considered as building upon the Seireg and Bass model since a flexed and a fixed elbow arm stroke were investigated by means of modeling. A three-link system for the arm was used to determine reactive forces and moments. Existing kinematic data, the Hanavan shapes, and experimental arm thrust data formed the basis for the model. Maximal moments were 50 nm at the shoulder with a fixed elbow condition, half as much at the shoulder under the flexed elbow condition. The moment at the elbow was half that of the shoulder during flexed conditions. Minimal moments were calculated for the wrist. Data in general appeared to agree with what is logical: drag forces were greater at the hand and minimal on proximal segments, and reactive forces were less during the flexed elbow position than the fixed elbow position. Percentage of error between experimental and mathematical modeling data were not reported.

Another example of the same type of modeling was conducted with the dolphin kick using a three-link system of the leg (Jensen and McIlwain, 1979). Kinematics of the motion were obtained from film data and anthropometric data were obtained from the subjects who were filmed performing the dolphin kick. Angular displacement at each joint was obtained and the following variables were calculated: drag forces acting at each segment; hip, knee, ankle, reactive forces and moments at each joint and the velocity at the hip. Implications of the data were presented with respect to performance and causes of acceleration of the body during the dolphin stroke.

The previous studies involved mathematical modeling based upon experimental data as well as theoretical data. The next two studies which will be described use physical models. Schleihauf (1979) determined lift and drag with respect to angles of pitch and sweepback of a model for a hand placed in a wind tunnel. Lift coefficients also were determined for various finger separation positions. Fingers should be no more than 1/8 inch apart to obtain benefits of lift. Data for various hand positions were used to determine resultant forces and were compared to positions of elite swimmers' hands. This was a comprehensive attempt to identify the effect of the position of the hand on force production and to relate different styles to these forces. A modeling of the stroke with more variables included in the model needs to be done to provide greater insight into the contributions of each variable. Validation of the force values during swimming also needs to be done.

Wood (1979) investigated the behavior of hand and forearm models in a wind tunnel. The results obtained were similar to those of Schleihauf

(1979). A more thorough extension of the physical model data, however, was conducted by Wood. Whereas Schleihauf investigated several swimmers and strokes, Wood modeled film data of one swimmer performing the crawl. Flow orientations were considered in the model. Actual lift and drag forces were calculated for the swimming situation and related to total body motion.

The final model is theoretical, or it might be viewed as philosophical, since Ungerechts (1979) presents concepts without actually performing the modeling techniques. Ungerechts proposed investigating the muscles' lines of action as each relates to the optimization of the hand pitch. Thus, propulsive forces may be optimized. Such an approach may also provide insight into causes of swimming injuries at the critical areas: shoulder, trunk, knee and metatarsal bones. Optimization and simulation of humans requires that the anatomical structure be considered.

In summary, modeling and simulation techniques are well developed. Researchers, however, are at the initial stages in determining what exactly is to be modeled and exactly which conditions should be simulated.

Major Problems for Future Modeling

The major problem is the inability to validate the model. I'm skeptical about the number of variables to be considered in a swimming model. Possibly a greater percentage of error will have to be accepted than is now considered desirable.

There are two approaches to mathematical modeling: (a) direct dynamics method in which the known or estimates of the known forcing functions are used to determine the resulting motion; and (b) the inverse method in which the known motion is used to determine the forcing functions. Researchers for swimming use a combination of these. Vaughan et al. (1982) offer guidelines of value to the researcher using modeling techniques in an effort to optimize the motion.

The other major problem is concerned with simulation techniques. Whenever one or more variable is manipulated the resulting simulation is subject to error. The body invariably modifies other segmental kinematics. For example, angular velocity is manipulated. Range of motion and angular velocity may change in other body segments in order to compensate for the manipulated change. The biological body does not respond as an inanimate object would respond.

Future Projections

A number of approaches are predicted for future use.
• The use of swimming treadmills will become an important adjunct in modeling research.

- Actual kinanthropometric data will be used to reduce error in the model. A library of phantoms for swimmers will be developed.
- A computerized data base of profiles on swimmers and ideal swimming styles for each profile subset will be developed.
- Modeling of joints and muscle forces to predict injury potential will be developed.
- Simulation techniques will be expanded to include the handicapped, development of new strokes, functional swimming techniques, and new devices or designs of existing devices.

Mathematical models of the mechanics of swimming movement will facilitate the construction of future achievement models. Craig and Pendergast (1979) have identified the relationships of stroke rate, velocity of swimming, and stroke distance and have postulated optimal stroke rate-stroke distance ratios. Craig et al. (1979) have constructed a nomogram to predict and assess swimming performance based on stroke rate and stroke distance.

The mathematical model may be illustrated as a physical one with the aid of computer graphics. The effect of simulation upon performance can be visually displayed for the teacher and coach. Thus, modeling may provide another link between the researcher and the practitioner.

References

BARTHELS, K.M. 1974. *Three Dimensional Kinematic Analysis of the Hand and Hip in the Butterfly Swimming Stroke.* Unpublished doctoral dissertation, Washington State University, Pullman.

BARTHELS, K.M., and Adrian, M.J. 1975. Three-dimensional spatial hand patterns of skilled butterfly swimmers. In: L. Lewillie and J.P. Clarys (eds.), *Swimming II*, pp. 154-160. University Park Press, Baltimore.

CARTER, J.E.L. 1966. The somatotype of swimmer. *Swim. Tech.* 3:76-80.

CHRISTIANSON, R., Weltman, G., and Egstrom, G. 1965. Thrust forces in underwater swimming. *Human Factors*, pp. 561-568.

CLARYS, J.P. 1979. Morphology and hydrodynamics. In: J. Terauds and E.W. Bedingfield (eds.), *Swimming III*, pp. 3-41. University Park Press, Baltimore.

CLARYS, J.P., Jiskoot, F., Rijken, H., and Brouwer, P.J. 1974. Total resistance in water and its relation to body form. In: R.C. Nelson and C.A. Morehouse (eds.), *Biomechanics IV*, pp. 187-196. University Park Press, Baltimore.

COOPER, J.M., Adrian, M., and Glassow, R.B. 1982. *Kinesiology.* C.V. Mosby, St. Louis.

CRAIG, A.B., Jr., Booder, W.L., and Gibbons, J.F. 1979. Use of stroke rate, distance per stroke, and velocity relationships during training for competitive swimming. In: J. Terauds and E.W. Bedingfield (eds.), *Swimming III*, pp. 265-274. University Park Press, Baltimore.

CRAIG, A.B., Jr., and Pendergast, D.R. 1979. Relationships of stroke rate, distance per stroke and velocity in competitive swimming. *Med. Sci. Sports* **11**: 278-283.

CZABANSKI, B., and Koszczyc, T. 1979. Relationship between stroke asymmetry and speed of breaststroke swimming. In: J. Terauds and E.W. Bedingfield (eds.), *Swimming III*, pp. 148-152. University Park Press, Baltimore.

DEGARAY, A.L., Levine, L., and Carter, J.E.L. 1974. *Genetic Anthropological Studies of Olympic Athletes.* Academic, New York.

DEVRIES, H.A. 1959. A cinematographical analysis of the dolphin swimming stroke. *Res. Q.* **30**:413-422.

diPRAMPERO, P., Pendergast, D., Wilson, D., and Rennie, D. 1974. Energetics of swimming in man. *J. Appl. Physiol.* **37**:1-5.

DUPUIS, R., Adrian, M., Yoneda, Y., and Jack, M. 1979. Forces acting on the hand during swimming and their relationships to muscular, spatial, and temporal factors. In: J. Terauds and E.W. Bedingfield (eds.), *Swimming III*, pp. 110-117. University Park Press, Baltimore.

EAVES, G. 1971. Angular momentum and the popularity of the six-beat crawl. In: L. Lewillie and J.P. Clarys (eds.), *First International Symposium on Biomechanics in Swimming, Waterpolo, and Diving*, pp. 143-144. Universite Libre De Bruxelles, Belgium.

HEBBELINCK, J., and Ross, W.D. 1974. Kinanthropometry and biomechanics. In: R.C. Nelson and C.A. Morehouse (eds.), *Biomechanics IV*, pp. 537-552. University Park Press, Baltimore.

HEBBELINCK, M., Carter, L., and DeGaray, A. 1975. Body build and somatotype of Olympic swimmers, divers, and water polo players. In: L. Lewillie and J.P. Clarys (eds.), *Swimming II*, pp. 285-305. University Park Press, Baltimore.

HIGGS, S.L., and Gallagher, H. 1979. The effect of arm position on strength of pull in freestyle and backstroke. *Swim. Tech.* **16**:24-27.

HOLMER, I. 1979. Analysis of acceleration as a measure of swimming proficiency. In J. Terauds and E.W. Bedingfield (eds.), *Swimming III*, pp. 118-124. University Park Press, Baltimore.

JENSEN, R.K., and Blanksby, B. 1975. A model for upper extremity forces during the underwater phase of the front crawl. In: L. Lewillie and J.P. Clarys (eds.), *Swimming II*, pp. 145-153. University Park Press, Baltimore.

JENSEN, R.K., and McIlwain, J. 1979. Modeling of lower extremity forces in the dolphin kick. In: J. Terauds and E.W. Bedingfield (eds.), *Swimming III*, pp. 137-147. University Park Press, Baltimore.

JISKOOT, J., and Clarys, J.P. 1975. Body resistance on and under the water surface. In: L. Lewillie and J.P. Clarys (eds.), *Swimming II*, pp. 105-109. University Park Press, Baltimore.

KARPOVICH, P.V. 1933. Water resistance in swimming. *Res. Q.* 4:21-28.

KARPOVICH, P.V., and Alteveer, R.J. 1940. *Natographic Analysis of the Butterfly Stroke.* Springfield College, Springfield, MA.

KENT, M.R., and Atha, J. 1975. Intracycle kinematics and body configuration changes in the breaststroke. In: L. Lewillie and J.P. Clarys (eds.), *Swimming II*, pp. 125-129. University Park Press, Baltimore.

MARTIN, B., Yeater, R.A., and White, M.K. 1981. A simple analytical model for the crawl stroke. *J. Biomech.* **14**:539-548.

NELSON, L.J. 1976. *Drag and Performance Analysis of a Resistance Device in Swimming*. MS thesis, Washington State University, Pullman.

PERSYN, U., Hoeven, R.G.C., and Daly, D.J. 1979. Evaluation center for competitive swimmers. In: J. Terauds and E.W. Bedingfield (eds.), *Swimming III*, pp. 182-198. University Park Press, Baltimore.

PERSYN, U., and Vervaecke, H. 1975. A model for a functional evaluation of full-synchronization data in the crawl stroke. *Hermes* **IX**:425-435.

PERSYN, H., Vervaecke, H., and Hoeven, R. 1980. Hydromechanical information obtained from artificially changed swimming styles and motor and anthropometric factors. In: U. Persyn, D. Daly, R. Hoeven, L. Van Tilborgh, D. Verhetsel, and H. Vervaecke (eds.), *Reader 2, Evaluation Center of Competitive Swimmers 10*. Katholieke Universiteit, Leuven, Belgium.

PLAGENHOEF, S. 1971. *Patterns of Human Motion, a Cinematographic Analysis*. Prentice-Hall, Englewood Cliffs, NJ.

RENNIE, D.W., Pendergast, D.R., and di Prampero, P.E. 1975. Energetics of swimming in man. In: L. Lewillie and J.P. Clarys (eds.), *Swimming II*, pp. 97-104. University Park Press, Baltimore.

ROSS, W.D. 1978. Kinanthropometry: An emerging scientific technology. In: F. Landry and W. Orban (eds.), *Biomechanics of Sports and Kinanthropometry*, pp. 269-282. Symposia Specialists, Miami.

SCHLEIHAUF, R.E. 1979. A hydrodynamic analysis of swimming propulsion. In: J. Terauds and E.W. Bedingfield (eds.), *Swimming III*, pp. 70-109. University Park Press, Baltimore.

SHELDON, W.H., Stevens, S.S., and Tucker, W.B. 1940. *The Varieties of Human Physique*. Harper and Brothers, New York.

SIEREG, A., and Baz, A. 1971. A mathematical model for swimming mechanics. In: L. Lewillie and J.P. Clarys (eds.), *First International Symposium on Biomechanics in Swimming, Waterpolo, and Diving*, pp. 81-104. Universite Libre De Bruxelles, Belgium.

STONER, L.J., and Luedtke, D.L. 1979. Variations in front crawl and back crawl arm strokes of varsity swimmers using hand paddles. In: J. Terauds and E.W. Bedingfield (eds.), *Swimming III*, pp. 281-288. University Park Press, Baltimore.

UNGERECHTS, B. 1979. Optimizing propulsion in swimming by rotation of the hands. In: J. Terauds and E.W. Bedingfield (eds.), *Swimming III*, pp. 55-61. University Park Press, Baltimore.

VAUGHAN, C.L., Hay, J.G., and Andrews, J.G. 1982. Closed loop problems in biomechanics, part II—An optimization approach. *J. Biomech.* **15**:201-210.

VERVAECKE, H., and Persyn, U. 1980. Some differences between men and women in various factors which determine swimming performance. In: U. Persyn, D. Daly, R. Hoeven, L. Van Tilborgh, D. Verhetsel, and H. Vervaecke (eds.), *Reader* **2(9)**. Katholieke Universiteit, Leuven, Belgium.

WELCH, J. 1981. Swimming with accessories: A filmed case study. *Swim. Tech.*, pp. 18-19.

WOOD, T.C. 1979. A fluid dynamics analysis of the propulsive potential of the hand and forearm in swimming. In: J. Terauds and E.W. Bedingfield (eds.), *Swimming III*, pp. 62-69. University Park Press, Baltimore.

Energetics and Mechanical Work in Swimming

Ingvar Holmér
National Board of Occupational Safety and Health,
Solna, Sweden

Swimmers continue to break world records more frequently and with greater margins than in most other sports. This is in part a result of greater training but also of a better understanding of rational principles of training. The physical and physiological requirements of a sport are the fundamental determinants of the training program design.

More than 10 years have passed since the first Biomechanics in Swimming Congress was held in Brussels (Clarys and Lewillie, 1971). During this period an impressive amount of scientific work on various aspects of swimming has emerged (Holmér, 1979b). This presentation reviews the energetics of swimming, the subject of several interesting and productive studies during the 1970s.

Buoyancy and Water Resistance

The main purpose of the propulsive work in swimming is to overcome the resistance of the water (drag) on the body. In addition, work has to be done to overcome some gravitational force acting on the immersed body.

Body density is slightly higher than that of water and is mainly determined by physical composition. Buoyancy, on the other hand, is not a well defined constant, but fluctuates with surface limb movements, body position and respiration. Many of these factors have been extensively reviewed by Miller (1975). A prone or supine floating position is not easily maintained without some effort. The relatively dense lower part of the body (legs) tends to sink and a torque is generated in relation to the center of buoyancy. This effect is more pronounced with male swimmers, whereas females have a more natural hoizontal floating position (Pendergast and Craig, 1974).

Water resistance of the body (drag) is a dynamic force which may be defined as a function of body motion, shape and position. Drag changes synchronously with stroke pattern. Average drag per stroke cycle or number of stroke cycles may be determined by different techniques; all more or less cumbersome (Clarys, 1979; diPrampero et al., 1974). Drag values, so obtained, are denoted as active drag values. Drag determined by towing subjects in an outstretched body position (passive drag) is not representative of the drag experienced by the swimmer during actual swimming and should be interpreted with some care. The relative importance of different factors determining drag may very well change from passive towing to free swimming. Due to the difficulties involved, measurements of active drag are very limited in number.

Active drag has been reported to be ca. 1.5-2 times greater than passive drag at corresponding velocities (diPrampero et al., 1974; Holmér, 1974a). On the average, women have significantly less drag than men. Such differences are reduced but not eliminated by correcting the data for body size differences (diPrampero et al., 1974; Pendergast et al., 1977). Better buoyancy and less tendency of the feet to sink are the primary explanations (Pendergast et al., 1978a).

Mechanical Work and Efficiency

If the velocity within a stroke cycle is assumed to be constant, the mechanical power related to the swimming speed, $\dot{W}$, can be estimated according to Equation 1 as proposed by diPrampero et al. (1974):

$$\dot{W} = Da * v \tag{1}$$

$$\dot{W} = \dot{E} * e \tag{2}$$

The proportion of the total energy cost per unit time, $\dot{E}$, that is spent to overcome the drag force is expressed by efficiency factor e in Equation 2. Hence, e can be expressed in terms of the ratio $(Da * v)/\dot{E}$.

So defined, overall efficiency has been reported higher than 15% in the front crawl (Pendergast et al., 1978a), whereas breaststroke efficiency is only about 5-6% (Holmér, 1974a). In general, overall efficiency is higher in competitive swimmers than in noncompetitive swimmers, and higher in women than in men (Pendergast et al., 1977).

Propulsion

Experimental studies on the water flow around and resultant forces on models of the human hand in a water channel (Schleihauf, 1979) and in a wind tunnel (Wood and Holt, 1979) have provided drag and lift coefficients for the hand in different positions and at different speeds of movement. It is now possible to roughly estimate propulsive forces during the stroke cycle from high-speed cinematographic recordings (Schleihauf, 1979). Using this technique Schleihauf has presented detailed analyses of stroke mechanics and hydrodynamic forces of top swimmers representing all strokes (Schleihauf, 1974, 1979). It is apparent that drag and lift forces combine to provide propulsion during the swim stroke. The relative importance of these forces changes within a stroke cycle, with the stroke and with the swimmer's skill and ability. Indeed, it is assumed that an optimal integration of drag and lift forces is one requirement for a good swimming technique.

Acceleration of the swimmer's body is synchronous with stroke rhythm. In the breaststroke, acceleration is great during the propulsive phases of both arm pull and leg kick, whereas in the front crawl acceleration within the stroke cycle is small (Holmér, 1979a). Similarly, intracycle velocity fluctuation is small in front crawl, and large in breaststroke (Craig and Pendergast, 1979; Holmér, 1979a; Schleihauf, 1979). Measurement of acceleration or velocity fluctuation within a stroke cycle has been suggested as an indicator of swimming proficiency (Holmér, 1979a; Kornecki and Bober, 1978). In a calculation of the total energy expenditure of swimming, the energy spent in accelerating the body is probably negligible in the front and back crawl. In the breaststroke, however, this energy cost might be significant.

In a swimming flume, it is possible to record the acceleration within a swimmer's stroke cycle by means of an accelerometer and a tape recorder (Holmér, 1979a). A frequency analysis of the acceleration signal presents additional information of: (a) the power loss due to fluctuations in velocity, (b) the origin of propulsive forces, and (c) the relative contributions to propulsion from arm and leg action (Holmér, 1979a). Peak accelerations coincide with the frequencies of arm stroke and leg kicking, respectively. It appears from Figure 1 that the contribution to propulsion from leg kicking in the front crawl increases at higher swim speeds, but is still small compared to the arm work.

Because of the inherent difficulties in taking measurements of swimmers in the water, significant data are lacking on propulsive and resistive forces in free swimming. The values presented are more or less reliable approximations obtained with rather simple methods. In mathematical modeling it is possible to derive expressions for almost any type of motion made by the swimmer. This may provide valuable information on the interaction of various factors and their relative importance (Adrian, 1983). On the other hand, the accuracy of a model is determined by the accuracy of the input data and the relevance of the basic assumptions necessary for any model. No model presented so far accounts for the interaction of drag and lift forces in propulsion.

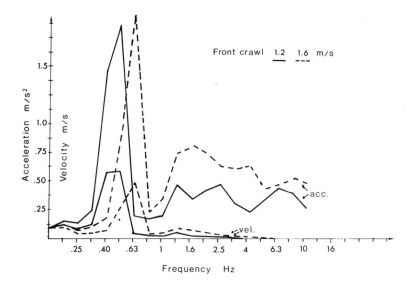

Figure 1—Frequency spectra of the acceleration and velocity signals for one swimmer at two different velocities (modified from Holmér, 1979a).

Energy Cost of Swimming

diPrampero and coworkers have presented a simple and illustrative model for the analysis of energy expenditure in swimming (diPrampero et al., 1974; Pendergast et al., 1977, 1978a). The power balance during steady-state swimming is described by

$$\dot{E} = Da/e * v \tag{3}$$

$$E/d = Da/e \tag{4}$$

Thus $\dot{E}$ at a given velocity is determined by the ratio Da/e. Furthermore, an estimate of Da/e is provided by the energy cost per unit distance (d) traveled (E/d). In fact these equations are only modifications of the formula defining overall efficiency in a previous section.

At submaximal velocities, E can be determined easily by measuring the subject's $\dot{V}O_2$. The amount of oxygen consumed per unit distance ($\dot{V}O_2/d$) is a quantitative measure of the economy of swimming or of the swimmer's technical ability (Da/e); values are higher for men than for women in competitive as well as noncompetitive swimmers (Pendergast et al., 1978a). This difference in $\dot{V}O_2/d$ can be attributed to better buoyancy and females' more favorable body position (Pendergast et al., 1978a). There is no difference in $\dot{V}O_2/d$ of young boys and girls (8-12 years) (Pendergast et al., 1978a), suggesting that body growth and devel-

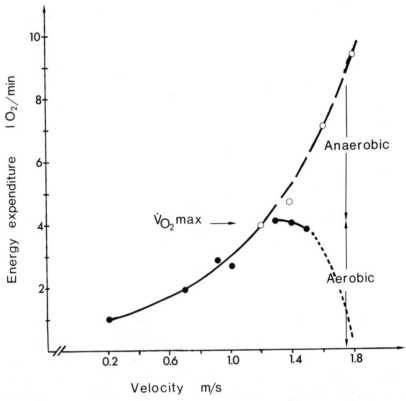

Figure 2 — Total energy expenditure expressed in L oxygen/min as a function of swimming velocity. Aerobic and anaerobic components are denoted (adapted from Pendergast et al., 1978b).

opment during and after puberty are responsible for the sex-related differences. For male distance swimmers, leg kicking is important in maintaining a more horizontal body position in the water which reduces the drag force accordingly.

Values of $\dot{V}O_2/d$ have been suggested for the evaluation of swimming proficiency (Pendergast et al., 1978a). The energy cost of swimming 1 km varies from ca. 300 to 2,000 kJ (75-500 kcal).

The energy cost of swimming at a given submaximal velocity is determined mainly by body drag, swimming technique, level of training, and swimming style (diPrampero et al., 1974; Holmér, 1974c; Pendergast et al., 1977). Substantial differences in energy cost are found among subjects of different swimming abilities. Energy expenditure rate increases exponentially with velocity (Figure 2). This is mainly from the exponential increase in drag. At very high velocities a decrease in efficiency may contribute to a sharp increase in energy expenditure (Pendergast et al., 1978b).

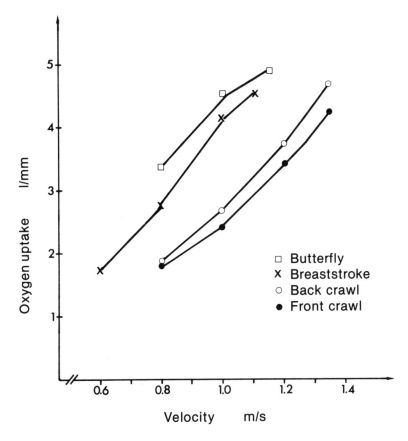

Figure 3—Mean values for oxygen uptake in relation to swimming velocity by male elite swimmers in the four competitive strokes (adapted from Holmér, 1974b).

Energy expenditures in the butterfly and breaststroke are almost twice that of the front and back crawls (Figure 3). This is valid within the constraints of comparable technique in the respective strokes. The energy cost of leg kick, arm stroke, and whole crawl stroke have been analyzed for the four competitive styles (Holmér, 1974b). Although the energy cost at a given submaximal velocity was independent of stroke for breaststroke and butterfly, it was higher during leg kicking and lower during arm swimming compared with swimming the whole stroke in the front and back crawls (Holmér, 1974b). Hence, there is a physiological basis for the common opinion that leg kicking is energy-demanding and should be reduced in distance swimming.

Swimming with controlled frequency breathing, popularly but erroneously called "hypoxic training" (Craig, 1979), has a certain influence on the energy cost. With more air in the lungs, buoyancy is increased and

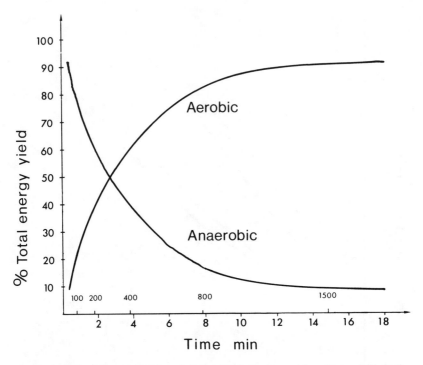

Figure 4 — Relative contributions by anaerobic and aerobic energy yield during swimming as a function of work time and swimming distances (adapted from data by Hermansen and Karlsson [1967] and Houston [1978]).

drag goes down. The energy cost of swimming at a given velocity is lowered (Holmér and Gullstrand, 1980). The effect of controlled frequency breathing should be small, but of practical importance for gaining speed. Of course the best effect may be achieved with a very pronounced reduction of respiration frequency. However, there are certain physiological limitations to this adaptation.

Aerobic and Anaerobic Energy Yield

The relative importance of anaerobic and aerobic metabolic reactions for the total energy yield with respect to maximal work time in swimming is illustrated in Figure 4 (Hermansen and Karlsson, 1967; Houston, 1978). It is apparent that in a 50-sec maximal exercise period (100-m front crawl), the anaerobic processes may account for ca. 80% of the total energy yield, whereas in maximal work periods exceeding about 3 min, the aerobic processes are responsible for more than 50% of the energy yield. Hence, in sprint and distance swimming the predominant metabolic reactions are of different types, power, and capacity. In 100-

and 200-m events which dominate competitive swimming, emphasis is on a large anaerobic capacity. For the 800- and 1,500-m races high aerobic power and capacity are required.

Maximal aerobic power is determined as oxygen uptake during maximal swimming. Anaerobic power is more difficult to measure. Oxygen debt and postexercise peak blood-lactate level are the most commonly used estimators of anaerobic power (diPrampero et al., 1978; Mader et al., 1978).

Values for $\dot{V}O_2$max up to 6 L/min have been measured. Table 1 summarizes maximal values for $\dot{V}O_2$ and blood lactate measured in Swedish elite swimmers at intervals of 3-5 years. It is interesting to note that in samples of male and female elite swimmers during a 10-year period, $\dot{V}O_2$max and maximal lactate values are unchanged. Twenty years ago, some girls with long training distances attained values for $\dot{V}O_2$max similar to those of today's female elite swimmers. The average Swedish elite swimmer has aerobic power slightly higher than 5 L/min (male) or about 3.2 L/min (female). Apparently the improved performance of swimmers today over that of swimmers 10 years ago has relatively little to do with maximal rates of energy exchange. Instead, this development is largely accounted for by improved technical ability, stroke mechanics, and other technical factors. Pendergast et al. (1977) noted that there is much greater potential for improvement in technical ability than for improvement in maximal power. This condition might also be one explanation for the higher frequency of world records being broken in swimming than in most other sports.

It has been claimed, but not proven, that swimming with controlled frequency breathing improves the anaerobic power (Counsilman, 1975).

Table 1

**Comparison of Maximal Values for Oxygen Uptake (L/min)
and Blood Lactate (mmol/L) during Swimming
in Different Samples of Elite Swedish Swimmers, 1961-78**

Year	Men		Women	
	$\dot{V}O_2$	Lactate	$\dot{V}O_2$	Lactate
1961 (Åstrand et al., 1963)	—	—	3.18	10.3
1967 (Hermansen and Karlsson, 1967)	5.16	14.0	—	—
1974 (Holmér et al., 1974b)	5.05	11.6	3.42	10.5
1978 (Gullstrand and Holmér, 1979)	5.08	11.1	3.21	9.2

This type of suppressed breathing, however, does not produce metabolic acidosis but respiratory alkalosis (Dicker et al., 1980; Holmér and Gullstrand, 1980). Hence, it would not affect maximal power output. On the other hand, there may very well be a biomechanical effect reducing drag. From this point of view, such a training program might be justified, the major effect being an improved tolerance to hypercapnia. Some support exists for this hypothesis in recent work on Japanese swimmers (Ohkuwa et al., 1980).

Essential to propulsion in swimming is high muscular power output. Several investigators have measured EMG and obtained valuable information on muscle recruitment, activity and coordination. In a recently published Swedish study (Bellbring et al., 1981) the EMG was recorded from four different muscle groups active during the crawl arm stroke. Recordings were obtained during different types of water and dryland exercises such as coll-craft, minigym, etc. It was shown that tethered swimming and swimming with hand paddles produced similar responses with respect to frequency, activity and coordination. For most dryland exercises the EMG showed similarities with natural swim movements but with significant differences in either frequency, activity or coordination.

The most significant feature of modern swim training is the popularity of strength training and the greater volume of work done by today's swimmers. Little data, however, are available on muscular strength of swimmers. Swedish elite swimmers have been tested regularly for maximal thrust in a tethered swim test using the swimming flume. This would be an integrated measure of the total muscular power of active swim muscles. The common trend is that swimmers have become stronger partly as a result of more dryland strength training (Gullstrand and Holmér, 1983).

Aerobic and anaerobic power probably are at optimal levels for the best top swimmers of today. Muscular strength apparently constitutes an underestimated determinant of performance, as do many biomechanical factors associated with technique. Training programs, certainly, develop the energy power of our swimmers. In order for improvements to continue more emphasis should be placed on technique and selective muscular strength in the training work.

References

ADRIAN, M.J. 1983. Biomechanics and mathematical modeling. In: A.P. Hollander, P.A. Huijing, and G. de Groot (eds.), *Biomechanics and Medicine in Swimming*, pp. 142-153. Human Kinetics, Champaign, IL.

ÅSTRAND, P.-O., Engström, L., Eriksson, B.O., Karlberg, P., Nylander, I., Saltin, B., and Thorén, C. 1963. Girl swimmers. *Acta Paediatr. Suppl.:147.*

BELLBRING, A., Holm, H., Hulten, B., and Vösu-Vangblad, M.L. 1981. Analys av muskelaktivitet vid olika typer av styrketräning för simmare. (Analysis of Muscular Activity during Strength Training for Swimmers.) Masters thesis, GIH, Stockholm.

CLARYS, J.P. 1979. Human morphology and hydrodynamics. In: J. Terauds and W. Bedingfield (eds.), *Swimming III*, pp. 3-41. University Park Press, Baltimore.

CLARYS, J.P., and Lewillie, L. 1971. (eds.), *Biomechanics in Swimming*. Université Libre de Bruxelles, Brussels.

COUNSILMAN, J.E. 1975. Hypoxic and other methods of training evaluated. *Swim. Tech.* **12**:19-26.

CRAIG, A.B., Jr. 1979. The fallacies of "hypoxic" training in swimming. In: J. Terauds and W. Bedingfield (eds.), *Swimming III*, pp. 235-239. University Park Press, Baltimore.

CRAIG, A.B., Jr., and Pendergast, D.R. 1979. Relationships of stroke rate, distance per stroke, and velocity in competitive swimming. *Med. Sci. Sports* **11**:278-283.

DICKER, S.G., Lofthus, G.K., Thornton, N.W., and Brooks, G.A. 1980. Respiratory and heart rate responses to tethered controlled frequency breathing swimming. *Med. Sci. Sports Exer.* **12**:20-23.

diPRAMPERO, P.E., Pendergast, D.R., Wilson, D.W., and Rennie, D.W. 1974. Energetics of swimming in man. *J. Appl. Physiol.* **37**:1-5.

diPRAMPERO, P.E., Pendergast, D.R., Wilson, D.W., and Rennie, D.W. 1978. Blood lactic acid concentrations in high velocity swimming. In: B.O. Eriksson and B. Furberg (eds.), *Swimming Medicine IV*, pp. 249-261. University Park Press, Baltimore.

GULLSTRAND, L., and Holmér, I. 1980. Maximal syreupptagning, del 1. (Maximal oxygen uptake, part 1.) *Simsport* **1**:22-24. (In Swedish).

GULLSTRAND, L., and Holmér, I. 1983. Physiological characteristics of champion swimmers during a 5-year follow-up period. In: A.P. Hollander, P.A. Huijing, and G. de Groot (eds.), *Biomechanics and Medicine in Swimming*, pp. 258-262. Human Kinetics, Champaign, IL.

HERMANSEN, L., and Karlsson, J. 1967. Detta är resultatet av fysiologernas undersökning av våra toppsimmare. (The results from the physiological investigation of our elite swimmers.) *Simsport* **22**:19-27.

HOLMÉR, I. 1974a. Propulsive efficiency of breaststroke and freestyle swimming. *Eur. J. Appl. Physiol.* **33**:95-103.

HOLMÉR, I. 1974b. Energy cost of arm stroke, leg kick, and the whole stroke in competitive swimming styles. *Eur. J. Appl. Physiol.* **33**:105-118.

HOLMÉR, I. 1974c. Physiology of swimming man. *Acta Physiol. Scand.* Suppl.:407.

HOLMÉR, I. 1979a. Analysis of acceleration as a measure of swimming proficiency. In: J. Terauds and W. Bedingfield (eds.), *Swimming III*, pp. 118-124. University Park Press, Baltimore.

HOLMÉR, I. 1979b. Physiology of swimming man. In: R.S. Hutton and D.I. Miller (eds.), *Exercise and Sport Sciences Reviews* (vol. 7). The Franklin Institute Press, Philadelphia.

HOLMÉR, I., Lundin, A., and Eriksson, B.O. 1974. Maximum oxygen uptake during swimming and running by elite swimmers. *J. Appl. Physiol.* 36:711-714.

HOLMÉR, I., and Gullstrand, L. 1980. Physiological responses to swimming with a controlled frequency of breathing. *Scand. J. Sports Sci.* 2:1-6.

HOUSTON, M. Metabolic responses to exercise, with special reference to training and competition in swimming. In: B.O. Eriksson and B. Furberg (eds.), *Swimming Medicine IV*, pp. 207-232. University Park Press, Baltimore.

KORNECKI, S., and Bober, T. 1978. Extreme velocities of a swimming cycle as a technique criterion. In: B.O. Eriksson and B. Furberg (eds.), *Swimming Medicine IV*, pp. 402-407. University Park Press, Baltimore.

MADER, A., Heck, H., and Hollman, W. 1978. Evaluation of lactic acid concentration of ear capillary blood in middle-distance runners and swimmers. In: F. Landry and W.A.P. Orban (eds.), *Exercise Physiology*. Symposia Specialists, Miami.

MILLER, D.I. 1975. Biomechanics of swimming. In: J.H. Wilmore and J.F. Koegh (eds.), *Exercise and Sport Sciences Reviews* (vol. 3). Academic Press, New York.

OHKUWA, T., Fujitsuka, N., Utsuno, T., and Miyamura, M. 1980. Ventilatory responses to hypercapnia in sprint and long-distance swimmers. *Eur. J. Appl. Physiol.* 43:235-241.

PENDERGAST, D.R., and Craig, A.B., Jr. 1974. Biomechanics of floating in water. *Physiologist* 17:305.

PENDERGAST, D.R., diPrampero, P.E., Craig, A.B., Jr., Wilson, D.R., and Rennie, D.W. 1977. Quantitative analysis of the front crawl in men and women. *J. Appl. Physiol.: Respirat. Environ. Exer. Physiol.* 43:475-479.

PENDERGAST, D.R., diPrampero, P.E., Craig, A.B., Jr., and Rennie, D.W. 1978a. The influence of selected biomechanical factors on the energy cost of swimming. In: B.O. Eriksson and B. Furberg (eds.), *Swimming Medicine IV*, pp. 367-378. University Park Press, Baltimore.

PENDERGAST, D.R., diPrampero, P., Craig, A.B., Jr., and Rennie, D.W. 1978b. Energetics of locomotion in man. In: F. Landry and W.A.R. Orban (eds.), *Exercise Physiology*. Symposia Specialists, Miami.

SCHLEIHAUF, R.E., JR. 1974. Biomechanical analysis of freestyle. *Swim. Tech.* 11:89-96.

SCHLEIHAUF, R.E., Jr. 1979. A hydrodynamic analysis of swimming propulsion. In: J. Terauds and W. Bedingfield (eds.), *Swimming III*, pp. 70-109. University Park Press, Baltimore.

WOOD, T.C., and Holt, L. Fluid dynamic analysis of the propulsive potential of the hand and forearm in swimming. In: J. Terauds and W. Bedingfield (eds.). *Swimming III*, pp. 62-69. University Park Press, Baltimore.

A Power Balance Applied to Swimming

H.M. Toussaint, F.C.T. van der Helm, J.R. Elzerman,
A. Peter Hollander, Gert de Groot, and G.J. van Ingen Schenau
Free University, Amsterdam, The Netherlands

Different approaches have been used to study the biomechanics and energetics of swimming, for example, balance of forces (Rackam, 1975). In this study, a power flow model was applied to swimming. At constant speed the total power (P_o) applied by the swimmer is:

$$P_o = P_d + P_k, \tag{1}$$

where P_d is the useful power to overcome drag and P_k is the kinetic energy flow to parts of the water which are accelerated as a result of the push-off. Hence, a propelling efficiency (e_p) can be defined as:

$$e_p = \frac{P_d}{P_d + P_k} . \tag{2}$$

When the fluctuations in speed (v) of the swimmer are neglected and $\bar{F}_d$ is the mean drag force, the useful external power of the swimmer is:

$$P_d = \bar{F}_d \cdot \bar{v} . \tag{3}$$

At constant speed the mean drag force ($\bar{F}_d$) on the swimmer will be equal to the mean propelling force ($\bar{F}_p$) of the swimmer. This mean propelling force is generated by giving a mass of water (Σm_i) a velocity change (Δu_i) in time T. Then,

$$\bar{F}_d = F_p = \frac{1}{T} \int_0^T \bar{F}_p dt = \frac{1}{T} \Sigma m_i \overline{\Delta u_i}, \tag{4}$$

where T equals the cycle time. Combining Equations 3 and 4 the useful external power then is:

$$P_d = f \cdot v \ \Sigma m_i \ \Delta u_i, \tag{5}$$

where $f \ (= \frac{1}{T})$ is the stroke frequency. The flow of kinetic energy lost to parts of the water is:

$$P_k = f \cdot \frac{1}{2} \ \Sigma m_i \ (\Delta u_i)^2. \tag{6}$$

The propelling efficiency can then be rewritten as:

$$e_p = \frac{P_d}{P_d + P_k} = \frac{v \ \Sigma m_i \ \Delta u_i}{v \ \Sigma m_i \ \Delta u_i + \frac{1}{2} \ \Sigma m_i \ (\Delta u_i)^2}. \tag{7}$$

In this study two groups of swimmers with different performance levels were compared in order to investigate possible differences in external power, aerobic capacity, stroke frequency and stroke length. Also under study were differences in anthropometric measures which could influence the flow of external power as well as the propelling efficiency in swimming.

Methods

To avoid possible changes due to physical conditioning or to technique during the swimming season, all measurements were performed within 2 months.

Subjects

The seven best 100-m freestyle female swimmers from The Netherlands (Olympic level) participated as the group of elite swimmers (100-m: 57.3 ± .98 sec; 200-m: 2:03.7 ± 1.9 sec). Seven female swimmers of a lower competitive level formed the trained group (100-m: 1:03.9 ± 2.6 sec; 200-m: 2:17.8 ± 4.0 sec).

Anthropometric Measurements

The following anthropometric measures were taken on all subjects: body weight, body length, arm length (tuberculum majus to tip of middle finger), upper arm length (tuberculum majus to caput radii), forearm length (caput radii to processus styloideus radii), hand length (processus styloideus radii to tip of middle finger), forearm and hand frontal area. The frontal area of hand and forearm were measured from the contour of frontal photographs (planimetry).

Distance Per Stroke and Stroke Frequency

During the 100- and 200-m races the subjects were filmed with a fixed videocamera, placed at the middle and 3 m from the edge of the pool's long side. Stroke frequency was calculated from the time required for the swimmer to perform 10 strokes. Average distance per stroke was calculated by counting the number of strokes per 15 m. This 15-m distance was indicated by markings on the ropes at the side of the lane. The data obtained from the 100- and 200-m freestyle films were first averaged for each subject and then for the entire group.

Oxygen Consumption Tests

Oxygen consumption and external power were measured for all subjects during 3 min of supramaximal arm cranking and during 3 min of supramaximal cycling, according to the test protocol described by Åstrand and Rodahl (1977, pp. 340-341). Both tests were performed within 4-7 days on an electromagnetically braked ergometer (Lode). Following the first minute of the 3-min test, a Douglas bag was filled with expired air every 30 sec until the subject was exhausted. The volume of expired air was measured in a calibrated volume meter (Dordrecht) and its oxygen and carbon dioxide content was analyzed with a paramagnetic O_2 (Mijnhardt, type UG 61) and an infrared CO_2 analyzer (Mijnhardt, type UG 51).

Differences between the groups were tested using t-statistics. The significance level was taken at $p < .05$, two-tailed.

Results

The mean values of the anthropometric variables measured are presented in Table 1. The mean values of stroke length and stroke frequency are presented in Table 2 and results of the arm cranking and cycling tests are given in Table 3.

The most striking differences between the two groups were found in arm length, forearm and hand frontal area, hand frontal area and stroke length. It was surprising that the results did not reveal any significant differences between the two groups in maximal aerobic power, total external power, and stroke frequency. When the anthropometric values were normalized for body length, a significant difference was found between the two groups in the hand frontal area.

Discussion

In this study no significant differences were found between the mean $\dot{V}O_2max$ and total external power of the two groups, either in the arm

Table 1

Anthropometric Data of the Subjects: Body Weight (BW), Body Length (BL), Total Arm Length (TAL), Upper Arm Length (UAL), Forearm Length (FAL), Hand Length (HAL), Forearm and Hand Frontal Area (FHFA) and Hand Frontal Area (HFA)

Group		BW (kg)	BL (m)	TAL (m)	UAL (m)	FAL (m)	HL (m)	FHFA (m²)	HFA (m²)
Elite	$\overline{X}$	63.21	1.7604	.7677	.3322	.2528	.1905	.3298	.1529
(n = 7)	SD	7.12	0.406	.0217	.0115	.0122	.0088	.0213	.0098
Trained	$\overline{X}$	63.64	1.6940	.7319	.3201	.2469	.1835	.3026	.1373
(n = 7)	SD	7.36	.0620	.0322	.0118	.0136	.0102	.0229	.0115
Difference (%)		−.67	3.8[b]	4.7[b]	3.6	2.3	3.7	8.3[b]	10.2[b]

[a]Means (X) and standard deviations (SD) are presented. Differences between the groups are expressed in percentage of the values of the top group.
[b]Indicates significant differences ($p < .05$).

Table 2

Stroke Frequency (f) and Distance per Stroke (d/s)[a]

Group		Stroke frequency (f)		Distance/stroke (d/s)	
		100 m (s^{-1})	200 m (s^{-1})	100 m (m)	200 m (m)
Elite	$\overline{X}$	1.667	1.487	.96	.95
($n = 7$)	SD	1.49	.099	.06	.04
Trained	$\overline{X}$	1.592	1.456	.85	.87
($n = 7$)	SD	.105	.088	.06	.06
Difference (%)		4.5	2.0	11.5[b]	8.4[b]

[a]Results are mean values ($\overline{X}$) and standard deviations (SD) of the two groups of swimmers of different performance levels. Differences between the groups are expressed in percentage of the values of the elite group.
[b]Indicates significant differences ($p < .05$).

test or in cycling (Table 3). However, Åstrand et al. (1963) have indicated that a high correlation exists between the $\dot{V}O_2$max measured in cycling and swimming.

The results of this study would indicate that no difference should exist in the capacity of the subjects to deliver external power (P_0). The total external power can be expressed as:

$$P_0 = A \cdot f, \tag{8}$$

where A is the amount of work per stroke and f is the stroke frequency.

As can be seen in Table 2, the stroke frequency (f) does not differ between the two groups. Since the total external power (for cycling) didn't differ either, it was assumed that there was no difference in the amount of work per stroke (A) between the groups. However, a significant difference was found in the stroke lengths.

At the same total external power (P_0), the combination of these results and Equations 1 and 2 leads to the conclusion that elite swimmers will utilize a greater part of A for propulsion, with less loss in kinetic energy (P_k) to the water. This means that elite swimmers have a higher propelling efficiency than trained swimmers.

According to Equations 4 and 7, the energy loss (P_k) can be decreased and e_p can be optimized in two ways:
- A greater distance should be covered underwater by the limbs to make the total amount of water acting against the push-off as large as possible (Counsilman, 1968). The same effect occurs when larger propelling surfaces (e.g., swim fins) are used (McMurray, 1975; Stoner and Luedtke, 1979).

Table 3

Data on Arm Cranking and Cycling Tests: Work Load Per Body Mass (P_c/BM), Maximal Oxygen Consumption Per Body Mass ($\dot{V}O_2max/BM$), Respiration Quotient (RQ), Heart Frequency (HF)

Group		Cycling				Arm cranking			
		P_c/BM (W)	$\dot{V}O_2max/BM$ (ml/min·kg)	RQ	HF (min^{-1})	P_c/BM (W)	$\dot{V}O_2max/BM$ (ml/min·kg)	RQ	HF (min^{-1})
Elite	X	3.63	48.9	1.17	187	1.58	31.6	1.03	180
(n = 7)	SD	.49	5.7	.08	5	.18	4.5	.11	10
Trained	X	3.44	47.9	1.09	190	1.49	31.1	1.01	176
(n = 7)	SD	.62	4.7	.17	5	.24	6.8	.07	13
Difference (%)		5.4	2	6.8	-1.5	5.7	1.6	1.9	2

- The push-off should be made against stagnant water. This follows from the fact that the losses (P_k) will be less when a change in water momentum ($\Sigma m_i - \Delta u_i$) is obtained by increasing Δu_i from 0 to Δu_i compared to the same change of momentum obtained from an increase in Δu_i from beginning velocity (Δw_i) to ($\Delta w_i + \Delta u_i$) since:

$$\tfrac{1}{2} \, m_i \, (\Delta w_i + \Delta u_i)^2 - \tfrac{1}{2} \, m_i \, \Delta w_i^2 =$$
$$\tfrac{1}{2} \, m_i \, \Delta u_i^2 + m_i \, \Delta w_i \, \Delta u_i > \tfrac{1}{2} \, m_i \, \Delta u_i^2. \tag{9}$$

The first statement is supported by the movement patterns described by several authors, including Schleihauf (1979) and Reischle (1979). Reischle (1979) found that skilled swimmers have less backward limb movement through the water at the same propulsive force from the "blading" movement of the limbs.

Table 1 shows that elite swimmers differed from trained swimmers in arm length and in frontal area of the forearm and hand. It is possible that these differences contributed to a difference in propelling efficiency and propelling force. As previously stated, there was no difference in the amount of work per stroke between the groups. A higher propelling efficiency means that a greater part of this amount of work done per stroke was used to overcome drag. This will result in a larger distance per stroke, which is in agreement with the results as shown in Table 2.

In the light of the theoretical considerations already discussed with respect to the propelling efficiency, a final remark should be made concerning the measurements of active drag reported in many other studies. In the past, several researchers assumed that the propelling efficiency did not change in experiments where active drag was calculated indirectly from oxygen consumption tests during swimming while extra external forces were applied (Clarys, 1978; diPrampero et al., 1974; Holmér, 1978; Pendergast et al., 1977). diPrampero et al. (1974) as well as Rennie et al. (1975) state that all external power in swimming contributes to propulsion. As previously explained this is not the case, as a fraction of $1 - e_p$ is lost as kinetic energy (P_k) to parts of the water. It is likely that e_p will not be constant when external loads are applied, since F_p and stroke frequency will change and thereby influence e_p. Moreover, even small changes in $\dot{V}_{O_2}$ due to small deviations in e_p will be amplified by the extrapolations which have been used in former studies. Further research is needed to clarify the extent to which a difference exists between active and passive drag.

From these results, it can be concluded that the propelling efficiency is a very important factor in swimming. Increasing the propelling efficiency by improving techniques should be an important objective in training for swimming.

References

ÅSTRAND, P.-O., Engström, L., Eriksson, B., Karlberg, P., Nylander, I., Saltin, B., and Thoren, C. 1963. Girl swimmers. *Acta Paediatr.* (Suppl.) **147**:43-63.

ÅSTRAND, P.-O., and Rodahl, K. 1977. *Textbook of Work Physiology*, pp. 340-341. McGraw-Hill, New York.

CLARYS, J.P. 1978. Relationship of human body form to passive and active hydrodynamic drag. In: E. Asmussen and K. Jørgensen (eds.), *Biomechanics VI-B*, pp. 120-125. University Park Press, Baltimore.

COUNSILMAN, J.E. 1968. *The Science of Swimming*. Prentice-Hall, Englewood Cliffs, NJ.

CRAIG, A.B., Jr., Boomer, W.L., and Gibbons, J.F. 1979. Use of stroke rate, distance per stroke, and velocity relationships during training for competitive swimming. In: J. Terauds and E.W. Bedingfield (eds.), *Swimming III*, pp. 265-274. University Park Press, Baltimore.

diPRAMPERO, P.E., Pendergast, D.R., Wilson, C.W., and Rennie, D.W. 1974. Energetics of swimming in man. *J. Appl. Physiol.* **37**:1-5.

HOLMÉR, I. 1978. Time relations: Running, swimming and skating performances. In: B. Eriksson and B. Furberg (eds.), *Swimming Medicine IV*, pp. 361-366. University Park Press, Baltimore.

McMURRAY, R.G. 1977. Comparative efficiencies of conventional and superswim fin designs. *Human Factors* **19**:495-501.

PENDERGAST, D.R., diPrampero, P.E., Craig, A.B., Wilson, D.R., and Rennie, D.W. 1977. Quantitative analysis of the front crawl in men and women. *J. Appl. Physiol. Respirat. Environ. Exercise Physiol.* **43**:475-479.

RACKAM, G.W. 1975. An analysis of arm propulsion in swimming. In: L. Lewillie and J.P. Clarys (eds.), *Swimming II*, pp. 174-179. University Park Press, Baltimore.

REISCHLE, K. 1979. A kinematic investigation of movement patterns in swimming with photo-optical methods. In: J. Terauds and E.W. Bedingfield (eds.), *Swimming III*, pp. 127-136. University Park Press, Baltimore.

RENNIE, D.W., Pendergast, D.E., and diPrampero, P.E. 1975. Energetics of swimming in man. In: L. Lewillie and J.P. Clarys (eds.), *Swimming II*, pp. 97-104. University Park Press, Baltimore.

SCHLEIHAUF, R.E. 1979. A hydrodynamic analysis of swimming propulsion. In: J. Terauds and E.W. Bedingfield (eds.), *Swimming III*, pp. 70-109. University Park Press, Baltimore.

STONER, L.J., and Luedtke, D.L. 1979. Variations in front crawl and back crawl arm strokes of varsity swimmers using hand paddles. In: J. Terauds and E.W. Bedingfield (eds.), *Swimming III*, pp. 281-288. University Park Press, Baltimore.

Three-Dimensional Analysis of Hand Propulsion in the Sprint Front Crawl Stroke

Robert Schleihauf, Lisa Gray, and Joseph DeRose
Columbia University, New York, USA

Previous work from this laboratory has involved the study of swimming film data in conjunction with background research from fluid laboratories. This research strategy allows the estimation of hand and forearm propulsive forces from film in any style of stroke, and the results have been shown to be reasonably accurate using a variety of tethered swimming experiments (Schleihauf, 1979).

The current research on swimming propulsion has been designed to extend previous work in two ways. First, the accuracy of the propulsive force estimations have been improved with a more rigorous three-dimensional data analysis procedure. Second, a sampling of 25 highly skilled freestylers has been analyzed and estimates of the hand and forearm propulsive forces and arm joint torques were obtained for each of the subjects. The kinematic and kinetic data of the sample have been surveyed and four measures which seem to characterize highly skilled sprint crawl stroke technique have been isolated. The four measures stand out so clearly in the data that it is felt they can be used with confidence in the design of future stroke instruction and stroke correction programs.

It should be noted that the data reduction and analysis procedures which have been applied to this freestyle study may also be applied to a wide range of questions on swimming performance. As a result, a description is given of the steps through which triaxial (or biaxial) film data may be analyzed to yield estimates of the most important kinetic variables associated with propulsive arm motions.

Three-Dimensional Film Data Analysis Procedures

The swimmers studied in this article were filmed on location at Princeton University, Columbia University, and Fairfield Preparatory

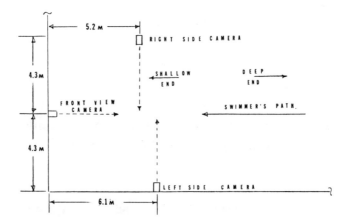

Figure 1 — Tri-axial camera set-up.

School. The "highly skilled" sample was defined as only those swimmers whose competitive best time was less than or equal to 49.9 sec in the 100-yd freestyle.

Three battery-operated movie cameras and underwater housings were set up as shown in Figure 1. The swimmers swam three to five 25-yd sprints toward the front view camera, and the trial with the best centered arm stroke data was selected for analysis.

Eight points were studied from the front and side view data on each arm. The body landmark points were: I, long finger tip (lighted with sub-miniature bulb); W, wrist joint center (lighted); T, index finger metacarpeal phalangeal (MP) joint (lighted); P, little finger MP joint (lighted); E, elbow joint (not lighted); S, shoulder joint (not lighted); N, clavicular notch (not lighted); and W, waist (lighted).

An estimate of the XYZ data on the pull was determined by a simple method which took into account the phase and scale differences between the cameras. A more accurate film data reduction procedure, such as the "DLT" method would be preferred in future work, although the necessary, large rigid reference cube would be difficult to use under field conditions.

Hand Motion Analysis

In order to use the Schleihauf data (1979) to estimate propulsive hand force, it was necessary to first determine the hand angle of pitch and sweepback from the film data. The hand's angle of pitch was defined as the angle between the hand plane and its line of motion. The estimation of hand pitch angle from the XYZ coordinate data on the four hand points was determined as follows.

Figure 2a shows that the cross product of vectors IW and TP yields HP, a vector perpendicular to the hand plane. Figure 2b shows that the

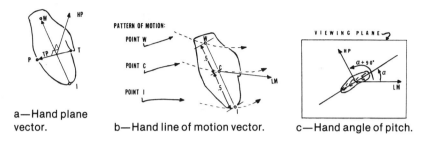

a—Hand plane
vector.   b—Hand line of motion vector.   c—Hand angle of pitch.

Figure 2—Hand angle of pitch.

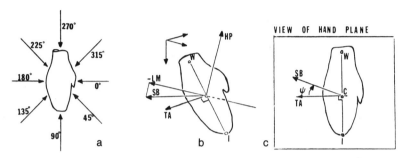

Figure 3—Hand sweepback angle—ψ.

first derivative of the position vector to point C determines the LM (line of motion) vector of the hand. Further, Figure 2c shows that the viewing plane which includes the two vectors LM and HP isolates the hand in edge view. Inspection of Figure 2c shows that the angle of pitch of the hand (α) is the angle between LM and HP less 90°.

$$\alpha = \text{TAN}^{-1}\ [(|\overrightarrow{\text{LM}} \times \overrightarrow{\text{HP}}|)/(\overrightarrow{\text{LM}} \times \overrightarrow{\text{HP}})] - 90°. \qquad (1)$$

The hand sweepback angle defines the leading edge of the hand. The measurement convention for sweepback is shown in Figure 3a, and the calculation procedure is as follows.

Figure 3b illustrates the $\overrightarrow{\text{SB}}$ vector, which is defined as the projection of the $-\overrightarrow{\text{LM}}$ vector in the HP plane. The $\overrightarrow{\text{TA}}$ (transverse axis) vector is perpendicular to vector $\overrightarrow{\text{IW}}$ and falls in the hand plane. The sweepback angle becomes the angle measured in a clockwise direction between the vectors $\overrightarrow{\text{TA}}$ and $\overrightarrow{\text{SB}}$ (for the right hand).

Given the angle of pitch, sweepback, and the hand speed at its aero-dynamic center, the magnitude of the lift and drag forces acting on the hand may be estimated using the data presented in Schleihauf (1979) and Equations 2 and 3. (Note: The actual location of the hand aerodynamic center will change with varying angles of pitch and sweepback. For our purposes, the aerodynamic center was estimated as being fixed at a point which was .6 of the distance between the wrist and long finger tip points.)

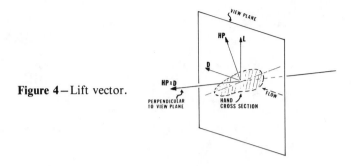

Figure 4—Lift vector.

$$|L| = \tfrac{1}{2}\varrho V^2 C_L S \tag{2}$$

$$|D| = \tfrac{1}{2}\varrho V^2 C_D S, \tag{3}$$

where $|L|$ = magnitude of hand lift force; $|D|$ = magnitude of drag force; ϱ = density of water; V = hand speed; C_L = coefficient of lift; C_D = coefficient of drag; and S = hand plane area. The drag force vector is given by Equation 4:

$$\vec{D} = |\vec{D}|\left(-\frac{\vec{LM}}{|\vec{LM}|}\right). \tag{4}$$

Figure 4 shows that the lift vector falls in the plane "VP" and is therefore perpendicular to HP × D. The lift vector is also perpendicular to the drag force vector D. As a result, the lift vector is given by Equation 5:

$$\vec{L} = |\vec{L}|\,[(\vec{D} \times (\vec{HP} \times \vec{D}))/|\vec{D} \times (\vec{HP} \times \vec{D})|]. \tag{5}$$

Next, the resultant hand propulsive force vector (P) is given by Equation 6:

$$\vec{P} = \vec{L} + \vec{D}. \tag{6}$$

Forearm Motion Analysis

The critical parameters of forearm propulsion may be determined through procedures virtually identical to those used for the hand. For the purposes of this study, preliminary data on forearm C_L and C_D values were used to determine approximate $\vec{L}$, $\vec{D}$, and $\vec{P}$ force vectors.

The forearm forces, combined with the hand forces, will account in large part for the total arm propulsion. More details from the fluid lab on the upper arm characteristics and the interaction of the various arm segments on each other will be needed to extend this work in the future.

Arm Joint Reaction Force/Joint Torque Computation

The computation of joint reaction forces and torques in three dimensions was accomplished through procedures specified by Andrews (1974). In our calculations, all point velocity and acceleration vectors were determined through differentiation of the position vectors using a digital-filtering data-smoothing program. The following simplifying assumptions were also made: (a) the angular velocity and acceleration component about each segment's long axis was set equal to zero; (b) the buoyant and gravitational forces were assumed equal, opposite and co-linear; (c) the forearm propulsion was assumed to act at the forearm center of mass; and (d) the upper arm propulsive force was ignored.

Results and Interpretation

In order to illustrate the measures computed on all subjects, the data output of a single "example" subject will be used. In the example, the swimmer had the following characteristics: height, 1.88 m; weight, 70.3 kg; best time for 100 yd, 46.3 sec.

Concurrent with the description of example swimmer's data, the trends observed in the entire sample will be reported and the findings on swimming propulsion which seem to be characteristic of highly skilled swimmers as a group will be stressed. Further, the interpretation of hand propulsive force data will be emphasized, for it is felt that in any stroke correction process the swimmer's attention is most easily focused on the control of hand motions.

Hand Speed Data

The typical form of the hand speed versus time curve, plus the front, side and bottom view pulling patterns is shown below for the swimmer's right arm pull. With this swimmer, "propulsive" hand speed points were defined as occurring at film frames 5-18. In the remaining frames the hand is sliding through the water, with high speed but low force. In previous research (Schleihauf, 1979), it has been hypothesized that highly skilled swimmers choose to deliver their highest values of propulsive hand speed at points in the stroke where diagonal pulling patterns are being followed. To determine the "diagonality" of pulling patterns, a pattern angle statistic was computed as follows:

$$PA = [(\frac{PA_1 + PA_2 + PA_3}{3})_{right} + (\frac{PA_1 + PA_2 + PA_3}{3})_{left}] \div 2, \quad (7)$$

where $PA_{1,2,3}$ = the angle between the $-\overrightarrow{LM}$ vector and the forward

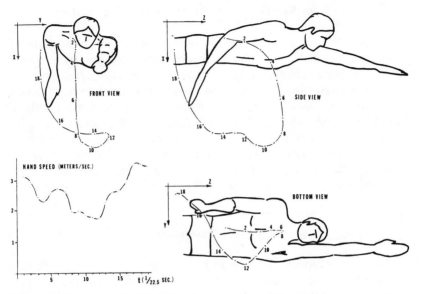

Figure 5—Example swimmer fingertip pattern/hand speed data.

direction at the first, second and third fastest propulsive hand speeds, on the right or left arm pull.

The swimmer's PA statistic was computed as 66.9°. The same measure of pulling pattern angle at key velocity points was computed for swimmers in the entire sample. The final result was:

$$\text{sample pattern angle} = 63.1 \pm 6.8°.$$

As a result, it can be concluded that highly skilled swimmers, as a group, tend to deliver their highest propulsive hand speeds at points in their stroking patterns aimed about 63° diagonal to their bodies' line of motion.

Hand Force Data

Figure 6 shows the hand lift, drag and propulsive force vectors at three selected points in the right side view. Figure 7 shows two curves of the propulsive force values calculated at each frame in the right arm underwater pull. The upper curve represents the hand force vector magnitude (total hand force), and the lower curve represents the component of the hand propulsion vector in the forward direction (effective hand force).

These data on the right arm show that a pulse of force is delivered on the last one-third of the stroke. In order to quantify the relative size of the force peak used in each arm stroke, a "peak force index" (PFI) was defined as follows:

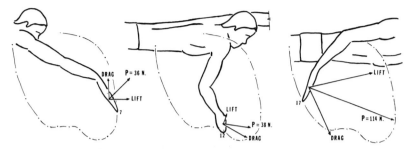

Figure 6—Hand propulsive force diagram.

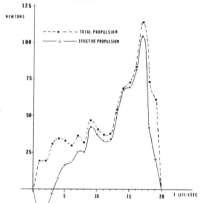

Figure 7—Right hand propulsive force.

$$PFI = [(\frac{P_{MAX}}{P_{AVE}})_{Right} + (\frac{P_{MAX}}{P_{AVE}})_{Left}] \div 2, \qquad (8)$$

where, for the single arm pull: P_{MAX} = the maximum hand force magnitude and P_{AVE} = the average hand force magnitude.

For this swimmer, the average Peak Force Index was 2.28. For the entire sample, the average Peak Force Index was:

Sample Average Peak Force Index = 2.37 ± .32.

Given these data, it is clear that highly skilled swimmers use force distributions which involve peak forces more than twice as large as the average hand force.

Given the information that good swimmers use a force peak in their propulsive curves, the "location" of this force peak during the course of the pull needs to be defined. In order to quantify the peak force location the Peak Force Distribution Index (PFD) was computed as follows:

$$PFD = [(\frac{t_1 + t_2 + t_3}{3} \div t_T)_{Right}$$
$$+ (\frac{t_1 + t_2 + t_3}{3} \div t_T)_{Left}] \div 2, \tag{9}$$

where t_1 = time to maximum total hand force; t_2 = time to second largest total hand force; t_3 = time to third largest total hand force; and t_T = total time of the pull (from fingertip entry to fingertip exit).

The PFD was .79 for this swimmer. Thus, the swimmer's largest hand forces occurred at a point about 79% of the way into the stroke. For the entire sample, the Hand Force Distribution Index was:

Sample Hand Force Distribution Index = .78 ± .08.

Next, the lift/drag ratios used at the three largest total hand propulsive forces on each arm must be defined. As a result, we calculated a "Scull Index" (SI) as follows:

$$SI = [(\frac{(L/D)_1 + (L/D)_2 + (L/D)_3}{3})_{Right}$$
$$+ (\frac{(L/D)_1 + (L/D)_2 + (L/D)_3}{3})_{Left}] \div 2, \tag{10}$$

where $(L/D)_{1,2,3}$ = the lift drag ratios at the points of the first, second and third largest total hand propulsive forces.

Substitution into Equation 10 yielded a Scull Index of 1.11 for the sample swimmer. The Scull Index for the entire sample was:

Sample Scull Index = 1.0 ± .19.

As a result, it should be noted that the key propulsive forces produced by highly skilled swimmers are produced by approximately equal combinations of lift and drag forces.

Finally, the net effective hand propulsion produced by the combined action of both arm pulls may be computed through superimposition of data on the right and left hand force curves. Further, the net effective hand force curve per unit time may be computed. For the entire sample, the average net effective hand force per unit time was:

Sample average NP_E/time = 48.0 ± 17.7 Newtons.

Note that the standard deviation for this measure was quite large. The variation in the average hand force data was primarily due to two sources: (a) while all swimmers were asked to sprint, not all achieved the same speed (the average velocity ranged from 1.48 to 1.92 m/sec). Slower body velocities will generally be related to less propulsive force; (b) not all swimmers used equally streamlined body position in their swimming motions.

The "average" swimmer in the sample swam at 1.66 m/sec and produced 48 Newtons of effective hand propulsion. The average effective forearm propulsion was ca. 24 Newtons. In steady-state (uniform average velocity) swimming, the total propulsive force produced must equal the total active body drag. The equation is:

$$P_{EH} + P_{EF} + P_{EU} + P_{EK} + P_{EINT} = D_T, \qquad (11)$$

where P_{EH} = the effective hand propulsion;[1] P_{EF} = the effective forearm propulsion; P_{EU} = the effective upper arm propulsion; P_{EINT} = the effective interaction effect at all segments to be determined by future fluid lab work); P_{EK} = the effective kicking propulsion; and D_T = drag due to trunk and head motion. Approximate values for the terms in the equation are: $P_{EH} \sim 48$ Newtons; $P_{EF} \sim 24$ Newtons; $P_{EU} + P_{EK} \sim 0$; $P_{EINT} \sim 0$; $D_T \sim$ the passive drag of the body = 76 Newtons (Clarys, 1979: 24°C, V = 1.66 m/sec). Substitutions of the estimated values into Equation 11 yields:

$$P_{EH} + P_{EF} + P_{EU} + P_{EK} + P_{EINT} = D_T$$
$$48 + 24 + 0 + 0 \sim 76$$
$$72 \sim 76.$$

These results show that passive drag values, when combined with effective propulsive force values, yielded results which reasonably approximated the findings expected theoretically. This is, of course, a very rough computation procedure. It is encouraging, however, to see that with this type of approach it may soon be possible to achieve the integration of research findings in the two fields of body drag and swimming propulsion.

Arm Joint Torque

The arm joint torques computed in this study were approximate, as simplifying assumptions were made. We intended to make only a first step in the estimation of swimming joint torques in three dimensions. However, the results will be of value in the qualitative interpretation of swimming data, particularly with reference to specificity of strength training (Schleihauf, 1983, this volume).

Figure 8 shows the magnitude of the estimated joint torque vectors, plotted versus time. It should be noted that the total elbow joint torque

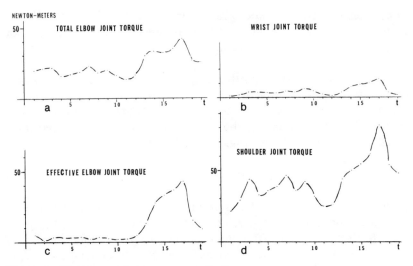

Figure 8—Right arm joint torque magnitudes.

vector includes a component which acts along the joint axis. This torque component reflects the net muscular forces (the effective elbow joint torque) acting at this hinge joint. Figure 9 illustrates that the actual torque vectors acting at the elbow and shoulder are very much three-dimensional quantities. The side view (Figure 9a) shows the X and Z vector components of the effective elbow and shoulder joint torques at the point of peak propulsive hand force for the sample swimmer. The bottom view (Figure 9b) shows the Y and Z components of the same vectors. Finally, Figure 9c is a diagonal view showing all three vector components on an identical scale.

Conclusion

A detailed understanding of the biomechanics of highly skilled sprint freestyle will be of value to swimmers, coaches and researchers at a number of different levels. First, the objectives of swimming instruction programs should become more clearly defined with the aid of the findings presented in this article. Further, it is hoped that the analytic procedure described may be used to help answer a wide variety of questions on swimming performance in the future.

Acknowledgments

The authors are indebted to Joseph Higgins (Teacher's College, Columbia University, New York City), John Hollerbach (Massachusetts Institute of Technology, Cambridge, MA), and Jesus Dapena (University of Massachusetts, Amherst, MA) for their helpful advice.

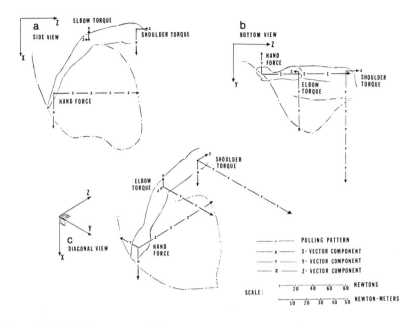

Figure 9 — Hand force — arm joint torque vector components.

Note

1. The active drag due to hand, forearm, upper arm and kicking motions are normally placed on the right-hand side of Equation 11. However, the calculation of *effective* propulsive forces takes into account both negative (active drag) and positive contributions caused by body part motions. Thus, the active drag measures are implicitly included on the left-hand side of Equation 11.

References

ANDREWS, J.G. 1974. Biomechanical analysis of human motion. *Kinesiology Review IV*, pp. 32-42. AAHPER.

CLARYS, I.P. 1979. Human morphology and hydrodynamics. In: J. Terauds and W. Bedingfield (eds.), *Swimming III*, pp. 3-41. University Park Press, Baltimore.

SCHLEIHAUF, R.E. 1979. A hydrodynamic analysis of swimming propulsion. In: J. Terauds and W. Bedingfield (eds.), *Swimming III*, pp. 70-109. University Park Press, Baltimore.

SCHLEIHAUF, R.E. 1983. Specificity of strength training in swimming: A biomechanical viewpoint. In: A.P. Hollander, P.A. Huijing and G. de Groot (eds.), *Biomechanics and Medicine in Swimming*, pp. 184-191. Human Kinetics, Champaign, IL.

Specificity of Strength Training in Swimming: A Biomechanical Viewpoint

Robert E. Schleihauf, Jr.
Columbia University, New York, USA

Specificity of strength training has traditionally been investigated by the exercise physiologist. Studies by Ikai (1970), and Lesmes et al. (1978) have yielded important information for use in the design of strength training programs. It should be noted that specificity of strength training may also be evaluated from a biomechanical viewpoint.

An underlying principle in strength training specificity is that maximal benefit may be derived from exercise motions which closely simulate those used in performance (Costill, 1980). In the analysis of swimming strength training, we are in a position to evaluate this principle objectively in light of recent biomechanical studies of the swimming arm motion (Schleihauf, 1983, this volume). Detailed information on the pulling motions, hand forces and arm joint torques used by skilled swimmers may help point the way toward more specific strength training mechanisms.

In the discussion of current strength training methods, reference is made to the popular swimming bench exercisers which use "isokinetic" resistance. At the outset it should be stressed that these "bench exercisers" provide the best type of strength training currently available to swimmers. Further, the design of these devices is in many respects ingenious. Nevertheless, the writer feels that the design of future strength training devices will allow for marked improvements in the specificity of swimming strength training.

In particular it must be recognized that the basic design of bench exercisers was derived before sculling motions were recognized as important. The fundamental differences between straight-back exercise motions and diagonal swimming motions may, in fact, explain the recent findings of Olbrecht and Clarys (1983, this volume). Their research has shown that the EMG records of arm motions used in exercise are distinctly dissimilar to those used in swimming performance.

This article presents reasons for the "nonspecific" EMG records observed in strength training. Further, it describes a new training mechanism which may be used in the future to achieve a high degree of strength training specificity for competitive swimmers.

Training for Movement Speed Specificity

A common approach used to gauge ideal movement speeds on a bench exerciser is to measure the stroke frequency used in performance and duplicate this frequency in exercise. The movement time of the pull in exercise should therefore approximately equal the time spent on the pull during swimming. However, the hand speeds actually used will differ significantly between swimming and exercise for two reasons.

First, the distance traveled by the hand, measured relative to the body, will be greater in the water where diagonal motions and longer pulling paths are used. On the bench, the single rope between the hand and pulley can only offer resistance on a straight line, and therefore, the pull will be straighter and consequently shorter. Thus, although the time of pull may be the same in each situation, the distance traveled in exercise is less than in swimming, and therefore the speed (= distance/time) must also be less.

Second, the uniform movement speed demanded by isokinetic resistance will not allow duplication of the peak hand speeds, which are the most critical. Figure 1 shows the hand velocity curve, calculated relative to the body, for a typical stroking action. The critical movement speeds, which involve the stroking actions that require the most strength, are shown by line A. Line B represents the average hand speed based on the true distance of pull used in swimming, measured relative to the body. Finally, line C shows the exercise movement speed which would result from straighter pulling motions, performed at the same stroke frequency on the exerciser as those in the water.

Figure 1 shows that exercise hand speeds will be 2.4 times slower than the critical hand speeds which occur in swimming even though identical pulling frequencies would be used in each case.

Exercise Resistance Specificity

Isokinetic resistance requires that a uniform, 100% effort be applied throughout the course of the exercise motion. Data in Schleihauf et al. (1983, this volume) indicate that distinct peaks are evident in the hand force and joint torque vs time curves of skilled swimmers. This information strongly implies that nonuniform "effort" distributions are used in swimming.

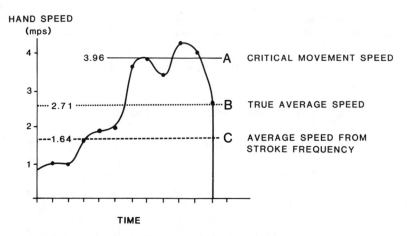

Figure 1 — Hand speeds calculated relative to the body.

One can assume that near maximal effort is expended at the finishing peak of a joint torque curve. However, the much lower values found at midstroke imply that submaximal effort expenditure is used. In Schleihauf et al. (1983) Figure 8d shows that at frame 11 (mid-stroke), the swimmer used a shoulder joint torque of 24.8 N•m. At frame 17 (on the finish), the shoulder joint torque magnitude was much larger, 81.7 N•m. There is no question that the sharp increase from 24.8 to 81.7 N•m within the space of .27 sec was due to an increase in effort by the swimmer moving into the last one-third of the stroke movement. This information implies that a uniform, 100% effort contraction on dry land would yield much higher force output at the middle of the stroke than is actually used in swimming. As a result, isokinetic resistance will produce distributions of pulling force in exercise which will be markedly dissimilar to those used in swimming performances.

Of course, doing more work than necessary at the middle of the pull may be ignored as a training deficiency as long as the more critical finishing actions of the stroke are overloaded properly. Unfortunately, traditional bench exerciser designs may not create this necessary overload at the end of the pull.

Figure 2a shows the approximate pulling pattern followed on a bench exerciser. The curved pattern on the finish of the pull (frames 4-7) is similar to a true swimming motion. However, the resistance provided by isokinetic exercisers acts only on the straight line between the hand grip and pulley mechanism. Further, the magnitude of the resistance is dependent on the rate at which the rope is pulled away from the resistance device.

Inspection of Figure 2a shows that the length of rope pulled from the resistance device between frames 5 and 6, and 6 and 7 is much less than at earlier frames. As a result, the resistance offered swimmers will be much

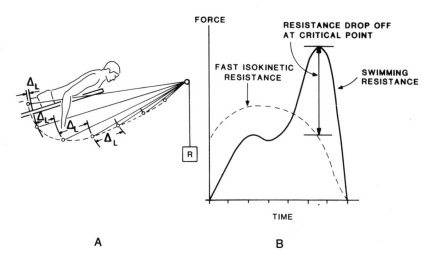

Figure 2—Effect of curvilinear pull on exercise resistance.

less at the end of the exercise pull if their motions are done smoothly. Figure 2b shows the swimming hand force output curve, and a hypothetical curve representing the exercise hand force output. Note the difference between the curves at the point where peak propulsive forces are used. This result implies that the muscle groups of critical importance in swimming propulsion will not be overloaded by traditional bench exercisers.

The problem with the exercise resistance is that it can only act in a straight line. Even if curved patterns are used, as in Figure 2a, the rope cannot resist any component of motion which is perpendicular to the line between the hand grip and pulley. Of course, it would be possible to maintain a high exercise resistance if the swimmer was forced to pull in a straight line away from the pulley (see Figure 3). Unfortunately, the pull in Figure 3 in no way approximates the curvilinear pattern used in swimming, especially in the critical finishing motion where the hand sweeps upward toward the surface.

The fact is, no single straight line could ever be expected to yield an approximation of the ever changing directions of pull used in swimming. However, Schleihauf et al. (1983, this volume) has shown that the most strenuous pulling motions occur within a limited segment at the end of the pulling pattern. Therefore, a straight-line resistance tangent to the pulling pattern at the critical range of the pull would seem to better suit the needs of the swimmer. Figure 4 shows how a straight line resistance would be best applied to freestyle and breaststroke motions.

The lines of pull shown in Figure 4 would allow maximal resistance to be applied with patterns of motion similar to those used in swimming. Further, only the critical range of motion would be exercised. The middle

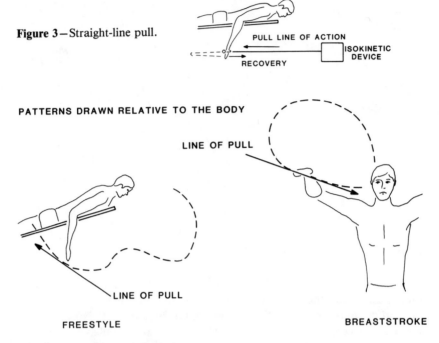

Figure 3—Straight-line pull.

PATTERNS DRAWN RELATIVE TO THE BODY

LINE OF PULL

LINE OF PULL

FREESTYLE   BREASTSTROKE

Figure 4—Critical stroking actions.

and beginning parts of the stroke, which involve submaximal efforts, would be eliminated from the exercise routine.

Let us now consider in detail the specificity of exercise which would be achieved with a breaststroke exercise motion. Note: the breaststroke was chosen because it provides the simplest and clearest example of the points to be emphasized. The more complicated freestyle example is discussed immediately after the breaststroke.

Figure 5 shows a typical hand force output curve for the breaststroke, along with the approximate exercise resistance "felt" by the swimmer. At first glance, it would appear that the exercise motion of Figure 5a is virtually identical to that used in swimming (e.g., see exercise line of motion). Further, the speed of the exercise motion could be selected to be close to that used in swimming. Finally, the exercise resistance magnitude is nearly identical to that used in swimming (Figure 5b).

There is, however, an important aspect of the exercise motion which is markedly dissimilar to the swimming action. The resistance *vector* is not at all the same when the two are compared. With the exercise motion, the resistance vector must fall on the straight line shown in Figure 5a. The joint torque produced with the exercise resistance will be primarily in the elbow joint and will produce a twisting effect in the plane of the forearm motion.

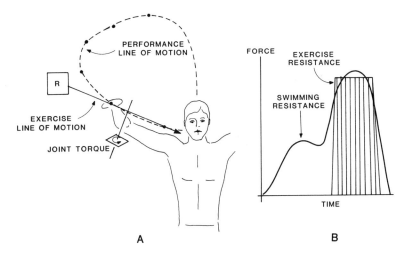

Figure 5—Breaststroke strength training.

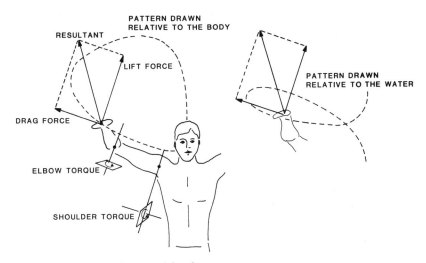

Figure 6—Breaststroke propulsive forces.

In swimming, the resistance vector occurs in three-dimensional space and includes a large component at right angles to the line of motion. Figure 6a shows that the forces produced in breaststroke swimming will be derived in part from a large shoulder joint torque which will balance the lift component of hand force. The net muscular action at the shoulder joint will cause a twisting force about the long axis of the upper arm. This important upper arm rotation torque will in no way be approximated by the exercise resistance of Figure 5a.

As a result, it is apparent that a single-line, single-dimension resistance device will never be able to duplicate the three-dimensional hand

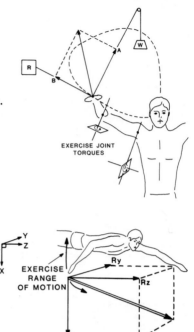

Figure 7—Two-dimensional resistive force.

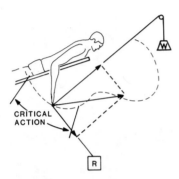

Figure 8—Two-dimensional freestyle training.

Figure 9—Three-dimensional exercise resistance.

resistance which occurs in actual swimming. Fortunately, there is a solution to the exercise resistance problem, allowing the three-dimensional joint torques used in swimming to be closely approximated by those used in exercise.

Multidimensional Exercise Resistance

Figure 7 shows a two-dimensional resistance device which will simultaneously duplicate the lift and drag components of swimming propulsive force. Resistance A in the figure must actively "pull" on the swimmer and could be either a pulley weight, stretch cord or spring. Resistance B could be any type of resistance, including isokinetic type.

Similarly, Figure 8 shows how a two-dimensional resistance setup could be applied to the finishing action of the freestyle arm pull. Further, three-dimensional resistance could be generated by adding a third line of resistance as shown in Figure 9.

Guided by the present knowledge of swimming biomechanics, the multidimensional exercise resistances used in training could be "tuned" to provide a combination of force components similar to those used in actual performances. The specific arrangement of the resistances could be adjusted to stress the patterns of motion preferred by an individual swimmer. Further, the magnitudes of resistance could be varied to provide overload training or speed-specific training designed for neuromuscular specificity.

Conclusions

It is clear that the single-dimensional training techniques fall far short of simulating the three-dimensional resistance encountered in water. We hope the concept of multidimensional exercise resistance will allow dramatic improvement in swimming training programs in the future. For the present, the most important implication of this article is that research in swimming must involve the integration of biomechanical and physiological viewpoints. Such an integrated approach will increase the quality of research findings and, in turn, competitive swimmers' performances.

References

COSTILL, D., Sharp, R., and Troup, T. Feb. 1980. Muscle strength: Contributions to sprint swimming. *Swim. World*, pp. 29-34.

IKAI, M. Sept. 1970. Training of muscle strength and power in athletes. Paper presented at the World Congress of Sports Medicine, Oxford, England.

LESMES, G.R., Costill, D.L., Coyle, E.F., and Fink, W.I. 1978. Muscle strength and power changes during maximal isokinetic training. *Med. Sci. Sport* **10**:266-269.

OLBRECHT, J., and Clarys, J.P. 1983. EMG of specific strength training exercises for the front crawl. In: A.P. Hollander, P. Huijing, and G. de Groot (eds.), *Biomechanics and Medicine in Swimming*, pp. 136-141. Human Kinetics, Champaign, IL.

SCHLEIHAUF, R.E., Gray, L., and DeRose, J. 1983. Three-dimensional analysis of hand propulsion in sprint front crawl stroke. In: A.P. Hollander, P. Huijing, and G. de Groot (eds.), *Biomechanics and Medicine in Swimming*. pp. 173-183. Human Kinetics, Champaign, IL.

Propulsive Force Generated by Swimmers during a Turning Motion

Goro Takahashi, Akira Yoshida, and Shozo Tsubakimoto
University of Tsukuba, Ibaraki, Japan

Mitsumasa Miyashita
University of Tokyo, Japan

Scientific research in swimming originated more than 70 years ago. Since that time, many research results about swimming have been published. Recently, Miller (1975), Clarys (1979) and Holmér (1979) reviewed the studies on swimming from various standpoints. However, they did not describe the swimmer's turn; in fact, only a few scientific investigations (Nicol and Krüger, 1979) on this aspect of competitive swimming have been done.

The main purpose of this study was to investigate the relationship between the force generated by the swimmer against the wall during a turning motion and the horizontal velocity of swimmers after turning.

Methods

The subjects were six male adults—three highly trained and three recreational swimmers. Their mean height and weight were 171.0 cm (range 160.0-181.0 cm) and 70.7 kg (range 65.0-85.0 kg), respectively.

In the first condition, the subject was asked to perform the glide (static start) under the surface of the water. The swimmer exerts force against the wall with his best effort and glides as far as possible with no stroke motion. In the second condition, the subject performed the flip turn 10 m away from the wall with his best technique, and after the turn, glided the same way as in the first condition. Three trials of each glide and flip turn were recorded for each subject, and the best performance was selected for subjective analysis by the coach monitoring the video film.

A waterproofed stainless steel force platform was devised (Takei-Kiki, Tokyo) to measure the force generated by the swimmer on the wall. The size of the platform was 120 cm width × 80 cm length × 11 cm thick. The force applied to the platform was detected by four piezoelectric sensors and recorded on magnetic tape (Sony, Tokyo). The data recorded on tape was analyzed by computer using A-D converters (Nippon Koden model ATAC 2300, Tokyo). The static calibrations were performed on dry land by several known weights before and after the measurements. In this study, the water pressure was neglected because the feet were positioned near the surface of the water.

In order to measure the horizontal velocity of the swimmer, a speed meter (Ohmich and Miyashita, 1981) (Takei-Kiki, Tokyo) was attached to the subject's waist. These measurements could be performed only during the glide (static start).

An electrogoniometer was attached at the subject's right knee in order to record the change in the knee joint angle. In order to monitor the turning motion a video camera was set inside the swimming pool.

Results and Discussion

The typical example of the changes in force on the platform, horizontal velocity of the swimmer's waist and knee joint angle during the glide (static start) is demonstrated in Figure 1. The subject takes a ready position; in this figure, the knee joint was slightly flexed and the waist was already moving forwards before the feet touched the wall. After the feet were against the wall, velocity increased and the knee joint was extended almost linearly up to the release. On the other hand, the force increased in two increments up to the peak force (833 N) at 0.07 sec before the release, and then rapidly decreased.

The knee joint was at about 120° of flexion when the peak force was observed. Ae (1982) reported that the peak force during the vertical jump was recorded in the range of knee angle from 120 to 140°. Though the peak force in vertical jumping is greater than in the push-off for the glide in water, it is interesting that the peak forces were observed in both cases at approximately the same angle of the knee joint. The same range of knee extension has been reported during maximal isokinetic contraction, that is, dynamic peak torque values occurred in a relatively narrow range of movement (114-125°) (Thorstensson et al., 1976).

There was a statistically significant, positive relationship between the initial velocity of the swimmer's waist and the impulse generated by the swimmer against the wall (Figure 2). The three highly trained swimmers showed the greater impulses and higher initial velocities than the three recreational swimmers (see Table 1).

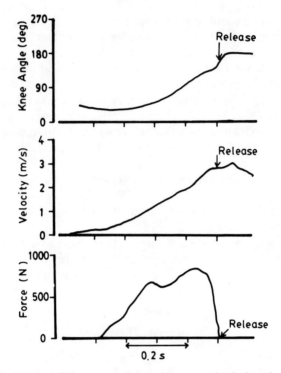

Figure 1 — Variations of force, velocity and knee angle during the glide (static start).

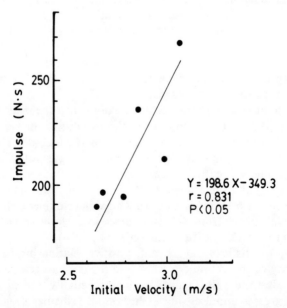

Figure 2 — Relationship between impulse and initial velocity during the glide.

Table 1

Means and Standard Deviations of Impulse, Peak Force, Initial Velocity, Maximal Flexion Angle of the Knee and Duration of Push-off[a]

Subjects[b]	Impulse (N·sec) G	Impulse (N·sec) FT	Peak force (N) G	Peak force (N) FT	Initial velocity (m/sec) G	Initial velocity (m/sec) FT	Maximal flexion angle of the knee (deg.) G	Maximal flexion angle of the knee (deg.) FT	Duration of push-off (sec) G	Duration of push-off (sec) FT
1	236.9	249.5	804	1176	2.87	—	65	82	0.41	0.35
2	268.8	351.1	1205	1999	3.07	—	61	98	0.38	0.29
3	213.1	304.8	833	1960	2.99	—	41	49	0.38	0.44
4	189.9	230.2	764	862	2.67	—	41	33	0.36	0.44
5	194.9	215.4	1352	1323	2.80	—	57	45	0.31	0.57
6	196.7	225.1	803	1019	2.70	—	49	49	0.45	0.44
$\bar{X}$	216.7	262.7	960	1390	2.85	—	52.3	59.3	0.38	0.42
SD	30.8	53.8	230	440	0.12	—	9.4	22.8	0.04	0.09
t	a		NS		—		NS		NS	

[a] $t = 3.095$; $p < 0.05$, NS = no significance; G = glide; FT = flip turn.
[b] Subjects 1-3: highly trained swimmers; subjects 4-6: recreational swimmers.

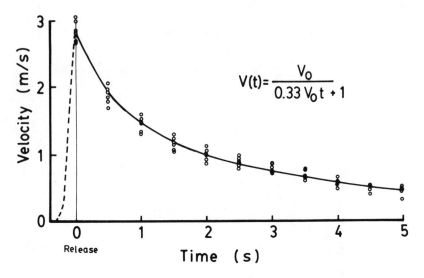

Figure 3 — Change in velocity of the swimmer after the static start.

The velocity variations throughout the glide after the static start are shown in Figure 3. The velocity decreases with time hyperbolically, which is almost the same as was demonstrated by Karpovich and Pestrecov (1939) for a glide on the water's surface.

The following hyperbolic equation was determined for the six subjects by the least squares method:

$$V = \frac{V_0}{0.33 \, V_0 \, t + 1}, \tag{1}$$

where V is the velocity at time of t and V_0 is the mean initial velocity (2.85 m/sec). The constant value of 0.33 was very similar to the value (0.37) calculated from the data reported by Karpovich and Pestrecov (1939).

During the flip turn, quite different force curves were obtained (Figure 4). When the feet were against the platform, a large force was recorded, but almost immediately it decreased to zero. Then, 0.08 sec later the force curve with three peaks appeared. These force variations might have been due to the complicated motion of the flip turn, that is, sculling the hands, stretching the arms, rotating the trunk, etc. This force curve with four peaks was integrated over time to determine the impulse during the flip turn.

The means and standard deviations of the impulse, peak force, maximal flexion angle of knee joint and duration of generating the force against the wall are summarized in Table 1. During the flip turn, the highly trained swimmers showed greater impulses than the recreational

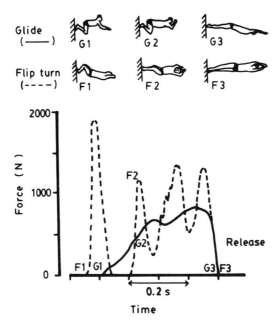

Figure 4—Comparison of force during the flip turn with force during the glide.

swimmers. However, the maximal knee flexions of the highly trained swimmers were clearly less than those of the recreational swimmers. Also, the time duration for exerting the force—push-off—seemed to be shorter for the highly trained swimmers.

We found no significant difference in peak force, maximal flexion angle of knee joint and duration of push-off between the glide and the flip turn. However, the impulse during the flip turn was significantly greater ($p < 0.05$) than that during the glide. Also, we found a significant positive relationship between the two impulses (Figure 5).

In this study, the swimmer's velocity after the release could not be measured for the flip turn. But it might be expected from the results shown in Figure 2, where even in the flip turn the greater the impulse, the faster the initial velocity.

The wide fluctuations seen in the force platform readings for the flip turn were not explained by the data obtained in this study. To do so will require further research including electromyography to study which muscle groups were involved. Perhaps those results could suggest a technique to eliminate or reduce these fluctuations.

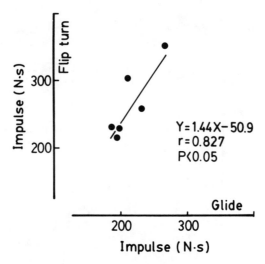

Figure 5—Relationship of impulses between the glide and the flip turn.

References

AE, M. 1982. A biomechanical study on jump for height contributions, body segments and the mechanism of the take-off. Unpublished doctoral dissertation, University of Tsukuba, Japan.

CLARYS, J.P. 1979. Human morphology and hydrodynamics. In: J. Terauds and E.W. Bedingfield (eds.), *Swimming III*, pp. 3-41. University Park Press, Baltimore.

HOLMĒR, I. 1979. Physiology of swimming man. In: R.S. Hutton and D.I. Miller (eds.), *Exercise Sport Sciences Review* (vol. 7), pp. 87-123. Franklin Institute Press, Philadelphia.

KARPOVICH, P.V., and Pestrecov, K. 1939. Mechanical work and efficiency in swimming crawl and back strokes. *Arbeitsphysiol.* **10**:504-514.

MILLER, D.I. 1975. Biomechanics of swimming. In: J.H. Wilmore and J.F. Koegh (eds.), *Exercise and Sport Sciences Review* (vol. 3), pp. 219-248. Academic Press, New York.

NICOL, K., and Krüger, F. 1979. Impulse exerted in performing several kinds of swimming turns. In: J. Terauds and E.W. Bedingfield (eds.), *Swimming III*, pp. 222-232. University Park Press, Baltimore.

OHMICH, H., and Miyashita, M. 1981. Analysis of the external work derived from the kinematics of human walking. In: A. Morecki, K. Kedzior, and A. Wit (eds.), *Biomechanics VII-B*, pp. 184-189. University Park Press, Baltimore.

THORSTENSSON, A., Grimby, G., and Karlsson, J. 1976. Force-velocity relations and fiber composition in human knee extensor muscles. *J. Appl. Physiol.* **40**:12-16.

Total Efficiency and Swimming Drag in Swimming the Front Crawl

Han C.G. Kemper and Robbert Verschuur
University of Amsterdam, The Netherlands

Jan Pieter Clarys
Vrije Universiteit Brussel, Belgium

Jan Jiskoot
Academy of Physical Education
Amsterdam, The Netherlands

Studies on the propulsive force of a swimming body can be divided into three different approaches: (a) tethered swimming, that is, recording a swimming body at zero velocity; (b) propulsive force recordings of a swimming body at a velocity greater than zero; and (c) measurement of the energy consumption during swimming (Clarys, 1981).

In this study, measurement of the propulsive force was combined with measurement of the energy consumption in order to establish the total efficiency (E_t) during free swimming. The total efficiency of subjects swimming the front crawl at a constant velocity was calculated by means of oxygen consumption ($\dot{V}O_2$) and mechanical work (W). Two fundamental criteria must be considered in order to obtain reliable measurements of energy consumption: (a) measurements must be made during constant speed under steady-state conditions and (b) natural swimming conditions must exist (Holmer, 1974).

Methods

Subjects

The subjects were 49 male physical education students (Academy of Physical Education in Amsterdam). The students had different degrees of swimming abilities, varying from poor to Olympic level performances. All subjects were between 18 and 24 years of age and were familiar with the procedure, having participated in previous experiments (Clarys and Jiskoot, 1975). The subjects' physical characteristics are shown in Table 1. Drag is related to body dimensions, of which the following seemed to be most relevant and were therefore measured: (a) body height, (b) body weight and (c) body surface area (calculated from a graphic plot of 35 circumferences and the respective height of the body) (Kemper et al., 1976).

Procedures

All swimming tests were carried out in a ship model towing tank (Martim, Wageningen) of $200 \times 4 \times 4$ m, as previously described (Clarys et al., 1974). During the experiments, water temperature varied from 24-28°C.

Total efficiency (E_t) was given by the ratio between mechanical work (W) and energy expenditure (M):

$$E_t = W/M \times 100\% \qquad [1]$$

Mechanical work was determined by the product of swimming drag (D_s) and speed. For the measurement of drag, a towing carriage driven on rails (Figure 1) with controllable speed and a device for automatic recording of drag (N) and velocity (m/sec) was used. The forces were measured using a telescopic rod system through which they were converted into electrical signals by strain guages and amplified. Swimming drag (D_s) refers to the drag actually measured during swimming. Swimming drag at a speed of 0.75 $m \cdot sec^{-1}$ was estimated as previously reported (Clarys, 1981). The forces recorded during swimming can be

Table 1

Anthropometric Data for Subjects[a]

	Height (cm)	Weight (kg)	Surface area (m²)
X̄	180.0	75.3	1.64
SD	6.5	9.3	0.14
Min	164.0	55.0	1.3
Max	195.0	115.0	2.0

[a]Mean (X̄), standard deviation (*SD*), minimal (min.) and maximal (max.) values of the anthropometric data for all subjects ($n=49$).

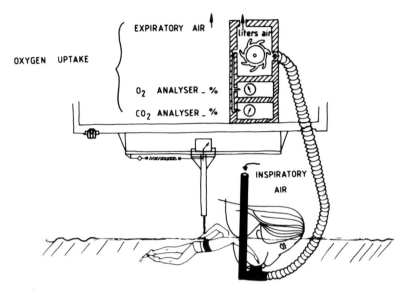

Figure 1—Schematic representation of the measurement procedures. The swimmer was connected to a telescopic rod system equipped with strain gauges and to the Ergo-analyzer apparatus with a breathing valve and tube.

either positive or negative. The force recordings of the crawl movement became positive as soon as the subject was unable to keep up with the pace of the towing carriage.

Positive forces were indicated by passive drag on the one hand and a swimming drag on the other. This swimming drag corresponded to a towing force, which was additional to the propulsive force developed by the subjects. Thus, this force was referred to as added drag $(D_{A(+)})$. Negative forces always reflected a propulsive force, which was being developed in addition to the subjects' overcoming their drag. At a certain velocity $D_{A(-)}$ will change to $D_{A(+)}$: At that velocity, propulsion of the swimmer equalled drag and no force was registered. A minimum of six data points, three below and three above the individual maximal swimming velocity (v_{max}) of each subject were measured. Individual curve fitting was done with polynomial functions of different degrees (Clarys, 1981). In order to obtain the swimming drag this function was extrapolated to zero velocity. The extrapolated force found at zero velocity (D_0) was added to the original curve to obtain the swimming drag $(D_s$ see Figure 2) (Clarys, 1979). Mechanical work (W) was calculated in Watts:

$$W = D_s \times 0.75. \qquad [2]$$

For comparison, the same subjects were also measured for: (a) maximal propulsive force (D_{th}) at zero velocity, also called tethered swim-

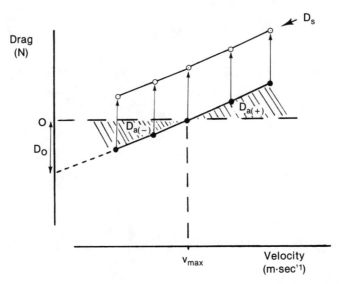

Figure 2—Determination of swimming drag D_s by extrapolation of the drag $(D_{A(+)})$ and added propulsion $(D_{A(-)})$ curve to D_0 at zero velocity.

ming, and (b) passive drag (D_p) by towing the body at a speed of 0.75 m·sec⁻¹ through the water in a streamlined, prone position with the arms extended forward and the legs unsupported.

Energy expenditure (M) was calculated from the amount of oxygen consumed above resting level:

$$\dot{V}O_2net = \dot{V}O_2swim - \dot{V}O_2rest, \qquad [3]$$

and transferred into Watts, assuming that 1 L O_2 will release 21 kJ of energy (only carbon oxidation).

Oxygen consumption was measured (a) at rest ($\dot{V}O_2rest$) with the subject hanging on to the towing device in a vertical, relaxed position in the water and (b) while swimming the front crawl at a constant velocity of 0.75 m·sec⁻¹ ($\dot{V}O_2swim$). This swimming velocity was chosen at 75% of the lowest maximal swimming speed (v_{max}) of the swimmers, a velocity at which all swimmers would be able to swim continuously for at least 4 min. Oxygen uptake obtained in the fourth minute was taken as the $\dot{V}O_2swim$.

Oxygen uptake was analyzed throughout the test by the open-circuit technique using an ergo-analyzer (Mijnhardt B.V., Odijk) installed on the towing carriage (see Figure 1). Measurement of the oxygen uptake with the ergo-analyzer has been shown to provide values comparable to those obtained by the classic method, that is, collecting expired air in Douglas bags and analyzing O_2 and CO_2 contents by the Scholander technique (Kemper et al., 1976).

Results

The mean, standard deviation, minimal and maximal values of swimming drag (D_s), mechanical work (W), energy expenditure (M) and total efficiency (E_t) of all subjects are given in Table 2. From the 49 subjects, two extreme groups were selected on the basis of their maximal swimming speed: 11 skilled swimmers with a v_{max} higher than 1.68 m•sec^{-1} and 11 unskilled swimmers with a v_{max} lower than 1.30 m•sec^{-1} (Table 3). Comparison of these two contrasting groups revealed the following: (a) a significantly higher D_s and as a consequence higher W in unskilled swimmers; (b) no significant differences in energy expenditure (M); and (c) no significant differences in total efficiency (E_t) between the groups.

Table 2

Swimming Drag and Total Efficiency[a]

	D_s (N)	W (W)	M (W)	E_t (%)
$\overline{X}$	47.2	34.7	721	4.99
SD	15.2	11.1	181	1.82
Min	12.8	9.4	390	1.54
Max	80.4	59.0	1140	11.44

[a]Mean ($\overline{X}$), standard deviation, minimum and maximum values of swimming drag (D_s), mechanical work (W), energy expenditure (M) and total efficiency (E_t) of all subjects at a speed of 0.75 m•sec^{-1}.

Table 3

Differences Between Contrasting Groups[a]

	Skilled swimmers (n=11)		Unskilled swimmers (n=11)		Probability of the difference
	$\overline{X}$	SD	$\overline{X}$	SD	(p)
V_{max} (m•sec^{-1})	1.73	(0.08)	1.15	(0.09)	< 0.01
D_s (N)	32.2	(14.3)	57.0	(16.2)	< 0.01
W (W)	23.6	(10.5)	41.8	(11.9)	< 0.01
M (W)	615	(146)	787	(190)	
W_t (%)	3.88	(1.42)	5.39	(1.41)	

[a]Mean ($\overline{X}$) and standard deviation (SD) of the same characteristics in Table 2 for the two contrasting groups. Significant ($p < 0.01$) differences between the groups are indicated.

Discussion

The mean E_t in our subjects was 4.99% ($\pm$ 1.82). This value was close to those reported in the literature (diPrampero et al., 1974; Holmer, 1974). Holmer et al. (1974) reported a value of 4.2%. These mean values were calculated from the force curves on the basis of swimming the front crawl at the same speed of 0.75 m$\cdot$sec^{-1} as was done in this study. Besides D_s, passive drag at 0.75 m$\cdot$sec^{-1} (D_p) and drag during tethered swimming (D_{th}) were also measured in the same subjects. The mean and standard deviation of these parameters and D_0 are given for the two contrasting groups in Table 4. Comparison of the mean swimming and passive drag revealed that in the unskilled swimmers, D_s (57.0) was more than twice as high as D_p (21.2). Between skilled and unskilled swimmers there was a significant difference in D_s but not in D_p (see Tables 3 and 4). Using this method and the interpretation of D_0 given in Figure 2, no difference was found in D_0 between the skilled (with a high v_{max}) and the unskilled swimmers (with a low v_{max}) (Table 4). Then, at the same submaximal speed the higher D_s value of the unskilled swimmers compared to the skilled swimmers is easy to explain. This difference in D_s and the same value of D_p for both groups indicates that swimming technique is a more important drag factor during swimming than body form. In some unskilled swimmers, D_s was as much as four times higher than D_p. Surprisingly, some skilled swimmers had lower D_s than D_p, although this only occurred in three top-class swimmers and could have been the result of a better horizontal position during swimming than during towing with unsupported legs.

In general, D_0 appeared higher than D_{th}, with this difference significant in the unskilled swimmers. Unlike D_0, a difference between D_{th} of

Table 4

Drag Values for the Two Groups[a]

	Skilled swimmers ($n=11$)		Unskilled swimmers ($n=11$)		Probability of the difference
	$\overline{X}$	SD	$\overline{X}$	SD	p
D_p (N)	22.5	(3.7)	21.2	(4.3)	
D_{th} (N)	104.0	(20.6)	76.5	(23.5)	$p < 0.01$
D_0 (N)	117.7	(40.2)	100.1	(27.5)	

[a]Mean ($\overline{X}$) and standard deviation (SD) of passive drag (D_p) at v = 0.75 m$\cdot$sec^{-1}, tethered swimming (D_{th}) and drag at zero velocity, extrapolated from the added force curve (D_0) in the two experimental groups.

the skilled and unskilled swimmers was observed. The relationship between D_{th} and D_0 needs further research. Energy expenditure was measured from the oxygen consumption during the fourth minute of the swimming test. The increase in oxygen consumption from the third to the fourth minute was not significant, indicating that the majority of the swimmers had reached a steady-state level in their oxygen uptake after 3 min. This statement is confirmed by the mean values of the expiratory exchange ratio (R) of ca. 1.0 as reported earlier (Kemper et al., 1976). However, in some unskilled swimmers R was considerably higher than 1.0 which means that part of the energy was derived from anaerobic sources. These subjects performed at a rate near to their maximum and consequently, their oxygen consumption underestimates total energy expenditure. This phenomenon could explain the nonsignificant difference in energy expenditures between skilled and unskilled swimmers (see Table 3). The underestimation of energy expenditure in the unskilled swimmers in connection with the low mechanical work in the unskilled swimmers could explain why the difference in total efficiency between skilled and unskilled swimmers was not statistically significant. This was an unexpected result. In 1976 an E_t calculated from passive drag in the same subjects was significantly lower in unskilled swimmers than in skilled swimmers. The explanation presented for this fact was that the chosen velocity of 0.75 m•sec^{-1}, a compromise, was too low for the skilled swimmers and therefore did not result in the highest total efficiency, and in contrast, too high for the unskilled swimmers, who did not reach a steady state in oxygen consumption but only a normal value.

Conclusions

Measurements of total efficiency (E_t) in 49 subjects, swimming the front crawl with a constant speed of 0.75 m•sec^{-1} during 4-5 min revealed a mean value of 4.99% ($\pm$ 1.82). Although the mechanical work was almost twice as high in the unskilled swimmers (41.8 W) compared to the skilled swimmers (23.6 W) the difference in energy expenditure was not significant. This resulted in a nonsignificant difference in E_t between the two contrasting groups at a velocity of 0.75 m•sec^{-1}, probably due to an underestimation of the energy expenditure in the unskilled swimmers.

Acknowledgment

The authors acknowledge the assistance of Jan Willem Ritmeester in data analysis for this study.

References

CLARYS, J.P., Jiskoot, J., Rijken, H., and Brouwer, P.J. 1974. Total resistance in water and in relation to body form. In: R.C. Nelson and C.A. Morehouse (eds.), *Biomechanics IV*, pp. 187-196. University Park Press, Baltimore.

CLARYS, J.P., and Jiskoot, J., 1975. Total resistance of selected body positions in the front crawl. In: L. Lewillie and J.P. Clarys (eds.), *Swimming II*, pp. 110-117. University Park Press, Baltimore.

CLARYS, J.P. 1979. Human morphology and hydrodynamics. In: J. Terauds and E.W. Bedingfield (eds.), *Swimming III*, pp. 3-41. University Park Press, Baltimore.

CLARYS, J.P. 1981. *The Biohydrodynamics of Swimming*. Australian Sports Biomechanics Lecture Tour.

DIPRAMPERO, P.E., Pendergast, D.R., Wilson, D.W., and Rennie, D.W. 1974. Energetics of swimming in man. *J.App.Physiol.* **37**:1-5.

HOLMÉR, I. 1974. Physiology of swimming man. *Acta Physiol. Scand.* **407** (suppl.)

KEMPER, H.C.G., Verschuur, R., Clarys, J.P., Jiskoot, J., and Rijken, H. 1976. Efficiency in swimming the front crawl. In: P. Komi (ed.) *Biomechanics V.B.* pp. 243-249, University Park Press, Baltimore.

KEMPER, H.C.G., Binkhorst, R.A., Verschuur, R., and Vissers, A.C.A. 1976. Reliability of the Ergo analyzer-a method for continuous determination of oxygen uptake. *J. Cardiovasc. Pulmon. Technol.* July/August:27-30.

The Influence of Some Somatic Factors
on Passive Drag, Gravity and Buoyancy Forces
in Competitive Swimmers

Luc Van Tilborgh, Daniel Daly, and Ulrik Persyn
Katholieke Universiteit Leuven, Heverlee, Belgium

A swimmer's velocity is determined by the combined effects of propulsion and drag. Drag can be regarded as a function of the movement and as a function of somatic characteristics of a "rigid" body. It can be assumed that the "rigid body" as a contributor to the drag becomes relatively more important as the swimming style improves. To study the swimmer's rigid body drag, two different approaches are available. First, mechanical properties of the body, such as buoyancy and passive drag, can be measured directly in specific testing situations. Second, somatic measurements which are expected to influence drag can be taken. These can be divided into external (shape and size) characteristics and internal (body composition) variables.

The purpose of this study was to determine within a group of competitive women swimmers the relationship between some mechanical properties of swimmers' rigid bodies and some currently used somatic variables and indices. Next, the dependence of swimming velocity at several distances using different strokes on the measured mechanical properties was assessed.

Of course, swimming velocity can be explained to a large part in terms of propulsive variables, such as strength, flexibility, size of hands and feet, etc. Therefore, this study must be seen rather as a search for a piece of the puzzle in an evaluation system. In this sense, even low correlations may be considered interesting.

Measuring Procedures

The data were gathered in a global project dealing with the evaluation and selection of competitive swimmers of at least national level age groups (Persyn et al., 1979). The specific tests discussed were only included in the later stages of this project. To reduce the influence of growth and maturity on the results, the majority of the subjects studied in this investigation were from the age group of 13 to 15 years ($n = 32$ females). Some body build and swimming performance characteristics of this group can be found in Tables 1 and 2, respectively (second column).

Measurement of Passive Drag

Passive drag was determined from film analysis of a push-off and glide test. This method was adapted from that presented by Klauck and Daniel (1976). The swimmer was asked to push-off from the wall as hard as possible in a completely extended position underwater with the hands in front of the head. This was filmed from a side view at 50 frames/sec, using a 16-mm Bolex EL battery-powered camera fixed perpendicular to and 6 m from the plane of motion. Horizontal and vertical length references were visible in each frame. The water temperature was 28°C. Film speed was controlled as in a previous study and has been shown to be constant (the measurement errors caused by inaccurate film speed are far smaller than those due to digitizing errors). The film was then analyzed, frame by frame, for a single point on the hip using a Vanguard motion analysis projector and an ultrasonic digitizing table of 100 × 100 cm with 13-bit resolution (accuracy .1 mm). More information and a discussion of the digitizing accuracy of the equipment are available in Spaepen (1980). The displacement data were then recorded on tape by a microprocessor, and transferred to a desk-top computer for further processing.

This processing included a mathematical check for digitizing errors followed by smoothing with third-degree polynomials over seven points and calculation of first and second derivatives from displacement data (Fritz, 1979). Then, the mathematical function:

$$D = \frac{C \cdot S \cdot V^2}{2}, \tag{1}$$

where D = drag force at given V, V = velocity, C = body shape constant and S = surface area perpendicular to the direction of motion, was fitted to the data, yielding a force-velocity relationship. The product C • S was calculated for each swimmer, taking the best of at least two glides.

Measurement of Buoyancy and the Relationship of the Forces of Gravity and Buoyancy

The relationship between the forces of gravity and buoyancy was determined using an adapted balance board technique. The method has been presented in more detail at the sixth "Congrès de Biomécanique" in

Table 1

Mean Values and Correlations Between "Rigid Body" Tests and Anthropometric Data
(n = 32 Female Swimmers, Mean Age 14.29 yr)

	$\overline{X}$ unit[b]	Inspired		Expired		Passive drag[a]		
		Weight	Torque	Weight	Torque	CS	CS/WEI	CS/DSI
		-1.21 (kg)	1.34 (kgm)	1.17 (kg)	0.58 (kgm)	122 (Nm/sec^2)	2.26 (m/sec^2)	0.15 (N/cm^2)
Height	164.0	$-.35^*$	.38*			.54**		.46**
Sitting height	86.1		.41*		.45**	.48**		.34*
Weight	54.0	$-.46^{**}$	.39*			.63**		.41*
Skinf. scap.	.93							
Skinf. calf	1.14		.36*					
Biacr. width	36.8		.49**		.35*	.59**		.38*
Bidelt. width	41.2	$-.34^*$	.37*			.62**		.39*
Biiliac width	25.9	$-.42^*$	.41*		.38*	.37*		
Chest depth	18.1					.55**		.38*
Bicond. humer.	6.00					.62**	.55**	.64**
Bicond. femur	8.2					.45**		
Delta circum.	102.0					.58**		.42*
Hip circum.	78.9	$-.51^{**}$	.41*			.51**		.37*
Calf circum.	33.6					.54**		.38*
Latiss. circ.	85.5		.42*			.42*		.41*
Leg length	77.9					.47**	.36*	.38*
Arm length	74.4	$-.35^*$						.38*
Body surface	157.0	$-.36^*$	.45*			.63**		.42*
Drag surf. ind.	79.6	$-.36^*$	.39*			.67**	.35*	.43*

[a]CS = drag coefficient (Equation 1). CS/WEI = drag divided by weight; CS/DSI = drag divided by drag surface index.
[b]Units for anthropometric measurements are: lengths, skinfolds, circumferences in cm, weight in kg, and surfaces in cm^2.
* 5% and ** 1% significance levels, respectively.

Table 2

Mean Values and Correlations Between "Rigid Body" Variables and Swimming Performance Data
(n = 32 Female Swimmers, Mean Age 14.29 yr)

	$\bar{X}$ (s)	Inspired Weight (kg)	Inspired Torque (kgm)	Expired Weight (kg)	Expired Torque (kgm)	CS (Nm/sec²)	Passive drag[a] CS/WEI (m/sec²)	Passive drag[a] CS/DSI (N/cm²)
$\bar{X}$		−1.21	1.34	1.17	0.58	122	2.26	0.15
Breast 100 M	84.3	.11	.18	.15	.15	.35	.43*	.31
Breast 200 M	177.4	.54**		.46*		.17	.30	.26
Butt 100 M	72.7	−.15					−.26	−.21
Butt 200 M	161.0	−.45*	−.25	−.44*	−.21	−.26	−.31	−.30
Back 100 M	77.7	−.17			.15			
Back 200 M	162.2	−.43*	.27		.11	.14		
Crawl 100 M	65.4	−.19	.17	−.21			−.19	−.15
Crawl 200 M	140.9	−.35*	.10	−.36*	.14		.14	
Crawl 400 M	292.7	−.33		−.35*	−.21		−.21	−.20
Crawl 800 M	599.0	−.39		−.45**	−.17		−.20	−.21

[a]CS = drag coefficient (Equation 1). CS/WEI = drag divided by weight; CS/DSI = drag divided by drag surface index.
* 5% and ** 1% significance levels, respectively.

Brussels (Daly, Note 1). From measurements out of and in the water, the center of gravity and the point of application of the resultant of gravity and buoyancy forces, as well as the underwater weight, were determined during inspiration and expiration. From these data, the moment of the resultant of gravity and buoyancy forces around the center of gravity was calculated. This corresponds to the torque caused by the upward pressure force around the center of gravity.

Anthropometric Variables

Twenty-eight anthropometric measurements were used. These included body widths, lengths and circumferences hypothesized to be related to either propulsion or drag, or else necessary for determining somatotype (Heath-Carter method). They are described in more detail in Vervaecke and Persyn (1981). Table 1 gives average values for the present sample.

Performance

Swimming velocity data for the various strokes and distances were obtained from official, published results of Swimming Federations.

Results and Discussion

In Tables 1 and 2 the mean values of all variables, and of product-moment correlations are presented. The columns list the various buoyancy and drag data: immersed weight and torque in inspiration and expiration, the CS drag coefficient (cf. Equation 1) as well as two relative passive drag coefficients — CS divided by weight and CS divided by a drag surface index (DSI) (i.e., the average of the surfaces covered by a circle with diameter equal to the bideltoid width and one with diameter equal to the chest depth). These two indices were constructed primarily because passive drag is related to many body build characteristics that influence the performance positively (e.g., height), thus confounding the analytical results for the negative effects of drag on performance.

As a first, general result it should be mentioned that no significant correlation was found between swimming speed and chronological and skeletal age. This is important because it eliminated the necessity of correcting for growth or maturity in the following statistical analyses.

Correlations Between Body Build Characteristics and the Buoyancy and Drag Data

Table 1 shows correlations between body build variables and the test results. Anthropometric variables with no significant correlations for any dependent variable were omitted, and only significant correlations are shown for the other variables.

The inspired weight and torque are correlated significantly with a number of anthropometric variables. It can be hypothesized that they vary with "general body structure." Immersed weight tends to be less for subjects with larger dimensions, and most significantly with a large reading for scapular skinfold and for hip circumference. However, larger dimensions are related to a greater torque (in the sense of causing the legs to sink). The correlation between inspired weight and torque is negative ($r = -.36$ at the 5% significance level), as could be expected from the foregoing discussion.

Although inspired weight and expired weight are positively correlated ($r = .63$ at the 1% significance level), the correlations between anthropometric variables and expired weight are all nonsignificant (Table 1). This could be due to insufficient expiration for psychological reasons.

The expired torque, however, does show significant correlations with three "trunk" variables: sitting height, biacromial width and biiliac width.

As might be expected, passive drag during push and glide (CS) was significantly correlated (at 1% level) with most of the anthropometric data; the highest correlation was that with the drag surface index, derived from bideltoid width and chest depth. These results indicate the possible usefulness of the index. Other significant correlations were found with body surface, body weight, bicondylar humerus width and bideltoid width.

The passive drag index (CS/WEI) showed lower correlations with anthropometric variables, indicating that weight is an effective corrector to remove the influence of general body build on passive drag results. The significant correlations remaining after correction were with bicondylar humerus width, leg length and drag surface index.

By dividing drag by the drag surface index (CS/DSI), an estimate of C (the body shape constant) was obtained. This yielded a correlation with (again) bicondylar humerus width and with body height, and also with most of the other variables that are related to the raw passive drag score.

Correlations Between Buoyancy and Drag Test Results and Performance

Table 2 shows correlations between the "rigid body variables" and performance. Here some nonsignificant correlations also were included and discussed for the reasons mentioned in the introduction.

Although the correlations on all three types of variables confirm each other, immersed weight appears to be the most interesting "rigid body" variable studied. This result suggests that "heavy legs" and a "dragging body structure" are more easily compensated than a heavy underwater weight in this (very select) group of competitive female swimmers. A possible interpretation is that these females were homogeneous with regard to passive drag and torque because subjects having poor scores on these variables drop out of competitive swimming. To resolve this question, a reference group should be studied.

It is remarkable to observe the similarity in the correlations of the two immersed weights for all performances, though they show totally different degrees of dependence from body build.

The breaststroke events showed consistently positive correlations where the other strokes were mostly correlated negatively. "Light" swimmers perform best in the other strokes, especially in the longer distance events. Looking at the 200-m events, one might conclude that "heavy" swimmers can only be successful in the breaststroke. The measurements thus seem to be useful in guiding a swimmer to compete in breaststroke or other events, or in giving some indication of an optimal distance.

Conclusion

In a select group of young female swimmers, the interrelationship between some mechanical "rigid body" characteristics, some current somatic variables and swimming velocity in diverse events was studied. Although the small number of subjects did not permit us to make conclusive statements, the results are promising in that a part of swimming performance in this sample might be attributed to body characteristics which cannot be altered by training, thus providing a possible basis for orientation and selection.

Therefore, it is anticipated that the buoyancy and gravity test procedure will be incorporated permanently in the Leuven Test Battery for Competitive Swimmers. As more groups are measured in subsequent evaluation sessions, results concerning other age and sex groups and levels of performance will become available.

Reference Note

1. Daly, D., Van Tilborgh, L., Riemaker, D., and Persyn, U. Sept. 1981. [*The Measurement of Gravity and Buoyancy Forces in Swimmers.*] Presentation at the sixth meeting of the "Société de Biomécanique," Brussels.

References

FRITZ, M. 1979. *Berechnung der Auflagerkrafte und der Muskelkrafte des Menschen bei ebenen Bewegungen aufgrund von kinematographischen Aufnahmen.* (Measurements of Human Movement Forces Determined by Cinematographic Analysis.) Ruhr-Univ. Bochum, Federal Republic of Germany.

KLAUCK, J., and Daniel, K. 1976. The determination of man's drag coefficients and effective propelling forces in swimming by means of chronocyclography. In: P. Komi (ed.), *Biomechanics V-B*, pp. 250-257. University Park Press, Baltimore.

PERSYN, U., Hoeven, R., and Daly, D. 1979. An evaluation center for competitive swimmers. In: J. Terauds and W. Bedingfield (eds.), *Swimming III*, pp. 182-195. University Park Press, Baltimore.

SPAEPEN, J. 1980. *Tweedimensionele Simulaties voor Afstoot- en Zweeffasen Van Menselijke Bewegingen.* (Two-Dimensional Simulation of Human Motions.) Unpublished doctoral thesis, Katholieke Universiteit Leuven, Heverlee, Belgium.

VERVAECKE, H., and Persyn, U. 1981. Some differences between men and women in various factors which determine swimming performances. In: J. Borms, M. Hebbelinck, and A. Vernerando (eds.), *The Woman Athlete: Medicine and Sport* (vol. XV), pp. 150-156. Karger, Basel.

A Comparison of the Movements of the
Rear Parts of Dolphins and Butterfly Swimmers

Bodo E. Ungerechts
Universität Bielefeld, West Germany

The locomotion of dolphins attracts attention in some respects, as it is harmonic and results in very high swimming speeds. The adaptation of this movement in a competitive swimming stroke for humans such as the butterfly stroke is therefore plausible. The body movements of the rear parts of both dolphins and butterfly swimmers, respectively, result in the production of drag and thrust in a unique situation. Whereas the dolphin's tail and fluke movements result solely in a powerful thrust, the effect of a swimmer's dolphin kick is discussed with more controversy.

Barthels and Adrian (1975) suggested that the down-beat contributes to the propulsion of the body. Makarenko (1978) claimed that the dolphin kick sometimes has a propulsive effect and that in some swimmers, leg movements stabilize the body by elevating the hips. Jensen and McIlwain (1979) demonstrated, on the basis of an estimate for joint reaction forces, that the first kick may accelerate the swimmer and elevate the hips. The joint reaction was calculated on the assumption that the production of propulsive forces depends on surface area, angular velocity of the body part considered, density of water, and drag coefficient. In this approach, the forces due to the interaction of the whole body and the water are treated as if every part of the body is counteracted by resistive forces. Therefore, this concept was called a "resistive model."

For the propulsion of dolphins, another model is taken into consideration, called a "reactive model." It is based on the reaction forces from the mass of water accelerated by the body's deflection. These forces are neglected in the resistive model. In order to extend the reactive model as developed for the movements of fast-swimming vertebrates to the biomechanics of human competitive swimming, it is first necessary to see if there are similar patterns in their movements. The purpose of this pilot study was to compare the movements of dolphins' rear parts with those of butterfly swimmers.

As Videler (1981) mentioned in discussing dolphins and fishes, the propelling movements are caused by cyclic muscle contractions, resulting in dorsal-ventral oriented waves along the body in a caudal direction at a velocity v_b with wavelength λ_b and wave period T, where:

$$v_b = \lambda_b \cdot T^{-1}. \tag{1}$$

As the velocity of the body wave is a basic parameter in connection with the swimming vertebrates' propelling movement, this parameter was compared. Because it is known that dolphins' body waves result in temporal, asymmetrical beats, this was compared as well. According to Purves (1963) the up-beat is performed more quickly than the down-beat. When learning the dolphin kick, therefore, the swimmer is told to emphasize the down-beat, which is, of course, controversial. Measurements for the duration of the up-beat were also obtained and compared.

Procedures

Velocity of the body wave and the duration of the up-beat were obtained from kinematic analyses of underwater films showing six dolphins in a German marineland and of seven butterfly swimmers at the world championships in Berlin during 1978. The camera frame rate in filming the swimmers was 24 fps; that for the dolphins was 18 fps.

The amplitude of two body points were measured frame by frame over one cycle relative to a moving reference system, with a velocity equal to the swimming velocity. For the dolphins the two points were (a) a body point, defined as $0.73 \times L$ (L = body length) behind the rostrum, and (b) the base of the fluke; for swimmers: (a) the knee and (b) the ankle.

The digitized film coordinates of the knee (body point) and ankle (base of the fluke) were used to provide continuous functions of displacement with time. The curves of the different points were plotted in single reference systems (Figure 1). From these diagrams the period (T) and the durations of the up- and down-beats were taken as well as the time lag (t). In a wave motion, two points in line reach their maximal limits of displacement with a phase shift, represented by the time lag (t). The distance between the two points divided by the time lag (t) results in the velocity of the body wave (v_b). The distance between the knee and the ankle related to the body length (L) was about $0.25 \times L$. The distance between the body point and the base of the fluke was about $0.19 \times L$. The wave velocity, normalized for body length can be calculated:

$$\begin{aligned} V_b/L &= 0.19 \times t^{-1} \\ &= 0.25 \times t^{-1} \end{aligned} \tag{2}$$

for dolphins and for swimmers. After the calculation of V_b/L and with

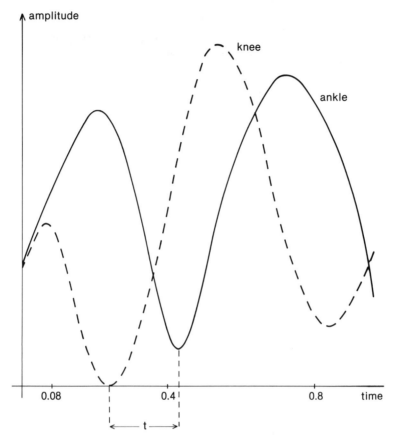

Figure 1 — Continuous displacement-time curves of the knee and ankle of a swimmer: t = time lag by which knee and ankle reach their maximal displacement.

T, the wavelength relative to body length (λ_b/L) was calculated using Equation 1.

Statistical significance was tested using the sign test or the Mann-Whitney U-test ($p \leq 0.05$, two-tailed). The number of positive and negative individual differences follow a binomial distribution and, under the null hypothesis, the different directions are equally likely. For comparing swimmers and dolphins, the observations were ranked in order of magnitude; for $n_1 = 6$ and $n_2 = 7$ the critical value of the statistic U is equal to 7.

Results

The parameters of the body wave (v_b, λ_b, T) of seven swimmers and six dolphins are presented in Table 1 (columns 1-4). In columns 5 and 6 the duration of the up-beat (t_u) and of the down-beat (t_d) are listed. The ac-

Table 1

Kinematic Analysis Results for the Movements of Rear Parts: Dolphins and Swimmers[a]

	t (sec)	v_b/L (sec^{-1})	T (sec)	λ_b/L	t_u (sec)	t_d (sec)
S_1	0.15	1.66	0.55	0.91	0.29	0.27
S_2	0.20	1.25	0.66	0.82	0.32	0.34
S_3	0.18	1.39	0.77	1.03	0.47	0.29
S_4	0.19	1.32	0.56	0.73	0.30	0.26
S_5	0.15	1.66	0.59	1.00	0.31	0.28
S_6	0.14	1.79	0.63	1.13	0.35	0.29
S_7	0.14	1.79	0.65	1.20	0.30	0.36
D_1	0.08	2.38	0.52	1.12	0.24	0.28
D_2	0.11	1.73	0.64	1.08	0.24	0.40
D_3	0.07	2.71	0.54	1.46	0.23	0.31
D_4	0.10	1.91	0.73	1.35	0.35	0.38
D_5	0.14	1.35	0.67	0.93	0.28	0.39
D_6	0.10	1.91	0.55	1.02	0.27	0.28

S_1 to S_7 = swimmers; D_1 to D_6 = dolphins; t = time lag, v_b/L = velocity of the body wave relative to body length; T = period of the total cycle; λ_b/L = length of the body wave relative to body length; t_u = duration of the up-beat; and t_d = duration of the down-beat.

curacy of the given time intervals is estimated at 0.02 sec, which is equal to about ½ of the sample interval determined by the film speed.

Comparison of the Body Wave Velocities

Body wave velocities, normalized to body length, ranged from 1.25 to 1.79 sec^{-1} for the swimmers, and for the dolphins, from 1.35 to 2.71 sec^{-1}. In the test for whether this variable was significantly different for dolphins and butterfly swimmers, a U = 7 (equal to the critical value) was obtained. Consequently, one cannot state that the body wave velocities of dolphins and butterfly swimmers are different. However, this outcome requires further study.

Duration of the Up-Beat and Down-Beat of the Dolphin Kick for Swimmers

Referring to the first kick, the amplitudes of the up-stroke and downstroke were equal. The second kick sometimes showed greater amplitude, especially when the feet broke through the surface. For the first kick, the duration of the up-beat, t_u, and the down-beat, t_d, were measured (columns 5 and 6). The data varied as follows: $0.29 < t_u < 0.47$ sec and $0.26 < t_d < 0.36$ sec; the means and standard deviations of the times were: $t_u = 0.33 \pm 0.06$ sec and $t_d = 0.30 \pm 0.04$ sec. The sign test, applied to the individual differences of duration for up- and down-beats, did not yield a statistically significant result. Therefore, the hypothesis of equal duration for up- and down-beats was retained.

For swimmer S_3 the velocity-time curve of the first dolphin kick was calculated by differentiating the fitted displacement-time curve. The maximal velocity during the up-beat was $V_u max/L = 0.66 sec^{-1}$ and was reached in 0.23 sec after the feet left the ventral turning point; the maximal velocity of the down-beat was $V_d max/L = 1.08 sec^{-1}$ in 0.16 sec after the dorsal turning point. The maximal velocity of the down-beat exceeded that of the up-beat by a factor of 1.63.

Durations of the Up-Beat and Down-Beat of the Dolphin's Fluke

The traces of the fluke seemed to be more symmetrical than those of the swimmers. This could be attributed to the greater flexibility of the fluke. The traces in the ventral and dorsal directions were equivalent. The data for the up-beat ranged from $0.23 < t_u < 0.35$ sec and for the down-beat from $0.28 < t_d < 0.40$ sec; the means and standard deviations were $t_u = 0.27 \pm 0.05$ sec and $t_d = 0.34 \pm 0.06$ sec. Using the sign test, this difference was statistically significant. Consequently, it was concluded that the up-beat was performed more quickly than the down-beat, which differed from the results obtained for swimmers.

The maximal velocity during the up-beat was $V_u max/L = 2.5 sec^{-1}$ and was reached in 0.13 sec after the ventral turning point. The maximal velocity of the down-beat was $V_d max/L = 1.87 sec^{-1}$, and was achieved in 0.10 sec after the dorsal turning point. The maximal velocity of the up-beat exceeded that of the down-stroke by a factor of 1.33.

In order to estimate the magnitude of the possible acceleration, the velocity-time curve for dolphin D_3 was differentiated. The value of the maximum during the up-beat was $a_u max/L = 25 sec^{-2}$, twice the value of the down-beat. The maximal acceleration in both cases occurred right after the dolphin left the turning point.

Comparison of Up-Beat Durations: Dolphin vs Swimmer Movements

Inspection of Table 1 shows that no differences existed in the movement frequencies for dolphins and swimmers, and that the time period for one cycle (T) differed between subjects. Therefore, the duration of the up-beat, t_u, is related to T and t_u/T was compared between the dolphins and swimmers. Using the Mann-Whitney U-test, a significant difference was found (U = 4); for swimmers $t_u/T = 0.53 \pm 0.05$ and for dolphins $t_u/T = 0.44 \pm 0.04$. Therefore, it can be stated that the up-beat of the fluke is faster than the up-beat of swimmer's feet at equal movement frequencies.

Discussion and Conclusions

The comparison of dolphin and butterfly swimmers' movements was based on body wave velocity and duration of the up-beat. The findings indicated that the body wave velocities were statistically similar. The duration of the up-beat, however, was statistically different.

Slow film speeds handicapped the determination of small time intervals, but it must be noted that the study was only a pilot study for generating a hypothesis about human and dolphin movement to be used in further investigations.

The findings for the up-beat duration during butterfly swimming were not substantiated in the literature. Makarenko (1978), who studied the movements of world-ranked swimmers, found values for the ratio t_u:t_d in the first dolphin kick ranging from 1.35 to 2.67.

As in this study with dolphins, Purves (1963) found that the up-beat was performed more quickly than the down-beat. This seems to be quite natural, because in cetaceans the muscle masses used in the up-stroke are substantially greater than those involved in the down-stroke. Moreover, it is apparent that in cetaceans the up-stroke would be important in surfacing very easily because they are mammals and must breathe oxygen from the air.

From a hydromechanical viewpoint, it has been stated that when swimming on the surface, a powerful down-stroke would risk the uptake of air bubbles, as seen quite often in competitive swimming. Although no difference exists in the duration of the up-beat, it remains to be proven that a difference is more favorable hydrodynamically. Ungerechts (unpublished) demonstrated that an asymmetrically oscillating fluke may produce propulsive power. In that experimental situation, no difference was found with respect to the flow conditions behind the fluke when the plane of the tail beat was changed from dorso-ventral to lateral. The difference in accentuation is merely due to an anatomical feature. The asymmetrical stroke, generally associated with yawing motions of the upper body, might support the actions of the ventral muscles. As the recoil motions lag in phase by 90° behind the kick, they may prestretch the ventral muscles in such a way that their efficiency may be increased.

The magnitude of acting on the oscillating body depends on the rate of changes in the body's velocity with respect to the water and to the mass of water accelerated. As already mentioned, the inertial components, which are attributed to the mass of the water, are neglected by the resistive theory. Lighthill (1969) explained the virtual mass of water crudely as follows:

> If any body in water starts moving, the water near the body is set instantaneously in motion, and so a momentum has to be given to the body equal to its velocity times the mass of the body augmented by an additional virtual mass of water.

Thus it is clear that the virtual mass of water might be different from the mass of the body segments, although it can be related to the body mass. If the body form is cylindrical, the virtual mass happens to be twice the mass of the body.

In conclusion, it can be stated that the flow along bodies which change their body form is beyond the scope of the resistive theory. In future estimations of forces acting on the body (or parts of it) in water, emphasis must be placed on evaluating the virtual mass, which is at present unknown for human bodies performing the butterfly stroke and, of course, is absent during dryland exercises.

References

BARTHELS, K., and Adrian, M. 1975. Three-dimensional spatial hand patterns of skilled butterfly swimmers. In: J.P. Clarys and L. Lewillie (eds.), *Swimming II*, pp. 154-160. University Park Press, Baltimore.

JENSEN, R.K., and McIlwain, J. 1979. Modelling of lower extremity forces in the dolphin kick. In: J. Terauds and E.W. Bedingfield (eds.), *Swimming III*, pp. 137-147. University Park Press, Baltimore.

LIGHTHILL, J. 1969. Hydrodynamics of aquatic animal propulsion. *Ann. Rev. Fluid Mech.* 1:413-446.

MAKARENKO, K.P. 1978. *Schwimmtechnik*. Berlin, Sportverlag.

PURVES, P.E. 1963. Locomotion in whales. *Nature* 197:334-337.

VIDELER, J. 1981. Swimming movements, body structure and propulsion. In: *Cod Gadusmorhua, Symposia of the Zoological Society of London* 48:1-27.

Backward Extrapolation of $\dot{V}O_2$ from the O_2 Recovery Curve after a Voluntary Maximal 400-m Swim

Jean-Marc Lavoie, L.A. Léger, R.R. Montpetit, and S. Chabot

Université de Montréal, Canada

Backward extrapolation (BE) of the O_2 recovery curve at time zero of recovery, first reported by diPrampero et al. (1976), has been reported to be a valid estimate of $\dot{V}O_2$ in maximal effort (Léger et al., 1980). This method is particularly useful in field situations such as swimming, where the subjects may be hindered by equipment. Montpetit et al. (1981) recently demonstrated that the BE method is a reliable and valid way to estimate peak $\dot{V}O_2$ in maximal swimming. As pointed out by these authors, the validity of the BE method is, however, based on the condition that the exercise is *not* of supramaximal intensity or of short duration (< 5 min). This condition is established in order to avoid a delay in the onset of O_2 recovery (diPrampero et al., 1973; Roberts and Morton, 1978).

Considering this particular aspect and the fact that the majority of well trained swimmers reach their maximal O_2 consumption at speeds much lower than maximal (diPrampero et al., 1978), a study was designed to determine if the delay in the onset of O_2 recovery after supramaximal exercise, namely a voluntary maximal 400-m swim, could be used to obtain an easier estimate of $\dot{V}O_2$max in swimming.

Subjects and Methods

Canadian national swimmers ($n = 15$), eight males and seven females, participated in the study (Table 1). These subjects performed two series of experiments in which they swam a voluntary maximal 400-m distance using the front crawl stroke. In the first series (A), $\dot{V}O_2$ peak was measured during free swimming using the Douglas bag method and im-

Supported by a grant from Alma Mater, Université de Montréal.

Table 1

Characteristics of Subjects[a]

	Age (yr)	Height (cm)	Weight (kg)	Velocity max (m·sec⁻¹) Series A	Velocity max (m·sec⁻¹) Series B
Males (*n* = 8)	16.2	173	70.7	1.25	1.45[b]
	0.6	2	1.8	0.02	0.01
Females (*n* = 7)	15.1	165	58.1	1.18	1.33[b]
	0.4	2	2.8	0.02	0.03

[a]Values are means ± *SE*.
[b]Significant difference versus series A; $p < 0.01$.

mediately after the swim using the backward extrapolation method. In the second series (B), the swimmers were free of equipment and $\dot{V}O_2$ was measured using the BE method only. Mean speed was calculated from the 400-m times in both experiments. A period of ca. 60 min separated the two maximal swims. The order of the swims was randomized.

Expired air was collected during swimming in Douglas bags attached to a cart which followed the swimmer along the side of the pool. Duplicate collections were made during the last 2 min of the swim. Immediately following the cessation of exercise in both series of experiments, four consecutive collections were made to permit the calculation of $\dot{V}O_2$ using the BE method. The collection period was carefully timed from the beginning of expiration and the end of expiration some 20 sec later. The BE method has been described elsewhere (Léger et al., 1980) and has been shown to be valid for the measurement of peak $\dot{V}O_2$. High reliability and reproducibility in using this method for the evaluation of peak $\dot{V}O_2$ after free swimming has also been reported (Montpetit et al., 1981).

The same breathing valve (Daniels) was used for all tests in both series. Expired air volumes were measured in a Tissot spirometer. Oxygen and carbon dioxide fractions in expired air samples were determined using Beckman E-2 and LB-1 gas analyzers, respectively. Both analyzers were calibrated before each experiment with gases of known concentrations. Water temperature was maintained at 27°C for all experiments. Statistical evaluations of the data were made using an analysis of variance for repeated determinations and a *t*-test for paired comparisons.

Results

The maximal speed at which peak $\dot{V}O_2$ was reached was significantly ($p < 0.01$) lower in the first (A) than in the second (B) series of experiments (Table 1). $\dot{V}O_2$ peak measured for the entire group of swimmers was significantly higher ($p < 0.01$) using the BE rather than the Douglas bag method (Table 2). However, when the value measured during the first 20 sec of recovery (20 sec R) was compared to the value measured with the Douglas bag method, no significant difference was found (Table 2).

The $\dot{V}O_2$ peak for maximal unimpeded swims (series B), using the BE method or the 20 sec R value, was significantly higher ($p < 0.01$) than corresponding $\dot{V}O_2$ peak measured in series A (Table 2). Similarly, pulmonary ventilation ($\dot{V}e$) and respiratory exchange ratio (RER) measured during the first 20 sec of recovery were significantly higher ($p < 0.01$ and $p < 0.05$, respectively) in series B than in series A (Table 3).

Discussion

The results of this study show that the BE as compared to the Douglas bag method leads to an overestimation of peak $\dot{V}O_2$ during a voluntary maximal 400-m swim. This overestimation, equivalent to ca. 20% in series A, strongly suggests a delay in the onset of O_2 recovery, as has been reported after supramaximal exercise (diPrampero et al., 1973; Roberts and Morton, 1978). The maximal mean velocities reached during the 400-m swim with the Douglas technique in the present study were 1.25 and 1.18 m•sec^{-1} for the male and female swimmers, respectively

Table 2

Comparisons of $\dot{V}O_2$ Peak (L•min^{-1})
During the Two Series of Experiments

	Series A			Series B	
	Douglas bag method	BE method[a]	20 sec after the end of exercise[b]	BE method[a]	20 sec after the end of exercise[b]
Males ($n = 8$)	3.97	4.65[c]	3.62	5.32[d,e]	4.34[e]
	0.4	0.3	0.1	0.2	0.2
Females ($n = 7$)	2.28	2.80	2.16	3.11[c]	2.72
	0.1	0.1	0.1	0.2	0.1
Males and females ($n = 15$)	3.13	3.73[d]	2.89	4.22[d,e]	3.54[f]
	0.2	0.2	0.1	0.2	0.2

Values are means ± SE.
[a]$\dot{V}O_2$ peak measured by the backward extrapolation method (BE).
[b]$\dot{V}O_2$ for the first collection immediately following the end of exercise.
[c]Significant difference versus Douglas bag method, $p < 0.05$; [d]$p < 0.01$.
[e]Significant difference versus corresponding value in series A, $p < 0.05$; [f]$p < 0.01$.

Table 3

Comparison of Maximal Pulmonary Ventilation (Ve) and Respiratory Exchange Ratio (RER) for the First Collection Immediately Following the End of Exercise in Both Series[a]

	Ve, L·min⁻¹ BTPS		RER	
	Series A	Series B	Series A	Series B
Males ($n = 8$)	83	121[b]	1.02	1.14[c]
	4	10	0.02	0.04
Females ($n = 7$)	50	71[b]	0.98	1.07
	5	3	0.06	0.02
Males and females	66	96[b]	1.00	1.10[c]
($n = 15$)	5	8	0.03	0.02

[a]Values are means ± SE.
[b]Significant difference versus series A, $p < 0.01$; [c]$p < 0.05$.

(Table 1). These swimming velocities could be considered as supramaximal exercise intensities based on the report that the majority of well trained swimmers reach their maximal O_2 consumption at speeds between 0.9 and 1.2 m·sec⁻¹ (diPrampero et al., 1978). However, the application of this statement to these swimmers has not been verified.

Supporting the overestimation found with the BE method is the finding that the $\dot{V}O_2$ values measured during the first 20 sec of recovery were not significantly different than the values obtained with the Douglas bag method. A correlation coefficient of 0.92 was calculated between the Douglas bag and the 20 sec R $\dot{V}O_2$ values for the whole group of swimmers (series A). These data suggest that following an all-out exercise, the BE method could be simplified by taking only one measurement during the sustained postexercise $\dot{V}O_2$ period. Whether 20 sec is an appropriate recovery time for such a measurement is uncertain, however. For example, a period of delay less than 20 sec before the onset of O_2 recovery might have led to an underestimation of the 20 sec R values measured in the present study. The delay in the decline of the $\dot{V}O_2$ toward rest after supramaximal exercise has been consistently described as lasting ca. 15 sec (diPrampero et al., 1973; Katch, 1973; Margaria, 1972). In addition to the precision of the time lag to the onset of O_2 recovery, the estimation of peak $\dot{V}O_2$ from just one postexercise collection would also require that two other test conditions be scrupulously observed: first, that no delay exists between the end of the exercise and the beginning of the gas collection; and second, that great care is taken not to cut respiratory cycles during the gas collection.

Comparisons of peak $\dot{V}O_2$, $\dot{V}e$, and RER for the first 20 sec of recovery show higher values for the series without the respiratory equipment than the series with it (Tables 2 and 3). The speed at which peak $\dot{V}O_2$ was reached was greater when swimming without the equipment than during the conventional test involving a mouthpiece and tubing ($+16$ and $+13\%$ for the males and females, respectively). These data directly support the allegations of restriction of equipment in conventional testing conditions, first suggested by Montpetit et al. (1981). These restrictions include modifications of the swimming technique and limitations in the full use of the specifically trained muscle mass of these individuals. Although it can be argued that the peak $\dot{V}O_2$ measured with the Douglas bag method could be lower for reasons other than equipment restriction, such as swimmers' lack of motivation in this testing condition, it must be emphasized that the peak $\dot{V}O_2$ values measured for the male group in the present study (3.97 L•min^{-1}) were in the same range as those reported in many different studies (Lavoie et al., 1981). In addition, lactate values of more than 100 mg•dL^{-1} have previously been measured in the laboratory (Lavoie and Thibault, 1981) with the same type of protocol.

In summary, the results of this study show that using the BE method after a voluntary maximal 400-m swim leads to an overestimation of peak $\dot{V}O_2$. The measure of the sustained $\dot{V}O_2$ after the end of exercise (20 sec or less) is, however, a good indicator of the exercise peak $\dot{V}O_2$ and presents the advantage of reducing the use of the BE method to only one sample collection.

References

diPRAMPERO, P.E., Cortili, G., Magnani, P., and Saibene, F. 1976. Energy cost of speed skating and efficiency of work against air resistance. *J. Appl. Physiol.* **40**:584-591.

diPRAMPERO, P.E., Peeters, L., and Margaria, R. 1973. Alactacid oxygen debt and lactacid production after exhausting exercise in man. *J. Appl. Physiol.* **34**:628-632.

diPRAMPERO, P.E., Pendergast, D.R., Wilson, D.W., and Rennie, D.W. 1978. Blood lactic acid concentrations in high velocity swimming. In: B. Eriksson and B. Furberg (eds.), *Swimming Medicine IV*, pp. 249-261. University Park Press, Baltimore.

KATCH, V.L. 1973. Kinetics of oxygen uptake and recovery for supramaximal work of short duration. *Int. Z. Angewand. Physiol.* **31**:197-207.

LAVOIE, J.-M., Taylor, A.W., and Montpetit, R.R. 1981. Physiological effects of training in elite swimmers as measured by a free swimming test. *J. Sports Med. Phys. Fitn.* **21**:38-42.

LAVOIE, J.-M., and Thibault, G. 1981. Specificity of swim training on maximal oxygen uptake: An inter-sex comparison. In: J. Borms, M. Hebbelinck and A.

Venerando (eds.), *Medicine and Sport Series* (vol. 14), pp. 112-119. Karger, Basel.

LÉGER, L.A., Seliger, V., and Brassard, L. 1980. Backward extrapolation of $\dot{V}O_2$max values from the O_2 recovery curve. *Med. Sci. Sports Exercise* **12**:24-27.

MARGARIA, R. 1972. Sources of muscular energy. *Sci. Am.* **226**:84-91.

MONTPETIT, R.R., Léger, L.A., Lavoie, J.-M., and Cazorla, G. 1981. $\dot{V}O_2$ peak during free swimming using the backward extrapolation of the O_2 recovery curve. *Eur. J. Appl. Physiol.* **47**:385-391.

ROBERTS, A.D., and Morton, A.R. 1978. Total and alactacid oxygen debts after supramaximal work. *Eur. J. Appl. Physiol.* **38**:281-289.

Aerobic Energy Cost of Swimming the Front Crawl at High Velocity in International Class and Adolescent Swimmers

R.R. Montpetit and Jean-Marc Lavoie
University of Montreal, Canada

Georges A. Cazorla
National Institute of Sport and Physical Education
Paris, France

The energetics of swimming has been the object of sporadic investigations since the beginning of this century (Karpovich and Millman, 1944; Liljestrand and Stenstrom, 1919; Pugh and Edholm, 1955). These early writings led to the belief that oxygen uptake is related to swimming velocity in an exponential manner. More recently, however, a number of authors (Faulkner, 1968; Holmer, 1974; LePere and Porter, 1975; McArdle et al., 1971) have provided evidence in support of a linear relationship. A closer look at these studies reveals that with one exception (Holmer, 1974), the velocities investigated were rather low compared to today's swimming standards.

Aside from understanding the true relationship of oxygen uptake to swimming velocity, some other points need to be addressed. For example, no published regression equations exist for any stroke in swimming and only one study (Pendergast et al., 1977) has compared the oxygen uptake during swimming at various velocities for male competitive swimmers to that of female competitive swimmers.

In this study, we examined the relationship between oxygen uptake and swimming velocity and tested for linearity by decomposing the curves into constant, linear, and quadratic components using orthogonal polynomials. Additional objectives of this study were: (a) to compare the aerobic energy cost of swimming as it related to velocity among four groups—elite male swimmers (Em), elite female swimmers (Ef), young male hopefuls (Ym) and young female hopefuls (Yf); and (b) to test for a common slope.

Subjects

The oxygen uptake as a function of swimming velocity was determined on 68 subjects. These swimmers comprised two distinct groups: an elite group, including five world-ranked swimmers and a group of hopefuls, that is, very promising swimmers of a younger age. The number of subjects in each group, their physical characteristics and maximal oxygen uptake in free swimming are shown in Table 1. These swimmers trained regularly twice a day for an average of 11 training sessions a week.

Methods

All swimming experiments were performed in a 50-m pool in which the water temperature was 26-27°C. All swimmers used the front crawl stroke, with each subject swimming at three to five submaximal velocities for at least 4 min. A rest of 5 min was given between each velocity level. To ensure constant velocity for each level, pylons were placed at the bottom of the pool at every 10 m. The subject's passing over each pylon had to coincide with an underwater audio-signal. To ascertain precisely the velocity at each level, the middle 40-m distance was timed to the nearest 0.1 sec. The starting speed was 0.9 m•sec^{-1} with increments of 0.2 m•sec^{-1} at each level. Expired gas was collected in meteorological balloons placed in a free-wheeling cart that followed the swimmer alongside the pool. The tubing extended from the breathing apparatus to a wooden pole that projected 90° from the cart and directly over the swimmer. Duplicate collections were made during the last 2 min at each velocity. Expired ventilation was measured by evacuating the contents of the balloon in a balanced spirometer. Gas samples drawn from the bags were analyzed for oxygen and carbon dioxide using Beckman E-2 and LB-1 analyzers. Both analyzers were calibrated before and after each experiment with gases of known concentrations (micro-Scholander technique). All swimmers were familiar with the testing procedure and apparatus as they had all been tested for $\dot{V}O_2$max at least once prior to this investigation.

Table 1

Characteristics of Subjects

Subjects	Sex (n)	Age (yr)	Height (cm)	Mass (kg)	$\dot{V}O_2$max (L•min^{-1})
Hopefuls	M (24)	14.7 ± 0.9	173.8 ± 6.2	63.8 ± 8.2	3.93 ± 0.45
(crawl)	F (17)	14.7 ± 0.8	164.2 ± 6.3	53.1 ± 5.9	2.82 ± 0.34
Elite	M (15)	18.4 ± 1.8	183.1 ± 4.9	74.9 ± 6.3	4.65 ± 0.38
(crawl)	F (12)	17.7 ± 2.5	168.6 ± 6.9	60.6 ± 8.1	3.30 ± 0.30

Free swimming maximal oxygen uptake was determined by the direct method as described previously (Montpetit, 1981). Body weight in water (Ww) of subjects completely submerged 10 cm beneath the surface after a maximal expiration was measured in nine elite swimmers according to the Wilmore and Behnke procedure (1969).

Statistical Analysis

A multivariate analysis of variance for repeated measures was used to test for differences in slopes as well as between the sexes and ability groups. In addition, an analysis of trend was performed to provide information about the form of the oxygen uptake/velocity relationships. This involved a curve-fitting procedure using orthogonal polynomials up to the cubic degree. Means and standard deviations were computed for all variables. In all statistical analyses, the 0.05 level of significance was used. Nonsignificant differences have been denoted by NS.

Results

Both male and female elite swimmers had a significantly higher $\dot{V}O_2$max values than their younger (hopeful) counterparts ($p < .01$). Data on the relationship between oxygen uptake and swimming velocity for all the experiments are depicted in Figure 1. The higher order polynomials were not significantly different from the linear equation. Thus, the relationship could be explained as a linear function. The linear regression lines shown in Figure 2 are the best least-squares fit. The regression equations are presented in Figures 1, a-d.

Figure 2 shows the relative position of the four regression lines for crawl swimming. A significant difference was observed among the slopes, indicating that the rate of increase of $\dot{V}O_2$ in $L \cdot min^{-1}$ for a given increase in velocity was higher for the males than for the females. When the data were grouped by levels of ability (elite M and F vs hopeful M and F), the slopes were not significantly different. Significant differences were observed among the adjusted means for a given velocity. The mean oxygen uptake of the elite at a given velocity (v) was significantly higher than for the younger swimmers. The male swimmers also had a significantly higher $\dot{V}O_2$ at a given v than the females. In addition, a significant interaction was found, indicating that the differences between males and females were greater in the elite group than in the group of hopefuls. The MANOVA summary is shown in Table 2.

There was a considerable range of oxygen uptakes for a given velocity within the four groups, which was emphasized by the results of two male elite subjects in the front crawl. At a velocity of 1.2 $m \cdot sec^{-1}$, these subjects had an oxygen uptake which differed by 1.16 $L \cdot min^{-1}$.

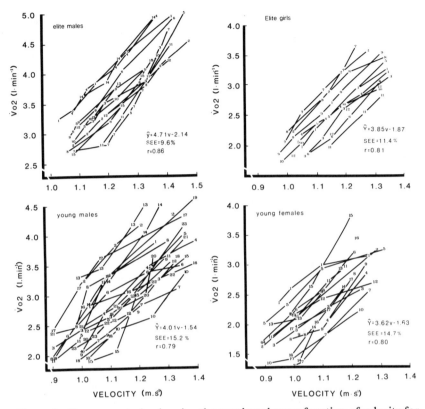

Figure 1 — Oxygen cost of swimming the crawl stroke as a function of velocity for (a) elite male swimmers, (b) elite females; (c) young male hopefuls; and (d) young female hopefuls.

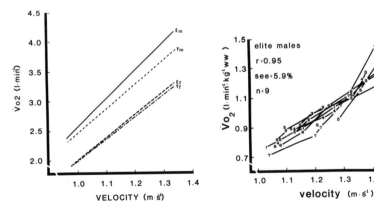

Figure 2 — The derived regression line for the $\dot{V}O_2$ swimming velocity relationship of the four experimental groups.

Figure 3 — Oxygen uptake expressed per kg weight in water as a function of swimming velocity for nine of the elite males shown in Figure 1a.

Table 2

Multivariable Analysis of Variance

Source of variation	F
Ability level	38.2[a]
Sex	129.8[a]
Level × sex (interaction)	4.12 NS
Velocity (constant)	332.4[a]
Ability level × speed (slope)	.24 NS
Sex × speed (slope)	4.93[a]
Ability level × sex × speed	1.63 NS

[a]$p < 0.01$.

For the nine elite swimmers in whom we measured weight in water the standard error of the estimate (SEE) of the regression line was 9.3%. When the $\dot{V}O_2$ data was normalized for body weight in water, the SEE of the new regression line was reduced to 5.9% (Figure 3).

Discussion

The results of this study indicate that $\dot{V}O_2$ increases linearly with swimming speed, (from 1.0 to 1.5 $m \cdot sec^{-1}$) regardless of age or sex. This agrees with previously reported studies on man by Holmer (1974), LePere and Porter (1975) and McArdle et al. (1971), although only Holmer studied the same subjects through a wide range of velocities (up to 1.5 $m \cdot sec^{-1}$). Unfortunately, no data exist for females relating $\dot{V}O_2$ to a wide range of speeds measured using the same subjects.

The regression lines indicate that the trained hopefuls swim more economically than the trained elite, particularly the females. This can be explained by the fact that a large part of the cost of swimming is influenced by drag and by weight in water, both of which are expected to be smaller in the groups of hopefuls. This does not imply, then, that their swimming proficiency is greater than that of the elites.

The aerobic energy cost of swimming has been shown to be significantly higher for men than for women of similar swimming experience (diPrampero et al., 1974; Pendergast et al., 1977). Again, these differences have been attributed to greater body size (reflected in drag), density (Pendergast et al., 1977) and the greater torque about the human center of volume (Gagnon and Montpetit, 1981). This investigation showed a significant difference between males and females in the actual cost of swimming at any measured speed.

As reported by diPrampero et al. (1974) and McArdle (1971), it was observed that despite the high proficiency of the swimmers, a considerable variation in energy cost was required to swim at a given speed. However, interindividual differences in energy cost were strikingly reduced when $\dot{V}O_2$ was related to body weight in water (Figure 3). The same finding was reported by Holmer (1972).

A useful quantity for comparing the energetics of locomotion in different animals is the specific energy cost of transport (E_t). This is defined as the energy used per unit body mass while walking, running, flying or swimming 1 m at a particular speed (Schmidt-Nielson, 1972). For example, for man with a mass of 70 kg running at 14 km hr^{-1}, E_t is 4.2 $J \cdot kg^{-1} \cdot m^{-1}$ (Margaria et al., 1963). diPrampero (1974) and Pendergast (1977) have reported values for net specific cost of swimming at 1.0 m·sec^{-1} between 15 and 17.4 $J \cdot kg^{-1} \cdot m^{-1}$ for men and 12.3-16.7 for women, respectively. In this study, the specific cost of swimming at 1.2 m·sec^{-1} was 11.9, 11.8, 13.1 and 13.2 $J \cdot kg^{-1} \cdot m^{-1}$ for male and female elite and male and female hopefuls, respectively. These values represent an exenditure of 2.8-3.0 times that for running, which is lower than that found by diPrampero et al. (1974). Our subjects were highly trained, especially the elite who all had had international experience. All subjects trained 11-12 sessions per week and covered an average of 10 km per day throughout the year. Differences in technique may account for the lower cost of swimming for the elite subjects and the differences between our data and those of others.

In summary, there is a linear relationship between $\dot{V}O_2$ and speed of swimming for a specific range of speeds (1.0-1.5 m·sec^{-1}) and this relationship holds regardless of sex or age in well trained swimmers. Variations are considerable among subjects in the cost of swimming at a given velocity, and much of these differences can be accounted for by the swimmer's size and weight in water.

References

diPRAMPERO, P.E., Pendergast, D.R., Wilson, D.W., and Rennie, D.W. 1972. Energetics of swimming in man. *J. Appl. Physiol. Respirat. Environ. Exercise Physiol.* **33**:502-509.

FAULKNER, J.A. 1968. Physiology of swimming and diving. In: H. Falls (ed.), *Exercise Physiology.* Academic Press, New York.

GAGNON, M., and Montpetit, R.R. 1981. Technological development for the measurement of the center of volume in the human body. *J. Biomech.* **14**:235-241.

HOLMER, I. 1972. Oxygen uptake during swimming in man. *J. Appl. Physiol.* **33**:502-509.

HOLMER, I. 1974. Energy cost of arm stroke, leg kick, and the whole stroke in competitive swimming styles. *Eur. J. Appl. Physiol.* **33**:105-118.

KARPOVICH, P.V., and Millman, N. 1944. Energy expenditure in swimming. *Am. J. Physiol.* **142**:140-144.

LePERE, C.B., and Porter, G.H. 1975. Cardiovascular and metabolic response of skilled and recreational swimmers during running and swimming. In: A.M. Taylor (ed.), *Application of Science and Medicine to Sport*. Charles C. Thomas, Springfield, IL.

LILJESTRAND, G., and Stenstrom, N. 1919. Studien uber die Physiologie des Schurmmens. *Skand. Arch. Physiol.* **39**:1-63.

MARGARIA, R.P., Cerretelli, P., Aghemo, P., and Sassi, G. 1963. Energy cost of running. *J. Appl. Physiol.* **18**:367-370.

McARDLE, W.D., Glaser, R.M., and Magel, J.R. 1971. Metabolic and cardiorespiratory response during free swimming and treadmill walking. *J. Appl. Physiol.* **30**:733-738.

MONTPETIT, R.R., Léger, L., Lavoie, J.-M., and Cazorla, G. 1981. $\dot{V}O_2$ peak during free swimming using the backward extrapolation of the recovery curve. *Eur. J. Appl. Physiol.* **47**:385-391.

PENDERGAST, D.R., diPrampero, P.E., Craig, A.B., Wilson, D.R., and Rennie, D.W. 1977. Quantitative analysis of the front crawl in men and women. *J. Appl. Physiol. Respirat. Environ. Exercise Physiol.* **43**:475-479.

PUGH, L.G.C., and Edholm, O.G. 1955. The physiology of channel swimmers. *Lancet* **II**:761-768.

SCHMIDT-NIELSEN, K. 1972. Locomotion: Energy cost of swimming, flying, and running. *Science* **177**:222-228.

WILMORE, J.H., and Behnke, A.R. 1969. An anthropometric estimation of body density and lean body weight in young men. *J. Appl. Physiol.* **27**:25-31.

A Comparison of the Anaerobic Threshold and Blood Lactate Increases during Cycle Ergometry and Free Swimming

Jay E. Caldwell and Heikki Pekkarinen
University of Kuopio, Finland

Although maximal oxygen consumption ($\dot{V}O_2$max) during swimming approaches that of most other endurance activities (Åstrand and Rodahl, 1977; Holmér, 1974), the efforts of the muscles receiving this increased oxygen supply are dedicated almost entirely to overcoming frictional forces (Pendergast et al., 1978). Furthermore, the muscles involved in this activity are predominantly those of the body's upper half.

For these reasons, physiological measurements and performance tests made on swimmers out of their normal athletic milieu are suspect. Most dryland tests of aerobic and anaerobic performance evaluate primarily the musculature of the lower body and most include gravity as a factor.

Recently, measurement of the anaerobic threshold (AT) has come to be important in athletics (Kindermann et al., 1979; Wasserman et al., 1973). The AT represents that intensity of exercise at which energy requirements exceed the capability of the aerobic system so that anaerobic processes become increasingly important. As anaerobic glycolysis escalates, pyruvate is converted to lactate. The lactate level rises when its rate of conversion from pyruvate in hypoxic muscle exceeds the capacity of the aerobic processes to metabolize it (Skinner and McLellan, 1980). During an exercise test, the elevated blood lactate can be measured directly, or the accompanying increase in ventilation (the hyperventilation threshold) can be utilized.

Intramuscular and intracellular processes are the most important determinants of AT so that its measurement is even more exercise-mode and muscle-group specific (Davis et al., 1976) than is evaluation of $\dot{V}O_2$max, in which centrally limiting cardiorespiratory factors play a more important role. Shephard et al. (1974) have suggested that it is appropriate to determine the $\dot{V}O_2$max of swimmers with cycle ergometry because in trained, motivated individuals, ergometry stresses central responses in addition to peripheral ones.

Because AT determination from gas exchange data is technically difficult in a swimming pool, the use of blood sampling for lactate determinations has been tried (diPrampero et al., 1978; Mader et al., 1978; Torma and Szekely, 1978; Treffene et al., 1980). Reported herein are the results of a pilot study undertaken to determine the efficacy of predicting the lactate threshold during free swimming from the hyperventilation threshold determined during cycle ergometry. If a correlation should exist, a larger study attempting to refine the relationship further, as has been done for runners (LaFontaine et al., 1981), would be justified. However, such a relationship was not found in this sample.

Material and Methods

Data were collected on nine members (four male and five female) of the Finnish National Swim Team during a routine performance testing camp. At the time of testing, the swimmers were in the middle of their short-course competitive season. Their anthropometric and physiological profiles can be found in Table 1. Details of the tests and protocol follow.

Anthropometric and hematologic data were obtained by standard methods (Durnin and Wormersley, 1974, for skinfolds).

Table 1

**Anthropometric and Physiological Profile
of the Finnish National Swim Team**

	Women (n = 5)	Men (n = 4)
Age (yr)	16.7 ± 2.4	19.2 ± 1.4
Height (cm)	170.1 ± 2.7	177.9 ± 7.8
Weight (kg)	62.1 ± 5.9	70.3 ± 6.4
Fat (%)	28.7 ± 4.5	12.6 ± 0.7
Hematocrit (%)	41.2 ± 2.4	47.3 ± 0.5
Hemoglobin (g/L)	14.1 ± 0.9	15.8 ± 0.4
AT (L/min)[a]	2.06 ± 0.39	2.35 ± 0.39
AT (ml/kg/min)[a]	33.2 ± 5.4	33.5 ± 5.8
AT (%$\dot{V}O_2$max)[a]	57.8 ± 6.4	54.7 ± 3.8
$\dot{V}O_2$max (L/min)[a]	3.57 ± 0.47	4.30 ± 0.70
$\dot{V}O_2$max (ml/kg/min)[a]	57.6 ± 6.4	61.1 ± 9.1

All values are expressed as mean ± *SD*.
[a]Anaerobic threshold (AT) and $\dot{V}O_2$max as determined by cycle ergometry.

Free-Swimming Anaerobic Threshold (Day 1)

Approximately 30 min prior to the test each swimmer applied a small amount of Finalgon salve (Boehringer Ingelheim), which contains β-butoxiaethylnicotin, a vasodilating agent, to each earlobe. Before the first min following each, and 4 min after the final swim, the earlobe was dried and pricked with a sterile blood lancet. Arterialized capillary blood (0.1 ml) was drawn into a nonheparinized capillary tube from which it was immediately pipetted into 0.6 ml of ice cold 0.6 N perchloric acid for deproteinization. These samples were later analyzed using the method described by Gutmann and Wohlefeld (1974).

Following a self-selected "very easy" warm-up, 10 consecutive, constant-pace, 100-m swims of progressively increasing intensity were made in a 25-m indoor swimming pool (25-26°C) with lane buoys. Each swimmer selected one stroke to be used throughout the test. The first swim was made at a pace which was estimated to be about 22 sec slower than the fastest time of which the swimmer thought him/herself capable that day. Each ensuing swim was performed 2-3 sec faster than the previous one. The final swim was at maximal pace.

At the conclusion of each swim, the swimmer promptly sat on the edge of the pool for blood collection. All blood samples were collected within 60 sec of completing the swim. The interval between swims was about 90 sec.

Blood lactates were graphically plotted against swim velocities. The AT was defined as the swimming velocity above which the blood lactate began a progressive rise above the baseline value.

Ergometry (Day 2)

Ergometry was performed on a Siemens 380B cycle ergometer in a well ventilated room (17-19°C). Direct oxygen and carbon dioxide concentrations as well as gas volume measurements were made with a Mijnhardt Oxycon-2 System on gas collected through an inflatable rubber face mask assembly and were recorded at the end of each minute.

After warming up for 5 min at 20 W, the test was started at a load of 20 W. At the end of each 2-min stage, the load was increased 40 W to volitional fatigue or until the requisite pedal cadence (60 rpm) could not be maintained. The AT was defined as the $\dot{V}O_2$ just prior to the loss of or change in linearity of the $\dot{V}E/\dot{V}O_2$ line.

Before and after the warm-up, at the end of the 200-W stage, and 4 min after the completion of the test, arterialized capillary blood was obtained from a finger tip for lactate determination as previously described.

Statistics and Calculations

Comparisons of cycle ergometer with free swimming values were made using a two-tailed Student's t-test for pairs and Pearson product-moment correlations. In order to determine %AT during free swimming three sets of assumptions were tested: (a) that workload was linearly related to swim speed, $V_{at}/V_{max} \times 100$; (b) that workload was related to the square of the swim speed, $V_{at}^2/V_{max}^2 \times 100$; and (c) that workload was related to the cube of the swim speed, $V_{at}^3/V_{max}^3 \times 100$, where V_{at} and V_{max} represent the velocities at AT and at maximum, respectively.

The swim speed corresponding to a workload of 200 W on the ergometer was determined assuming the V^2 and V^3 relationships. First the ergometry percentage Wmax was determined ($W_{at}/W_{max} \times 100$; where W_{at} and W_{max} are the workloads in W at AT and max, respectively). The decimal fraction was then multiplied by the square or cube of V_{max}, and finally the square or cube root of the entire term was extracted. This was the V_{200}. The lactate response at this speed could then be interpolated from the individual lactate-vs-speed plots.

Results and Discussion

Table 2 (upper part) gives the t values from the paired Student t-tests and their corresponding p values for comparisons between various expressions of the AT determined during cycle ergometry and free swimming. The ergometric AT occurred at $51.5 \pm 6.3\%$ of the maximal workload achieved. When expressed as a fraction of $\dot{V}O_2max$, the percentage was $56.4 \pm 6.8\%$. These values differ ($p = 0.031$), but are correlated ($r = 0.627$, $p = 0.035$).

Expressing the AT as a percentage of the maximal swimming load is more difficult (Holmer, 1978; Karpovich, 1933). Miyashita and Tsunoda (1978) suggest that the following relationships apply:

$$\text{Work (W)} \approx \text{Drag (D)}$$
$$\text{Work Rate } (\dot{W}) \approx \text{Drag} \times \text{Velocity (V)}$$
$$\text{Drag} = K \times V^n,$$

where K is $1.81 - 5.39$, and n is $1.18 - 2.37$, inversely related to K. Thus, $\dot{W} \propto V^{n+1}$, where n is 1-2.

Pendergast et al. (1978) explored this relationship further. They pointed out that although the above equations are valid, an additional one must be considered:

$$\dot{W} \approx \text{Energy Cost } (\dot{E} \text{ or } \dot{V}O_2) \times \text{Efficiency (e)}.$$

By combining the expression for $\dot{W}$, we have:

$$\dot{V}O_2 = (KV^{n+1})/e.$$

Table 2

**Comparison of Anaerobic Thresholds
Determined during Ergometry and Free Swimming**

Swimming $\%W_{max}$	Ergometry							
	$\%\dot{V}O_2max$ $(56.4+6.8\%)$				$\%W_{max}$ $(51.5+6.3\%)$			
	t	p	r	p	t	p	r	p
v $(89.4+5.0\%)$	-10.38	0.001	-0.291	0.223	-11.75	0.001	-0.468	0.102
v^2 $(80.1+8.9\%)$	-5.59	0.001	-0.293	0.222	-6.55	0.001	-0.468	0.102
v^3 $(72.0+12.1\%)$	-3.02	0.017	-0.295	0.221	-3.85	0.005	-0.468	0.102

Ergometry $\%\dot{V}O_2max$ = anaerobic threshold expressed as percentage of $\dot{V}O_2max$.
Ergometry $\%W_{max}$ = anaerobic threshold expressed as percentage of maximal workload.
Swimming $\%W_{max}$ = anaerobic threshold expressed as percentage of maximal workload as described in the Methods section.
t = t-ratios of differences between ergometry and swimming ATs (p is significance of differences).
r = correlation coefficients between ergometry and swimming ATs (p is significance of the correlation).

This would imply a relationship between energy cost and the cube of the swimming velocity except that swimming efficiency (e) is velocity-dependent. The faster one swims, the more efficient one becomes (up to a point) due to hydroplaning and diminished leg drag. Houston (1978) states that drag is related to a higher exponential value of the velocity at a very high speed than at a lower one. These results have been expressed by substitution of the exponents of 1-3 into the proportion $\dot{V}O_2 \propto V^{n+1}$.

Table 2 presents comparisons between the ergometric AT and three approximations of the swimming AT. In no case was there equality, nor was there a significant correlation. In fact, the lower the exponent, the greater was the %AT, and the greater the difference between it and the ergometry AT. For exponents of 1 to 3 the corresponding swimming %ATs were 89.4, 80.1, and 72.0. These values compare favorably with the 88% AT reported in competitive swimmers by Treffene et al. (1980). From the admittedly limited data, then, it would appear unsafe to transfer AT data obtained during dryland ergometry to swimming situations.

Next, the swimmers' responses to leg exercise on the ergometer were compared with their responses to total, but primarily upper body exertion in the pool, by obtaining blood at the end of the 200-W stage for lactate analysis. The method of determining the corresponding swimming lactate has been described in the previous section. There were two separate sets of calculations, one using the square of the velocity, and one using the cube. These data are presented in Table 3.

Several points deserve mention. First, the location of blood sampling differed between the two tests. During ergometry the blood came from a finger tip, whereas during swimming it came from an earlobe. The baseline values differed significantly ($p < 0.001$). In each case the blood for the baseline lactate level was obtained several minutes after a mild warmup: 50 W for 5 min before ergometry and a self-selected easy warm-up before the swim test.

For both approximations of the swim load corresponding to the 200-W ergometry load, lactate values were lower than during ergometry. The mean ergometry 200-W lactate value was 3.56 ± 0.61 mmol/L, whereas the value during the swim was 1.73 ± 0.44 mmol/L (V^2) or 2.57 ± 0.86 mmol/L (V^3). Both swimming values differed significantly from the ergometry value ($p < 0.001$, $p < 0.005$).

When the elevated baseline ergometry lactate was taken into consideration by expressing the blood lactate as a change from baseline (delta lactate, dLA) there was no difference between either of the swimming dLAs and the ergometry dLA (Table 3).

Table 3

Comparison of Blood Lactate Responses
Measured during Ergometry and Free Swimming

	Swimming[a]	Ergometry	p
	Absolute LA (mmol/L)		
Resting	1.21 ± 0.28	2.32 ± 0.35	0.001
200 W V^2	2.57 ± 0.86	3.57 ± 0.61	0.005
V^3	1.73 ± 0.44		0.001
Maximum	7.96 ± 2.42	8.85 ± 2.23	0.275
	dLA (change from baseline value; mmol/L)		
200 W V^2	1.31 ± 0.84	1.24 ± 0.65	0.828
V^3	0.47 ± 0.43		0.682
Maximum	6.75 ± 2.42	6.53 ± 2.14	0.795

All values expressed in mmol/L and as mean $\pm$ *SD*.
p is the significance of the difference between the ergometry and swimming values.
[a]Swimming 200W lactate derived from individual lactate vs velocity graphs as explained in the Methods section.

The mean maximal blood lactate produced by swimming was 7.96 ± 2.42 mmol/L and that from cycle exercise was 8.85 ± 2.23 mmol/L ($t = 1.17$, $p = 0.27$). When expressed as delta values the difference was negligible ($t = 0.26$, $p = 0.795$) (Table 3).

These lactate and AT data were internally consistent. During ergometry, ATs were low so anaerobic metabolism became predominant earlier than during swimming, in which ATs were much higher. During free swimming each athlete was able to work closer to his or her maximum before having to recruit the glycolytic pathway. As a result, lactates were lower during swimming than ergometry at roughly equivalent loads (maximum, and 200 W).

Summary and Conclusions

A method has been described for determining the lactate threshold during free swimming. Using this limited sample of excellent swimmers, it has been demonstrated that the ATs determined during ergometry were much lower than those found during free swimming. Consistent with this finding is the observation that blood lactates, both at maximal and submaximal loads, were lower during swimming than during ergometry. This may reflect the superior aerobic capacity of these swimmers' upper body musculature or a smaller active muscle mass. It would appear that although ergometry may provide valuable information about $\dot{V}O_2$max, application of data from the submaximal portion of the test to swim training is unwarranted.

Acknowledgments

We wish to thank Ingvar Holmér and Lennart Gullstrand (details of the swim test) in Stockholm, and Kari Keskinen (expression of lactate data) in Jyväskylä for their insight and advice. The authors also wish to thank the members and coaches of the Finnish National Swim Team for their cooperation in this study, and the staff of the Kuopio Municipal Swimming Hall for its assistance.

This study was conducted at the Kuopio Institute of Exercise Medicine, University of Kuopio, Finland.

References

ÅSTRAND, P-O., and Rodahl, K. 1977. *Textbook of Work Physiology* (2nd ed.). McGraw-Hill, Toronto.

DAVIS, J., et al. 1976. Anaerobic threshold and maximal aerobic power for three modes of exercise. *J. Appl. Physiol.* **41**:544-550.

diPRAMPERO, P.E., Pendergast, D.R., Wilson, D.W., and Rennie, D.W. 1978. Blood lactic acid concentrations in high velocity swimming. In: B. Eriksson and B. Furberg (eds.), *Swimming Medicine IV*, pp. 249-261. University Park Press, Baltimore.

DURNIN, J.V.G.A., and Wormersley, J. 1974. Body fat and skinfolds. *Br. J. Nutr.* **32**:77-97.

GUTMANN, I., and Wohlefeld, A.W. 1974. L-(+)-lactate determination with lactate dehydrogenase and NAD. In: H.U. Bergmeyer (ed.), *Methods of Enzymatic Analysis* (2nd ed.). Academic, New York.

HOLMÉR, I. 1979. Physiology of swimming man. In: R.S. Hutton and D.I. Miller (eds.), *Exercise Sports Sci. Rev.* **7**:87-124. The Franklin Institute Press, Philadelphia.

HOUSTON, M.E. 1978. Metabolic responses to exercise, with special reference to training and competition in swimming. In: B. Eriksson and B. Furberg (eds.), *Swimming Medicine IV*, pp. 207-232. University Park Press, Baltimore.

KARPOVICH, P.V. 1933. Water resistance during swimming. *Res. Q.* **4**:21-28.

KINDERMANN, W., Simon, G., and Keul, J. 1979. The significance of the aerobic-anaerobic transition for the determination of workload intensities during endurance training. *Eur. J. Appl. Physiol.* **42**:25-34.

LaFONTAINE, T.P., Londeree, B.R., and Spath, W.K. 1981. The maximum steady state versus selected running events. *Med. Sci. Sports Exercise* **13**:190-192.

MADER, A., Heck, H., and Hollmann, W. 1978. Evaluation of lactic acid anaerobic energy contribution by determination of post-exercise lactic acid concentration of ear capillary blood in middle-distance runners and swimmers. In: F. Landry and W. Orban (eds.), Proceedings of the International Congress of Physical Activity Sciences (Vol. 4).

MILES, M.E.M., Lipschitz, D.A., Bieber, C.P., and Cook, J.D. 1974. Measurement of serum ferritin by a 2-site immunoradiometric assay. *Analyt. Biochem.* **61**:209.

MIYASHITA, M., and Tsunoda, T. 1978. Water resistance in relation to body size. In: B. Eriksson and B. Furberg (eds.), *Swimming Medicine IV*, pp. 395-401. University Park Press, Baltimore.

PENDERGAST, D.R., diPrampero, P.E., Craig, A.B., and Rennie, D.W. 1978. The influence of selected biomechanical factors on the energy cost of swimming. In: B. Eriksson and B. Furberg (eds.), *Swimming Medicine IV*, pp. 367-378. University Park Press, Baltimore.

SAWKA, M.N., Knowlton, R.G., Miles, D.S., and Critz, J.B. 1979. Postcompetition blood lactate concentrations in collegiate swimmers. *Eur. J. Appl. Physiol.* **41**:93-99.

SHEPHARD, R.J., Godin, G., and Campbell, R. 1974. Characteristics of sprint, medium, and long-distance swimmers. *Eur. J. Appl. Physiol.* **32**:99-116.

SKINNER, J.S., and McLellan, T.H. 1980. The transition from aerobic to anaerobic metabolism. *Res. Q.* **51**:234-248.

TORMA, Z.D., and Szekely, G. 1978. Parameters of acid-base equilibrium at various swimming intensities and distances. In: B. Eriksson and B. Furberg (eds.), *Swimming Medicine IV*, pp. 274-281. University Park Press, Baltimore.

TREFFENE, R.J., et al. 1980. Lactic acid accumulation during constant speed swimming at controlled relative intensities. *J. Sports Med.* **20**:244-254.

WASSERMAN, K., Whipp, B., Koyal, S., and Beaver, W. 1973. Anaerobic threshold and respiratory gas exchange during exercise. *J. Appl. Physiol.* **35**:236-243.

The Influence of Active Recovery on Blood Lactate Disappearance after Supramaximal Swimming

G. Cazorla, C. Dufort, and J.-P. Cervetti
National Institute of Sport and Physical Education
Paris, France

R.R. Montpetit
University of Montreal, Canada

During swimming competition it is not unusual for an individual to participate in many races within a short time interval. Since races over short distances (100- to 200-m) result in high blood lactate (LA) levels (Sawka et al., 1979), this might adversely affect subsequent performances (Klausen et al., 1972). By the same token, in training, the chronology of a certain series of swimming exercises may induce fatigue which can negatively affect subsequent work. The question of how the swimmer can best recover from these workouts is nearly always a concern of the coaches.

Several studies have shown that the rate of lactate disappearance following heavy work may be facilitated by performing exercise during recovery (Bonen and Belcastro, 1977; Davis et al., 1970; Hermansen and Stensvold, 1972; Stamford et al., 1978; Weltman et al., 1979). The intensity of recovery exercise is thought to affect blood lactate disappearance (Belcastro and Bonen, 1975; Bonen and Belcastro, 1979; Stamford et al., 1978). However, no universal agreement exists regarding the optimal intensity for recovery exercise. Moreover, results obtained from laboratory ergometers such as the bicycle and treadmill cannot be applied readily to swimming. This investigation was undertaken to examine the efficacy of four recovery protocols with respect to blood lactate disappearance in swimmers.

Methods

Subjects

The experiments were performed on seven well trained swimmers (na-

244

tional level) using the front crawl in a 50-m pool at water temperatures of 26-27° C. The subjects' physical characteristics and other pertinent data are presented in Table 1.

Performance Tests

Each subject completed a criterion supramaximal work task and one of four recovery conditions per testing session. The order of recovery patterns was randomized and testing sessions were separated by a minimum of 2 days. The criterion task consisted of swimming 3 × 100 m (from a push-off start in the water) at maximal speed with a 5-min rest between trials. Following the initial performance, subjects recovered either passively (PR) during 60 min of sitting on a chair at pool side or actively under one of three conditions: (a) swimming at 60% of max speed (AR 60); (b) swimming at 75% of max speed (AR 75); or (c) swimming at a freely chosen speed (ARF) for 20 min duration. To maintain the assigned swimming speed in a constant manner, the subjects followed light pacers placed at the bottom of the pool. The speeds were also checked by timing the middle 40-m portion of each 50 m.

Lactate

Blood samples were drawn from the subjects' prewarmed earlobes at rest immediately after the criterion task, and sequentially during the four recovery conditions. Specifically, blood samples were obtained at 0-30

Table 1

Physical Characteristics of Subjects

Subject	Height (cm)	Body mass (kg)	Body fat (%)	Age (yr)	Best time in 100 m (sec)	$\dot{V}O_2max$[a] L·min^{-1}	$\dot{V}O_2max$[a] ml·kg^{-1}·min^{-1}	HR[b] max
1	181	80	11.1	19.75	54.70	4.45	55.3	185
2	186	80	13.2	19.25	56.35	4.51	56.4	170
3	180	63	10	19.75	55.89	4.59	72.8	178
4	174	66	10	19.75	56.40	3.63	55.0	175
5	176	69	9.3	19.00	55.68	4.41	63.9	175
6	176	72	10.7	18.10	55.18	4.46	61.9	174
7	180	73	10.6	20.75	53.7	4.43	60.7	184
M	179	71.9	11.1	19.5	55.1	4.35	60.9	177.3
± SD	4.0	6.5	1.8	0.8	0.9	0.32	6.3	5.5

[a]$\dot{V}O_2max$ free swimming.
[b]Maximal heart rate at $\dot{V}O_2max$.

sec after the end of the swim and thereafter at the 3rd, 5th, 7th, 10th, 15th and 20th min. For the passive recovery, sampling was continued for 60 min. The blood samples were subsequently analyzed for lactate (LA) concentration according to the technique of Hoborst (1962).

A preliminary series of experiments was performed to determine individual curves of $\dot{V}O_2$ vs heart rate and maximal aerobic-power free swimming ($\dot{V}O_2$max) for each subject. The method has been described elsewhere (Cazorla et al., 1982). Heart rate was monitored continuously using water-resistant electrodes and a battery-powered ECG recorder during the recovery exercises. The mean heart rate served to estimate the relative intensity in % $\dot{V}O_2$max of each recovery conditions using each subject's individual HR/$\dot{V}O_2$ curve.

Statistical Methods

A one-way analysis of variance (ANOVA) with repeated measures was performed to determine whether significant differences existed between the experimental conditions for each variable; that is, LA concentrations, LA half-times ($t^{1/2}$), and velocity constants. When significant differences were found, a Tukey HSD post-hoc test was performed. Regression equations were computed to obtain the slopes of recovery lines (constant velocity). In all analyses the 0.05 level of significance was used.

Results

The mean 100-m swim time for all subjects on the criterion task (3 × 100 m) was 1:02.38 ± 0.92 sec. The blood LA concentration measured after the maximal swims peaked between the second and sixth min ($\bar{X}$ = 3.04 ± 1.4) and on the average amounted to 11.3 ± 1.7 mM/L. There were no statistically significant differences in blood lactate across conditions throughout the initial 6 min of recovery.

Mean heart rate, measured swimming speed and estimated relative intensity (% $\dot{V}O_2$max) for the three active recovery conditions are presented in Table 2. Figure 1 shows the blood lactate removal patterns during recovery from the 3 × 100 m. The values for blood LA during the 20-min recovery period (60 min for passive recovery) were plotted on a semilogarithmic scale to give a straight line for the LA removal pattern. The slope of these lines represents the velocity of LA removal (or rate constant, K). In addition, the half-time for lactate removal was calculated. The mean half-time for the PR, AR60, AR75 and ART conditions were 27.1, 11.4, 11.9 and 11.9 min, respectively. The one-way ANOVA for repeated measures revealed significant differences between recovery conditions for both the velocity constants and half-times. Lactate removal in passive recovery was significantly slower than the other

Table 2

Physiological Variables during Active Recovery Conditions

	Recovery Conditions		
	60% v. max.[a] (AR 60)	75% v. max. (AR 75)	Free recovery (ARF)
% speed max.	59.4 ± 1.07	74.1 ± 0.99	71.4 ± 3.39
% $\dot{V}O_2$max.	54.9 ± 10.9	69.6 ± 11.6	73.2 ± 9.2
Heart rate (beats min^{-1})	122.3 ± 7.97	140.6 ± 12.2	144.0 ± 10.92

[a]v = percentage of max speed for best 100-m time.

conditions. The Tukey's HSD test showed that lactate removal for the three exercise recovery conditions did not differ significantly from each other in regard to both half-time and velocity constant.

Discussion

The postexercise lactate data of this study agreed well with those previously reported by Sawka et al. (1979) for 100-m crawl swimming. Previous data collected in this laboratory (Montpetit, 1982) and the data of Holmer (1974) have demonstrated similar $\dot{V}O_2$max levels for national caliber swimmers.

The major finding of this study was the lack of difference in removal rates of lactate between the three active recovery conditions. It appears that swimmers, like runners (Bonen and Belcastro, 1977) can regulate their own lactate recovery.

Previous investigations by Davies et al. (1970) and Belcastro and Bonen (1975) have shown that bicycle ergometer exercise during recovery at intensities ranging between 27 and 40% of $\dot{V}O_2$max is most effective in facilitating blood LA disappearance, whereas recovery at higher intensities (60-80% of $\dot{V}O_2$max) is not significantly different from passive recovery. However, Hermansen and Stensvold's data (1972), using running as the recovery work modality, show that an exercise intensity between 60-70% $\dot{V}O_2$max is optimal for "removing" lactate from the blood. Our results agree perfectly with the findings of Hermansen and Stensvold (1972) and the recent study of Stamford et al. (1981). In the Stamford et al. investigation, when measured baselines for each condition were taken into account, there were no significant differences in blood LA disappearance between the 40 and 70% of $\dot{V}O_2$max recoveries on the bicycle ergometer. Although in the present study no baseline

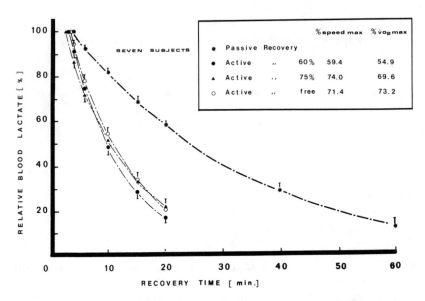

Figure 1—Relative blood lactate decrement as percentage of highest obtained value during recovery for all experimental conditions. Percentage speed max = percentage of best 100-m time, percentage $\dot{V}O_2$max = estimated percentage $\dot{V}O_2$max from heart rate values measured during the recovery swim.

measures were obtained, it is felt that even at the highest workload recoveries the subjects did not exceed their onset of blood lactate accumulation (OBLA). Recent results obtained in this laboratory indicate that OBLA occurs in swimming at speeds representing 85% of maximal velocity for 100 m (Montpetit, unpublished data). This finding suggests that if swimming recovery intensity is kept at high levels without lactate production, disappearance of LA from the blood probably will be optimal.

Additional support for this view comes from the observation that, in this study, the rates of lactate disappearance during swimming (5.3% • min^{-1} at 74% $\dot{V}O_2$max) were higher than rates observed in bicycling (2.90% min at 29% $\dot{V}O_2$max [Bonen and Belcastro, 1977; McGrail et al., 1978]) and slightly higher than those which occur in running (4.5%) at a recovery intensity (60-70% $\dot{V}O_2$max) similar to the intensity used in this study (Bonen and Belcastro, 1977; Hermansen and Stensvold, 1972). During resting recovery, the rate of removal of LA was 2.73% • min^{-1}, a value similar to that found in other experiments (Bonen and Belcastro, 1977; McGrail et al., 1978).

The rate of lactate removal is plotted as a function of swimming intensity (% $\dot{V}O_2$max) in Figure 2. The rate of lactate removal increased with increasing relative work up to a critical work level, representing 60% of the individual's maximal oxygen uptake. Beyond that point was a tenden-

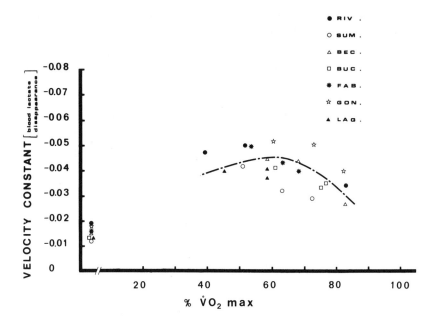

Figure 2—Relationship between velocity constant (log [HLa] in mM/L/min) and estimated % $\dot{V}O_2$max during swimming for 20 min. Values at the extreme left represent the passive recovery velocity constant. Each symbol represents a subject.

cy for the velocity constant to decrease. However, the rate of lactate removal was on the average significantly higher at the highest oxygen consumption than at rest.

The question may be asked whether low recovery intensities while swimming might be as effective as high intensities. The fact is that trained swimmers simply cannot swim at intensities that represent 30-50% of $\dot{V}O_2$max because at that speed it is impossible to maintain correct technique. Thus, it becomes highly impractical to impose such low-velocity swimming.

In summary, active recovery was more effective than rest in promoting blood lactate disappearance during recovery from swimming. The swimmers were able to freely choose an optimal swimming speed during recovery from supramaximal exercise. In practical terms, it means that if competitors swim for about 20 min at a speed equal to 60-70% of their best time for 100 m, their lactate level will have returned to resting value.

References

BELCASTRO, A.N., and Bonen, A. 1975. Lactic acid removal rates during controlled and uncontrolled recovery exercise. *J. Appl. Physiol.* **39**:932-937.

BONEN, A., and Belcastro, A.N. 1977. A physiological rationale for active recovery exercise. *Can. J. Appl. Sport Sci.* **2**:63-65.

CAZORLA, G., Montpetit, R.R., Fouillot, S.P., and Cervetti, J.-P. 1982. Etude méthodologique de la mesure directe de la consommation maximale d'oxygène au cours de la nage. *Cinésiologie* **21**:33-40.

DAVIES, C.T.M., Knibbs, A.V., and Musgrove, J. 1970. The rate of lactic acid removal in relation to different baselines of recovery exercise. *Int. Z. Angew. Physiol.* **28**:155-161.

HERMANSEN, L., and Stensvold, I. 1972. Production and removal of lactate during exercise in man. *Acta Physiol. Scand.* **86**:191-201.

HOBORST, H.J. 1962. Methods of Enzymatic Analysis (1st ed.), p. 622. Verlag Chimie, Weinheim.

HOLMER, I., Lundin, A., and Eriksson, B. 1974. Maximum oxygen uptake during swimming and running by elite swimmers. *J. Appl. Physiol.* **36**:711-714.

KLAUSEN, K., Knuttgen, H.G., and Forster, H. 1972. Effect of pre-existing high blood lactate concentration on maximal exercise performance. *Scand. J. Clin. Lab. Invest.* **30**:415-419.

McGRAIL, J.C., Bonen, A., and Belcastro, A.N. 1978. Dependence of lactate removal on muscle metabolism in man. *Eur. J. Appl. Physiol.* **39**:89-97.

MONTPETIT, R.R. 1982. Efficiency, economy and energy expenditure in swimming. In: R.M. Ousley (ed.), *American Swimming Coaches Association World Clinic Yearbook*. Fort Lauderdale, FL.

SAWKA, M.N., Knowlton, R.G., Miles, D.S., and Critz, J.B. 1979. Postcompetition blood lactate concentrations in collegiate swimmers. *Eur. J. Appl. Physiol.* **41**:93-99.

STAMFORD, A.B., Moffatt, R.J., Wittman, A., Maldonado, C., and Curtis, M. 1978. Blood lactate disappearance after supramaximal one-legged exercise. *J. Appl. Physiol. Respirat. Environ. Exercise Physiol.* **45**:244-248.

WELTMAN, A., Stamford, B.A., and Fulco, C. 1979. Recovery from maximal effort exercise: Lactate disappearance and subsequent performance. *J. Appl. Physiol. Respirat. Environ. Exercise Physiol.* **47**:677-682.

The Influence of Training and Age on $\dot{V}O_2$max during Swimming in Japanese Elite Age Group and Olympic Swimmers

Takeo Nomura

University of Tsukuba, Ibaraki, Japan

In competitive swimming, top performances often are attained at early ages. In some cases, world records have been achieved by girls at ages 12-14 years. Swimming records are broken as a combination of energy processes (aerobic and anaerobic capacities, techniques and psychological factors (motivation, tactics, etc.) (Åstrand, 1978). From this standpoint it is important to evaluate aerobic capacity in relation to the growth patterns among the same age-group of swimmers. This study deals with maximal oxygen uptake ($\dot{V}O_2$max), growth pattern and swimming records of Japanese elite, age-group swimmers.

Methods

The subjects were 66 male and 46 female elite age-group and Olympic swimmers, aged 10 to 23 years. All subjects were Olympic swimmers in Moscow during 1980, or were Japanese junior Olympic finalists. For comparison the subjects were divided into sprinters and distance swimmers. Sprinters comprised those who swam 100- and 200-m events and distance swimmers were those who swam 400 m or greater distances. The data were obtained by a cross-sectional study; $\dot{V}O_2$max was measured in a specially designed swimming flume similar to that of Åstrand and Englesson (1972). As water is circulated in a deep loop by a motor-driven propeller, the water velocity in the swimming flume can be varied from 0 to 2.5 m/sec in increments of 0.01 m/sec. The dimensions of the swimmers' section were 5.5 m long, 2.0 m wide and 1.2 m deep. Water temperature was kept between 26.0 and 27.0°C in this experiment. The testing workloads used were similar to those in Holmér's (1972) work. $\dot{V}O_2$max was determined using the Douglas bag technique. The volume of expired

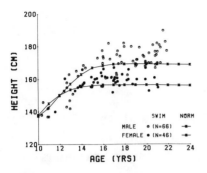

Figure 1 — The relationship between age and height.

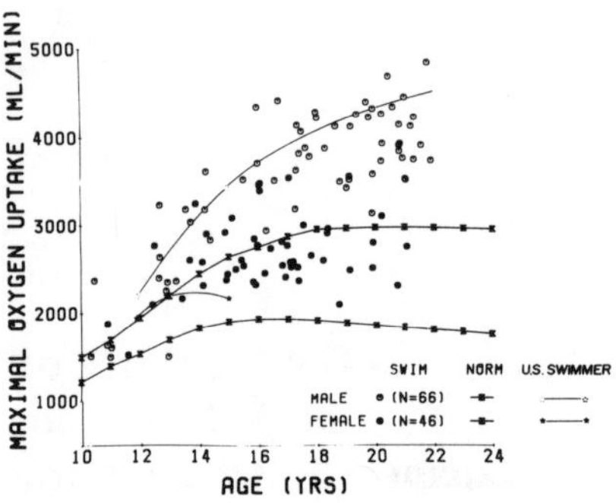

Figure 2 — Individual values in maximal oxygen uptake (ml/min) at different ages.

gas was measured in a calibrated, dry gas meter and samples were analyzed for O_2 and CO_2 content using a respiratory mass spectrometer (Perkin-Elmer, USA). Heart rate was recorded with an electrocardiogram (ECG) apparatus. Blood lactate concentrations in the blood were drawn from the brachial veins and were analyzed according to the electrochemical-enzymatic analysis (Roche model 640 lactate analyzer). Analysis of variance (ANOVA) was used to test the significance of differences among the observed means in a comparison of swimmers to Japanese normals (Meshizuka, 1980), and of sprinters to distance swimmers.

Results

Some anthropometric characteristics and physiological responses during maximal swimming are shown in Table 1. There were no significant differences in body height and weight up to the age of 13 years with respect to Japanese normal males and females; thereafter, the swimmers were taller (Figure 1) and heavier. $\dot{V}O_2$max increased to the age of 16 and thereafter seemed to plateau in males; for females, the plateau for $\dot{V}O_2$max occurred at the age of 14 (Figure 2). Significantly greater $\dot{V}O_2$max was observed with increasing age in the swim group. However, when $\dot{V}O_2$max was related to body size (ml/kg/min), no significant differences between ages were observed except in the youngest male's group (Figure 3). There were no significant differences between males and females in $\dot{V}O_2$max at the ages of 10-13 years. However, above the age of 13 years, the males' values were greater than those of the females.

The difference in $\dot{V}O_2$max (ml/kg/min) between sprint and distance swimmers was seen at early ages. However, there was no significant difference after the age of 14 years between the male and female swimmers (Figure 4). $\dot{V}O_2$max attained in the swimming flume was highly correlated with the 400-m freestyle swimming speed ($r = 0.75$; $p < 0.005$)

Table 1

Physical Characteristics and Physiological Responses of Subjects

Subjects (n)		Age (yr)	Height (cm)	Weight (kg)	$\dot{V}O_2$max (L/min)	$\dot{V}O_2$max (ml/kg/min)	RQ	HR (beats/min)	$\dot{V}E$ (L/min)	RR[a] (L/min)	TV[b] (L)	Lactate (mg%)
Male												
14	$\overline{X}$	12.2	149.1	41.4	2.3	54.2	1.06	183.0	68.1	50.0	1.36	53.4
	S	1.1	9.6	7.4	0.6	9.0	0.09	5.9	11.9	9.5	0.24	7.8
19	$\overline{X}$	16.4	171.1	63.2	3.7	58.0	1.04	179.7	109.6	47.6	2.33	64.7
	S	1.5	6.5	6.5	0.4	4.2	0.10	9.2	18.0	5.1	0.45	21.4
33	$\overline{X}$	20.2	174.3	68.0	4.0	58.4	1.08	177.9	122.2	49.7	2.48	73.9
	S	1.0	5.7	6.0	0.4	4.6	0.08	10.6	17.8	7.7	0.35	23.4
Female												
7	$\overline{X}$	12.6	151.4	41.1	2.3	56.4	1.09	191.5	77.8	46.0	1.76	69.8
	S	1.0	7.0	4.2	0.5	10.6	0.07	6.0	16.4	2.0	0.45	16.8
29	$\overline{X}$	16.0	159.8	54.4	2.7	49.2	1.01	179.5	80.5	52.8	1.58	52.7
	S	1.1	3.5	4.1	0.3	5.0	0.10	7.5	10.3	10.5	0.21	18.5
10	$\overline{X}$	19.5	159.9	55.4	2.7	47.7	0.96	178.5	74.3	48.6	1.64	67.4
	S	0.9	4.1	2.5	0.3	4.4	0.10	7.3	16.8	14.1	0.44	35.3

The means and standard deviations of males and females are given for three age groups.
[a]Respiratory rate.
[b]Tidal volume.

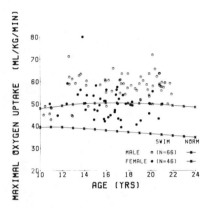

Figure 3—Maximal oxygen uptake per unit of body weight (ml/kg/min) at different ages.

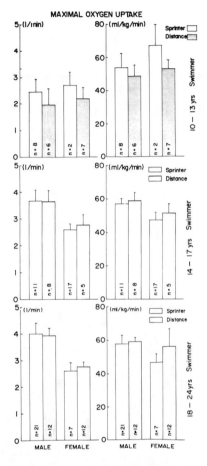

Figure 4—Comparison of maximal oxygen uptake between the sprinters and distance swimmers for different age groups.

(Figure 5). In a longitudinal study it was found that in female swimmers, ca. 2 years after the onset of menarche, body height and weight seemed to plateau (Figure 6). The swimmers experienced a delay in menarche of 6 months as compared to normals. Patterns of growth and swimming records did not differ, even though ages of menarche were different (Figure 7).

Discussion

$\dot{V}O_2$max of trained swimmers has been reported (Åstrand et al., 1963; Cunningham and Eynon, 1973; Miyashita et al., 1970; Nomura, 1978). However, the methods used to obtain $\dot{V}O_2$max were not the same and were not standardized. It is also important to evaluate a swimmer's aerobic capacity during swimming because the cardiopulmonary response to swimming is much different than that noted in land exercises,

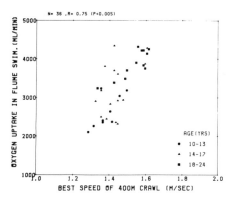

Figure 5—The relationship between maximal oxygen uptake (ml/min) and speed (m/sec) during a 400-m freestyle race by distance swimmers.

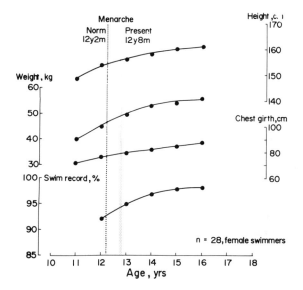

Figure 6—Longitudinal study of height, weight, chest girth and swimming records for 28 female swimmers.

such as those with the treadmill or bicycle ergometer. From that standpoint, the present results of $\dot{V}O_2$max were all attained from the maximal swimming tests using the swimming flume. Comparing the values of $\dot{V}O_2$max reported previously and those of Japanese swimmers (Miyashita et al., 1970), the Japanese swimmers were about 10-15% lower than American and European swimmers (Cunningham and Eynon, 1973; Holmér et al., 1972). However, when $\dot{V}O_2$max was expressed per unit of body weight, there was no significant difference. There was also no significant difference in $\dot{V}O_2$max for the boys aged 10-13 years compared to the Japanese normal values. However, when age increased, the $\dot{V}O_2$max of the present swimmers exceeded to a considerable extent the

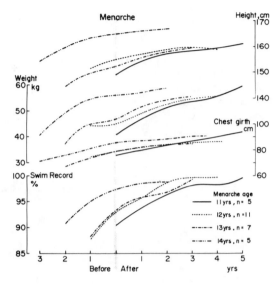

Figure 7—Different ages of menarche group of body height, weight, chest girth and swimming records were matched with the age of menarche.

normal values. This was also true when $\dot{V}O_2$max was corrected for differences in body weight. In our opinion, these results might suggest that swimming training during growth accelerated the development of body height and aerobic capacity. However, only a longitudinal study can confirm this theory. Ideal training prescriptions for developing aerobic capacity during growth are still required to improve swimming records.

During swimming, energy cost can be separated into two components: energy for propulsion and energy required to overcome drag. On land, the gravitational effects have a much greater influence on performance than when swimming. For that reason, swimming performance is more likely to be affected by absolute $\dot{V}O_2$max (L/min) than by $\dot{V}O_2$max per unit of body weight (ml/kg/min). A substantial relationship exists between 400-m freestyle swimming speed and $\dot{V}O_2$max (L/min) (Figure 5). Based on the relative contribution of aerobic and anaerobic metabolism to the total energy required during a 400-m freestyle at world record speed, anaerobic metabolism is assumed to be 12 L and aerobic metabolism would be estimated at 18 L (Houston, 1978). According to these data, in order to establish a world record, the swimmer should have a $\dot{V}O_2$max of at least 4.5 L/min or above. For the Japanese swimmers to attain this world record, they would need to increase their $\dot{V}O_2$max by at least 10-15% of their present values if the total efficiency is assumed to be equal.

Personal swimming records improved as body height and weight increased. Thereafter, records stayed about the same as height plateaued. Weight tended to increase a little more for 1-3 years after height plateaued. After ca. 2 years of menarche, the height and swimming records tended to plateau. Our subjects' (28 female swimmers) menarche occurred at the age of 12 years and 8 months, whereas Japanese standards were 12 years and 2 months (Hoshi, 1980). From the growth pattern such as height, weight and ages of menarche, development of $\dot{V}O_2$max and swimming records could be roughly estimated. It would be more accurate to estimate the pattern of the $\dot{V}O_2$max and swimming records by considering the percentage of body fat for the female swimmers; also for female swimmers, it is very important to consider the age of menarche. After menarche, hormonal response (FSH, LH) plays a large part in influencing body composition and strength per se. These characteristics might affect swimming performance and might be the main reason why female swimmers achieve world records prior to the increase in body fat or decline in body strength. Therefore, the following suggestions are proposed: (a) At the time of the menarche a program of weight control should be followed to prevent increases in body fat; (b) strenuous swim training should be continued; and (c) weight training should be included to prevent a loss of strength.

References

ÅSTRAND, P.-O., Engstrom, L., Eriksson, B.O., Karlberg, P., Nylander, I., Saltin, B., and Thoren, C. 1963. Girl swimmers. *Acta Paediatr. (Suppl.)*:147.

ÅSTRAND, P.-O., and Englesson, B. 1972. A swimming flume. 1972. *J. Appl. Physiol.* **33**:514.

ÅSTRAND, P.-O. 1978. Aerobic power. In: B.O. Eriksson and B. Furberg (eds.), *Swimming Medicine IV*, pp. 127-131. University Park Press, Baltimore.

CUNNINGHAM, D.A., and Eynon, R.B. 1973. The work capacity of young competitive swimmers, 10-16 years of age. *Med. Sci. Sports* **5**:227-231.

HOLMÉR, I. 1972. Oxygen uptake during swimming. *J. Appl. Physiol.* **33**:502-509.

HOSHI, H. 1980. On the study of Japanese age menarche with the change of time. *Jpn. J. School Health* (abstr.): 22-116.

HOUSTON, M. 1978. Metabolic responses to exercise, with special reference to training and competition in swimming. In: B.O. Eriksson and B. Furberg (eds.), *Swimming Medicine IV*, pp. 207-232. University Park Press, Baltimore.

MESHIZUKA, T. 1980. Physical fitness standards of Japanese people, pp. 30-31 (in Japanese).

MIYASHITA, M., Hayashi, Y., and Furuhashi, H. 1970. Maximum oxygen intake of Japanese top swimmers. *J. Sports Med. Phys. Fitness* **10**:211-216.

NOMURA, T. 1978. Maximal oxygen uptake of age group swimmers. *Jpn. J. Phys. Educ.* **22**:301-309.

Physiological Characteristics of Champion Swimmers during a Five-Year Follow-Up Period

Lennart Gullstrand
Karolinska Institute, Stockholm, Sweden

Ingvar Holmér
National Board of Occupational Safety and Health,
Solna, Sweden

In order to develop capacity profiles for swimmers of the Swedish National Team and to help coaches and swimmers be more effective in their training, a battery of physiological tests has been used since 1977. This study reports some results from this program and includes data of five male and five female subjects, several of whom have been medalists in major international championships. The tests were performed three to four times a year during periods of hard training as well as during the competitive periods (immediately after national/international championships). All physiological measurements were designed to be as swim-specific as possible, and were enhanced by the use of a swimming flume constructed by the Flygt Co., Stockholm (Åstrand, 1972).

Methods

Tests were conducted in a swimming flume, a 2.5-m wide and 4-m long test basin in which the water can be circulated accurately at speeds ranging from 0-2.0 m/sec. Hence, the subjects could swim at a predetermined speed in a stationary position (Holmér, 1972). Oxygen uptake ($\dot{V}O_2$) was calculated from expired air samples collected in Douglas bags, and was analyzed for O_2 and CO_2 in a Centronic mass spectrometer following volume determination with a balanced spirometer. Blood lactate levels were determined with the modified Baker-Summerson method (Ström, 1949).

Heart rate was calculated on the basis of electrocardiograms (swimming flume) or from the time taken to count 10 beats immediately after each 100-m repeat swim (25-m pool). Muscular force in the water was measured with a wire strain gauge (Bofors KRG 4) and recorded with a Honeywell recorder.

Procedure

The complete test protocol contained the following measurements, of which only selected parts are reported here: (a) $\dot{V}O_2$submax (standard speeds), pulse rate and blood lactate; (b) $\dot{V}O_2$max, pulse rate and blood lactate; (c) swimming force — pulling, kicking, whole stroke, and pulling aginst different water speeds; (d) blood lactate during a progressive series of 10 × 100 m freestyle trials in a 25-m pool; and (e) anthropometry — height, weight, skinfold measurements, circumferences of upper arms and legs, and underwater weight.

An individualized, progressive speed increase to total exhaustion was used to determine $\dot{V}O_2$max. The normal time for this exhaustive swim took 4-5 min. After subjects completed the swim, blood samples were collected at 1, 3, 5 and 7 min to find peak values. During both swims the pulse rate was recorded via telemetry on an ECG-recorder.

To find the aerobic/anaerobic threshold (Figure 1) for each swimmer, a series of 10 × 100-m freestyle swims were carried out in a 25-m pool. Each swim in the series was swum with gradually increased speed, 1.5-2 sec faster per repetition, until the tenth one was at maximal speed.

Blood samples were taken from the hyperaemisized earlobe after each repetition and at the first, third and fifth min following the last 100-m swim. After each repetition, the carotid artery heart rate was counted manually using a pulse watch based on 10 beats. The procedure took ca. 15-20 sec, which made it possible for elite male freestyle swimmers to start every 90 sec. These conditions simulated those which frequently occur in actual training situations.

Maximal swimming forces were measured in the flume in still water during a 10-sec tethered swim. The swimmer wore a belt which was connected by a line to an inelastic pulley system containing a strain gauge transducer. A double-pen recorder measured one original curve and another which was averaged using a time constant filter.

During the pulling tests, the swimmer's legs were fixed with an elastic band, and the body's normal swimming position was achieved by pull-buoys placed between the ankles and/or the thighs. Kicking tests were performed with the hands on a kickboard and the head out of the water.

Swimming force was also measured during a maximal 10-sec tethered pulling swim performed in the flume against a 1.2-m/sec water speed for males and 1.1 m/sec for females. Because tests of swimming skill need to be as specific as possible, the most important measurements are those which result from the forces produced during the tethered swim against the flowing water rather than the forces against the still water.

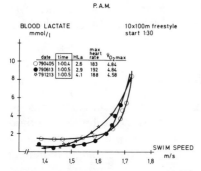

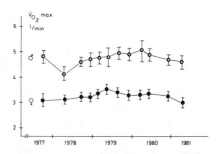

Figure 1—Blood lactate/velocity relationships for one competition period (open symbols) and two build-up periods (filled symbols) from a top male swimmer. In Table 1 swimming speed is denoted at all three occasions as compared to the corresponding blood lactate value.

Figure 2—Mean and standard deviations of VO₂max for Swedish male and female National Team swimmers.

Results

Measurements of $\dot{V}O_2$max for male and female swimmers are provided in Figure 2. Between 1977 and 1981, no great differences were seen. Nevertheless, some swimmers differed by about 15% in their $\dot{V}O_2$max values between tests carried out in periods of build-up training and those in competition periods. Interestingly, a few swimmers with a lowered $\dot{V}O_2$max broke good Swedish records of 200 and 400 m only a few days before the tests.

Peak blood lactate for males taken after $\dot{V}O_2$max swims are presented in Figure 3. Mean values show a distinct fluctuation pattern corresponding to competition and hard training periods, respectively. The same type of curve can be seen for the female swimmers, except that the girls in the study were younger than the boys and participated in the junior championships in December. Therefore they also attained their peak blood lactate concentrations in December.

Results of swimming force achieved by the male swimmers are also shown in Figure 3. Here a clear pattern can be identified which is related to the build-up and competitive periods of a swimming season. Peak blood lactate values vary inversely with the values of swimming forces (Figure 3).

Since the first measurements were taken in 1977, one can observe an increase of 25% in whole-stroke, 30% in pulling, 50% in pulling against 1.2 m/sec water speed and 25% in kicking for male swimmers. Females also improved their performances but by ca. 10% less in each test except kicking, where no improvement could be seen (Figure 4).

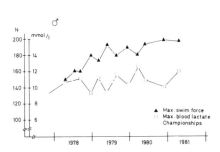

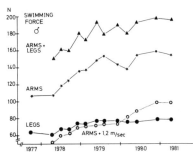

Figure 3—Mean values of peak blood lactate and maximal swimming force (whole stroke, freestyle) of male swimmers.

Figure 4—Mean values of maximal swimming force from a series of 10-sec maximal tethered swims of Swedish top male swimmers (freestyle).

Discussion

From a physiological viewpoint, this battery of tests provides some explanation for the progressive improvement of swimming records. Maximal $\dot{V}O_2$ revealed no significant changes during the follow-up period. It is also interesting to compare the actual data with the measurements of female and male Swedish National swimmers from 1961 to 1974 (Åstrand et al., 1961; Hermansson and Karlsson, 1967; Holmér et al., 1974). These results show almost the same mean values. The females attained a value slightly higher than 3 L/min and that of the male swimmers was ca. 5.0 L/min.

These data support the assumption that a highly developed aerobic capacity among Swedish National swimmers already existed during the 1960s. In fact, the group of females who were measured included Olympic medal winners and world record holders of the 400- and 1,500-m races, respectively. Therefore the recent development of Swedish records is obviously less dependent on VO_2max than other physiological factors.

The results of the tethered swim tests indicate clearly that increased swimming force probably is one of the most important factors behind the development of swimming records in recent years. This is possibly the result of a greater interest in different types of strength training, development of new training equipment and, of course, an overall increase in strength training. The decreased swimming force during the competitive period depends mainly on the traditional way of tapering-off a swimmer. Most swimmers stop their strength training abruptly about 4-6 weeks before the championships, which results in decreased muscular strength.

These results were reported in clinics for Swedish coaches during which participants were encouraged to let their athletes continue strength training but tapering off up to 10-14 days before the important meets.

This procedure was followed successfully, as evident in many ways. Several physiological factors reached top values during the subsequent test session. In the championships immediately preceding the tests, 17 Swedish records were broken. In an international meet with the Soviet Union a few days later five more Swedish national records were broken as the Swedish team dominated the meet. Although improved performance is caused by many different factors, test results indicate a significant contribution from physiological factors, as both swimming force and blood lactate values remained high during the competition period.

One explanation for the high blood lactate values during build-up periods could be that Swedish swimmers simply do a great volume of anaerobic work before the competitions and less in the other periods, and that the body quickly adapts to these conditions. This adaptation was also seen in the 10 × 100-m swims (Figure 1).

Swimmers in 18 of 23 races in national and international championships rely on anaerobic sources for 50% or more of the energy required (Houston, 1977). For this reason, swim training on a high level with pubertal and postpubertal athletes should include more time for development of their anaerobic capacities.

References

ÅSTRAND, P.-O., and Englesson, S. 1972. A swimming flume. *J. Appl. Physiol.* **33**:514.

ÅSTRAND, P.-O., Engström, L., Eriksson, B., Karlberg, P., Nylander, I., Saltin, B., and Thoren, C. 1961. Girl swimmers. *Acta Paediatr.* (Suppl.):147.

HERMANSEN, L., and Karlsson, J. 1967. Detta är resultatet av fysiologernas undersökning av våra toppsimmare. (The results of physiological research on several top level swimmers.) *Simsport* **22**:19-27.

HOLMÉR, I. 1972. Oxygen uptake during swimming in man. *J. Appl. Physiol.* **33**:502-509.

HOLMÉR, I., Lundin, A., and Eriksson, B. 1974. Maximum oxygen uptake during swimming and running by elite swimmers. *J. Appl. Physiol.* **33**:510-513.

HOUSTON, M.E. 1978. Metabolic responses to exercise, with special reference to training and competition in swimming. In: B.O. Eriksson and B. Furberg (eds.), *Swimming Medicine IV*, pp. 207-232. University Park Press, Baltimore.

STRÖM, G. 1949. The influence of anoxia on lactate utilization in man after prolonged muscular work. *Acta Physiol. Scand.* **17**:440-451.

Temperature Regulation and Immersion

Albert B. Craig, Jr.

University of Rochester School of Medicine and Denistry,
Rochester, New York, USA

A recently published bibliography titled *Man in the Cold Environment* contains about 500 abstracts, most of which have appeared in the literature since 1972 (Schilling, 1980). There were, of course, many other earlier publications which were not included. It is not possible to cover the entire subject of thermoregulation in a cold environment and my review must therefore be limited. The aim of this article is to discuss temperature regulation in water as it relates to competitive and recreational swimmers. Man's normal environment is air, but people enter the water for many reasons, including rehabilitation, recreation, and competitive sports. Many physiological responses are different in air than in water, but for swimmers the most important factor is heat exchange between the water and the body.

In both media, thermal balance is defined as the equality of heat production and heat loss. Heat production is related to resting energy expenditure plus any additional energy for activity and/or shivering. Heat is lost by conduction, radiation, convection, and evaporation. In air, conductive heat loss is so small that it is usually ignored, but in water this route is very important. Convective losses are also different between water and air (Boutelier et al., 1977). In air, increases in convective heat loss are related to movement of air past the surface. This route can be controlled by clothing which traps the air and conserves heat. In water, convective heat loss is unregulated because the swimmer usually does not wear protective clothing. In addition, there is almost always a significant movement of water around the body. Radiation and evaporation are important pathways of heat exchange in air but are not functional in water.

The maintenance of constant body temperature depends on the balance between heat production and heat loss. If production exceeds losses, the body temperature increases, and conversely, if losses are greater than production, temperature decreases. In air the most common regulation is behavioral; we adjust clothing to control heat losses. The development of protective devices for accidental immersion has produced some interesting results (Hayward et al., 1975), but clothing is irrelevant to recreational or competitive swimmers.

In addition to behavioral regulation, the body's insulation can be varied by physiological mechanisms that adjust blood flow to the peripheral parts of the body. The Fick Principle can be used to quantify these processes:

$$\text{Rate of heat loss} = Q_{skin} (T_{core} - T_{skin}) (.83),$$

where Q_{skin} is the blood flow in L/min to the skin and the constant .83 is the specific heat of blood expressed as kcal/(L × °C).

In a cool environment where the difference between core and skin temperatures may be great, a decreased blood flow to the skin is the major mechanism for heat conservation. In air this vasoconstriction is a function of both the skin and central body temperatures. During immersion, hand blood flow is minimal when the water temperature is between 30 and 31°C (Craig and Dvorak, 1976). This water temperature is significantly greater than that of most swimming pools. The recommended temperature for competitive swimming is between 26 and 27°C which is about the same temperature as when the pool is used for recreation. This writer measured the surface temperatures in several local lakes at a time when the residents said swimming was very pleasant. These temperatures varied between 20 and 23°C. Under most conditions, the water temperature experienced by swimmers will elicit maximal vasoconstriction.

Another basic response to exposure to a cold environment is shivering. This muscle activity increases heat production, but many people argue that as most muscles are relatively close to the surface much of the excess heat production is lost to the water. Therefore, there seems to be no significant benefit from the increased heat production in terms of achieving thermal balance. In our studies of head-out immersion at rest, the oxygen consumption was minimal in water between 32 and 36°C. In 30°C water, energy production did not increase until the last 20 min of the 1-hr immersion, but with 28°C it increased after 10 min (Craig and Dvorak, 1966). These and other studies (Burton and Bazett, 1936; Carlson et al., 1958; Cooper et al., 1976; Hayward et al., 1977; Keatinge, 1969; Nielsen, 1973; Rennie, 1965) indicate that, at rest, the cold stress which elicits shivering occurs at water temperatures only a few degrees less than the subject's core temperature.

In contrast to our studies of subjects at rest, it was found that during light work the oxygen consumption was about .7 L/min in water temperatures between 28 and 35°C, but was increased in 24 and 26°C water. At slightly greater workloads, the oxygen consumption was .9 L/min and was increased only in 24°C water (Craig and Dvorak, 1968). In another

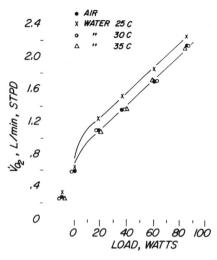

Figure 1—Relationships of rate of work to oxygen consumption in different environments. Points lying to the right of the zero workload indicate control measurements with the subjects at rest (Craig and Dvorak, 1969). Reprinted with permission of the American College of Sports Medicine.

study, a greater range of energy expenditure was obtained by using a bicycle-type ergometer with both arm and leg pedaling (Craig and Dvorak, 1969). This ergometer also had the advantage of producing the same oxygen consumption for a given workload in and out of the water. It was observed that the relationships between workloads in the range of 0-84 W oxygen consumption was no different in air of 22°C compared to 30 or 35°C water (Figure 1). In 25°C water, the oxygen consumption was increased by .14 L/min at all workloads even though the subjects did not report shivering. This increment in oxygen consumption probably reflects the increase in muscle tension that precedes recognizable shivering.

McArdle et al. (1976) used the same ergometer and extended the observations to greater workloads and colder water. Their results were similar to ours except at a work rate of 120 W the oxygen consumption was no different in 18°C water compared to warmer water or to air. Other studies have documented the increased energy costs of swimming in cool water (Hong and Nadel, 1979; Nadel et al., 1974; Nielsen, 1973; Pugh, 1965).

The rule specifying water temperature in the range of 26-27°C for competitive swimming was not based on the experimental results cited, but in retrospect it represents a good empirical decision. Several years ago a US national championship meet was held in a new, 50-m pool. The builders were late in completing the pool, and there was insufficient time to heat the water to the required temperature. The water temperature was 1.5°C less than the lower recommended standard. No national records were established during the meet despite the fact that many were broken at this meet the year before and the year after.

As previously mentioned, behavioral responses to both thermal stresses are very common, and this observation is also true in water. When most people enter the water, they begin to swim immediately, and they do not remain in the water for very long. Some years ago our family belonged to a swimming club with an outdoor pool. There was a rule excluding children from the water for 15 min out of every hour. When the "adult time" began a number of people entered the pool, but after 5 min the only ones still swimming were those doing so for exercise. If you use a watch to measure the time adults spend in a lake or in the ocean, you will find it is usually less than 2 min. In that period, considerable heat can be lost from the skin, and the subject is ready to regain the heat in the air environment.

In contrast to adults, children seem to adjust their behavior as a response to thermal stress. They usually are involved in games which demand considerable activity, and the consequent increased heat production probably balances heat losses. This is quite a common observation which many adults don't understand. Many adults also don't appear to understand that many children don't mind shivering even when they are active if they are having fun with their peers.

Methods of quantifying temperature regulation have been devised for subjects in the air environment. However, there are some serious reservations about using these techniques in water. Two approaches have been used, called direct and indirect calorimetry. In both methods heat production is assessed by measuring the oxygen consumption and by using a caloric equivalent of 4.8-5.0 kcal/L of oxygen. The methods of evaluating heat losses are quite different. Direct calorimetry involves enclosing a subject in a calorimeter capable of capturing and measuring the heat lost. Changes in heat stores are calculated as the differences between heat production and heat loss. In indirect calorimetry, heat losses are assessed as the sum of the heat production and the change in heat stores. This latter value is calculated from the changes in mean body temperature multiplied by the specific heat of body tissues, with the value of .83 kcal/(kg × °C) for specific heat usually used.

The use of direct calorimetry is limited because the methods are cumbersome, the conduct of experiments is tedious, and the expense is great (Burton and Bazett, 1936; Lefevre, 1911; Webb, 1973). Indirect calorimetry involves only the measurement of oxygen consumption, which has become relatively simple, as well as the recording of changes in temperature at specific sites. Formulas for calculating the change of mean body temperature from the changes in peripheral and core temperatures and expressing this change of temperature as heat loss or gain are comparatively easy to apply and are therefore inviting.

Since the temperature at different points in the body varies, the value for a mean body temperature is very difficult to assess. The most common solution to this problem is to use a simple, two-compartment model (Burton, 1935) which says there is a core at one temperature and the rest of the body, the periphery, is at another temperature. Although the temperature of each compartment may change, it must be assumed that size of the compartment is constant. Furthermore, it is assumed that each compartment is homogeneous in terms of the temperature. In order to use this model it is necessary to find a representative core temperature. The most common site of measurement has been the rectum, although in recent years the temperature of the outer surface of the tympanic membrane has been a useful site. A number of techniques have been used, including a small temperature sensor and radio transmitter which can be swallowed (Kuehn et al., 1977).

The most common solution to assessing the peripheral temperature is to measure the temperature at several representative sites on the surface of the skin and to calculate a mean temperature by using predetermined proportional sizes of each area. This final value is called weighted mean skin temperature (T_{skin}).

The final step in calculating mean body temperature involves using a factor for the size of each compartment. Various factors for the size of the core have been used ranging from .9 to .6 of the body mass (Burton and Bazett, 1936; Craig and Dvorak, 1966, 1968; Rennie, 1965). In this two-compartment model the size of the periphery is, by definition, 1 − core. These proportions were originally derived from data obtained by direct calorimetry (Burton, 1935). During periods of unsteady states, the differences between heat production and loss reflect changes in heat stores. In such periods, it is also necessary to measure the changes in core temperature and weighted mean skin temperature. The change in heat stores can be expressed as a change in mean body temperature by using .83 kcal/(kg × °C) for the specific heat of the tissue:

$$T_{body} = T_{core} \times f + T_{periphery} \times (1 - f),$$

where f is the proportional size of the core compartment.

If the changes in mean body temperature and in temperatures of the core and periphery are known, this equation can then be solved for f. Burton (1935) utilized data from experiments designed for quite a different purpose but felt the results were suitable for calculating the factor of proportionality. Calculations from ca. 40 such experiments suggested that the change in rectal temperature was representative of .65 of the total mass and the periphery, .35. In recalculating the data, this writer found that f was negative in about half of the experiments. This is a theoretically impossible result, and if these experiments are eliminated, quite different factors are derived.

In addition to these problems of using changes in core and peripheral temperatures to assess changes in heat stores, water immersion presents additional complications. It is almost impossible to know the temperature of the peripheral compartment. Measuring skin temperature necessitates insulating the measuring device from the water and thus insulating the area of the skin measured (Craig and Dvorak, 1966, 1968). Some in-

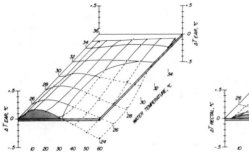 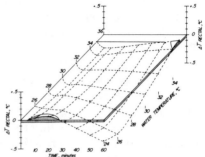

Figure 2 — Average changes in temperature of the insulated external auditory canal, T_e, of 10 subjects during light work and immersion in different water temperatures (Craig and Dvorak, 1968). Reprinted with permission of the American Physiological Society.

Figure 3 — Average changes in rectal temperature, T_r, for the same experiments shown in Figure 2 (Craig and Dvorak, 1968). Reprinted with permission of the American Physiological Society.

vestigators (Nadel et al., 1974) have inserted temperature probes just under the surface of the skin, but the number of sites studied by such techniques usually is very limited. In any case, the surface temperature of the immersed subject falls rapidly and is not measurably different from the water temperature. In addition, if you use the water temperature as the temperature of the periphery, there is no assurance that the size of this compartment is constant throughout the period of immersion.

Assessing the changes in heat content of the core also produces some problems in water. Rectal temperature may be influenced by cold venous blood returning from the extremities (Carlson et al., 1958; Cooper et al., 1976; Keatinge, 1969; Nadel et al., 1974; Nielsen, 1973). It has been reported that at the beginning of immersion the temperature in the insulated external auditory canal (T_{ear}) and that in the rectum (T_r) increased for the first 15-20 min before falling (Craig and Dvorak, 1966). When the subject was exercising, the increase in T_{ear} lasted longer, but the T_r decreased very quickly in almost all water temperatures (Figures 2 and 3) (Craig and Dvorak, 1968). These results could be explained by a cooling of the rectal site associated with increased blood flow from the legs. Webb (1973) used a unique water-heated garment to study rewarming after immersion in water of 5-15°C. He concluded that "none of the following body temperatures reliably indicated completion of rewarming: rectal, ear canal, esophageal, skin (mean or any of 8 sites), calf or chest subcutaneous temperature, or calculated mean body temperature."

Burton and Bazett (1936) addressed the problem of heat loss in water using direct calorimetry. They adjusted the electrical heaters in an insulated bathtub to maintain the water at a constant temperature and calculated heat loss as the difference between the heat needed to maintain

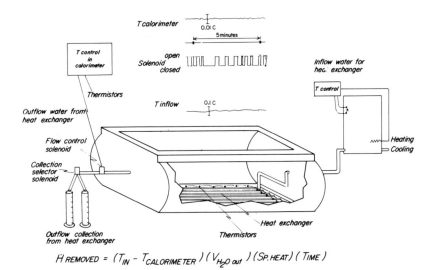

$$H_{REMOVED} = (T_{IN} - T_{CALORIMETER})(V_{H_2O\ out})(SP.HEAT)(TIME)$$

Figure 4—Schematic representation of the direct water calorimeter (Craig and Dvorak, 1976). Reprinted with permission of the Federation of American Societies for Experimental Biology.

Figure 5—Schematic representation of the water flow in the direct water calorimeter (Craig and Dvorak, 1976). Reprinted with permission of the Federation of American Societies for Experimental Biology.

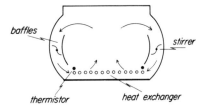

constant water temperature with and without the subject in the bath. Most of the experiments were done on one of four subjects, with the range of water temperatures between 31 and 36°C. They concluded that "temperature differences exceeding 4°C lead to an increased heat loss which exceeded normal heat production." They also used the factors of .65 and .35 to caculate the mean body temperature and the change in body heat stores after rapidly increasing or decreasing the water temperature and were satisfied that such indirect calculations adequately described the observations by direct calorimetry. Initial studies of responses to immersion by Craig and Dvorak (1966, 1968) and those of Rennie (1965) used indirect calorimetry and led to a discussion of the appropriate proportionality factor, f, to use in water. It was apparent that further experience with direct calorimetry during immersion was needed.

The calorimeter used by Craig and Dvorak (1973, 1976) used the same principle as that of Burton and Bazett (1936). The water temperature was maintained to within ±.002°C and heat losses were calculated as the amount of heat which came from the subject and was removed from the calorimeter (Figures 4 and 5). The heat exchange was accomplished by

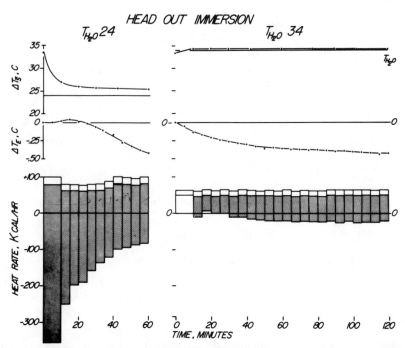

Figure 6 — Average heat balance during head-out immersion of 10 subjects in two water temperatures. The changes in mean skin temperature, T_s, and in temperature of the insulated external auditory canal, T_e, are shown at the top of the graph. Heat balance data are shown at the bottom. Heat production is indicated by the tops of the bars and the clear areas just below show the subtraction of calculated heat losses from the head and respiratory tract. The stippled areas represent heat losses to the water. The bottom lines which are below zero indicate heat losses from stores. The clear areas above zero during the first 30 min of immersion in 34°C water signifies heat gains by the body. Reprinted with permission of the Federation of American Societies for Experimental Biology.

controlling the flow of colder water through a series of copper tubes in the bottom of the bath. Stirring the water minimized the time delay between heat loss from the subject and its removal from the calorimeter, and the observations could be divided into 10-min periods (Craig and Dvorak, 1976). Heat production was assessed by continuous measurement of oxygen consumption. Heat losses were calculated as the sum of the heat lost to the water plus small additional losses from the respiratory tract and the head which was not immersed. Ten subjects were studied in water of 24, 26 and 28°C for 1 hr and 30, 32, 34, 35 and 36°C for 2 hr.

The results in two different water temperatures are shown in Figure 6. In the coldest water, 24°C, there was a great initial heat loss which decreased exponentially during the entire hour. T_{ear} showed an initial increase for 20 min followed by a decrease. T_{skin} decreased in the first 10 min. It is difficult to interpret the observation of a skin temperature

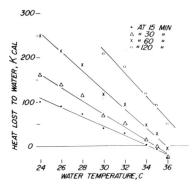

Figure 7 — Average heat lost (or gained) to water of different temperatures for 10 subjects at different times during immersion in the calorimeter (from Craig and Dvorak, 1976).

which remained about 1°C greater than the water, as it was necessary to insulate the thermisters from the water with closed-cell neoprene rubber. In 34°C water there was an initial small gain of heat in the first 20 min of immersion, but after 30 min and to the end of the 2 hr there was a negative heat balance.

A summary of these experiments is shown in Figure 7. Heat lost to the water was a direct, linear function of water temperature. Increased heat production by shivering did not significantly influence the heat balance. Peripheral vasoconstriction appeared to isolate the core from the periphery during the initial stages of immersion; however, this vascular response was ineffective in preventing heat loss during the later periods. Furthermore, it was not possible to calculate any proportionality factor, f, which would define the change in mean body temperature observed in this series of experiments. Despite physiological responses to the cold stress, the subject's heat exchange to the body resembled that of an inanimate body.

One implication of these findings is that during immersion in water, heat balance must be achieved by increased heat production. For unprotected swimmers this means they must exercise, and if the water temperature is cold as in the English Channel they must swim at a considerable pace (Pugh, 1965). Of course, the other alternative is to increase body fat which provides insulation or to wear protective clothing as divers do.

Another related observation is that the ingestion of alcohol which would be expected to cause a vasodilation and increased heat loss does not influence the changes in core temperature in either 10°C or in warmer water of 22 and 30°C (Keuhn et al., 1977; Martin and Cooper, 1978; Martin et al., 1977). The water is such an overwhelming heat sink that the anticipated pharmacologic effect of alcohol is either masked or overridden by the cold stress.

This thermal stress of immersion also makes acclimatization difficult. The only long-term effects of repeated exposure have been described in the diving women (Ama) of Korea. Rennie (1965) determined the water temperature necessary to prevent shivering during a 3-hr period of immersion. When corrected for skinfold thickness, this so-called "shivering threshold" was less for the Ama than for the control subjects. Recently these investigators have restudied the Ama who now use "wet suits" for diving and have found that the decreased "shivering threshold" is no longer observed (Rennie, personal communication).

However, repeated daily immersion in cold water does produce subjective evidence of acclimatization. When swimming in 16-18°C water, the pain and other discomfort limits immersion to 2-5 min for 3 or 4 days. After about 5 days, I find it possible to swim for 10-15 min before the sensations of cold force me to leave the water. We attempted to document this subjective evidence of acclimatization by repeated immersion in 20°C water in the laboratory, but did not find a good physiologic parameter to measure. The only change observed was that the temperature of the forehead skin increased in the first 20 min of immersion and this increase seemed to be faster at the end of 5 days. A possible interpretation of this observation is that acclimatization involves the speed of vasoconstriction and partial isolation of the periphery. If blood flow to the skin were decreased more rapidly with acclimatization, this change in response would permit the skin to cool faster. It has been shown (Keatinge, 1969) that at about 20°C nerve conduction from the "cold sensors" is blocked. This type of local anesthesia would decrease this source of discomfort. The remaining sensation of cold would depend on the hypothalmic sensors which would not respond until the temperature of the core decreased after the initial increase. This hypothesis of acclimatization to the cold stress of immersion is compatible with the current information but has not been tested.

For the competitive swimmer in water of 26-27°C, the implications for problems of heat exchange are that during practice, heat production usually balances losses. However, during the first 10-15 min, there is probably still a significant loss of heat from body stores. If you spend much time with swimmers, you will note that the entry into the water at the beginning of practice usually is characterized by hesitancy and verbal protests. It is also possible to observe anticipatory piloerection and it probably would be possible to show vasoconstriction even before entry.

We also have a few swimmers with very little subcutaneous fat, and they often take time out during practice for a warm shower. Children who have a less favorable mass-to-surface ratio cool faster than adults (Sloan and Keatinge, 1973), and in working with young swimmers the coach must consider these problems. If you attend these children in practice, you will observe many who are shivering. When not swimming, most will assume postures that may attenuate heat loss. They stand in a huddled position with the legs together and with the arms folded across the chest even if they are still in water. Young swimmers should probably be active continuously during practice and periods of verbal instruction with the subjects standing in the water should be minimized.

When subjects leave the water, they have a well documented further drop in core temperature (Carlson et al., 1958; Cooper et al., 1976; Keatinge, 1969). As the skin temperature and peripheral blood flow increase, cold blood from the extremities cools the core of the body, an observation which also has implications for the coach. Requiring young children to make frequent changes between the water and the air may result in more cooling than continuous immersion and activity. In preparation for competition, the swimmer usually has a "warm-up." After this time the swimmers leave the pool, dry, and sit around in their wet suits. Under such conditions one would predict a decrease in the core temperature. After the "warm-up" our swimmers dry off, put on their "warm-ups" (pants and jacket), and don woolen hats, mittens, shoes, and socks. Their appearance contrasts markedly to that of the opponents, but we are assured that they have rewarmed by the time of their event.

Many other undocumented and subjective observations are related to heat exchanges during immersion, with many experiments yet to be done. However, it is known that immersion in water less than 32°C constitutes cold stress, and that the physiological responses of vasoconstriction and shivering are ineffective in limiting the decrease of body heat. The only appropriate response is behavioral, that is, to swim.

References

BOUTELIER, C., Bougues, L., and Timbal, J. 1977. Experimental study of convective heat transfer coefficient for the human body in water. *J. Appl. Physiol. Respirat. Environ. Exercise Physiol.* **42**:93-100.

BURTON, A.C. 1935. Human calorimetry. II. The average temperature of the tissues of the body. *J. Nutr.* **9**:261-280.

BURTON, A.C., and Bazett, H.C. 1936. A study of the average temperature of the tissues, of the exchanges of heat and vasomotor responses in man by means of a bath calorimeter. *Am. J. Physiol.* **117**:36-54.

CARLSON, L.D., Hsieh, A.C., Fullerton, F., and Elsner, R.W. 1958. Immersion in cold water and body tissue insulation. *J. Aviat. Med.* **29**:145-152.

COOPER, K.E., Martin, S., and Riben, P. 1976. Respiratory and other responses in subjects immersed in cold water. *J. Appl. Physiol.* **40**:903-910.

CRAIG, A.B., Jr., and Dvorak, M. 1966. Thermal regulation during water immersion. *J. Appl. Physiol.* **21**:1577-1585.

CRAIG, A.B., Jr., and Dvorak, M. 1968. Thermal regulation of man exercising during water immersion. *J. Appl. Physiol.* **25**:28-35.

CRAIG, A.B., Jr., and Dvorak, M. 1969. Comparison of exercise in air and in water of different temperatures. *Med. Sci. Sports* **1**:124-130.

CRAIG, A.B., Jr., and Dvorak, M. 1973. Heat balance during head out immersion in water. *Fed. Proc.* **32**:391.

CRAIG, A.B., Jr., and Dvorak, M. 1976. Heat exchanges between man and the water environment. In: C.J. Lambertson (ed.), *Underwater physiology V*, pp. 765-773. Proc. of the Fifth Symposium on Underwater Physiology. Fed. Am. Soc. Exp. Biol. Bethesda, MD.

HAYWARD, J.S., Eckerson, J.D., and Collis, M.L. 1975. Effect of behavioral variables on cooling rate of man in cold water. *J. Appl. Physiol.* **38**:1073-1077.

HAYWARD, J.S., Eckerson, J.D., and Collis, M.L. 1977. Thermoregulatory heat production in man: Prediction equation based on skin and core temperatures. *J. Appl. Physiol. Respirat. Environ. Exercise Physiol.* **42**:377-384.

HONG, S., and Nadel, E.R. 1979. Thermogenic control during exercise in a cold environment. *J. Appl. Physiol. Respirat. Environ. Exercise Physiol.* **47**:1084-1089.

KEATINGE, W.R. 1969. *Survival in Cold Water: The Physiology and Treatment of Immersion Hypothermia and Drowning*. Blackwell, Oxford.

KUEHN, L., Livingstone, S., Limmer, R., and Weatherson, B. 1977. The effect of ethanol consumption on human heat exchange. *Can. J. Physiol. Pharmacol.* **8**:43.

LEFEVRE, J. 1911. *Chaleur Animale et Bioenergetique*. Masson, Paris.

MARTIN, S., and Cooper, K.E. 1978. Alcohol and respiratory and body temperature during tepid water immersion. *J. Appl. Physiol. Respirat. Environ. Exercise Physiol.* **44**:683-689.

MARTIN, S., Diewold, R.J., and Cooper, K.E. 1977. Alcohol, respiratory, skin, and body temperature changes during cold water immersion. *J. Appl. Physiol. Respirat. Environ. Exercise Physiol.* **43**:211-215.

McARDLE, W.D., Magel, J.R., Lesmes, G.R., and Pechar, G.S. 1976. Metabolic and cardiovascular adjustment to work in air and water at 18, 25, and 33 °C. *J. Appl. Physiol.* **40**:85-90.

NADEL, E.R., Holmér, I., Bergh, U., Åstrand, P.-O., and Stolwijk, J.A.J. 1974. Energy exchanges of swimming man. *J. Appl. Physiol.* **36**:465-471.

NIELSEN, B. 1973. Metabolic reactions to cold during swimming at different speeds. *Arch. Sci. Physiol.* **27**:A207-A211.

PUGH, L.G.C.E. 1965. Temperature regulation in swimmers. In: H. Rahn (ed.), *Physiology of Breath-hold Diving and the Ama of Japan*, pp. 325-348. Nat'l(U.S.) Acad. of Sci.-Nat'l Res. Council. Publ. no. 1341.

RENNIE, D.W. 1965. Thermal insulation of Korean diving women and non-divers in water. In: H. Rahn (ed.), *Physiology of Breath-hold Diving and the Ama of Japan*, pp. 315-324. Nat'l (U.S.) Acad. Sci.-Nat'l Res. Council. Publ. no. 1341.

SCHILLING, C.W. 1980. *Man in the Cold Environment: A Bibliography with Informative Abstracts*. Undersea Medical Society, Bethesda, MD. Publication no. 35 (Ce) 1-15-80.

SLOAN, R.E.G., and Keatinge, W.R. 1973. Cooling rates of young people swimming in cold water. *J. Appl. Physiol.* **35**:371-375.

WEBB, P. 1973. Rewarming after diving in cold water. *Aerospace Med.* **44**:1152-1157.

Effects of Swimming in Ice-cold and Warm Water on Changes in Plasma Volume and Free Fatty Acids

Václav Zeman and Václav Holeček
Faculty Hospital, Plzeň, Czechoslovakia

Jaroslav Novàk
Physical Culture Research Institute, Prague, Czechoslovakia

In the CSSR during recent years a special sport has been developing called "sports hardening" or winter swimming. It implies year-round outdoor swimming. During competition the athletes swim, depending on their degree of hardening and swimming fitness, 100-, 250-, 500-, 750-and 1,000-m races in water at temperatures of 0-8°C. The longest time permitted in water is 20 min. We were interested in the organism's response to this substantial cold stress and compared it with responses to swimming in warm water in a pool.

Material and Methods

We investigated four men who have participated regularly in 750-m races in water at temperatures of 0-4°C. Their mean age was 34 years, body weight 88.4 kg and body fat, according to Pařízková (1977), 21.0%. They have swum in ice-cold water for 2-12 seasons.

The examination was in three stages. Between each stage were 2-week intervals, with the investigation taking place in November and December 1980. We proceeded according to the following protocol which differed only as to the temperature of the water (T_w) in which the men swam and the air temperature (T_a). During the third stage, the subjects were examined at rest indoors. The three stages consisted of: (1) T_w 4°C, T_a 8°C, T_a indoors 20°C, waves 10-15 cm, swimming in a pond; (2) T_w 25°C, T_a 22°C, calm surface, swimming in an indoor pool; and (3) T_a 26°C, physical rest.

The athletes had a precisely outlined dietary regimen which was the same on all examination days. The swimming period was 20 min, which according to contest regulations is the longest permissible period that may be spent in ice-cold water. The men swam at a slow rate, with the distance covered about 600 m.

Fifteen min before and 15 min after swimming they engaged in warm-up exercises. The heart rate (HR), blood pressure (BP) and rectal temperature (T_r) were taken at rest, immediately after swimming and then 30 min, 1 and 2 hr after leaving the water. Blood was collected at rest, immediately after swimming and then 30 min, 2 and 4 hr after leaving the water. During the same time of day the data in stage 3 were gathered without swimming, indoors, at rest.

The BP was assessed by the auscultation method, the heart rate by palpation and the T_r by means of a thermometer inserted 5 cm into the rectum. The complete hemogram was assessed on a Coulter S apparatus. The hematocrite (Htc) was determined by a micromethod from samples. Free fatty acids (FFA) were determined by Duncombe's (1964) time method. Using the Htc and hemoglobin (Hb) values in Dill and Costill's (1974) equation V, changes in plasma volume were calculated as a part of the investigation. The assessed FFA values were corrected (Ohira et al., 1977) using percentage of the changes in plasma volume. Differences were tested using Student's t-test ($p \le .05$).

Results

The stresses in the different stages were characterized primarily by the rectal temperature (T_r) curve. After swimming in cold water the T_r declined on the average to 34.7°C, whereas it rose after swimming in the pool with warm water on the average to 38.3°C (Figure 1). According to the heart rate, which after emerging from the water was on the average 110 b/m, the load may be described as light (Seliger et al., 1966). A statistically significant increase in BP occurred only after swimming in ice-cold water (Figure 2). The diastolic pressure rose significantly only 30 min after swimming (Figure 3).

Changes in plasma volume are illustrated in Figure 4. Hemoconcentration develops after swimming in cold as well as in warm water, although in cold water it is more marked and reaches its peak after leaving the water. During the 4th hr in all stages, hemodilution occurred. A statistically significant increase in FFA also was recorded 30 min after emergence from the water (Figure 5). The increase is also similar and significant when corrected for changes in the plasma volume.

Discussion

Swimming for 20 min in water with a temperature of 4°C puts considerable demands on the thermoregulating capacity of the organism as it

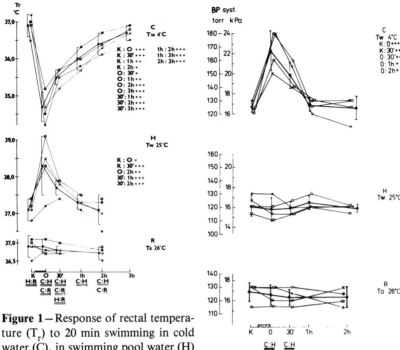

Figure 1 — Response of rectal temperature (T_r) to 20 min swimming in cold water (C), in swimming pool water (H) and at physical rest in a laboratory environment (R). Legend: K — rest values; O — values immediately after swimming; 30 min, 1 hr, 2 hr, 3 hr, 4 hr — values in 30 min and 1-4 hr after swimming. Data are given for four individual subjects. Filled circles and vertical lines illustrate mean values ± 1 standard deviation. Statistical significance: $p < 0.05$, underlined once or +; $p < 0.01$, underlined twice or + +; $p < 0.001$, underlined three times + + +.

Figure 2 — Response of systolic blood pressure (BP syst) to swimming in cold water (C), in swimming pool water (H) and at physical rest in a laboratory environment (R). Other abbreviations as in Figure 1.

attempts to restrict the heat output. Vasoconstriction of the periphery and centralization of the circulation develop (Itoh, 1974; Zeman and Novak, 1976, 1978). This reaction also is associated with a rise in BP. However, even adapted subjects cannot maintain a positive thermal balance and a decline in T_r occurs. Cold water is a potent stressing stimulus, followed by irritation of the sympathetic nervous system (sympathoadrenal system) (Itoh, 1974; Suzuki, 1972). Catecholamine release is the common denominator for the response of the BP and the FFA output.

The participation of noradrenaline (NA) in the rise of BP during cold exposure was shown by Itoh (1974) who eliminated the cold response of

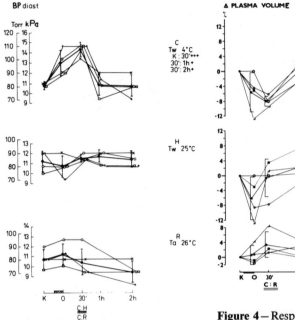

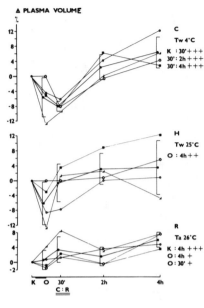

Figure 3 – Response of diastolic blood pressure (BP diast) to swimming in cold water (C), in swimming pool water (H) and at physical rest in a laboratory environment (R). Other abbreviations as in Figure 1.

Figure 4 – Response of plasma volume changes (plasma volume) to swimming in cold water (C), in swimming pool water (H) and at physical rest in a laboratory environment (R). Other abbreviations as in Figure 1.

BP by administering ganglioplegic hexamethonium. It is also known that FFA release from adipose tissue during exposure to cold is due to the action of catecholamines (Doi et al., 1974; Gilen et al., 1962; Inoue, 1972; Itoh, 1974). A rise in systolic and diastolic blood pressure along with a rise of FFA after a 2-min immersion of one forearm into water of 4°C was observed by Tsutsumi et al. (1970).

During swimming in ice-cold water, the mutual antagonistic action of the organism's thermoregulating reaction and response to physical stress is involved. Thermoregulation tends to restrict the blood flow through peripheral parts of the body, whereas the stress response tends to enhance the blood supply to the muscles. In our opinion, this was why the diastolic pressure rose markedly in these subjects only 30 min after they had left the water when only the thermoregulating processes were occurring and with no physical load. During these 30 min, all men also developed a more or less marked tremor.

The insignificant FFA rise in a warm environment and during swimming in warm water was, in our opinion, due to the fact that FFA are not

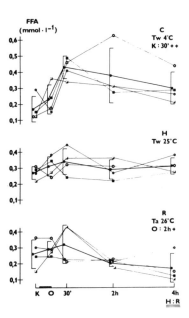

Figure 5 — Response of free fatty acids in blood (FFA) to swimming in cold water (C), in swimming pool water (H) and at physical rest in a laboratory environment (R). Other abbreviations as in Figure 1.

only mobilized during muscular activity but are also consumed. Thus, a significant rise was recorded only 30 min after cold exposure when the catecholamine output obviously proceeded without physical load as a response to the still-low body temperature, as illustrated by the low T_r. This fact is also confirmed by the higher diastolic pressure during this period.

Hemoconcentration in the cold could be the result of cold diuresis which can be inhibited by small doses of Pitressin (Bader et al., 1952), and thus must be due to reduced antidiuretic hormone (ADH) secretion (Itoh, 1974; Segar and Moore, 1968). This finding explains why cold-induced vasoconstriction causes a shift of blood from the periphery to the center, because volume receptors are stimulated and resulting in a lower ADH output. A significant rise in Htc and plasma proteins occurs on the average by about 10%. During a physical load such as swimming, the hemoconcentration moreover shifts to the working muscles (Poortmans, 1969).

Swimming in very cold water thus presents a high demand on the functional capacity of humans, not only from a thermoregulation viewpoint but in all other systems as well, including the sympathoadrenal system.

References

BADER, R.A., Eliot, J.W., and Bass, D.E. 1952. Hormonal and renal mechanisms of cold diuresis. *J. Appl. Physiol.* **15**:649-653.

DILL, D.B., and Costill, D.L. 1974. Calculation of percentage changes in volumes of blood, plasma and red cells in dehydration. *J. Appl. Physiol.* 37:247-248.

DOI, K., Kuroschima, A., and Itoh, S. 1972. Metabolic responses to whole body cold exposure in man. *Hokkaido J. Med. Sci.* 47:382; quoted by Itoh, S. 1974. Physiology of cold-adapted man. Hokkaido Univ., Sapporo, Japan.

DUNCOMBE, W.G. 1964. The colorimetric micro-determination of nonesterified fatty acids in plasma. *Clin. Chir. Acta* 9:122-125.

GILEN, A., Maickel, R.P., Nikodijevic, O., and Brodie, B.B. 1962. Essential role of catecholamines in the mobilisation of free fatty acids and glucose after exposure to cold. *Life Sci.* 12:708-715.

INOUE, T. 1972. Thermal regulation during water immersion. In: S. Itoh et al. (eds.), *Advances in Climatic Physiology*. Igaku Schoin, Tokyo.

ITOH, S. 1954. The release of antidiuretic hormone from the posterior pituitary body on exposure to heat. *Jpn. J. Physiol.* 4:185; quoted by Itoh, S. 1974. Physiology of cold-adapted man. Hokkaido Univ., Sapporo, Japan.

ITOH, S. 1974. Physiology of Cold-Adapted Man. Hokkaido Univ., Sapporo, Japan.

OHIRA, Y., Ito, A., and Ikawa, S. 1977. Correction of water content and solute concentration in blood during hemoconcentration. *J. Appl. Physiol. Respirat. Environ. Exercise Physiol.* 42:739-743.

PAŘÍZKOVÁ, J. 1977. *Body Fat and Physical Fitness*. Martinus Nijhoff, The Hague.

POORTMANS, J.R. 1969. Influence of physical exercise on proteins in biological fluids. In: J.R. Poortmans (ed.), *Biochemistry of Exercise*, pp. 312-327. S. Karger, Basel-New York.

SEGAR, W.E., and Moore, W.W. 1968. The regulation of antidiuretic hormone release in man. I. Effects of change in position and ambient temperature. *J. Clin. Invest.* 47:2143-2145.

SELIGER, V. et al. 1966. *Physiology of Physical Exercise* (in Czech). SZN, Praha.

SUZUKI, M. 1972. Thyroid activity and cold adaptability. In: S. Itoh et al. (eds.), *Advances in Climatic Physiology*. Igaku Schoin, Tokyo.

TSUTSUMI, T., Goto, Y., Aoki, K. 1970. Effect of one arm immersion into cold water upon serum free fatty acid, blood sugar and serum electrolytes. *Bull. Phys. Fitness Res. Inst.* Japan 19:1-10.

ZEMAN, V., and Novák, J. 1976. Comparison of the heart rate, blood pressure, skin and rectal temperature during a stay in cold water without exercise and when swimming (in Czech). *Teor. Praxe těl. Vých.* 24;619-622.

ZEMAN, V., Novák, J. 1978. Response of the organism to a stay in cold water. *Teor. Praxe těl. Vých.* 26:223-226.

Some Medical Observations
of Marathon Swimmers after the Race

Jaroslav Novák

Physical Culture Research Institute, Prague, Czechoslovakia

Václav Zeman and Jiri Berger

Faculty Hospital, Plzen, Czechoslovakia

Bohdan Semiginovsky

Institute of Physiology, Prague, Czechoslovakia

Marathon swimming represents a workload of medium intensity performed for a period of 1-10 hr, depending on the length of the race and the swimmer's performance. This type of event is often performed in cool water. In order to find out whether exposure to prolonged physical activity in a horizontal position in cool water has an unfavorable influence on the electrophysiological function of the myocardium, ECGs were examined in 25 swimmers who had finished the marathon (Zeman and Novák, 1975). No pathological changes were detected. This examination was exploratory only, and it is evident that this problem will have to be investigated in greater detail and on a larger sample.

Since many races take place in rather cold water (less than 20°C) one can expect body cooling to occur in some of the participants (Bergh et al., 1977; Holmér and Bergh, 1974; Kollias et al., 1974; Sloan and Keatinge, 1975; Wagner et al., 1974). Hence, it was decided to monitor rectal temperatures (T_r) of the marathon swimmers as well. Because very expressive disorders in body motion were sometimes noted in long-distance swimmers after finishing a race, it was decided to perform a neurological examination to objectify this phenomenon.

Subjects and Methods

The observations were made at a marathon in the Lipno Dam Lake which is organized every year at the beginning of September as an unofficial Czechoslovakian championship with international participation. The Lipno Dam Lake is situated in the Sumava mountains at 700 m above sea level; therefore, the climatic conditions may be rather severe in this locale at this time of the year. Conditions and distances for three successive years are presented in Table 1.

In 1977, 1978 and 1979 we examined, respectively, 24, 15 and 21 men and 5, 3 and 7 women. The mean ages of the men for the three races were 33, 30 and 34 years, respectively, and for women 26, 22 and 17 years. ECGs were recorded for 1 min in a horizontal position. The record was taken from the lead C5-S5R, which has previously been shown to be useful (Zeman and Novak, 1975; Zeman et al., 1977) and which is recommended by WHO for monitoring physical exercise (Lange-Andersen et al., 1971). The locations of the electrodes were marked on the skin so the records from both measurements could be compared. ECG signals were registered with a Startest I apparatus (Chirana-Czechoslovakia). The basic characteristics of the ECG and length of the electric systole (QT-interval) were evaluated. This interval was nearly always measured in three complexes and the means were calculated. The QT-interval was then corrected (QT_c) with respect to the heart rate (HR) according to Lepeschkin's homogram (Lepeschkin, 1957). In 1978 and 1979, percentage body fat (BF%) was calculated for each swimmer according to Pařízková (1977) on the basis of 10 skinfold thicknesses measured with a Best caliper. In 1978 and 1979, rectal temperature (T_r) was measured with a fast display thermometer (CSN 850537, range 31-42°C) which was placed in the rectum, ca. 5 cm deep. In order to compare swimmers with different performances, cooling rates (CR) were calculated as an average T_r-decrease per hour of swimming (Golden et al., 1979). In 1978, skin temperature also was measured on the forehead, forearm and shin with a battery-powered thermometer (Biotherm MB 5403 Medicor, Hungary, range 16-44°C). The sites for measurements were marked with color in advance.

In order to compare the results for the degree of adaptation to cold, the following criteria were used: no adaptation = 0, daily washing in

Table 1

Climatic Conditions and Distances during Three Marathons

Marathon	Water temperature (T_w-°C)	Air temperature (T_a-°C)	Distances (km)
1977	18	25	10, 20
1978	14	7 to 13	2.5*, 5, 10
1979	16 to 17	17 to 20	5*, 10, 20

*Women only.

cold water = 1, cold shower 2 times a week or more = 2, regular swimming in water of 10-15°C = 3; and for winter swimming, able to swim 100 m in water of 0-5°C = 4, able to swim 250 m in water 0-5°C = 5, able to swim 500 m in water 0-5°C = 6, able to swim 750 m in water 0-5°C = 7, able to swim 1,000 m in water 0-5°C = 8. Differences in data before and after the race were tested using the paired Student t-test. A correlation matrix was developed in order to detect mutual dependence of various variables.

In 32 swimmers participating in the 1979 marathon, eye bulb nystagmus, great asymmetry, diadochokinesis, elementary postural reflexes, and myotatic reflexes were examined a day before and within 20 min after the marathon. The Chi-square Test of Association was used for statistical evaluation of these variables.

Results

Significant protraction of QT_c appeared in all three marathon performances (Table 2). On the other hand, no difference could be shown in QT_c after swimming races of various lengths.

In 1977, QT_c was abnormal in two swimmers before the start (one shortened, one protracted); after the race, six swimmers showed abnor-

Table 2

Heart Rate (HR), Length of QT Interval (QT) in msec, and Corrected QT Interval (QT_c) Changes in Swimming Marathons: Men

Marathon	n	Before		After		Significance (p)
		X̄	SD	X̄	SD	
1977[a]	24					
HR		64	17	93	25	< 0.001
QT		0.37	0.03	0.34	0.03	< 0.01
QT_c		100.2	8.8	110.3	8.0	< 0.01
1978[b]	15					
HR		58	11	80	13	< 0.001
QT		0.36	0.03	0.35	0.04	NS
QT_c		93.5	5.4	102.8	8.1	< 0.001
1979[c]	21					
HR		66	8	85	15	< 0.001
QT		0.36	0.02	0.34	0.04	NS
QT_c		97.1	4.7	104.9	6.8	< 0.001

[a]Races were 10- and 20-km. Average time, 4 hr 35 sec (range 3:01-8:10).
[b]Races were 5- and 10-km. Average time, 2 hr 6 sec (range 1:05-3:57).
[c]Races were 10- and 20-km. Average time, 4 hr 57 sec (range 2:58-3:44).
NS = not significant.

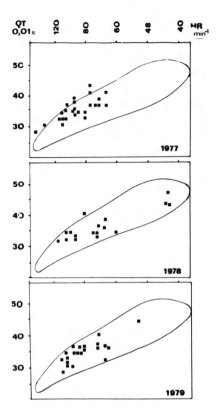

Figure 1—Corrected QT interval (QT$_c$) values in marathon swimmers (full squares) after the races in 1977 (upper part), 1978 (middle part) and 1979 (lower part) in Lepeschkin's nomogram as related to heart rate (HR) and QT interval (QT).

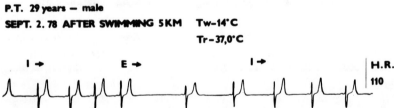

P.T. 29 years — male

SEPT. 2. 78 AFTER SWIMMING 5 KM   Tw–14°C

Tr–37,0°C

Figure 2—Respiratory arrhythmia in swimmer P.T. after the race.

mal QT$_c$ (protracted in all cases). Pathologically protracted QT$_c$ was revealed in men only (Figure 1). Minor arrhythmias were also detected in men only; one swimmer had ventricular extrasystoles (6 and 7 • min^{-1}) after a 10-km race. These swimmers also had pathologically protracted QT$_c$ values. Expressed respiration arrhythmia was detected in two cases after the competition. Swimmer P.T., 28 years old, had an expressed arrhythmia after 20 km race, but no other type of supraventricular arrhythmia (e.g., wandering pacemaker, sinoatrial block) could be detected. The finding was found repeatedly in the same swimmer even in subsequent marathons (Figure 2).

In 1978, QT_c was abnormal in one subject before swimming (shortened) and in one subject after swimming (protracted) in men (Figure 1). Some long-distance swimmers (three men and one woman) expressed respiration arrhythmias after the competition.

In 1979, QT_c did not deviate from the norm in any of the swimmers (Figure 1). Supraventricular extrasystoles were registered frequently (up to $4 \cdot min^{-1}$) in two women. After swimming, a PQ-interval of 0.24 sec was registered in one woman at a heart rate of $88 \cdot min^{-1}$, T_r being 33.8°C. Expressed respiration arrhythmias appeared in three men after 10 km and in two women after a 5-km swim. Significant correlations of ECG parameters with other variables are given in Table 3.

Figure 3 indicates the changes of rectal temperature (T_r). Four swimmers in the 10-km race had no decrease in T_r. Three of them were "winter" swimmers with an average percentage body fat of 22.5. All were well trained and had achieved top performances in this sport for many years. For swimmers in the 5-km race, the decrease in T_r was rather significant. T_r after the race went down to 33°C in some of the swimmers. Four of five female swimmers in 10-, 5- and 2.5-km races had a significant decrease in T_r. Increased T_r was registered in only two cases after the race. Both were "winter" swimmers, one a man with body fat of 28%, and the other a woman with 29% body fat.

The changes in skin temperature of the forehead, forearm and shin in men are indicated in Figure 4. There was a significant decrease for all locations in both races. For group swimmers in the 10-km race, where no decrease in T_r was observed, T_s values on the forearm and shin were not significantly lower if compared with the swimmers in the 5-km race.

Figure 5 compares the changes in T_r and T_s on the shin in "winter" swimmers with those of other marathon participants. Both groups had a significant decrease for both values, but in the group of "winter" swimmers the final temperature is significantly higher. Percentages of body fat and average swimming times didn't differ significantly.

Table 3

Correlations of ECG Parameters

Marathon	Variable 1	Variable 2	Significance
1977	Length of race	QT_c after finish	< 0.05 - neg.
	Heart rate	QT_c after finish	< 0.05 - pos.
1978	QT_c before start	QT_c after finish	< 0.01 - pos.
1979	T_r	QT after finish	< 0.1 - neg.
	T_r	QT_c after finish	< 0.1 - neg.

pos. = positive correlation; neg. = negative correlation.

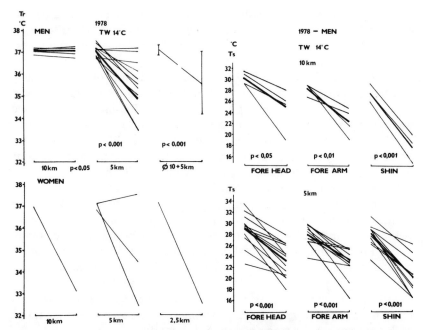

Figure 3—Rectal temperature changes (T_r) in the 1978 marathon. The lines connect the values before and after the race. The thicker line connects the mean values.

Figure 4—Skin temperatures (T_s) on the forehead, forearm and shin in the 1978 marathon. Thicker lines connect the mean values of individual measurements.

Figure 6 indicates T_r changes in the 1979 marathon. There was a significant decrease of T_r for swimmers in the 20- and 10-km races. The largest decreases were found in two swimmers with the lowest percentage of body fat (6.3 and 12.1%). An increase of T_r was registered in the same swimmers in the previous year's marathon. If comparing the changes of T_r in "winter" swimmers and "nonwinter" swimmers, the winter swimmers had a significantly higher T_r in the 20-km race. In this group, both percentage of body fat and swim time were higher. Significant correlations of T_r with other variables are presented in Table 4.

Higher incidence of nystagmus ($p < 0.05$), greater asymmetry ($p < 0.01$) and elementary postural reflexes ($p < .05$) were observed after the 1979 marathon. Incidence of increased myotatic reflexes was also observed, but the difference wasn't significant. This finding may be interpreted as an irritation of the vestibular apparatus, functional disorder of mid-brain and disorder of extrapyramidal system.

Discussion

No serious arrhythmias or ischemic changes appeared in the swimmers after finishing any of the three marathons. Supraventricular ex-

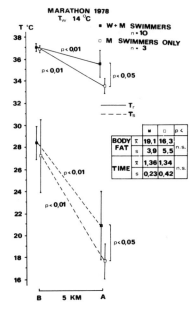

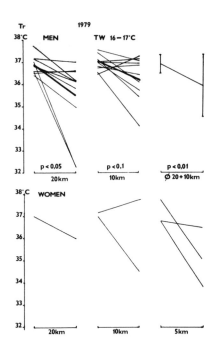

Figure 5 — Rectal temperature (T_r) and skin temperature (T_s) in winter and marathon swimmers (W + M) and in marathon swimmers only (M) in a 5-km race of the 1978 marathon. B = values before the race, A = values after the race, body fats = values given in percentage of body weight, time = average swimming time for the 5-km race (hr).

Figure 6 — Rectal temperature changes (T_r) in the 1979 marathon. For details, see Figure 3.

trasystoles appeared in individual cases, as they can be present even in quite healthy, trained persons in the recovery phase following exercise. They can be explained by a sudden predominance of the parasympathetic system after previous sympathetic irritation (Rous and Kocnar, 1978). Expressive respiration arrhythmia may be explained in the same way. We have not been able to show that these arrhythmias are connected with the cooling of the organism. Only a protracted PQ interval in a female swimmer was detected, together with the decrease of T_r to 33.8°C. This was, however, only an isolated finding, and no valid conclusions can be deduced from this observation.

In the literature (Zindler et al., 1966) reports on malignant arrhythmias (fibrillation of ventricles, asystole) during an operation performed under total anesthesia and hypothermia of 30-32°C appeared. In seven swimmers, T_r decreased to below 34°C, and in three swimmers it was even below 32.5°C. No serious arrhythmias were detected in any of these swimmers.

Table 4

Correlations of Body Temperature Parameters[a]

Marathon	Variable 1	Variable 2	Significance (p)
1978	Age	T_s forehead B	< 0.05 - neg.
	Age	T_s shin B	< 0.01 - neg.
	Age	T_r A	< 0.1 - neg.
	Length of race	T_r A	< 0.01 - pos.
	T_s forehead B	T_s forehead A	< 0.05 - pos.
	T_s shin B	T_s shin A	< 0.05 - pos.
	T_s forearm B	T_r B	< 0.01 - neg.
	Performance	Age	< 0.01 - neg.
	Performance	BF%	< 0.01 - neg.
	Hardening degree	T_r A	< 0.05 - pos.
	Hardening degree	T_r A	< 0.05 - pos.
	Hardening degree	Body cooling rate	< 0.05 - neg.
	Body cooling rate	BF%	< 0.05 - neg.
1979	T_r A	BF%	< 0.001 - pos.
	T_r A	Hardening degree	< 0.05 - pos.
	Hardening degree	BF%	< 0.1 - pos.
	Hardening degree	Body cooling rate	< 0.1 - neg.
	Body cooling rate	BF%	< 0.001 - neg.

[a]T_s = skin temperature; T_r = rectal temperature; BF% = body fat percentage; B = before the start; A = after the finish; pos. = positive correlation; neg. = negative correlation.

Protraction of QT_c after the finish was a regular finding. Schröder and Südhof (1971) considered this to be common in athletes after exercise. Busnengo and Rotta (1969) described QT_c protraction after an increasing bicycle ergometer load. Butschenko and Bürger (1965) observed QT_c protraction after exercise in untrained persons. Protracted QT_c in "winter" swimmers have been recorded after swimming in icy water (Zeman and Novak, 1976; Zeman et al., 1977) and in veteran runners after having finished a 25-km race (Novak and Kundrat, 1973).

The correlations revealed the influence of the length of a race on QT_c in one marathon only. In contrast to our original hypothesis, however, this correlation was negative. It may be explained by the fact that the more protracted QT_c in the shorter race was detected in a less highly trained person. Only in one marathon did QT and QT_c correlate negatively with T_r, which could indicate the possible influence of coolness on the protraction of QT_c. The influence of coolness on the protraction of QT_c was reported by Lepeschkin (1957).

The temperature of water is of prime importance for body temperature during marathon swimming. The data show that with a water temperature of 14°C there was a greater decrease in T_r than with a water temperature of 16-17°C, even when the swimming time was only a little more than half as long in the cooler water.

Humans are typical tropical animals in reacting to cold. The critical temperature of water (T_{wc}), for humans, is about 9°C higher than that of air and ranges between 32 and 35°C (Smith and Hanna, 1975; Wilkerson et al., 1974). The water temperature in marathon swimming in our country is below this level and requires intensive protective thermoregulatory mechanisms. These are either limitation of heat loss (fat, vasoconstriction) or increased production of heat (muscular work, shivering). These mechanisms do not have the same effect from the viewpoint of thermoregulation. Muscular work, and to a certain degree, even shivering, evoke increased blood flow through the superficial body regions. Due to this, the insulative ability of the body surface is decreased and the loss of body temperature is increased (Jansky, 1973; Keatinge, 1961; Nadel et al., 1974; Zeman and Novak, 1976).

Skinfold thickness is a significant factor in protection against cold. According to Smith's nomogram (Smith and Hanna, 1975), T_{wc} is 35°C in persons with 4% body fat whereas in persons with 20% body fat it is ca. 32°C. A number of authors (Bergh et al., 1977; Buskirk et al., 1963; Cannon and Keatinge, 1960; Kollias et al., 1974; Nadel et al., 1974; Sloan and Keatinge, 1975; Zeman and Novak, 1980) indicate a significantly higher decrease of body temperature in thin persons if in water below 20°C. Holmér and Bergh (1974) are of the opinion that in persons with up to 10% body fat, T_w has to be 18-20°C if the body temperature is to remain unchanged during swimming. In our investigaton as well, the skinfold thickness appeared to be an important factor in maintaining body temperature (see Table 4).

Peripheral vasodilation is not an unusual manifestation of acclimation to cold. It was observed by Hamel (1964) in the Eskimos, by Krog et al. (1960) in Norwegian fishermen, and by Paik et al. (1972) in Korean female divers. The increase of blood flow is, from the viewpoint of total thermoregulation, an unfavorable phenomenon, but may be advantageous as well in higher resistance to chilblain and in ensuring the realization of important functions of the hands in a cold environment (Lange-Andersen, 1970). Hamel (1954) indicates three main types of reactions in acclimatization to cold: (a) metabolic — increased production of heat; (b) isolation — the production of heat remains on the same level and isolation is increased (by vasoconstriction); (c) hypothermic — neither the production of the heat, nor vasoconstriction are increased, T_r is decreased.

All of these reactions were observed in our swimmers, namely in persons who are acclimated by "winter" swimming. The insulation and metabolic type prevents a decrease in T_r. In case of hypothermic reaction the organism is adapted to work under conditions of low body temperature by decreasing the thermal discomfort and sensations of cold (Bruck et al., 1976). From the correlation coefficients (Table 4) and from Figure 3 it is evident that our swimmers, evaluated as adapted, had higher T_r together with higher T_s values on the shin after swimming. This would indicate that a high degree of adaptation develops, above all, in the metabolic type of acclimation to cold. Higher T_r of cold-accustomed swimmers compared to unaccustomed ones at the end of the swimming in water temperature of 17°C was also described by Golden et al. (1979).

Exhaustion from swimming in waves may have been a factor in the T_r results in the 1978 marathon and also in the lack of significant correlation of T_r and percentage body fat in this race. The tolerance of long-distance swimmers to cold water generally is attributed to their combination of physical fitness and subcutaneous fat thickness (Pugh and Edholm, 1955).

Wagner et al. (1974) indicated that the loss of body temperature is lower in young people (20-29 years of age) due to higher vasoconstriction of the peripheral vessels. Older persons (46-67 years of age) do not increase their metabolism to the same extent as young persons and are not able to maintain their temperature by vasoconstriction.

Another investigation, similar to this study, was conducted by Bergh et al. (1977) on 41 men and 8 women in a race of 3.2 km and water temperature 19°C. The average T_r before the race was 37.7°C; after the race it was 36.4°C. The decrease in T_r was higher in slim persons, whereas in the obese ones T_r increased. The lower T_r in our swimmers corresponds to the cooler water and to the longer exposure.

References

BERGH, U., Ekblom, B., Gullstrand, L., and Holmér, I. 1977. Body temperature response to a long distance swimming race. *N. Z. J. Sports Med.* **5**:31.

BRÜCK, K., Baum, E., and Schwennicker, H.P. 1976. Cold-adaptive modifications in man induced by repeated short-term cold-exposure and during a 10-day and night cold-exposure. *Pflueg. Arch.* **363**:125-133.

BUSKIRK, E.R., Thompson, R.H., and Whedon, G.D. 1963. Metabolic response to cold air in men and women in relation to total body fat content. *J. Appl. Physiol.* **18**:603-606.

BUSNENGO, L.A., and Rotta, P. 1969. Modificazioni della durate dell intervallo QT nell electrocardiogramma durante lavoro muscolatore. (Modification of the duration of the QT interval in the electrocardiogram during muscular work.) *Med. Sport Torino* **22**:94-99.

BUTSCHENKO, L.A., and Bürger, H. 1965. Untersuchungen über Veränderungen des QT-Intervalls im Elektrokardiogramm von Sportlern. (Investigation of changes in QT intervals in electrocardiograms of sportsmen.) *Med. Sport* **5**:137-141.

CANNON, P., and Keatinge, W.R. 1960. The metabolic rate and heat loss of fat and thin men and heat balance in cold and warm water. *J. Physiol.* **154**:329-344.

GOLDEN, F.C., Hampton, I.F.G., and Smith, D. 1979. Cold tolerance in long distance swimmers. *J. Physiol.* **290**:48P-49P.

HAMMEL, H.T. 1964. Terrestrial animals in cold: Recent studies of primitive man. In: D.B. Dill (ed.), *Handbook of Physiology — Adaptation to the Environment*, pp. 413-414. Williams and Wilkins, Baltimore.

HOLMÉR, I., and Bergh, U. 1974. Metabolic and thermal response to swimming in water at varying temperatures. *J. Appl. Physiol.* **37**:702-705.

JANSKY, L. 1973. *Homothermia and Its Adaptability* (in Czech). Avicenum, Praha.

KEATINGE, K.R. 1961. The effect of work and clothing on the maintenance of the body temperature in water. *Q. J. Exp. Physiol.* **46**:69-81.

KOLLIAS, J., Barlett, L., Bergsteinova, V., Skinner, J.S., Buskirk, E.R., and Nicholas, W.C. 1974. Metabolic and thermal responses of women during cooling in water. *J. Appl. Physiol.* **36**:577-580.

KROG, J., Foekow, B., Fox, R.H., and Lange-Andersen, K. 1960. Hand circulation in the cold of Lappe and North-Norwegian fishermen. *J. Appl. Physiol.* **15**:654-658.

LANGE-ANDERSEN, K. 1970. Kälte-Anpassung. (Cold adaptation.) *Z. Physiol. Med.* **1**:117-132.

LANGE-ANDERSEN, K., Shephard, R.J., Denolin, H., Varnauskas, E., and Masironi, R. 1971. *Fundamentals of Exercise Testing*. WHO, Geneva.

LEPESCHKIN, E. 1956. *Das Electrokardiogram.* (The Electrocardiogram.) Steinkopf A., Dresden and Leipzig.

NADEL, E.R., Holmér, I., Bergh, U., Åstrand, P.-O., and Stolwijk, J.A.J. 1974. Energy Exchanges of swimming man. *J. Appl. Physiol.* **36**:465-471.

NOVAK, J., and Kundrat, M. 1973. The reaction of heart rate and ECG findings of veteran runners after 25 km race (in Czech). *Pracovni Lek.* **25**:283-287.

PAIK, K.S., Kang, B.S., Han, D.S., Rennie, D.W., and Hong, S.K. 1972. Vascular responses of Korean men to hand immersion in cold water. *J. Appl. Physiol.* **32**:446-450.

PAŘÍZKOVÁ, J. 1977. *Body Fat and Physical Fitness*. Martinus Nijhoff, The Hague.

PUGH, L.G.C., and Edholm, O.G. 1955. The physiology of channel swimmers. *Lancet*, pp. 761-768.

ROUS, J., and Kocnar, K. 1978. Sinoatrial blockade development during underwater swimming. *Swimming Medicine IV*, pp. 62-69. University Park Press, Baltimore.

SCHRÖDER, R., and Südhof, H. 1971. *The Evaluation of ECG in the Practice* (in Czech). Avicenum, Praha.

SLOAN, R.E.G., and Keatinge, W.R. 1975. Cooling rates of young people swimming in cold water. *J. Appl. Physiol.* **39**:93-102.

SMITH, R.M., and Hanna, J.M. 1975. Skinfolds and resting heat loss in cold air and water: Temperature equivalence. *J. Appl. Physiol.* **39**:93-102.

THAUER, R. 1965. Physiologie und Patophysiologie der Auskühlung in Wasser. (Physiology and pathology of cooling off in water.) In: *Uberleben auf See*, pp. 25-43. C.F. Boehringer, Mannheim.

WAGNER, J.A., Robinson, S., and Marino, R.P. 1974. Age and temperature regulations of humans in neutral and cold environments. *J. Appl. Physiol.* **37**:562-565.

WILKERSON, J.E., Raven, P.B., and Horvath, S.M. 1974. Critical temperature of unacclimatized Caucasians. *J. Appl. Physiol.* **37**:562-565.

ZEMAN, V., Holla, A., and Novak, J. 1977. Electrocardiographical changes after swimming in sportsmen adapted to cold water (in Czech). *Prakt. Lek.* **57**:16-18.

ZEMAN, V., and Novak, J. 1975. Electrocardiographical findings after performance of sports hardeners and endurance swimmers (in Czech). *Teor. Prax. tel. Vych.* **23**:465-469.

ZEMAN, V., and Novak, J. 1976. The influence of staying in cold water without movement and in connection with swimming on heart rate, blood pressure, skin and rectal temperature (in Czech). *Teor. Prax. tel. Vych.* **24**:619-622.

ZEMAN, V., and Novak, J. 1980. Body temperature of swimmers after competition in sports hardening (in Czech). *Theor. Prax. tel. Vych.* **28**:243-246.

ZINDLER, M., Dudziak, R., and Bunike, S. 1966. Erfahrungen bei 1290 Künstlichen Hypothermien für Herz und Gefässoperationen. (Experiences of 1290 artificial hypothermias of the heart and myocardium operations.)

Physiological Effects of a 24-Hour Swim

Jean-Claude Chatard, A. Geyssant, and J.R. Lacour
Laboratoire de Physiologie, Saint-Etienne, France

In May 1980 and March 1981, four attempts at the 24-hr world distance swimming record in a pool took place in St.-Etienne, France. Beyond the purely sporting aspect, this type of exercise poses a number of physiological problems and can even be dangerous to the competitor. It was felt it would be interesting to gather observations in order to be able to provide a few guidelines in helping reduce the dangers associated with these experiments.

Swimmers and Methods

Swimmers

The subjects included one woman and three men (one of whom had both legs amputated). See Table 1 for physical characteristics, $\dot{V}O_2$max, maximal heart rates and best swimming performance.

The tests were held in a covered pool, 50 m long. The temperature of the water was 26°C at the beginning of the test and was progressively increased to 31°C at the 20th hr. It was then maintained at that level until the end of the swim.

Every 20 min the swimmers took a nutritive solution of known caloric value. The quantity offered was related to their speed in an attempt to balance the energy expenditure. It was calculated as:

$$\overline{X} = \dot{V}O_2\text{max} \times P\% \times 21 \text{ kJ} \times 20 \text{ min.}$$

The subjects did not take all food offered but the quantities not ingested were measured precisely.

Measurements

Distances and times were collected by officials of the French Swimming Federation. The maximal oxygen uptakes ($\dot{V}O_2$max) were

Table 1

Characteristics of the Four Swimmers

Swimmer	Sex	Age (yr)	Height (cm)	Weight (kg)	$\dot{V}O_2$max (L·min^{-1})	HR max (bpm)	Best timing of the year (1,500 or 800 m)	Other details
BM	M	18	179	68	4.7	205	17 min 50 sec (1,500 m)	Hopes for international record in 1,500-m
MF	F	17	162	55	3.0	200	10 min 30 sec (800 m)	
AM	M	18	119	60	2.8	200	14 min 40 sec (1,500 m)	Both legs and left hand amputated. Medal in Olympic Games for the Handicapped, 1980.
PB	M	34	193	97	4.7	196	18 min 37 sec (1,500 m)	

measured during the week preceding the trial using a continuous test of increasing intensity on a treadmill for three of the competitors. For the fourth one (AM), $\dot{V}O_2$max was measured for his upper limbs on a cycloergometer, following the same procedure. During those preliminary tests, the maximal heart rates were also measured.

Blood samples were taken intravenously before the start of the experiment (D_1) and at the end (D_2). The following blood analyses were made: (a) plasma concentration in albumin and haptoglobin by radial immunodiffusion on M. Partigen® immunodiffusion slides (Behring); (b) hematocrit by centrifuging for 8 min at 8,000 rpm; (c) concentration of hemoglobin by the Drabkin method (1936); (d) deformation of red cells by measuring the time taken to cross the pores of a membrane 4 μm in diameter (hemorheometer prototype SP 001; Hanss, 1979); and (e) concentration of ATP in erythrocytes by the technique of bioluminescence with the complex luciferase-luciferin.

Methods of Estimation

Estimation of relative power of the swim (P%) was necessary because the conditions of the test precluded all types of direct measurement. The estimation was particularly detailed as a number of conclusions are based on this value. Relative power is the relationship between power developed during the swim at a given speed to maximal aerobic power (MAP) of the individual, measured using a bicycle or treadmill and two methods: (a) estimation by reference to the average speed over 800 and 1,500 m. During these 10- to 20-min long tests 90-95% of the energy was provided by aerobic processes. The power (P_1) corresponding to the average speed (S_1) sustained in this situation can be compared to the individual's MAP. P_2 is the power corresponding to the average speed (S_2) developed during the swim. If it is assumed that the mechanical efficiency is the same at both speeds, P_2 can be calculated by the following equation:

$$P_2 = P_1 \times S_2^3/S_1^3. \tag{1}$$

The other method was (b) estimation by reference to the relationship between heart rate and speed. This relationship was established for each of the swimmers after a 20-min warm-up using telemetry at increasing speeds (1-2 sec/100 m for each 100-m level), totaling a distance of 800-1,200 m. Since it is difficult to reach stable heart rates at low speeds, these tests were repeated two to three times at 24-hr intervals during the week preceding the trial. The final HR/speed curve was computed using all values obtained (15-25 points). The relative power (P%) corresponding to each speed was calculated as:

$$P\% = (HR \text{ measured} - \text{resting HR}) / (HR \text{ max} - \text{resting HR}) \tag{2}$$

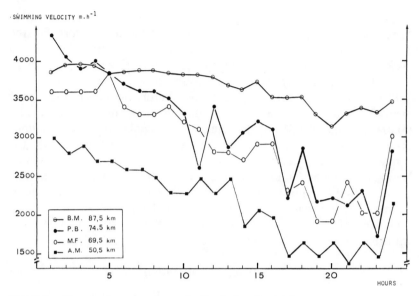

Figure 1—Changes in swimming velocity during the trial.

The heart rate at rest was fixed at 60 bpm. Maximal heart rate was established at 10 bpm below the maximum measured on the treadmill or cycle, applying the observations of Holmér (1974).

Results

Distances Covered and Speed Variations

The distances covered are indicated in Table 2. Subject BM's performance of 87.5 km was a world record for this type of trial. The speeds are indicated in Figure 1. For all swimmers, decreasing speeds were observed throughout the trial.

Each of the subject's swims was interrupted by a short pause. For BM the pauses were between 7 and 13 sec and came at 20-min intervals. These breaks were used to take in food; the other swimmers also stopped and came out of the water for 10- or 15-min massages (Table 2).

Relative Swimming Power

The two methods of estimation gave consistent results for all the competitors (Table 2). While swimming, the four competitors worked at a relative power between 30 and 40% of their MAP taking into account that the stops increased that difference. BM was particularly outstanding as the others swam at a lower relative power and stopped for longer periods.

Table 2

**Distance Covered, Average Speed, Overall Duration of the Stops
during the Trial and Relative Swimming Power**

Swimmer	Distance (km)	Average speed (km·hr⁻¹)	Overall duration of stops (min)	Relative power over 24 hr of swim (%)			
				(1) First method		(2) Second method	
				Without stops	With stops	Without stops	With stops
BM	87.5	3.646	15	39.5	39	41	
MF	69.5	2.896	80	30	28	29	
AM	50.5	2.104	142	36.5	31	31.5	
PB	74.5	3.104	145	35	32	36	

Energy Consumption

The energy expenditure of each competitor was calculated from the MAP and the relative power of the swim (Table 3). This energy consumption, whether expressed absolutely or corrected to a kg of body weight, was definitely higher for BM than for the other three swimmers. The regular feeding compensated more or less for this energy consumption. In one case (MF) feeding even overcompensated, since the decreasing speed after the 15th hr was not taken into consideration in determining the quantity of food offered to the swimmer. These results show that at these workloads it is possible to balance out and go beyond the energy expenditure of each individual.

Changes in Blood Variables

Table 4 shows the results of the blood sample measurements before the start (D_1) and at the finish (D_2) of the swim. In all swimmers the trial showed increases in plasma albumin concentration and hematocrit. The day following the event, however, revealed much lower readings of plasma albumin and hematocrit compared to initial readings. All swimmers' mean corpuscular volume (MCV) decreased during the trial.

Discussion

The methods of estimating the relative power of swim imply that MAP measured on a treadmill or bicycle is equal to the maximal power produced during an event of 800 or 1,500 m. We can assume that these values are close: In fact, the MAP achieved during swimming is 10% lower than that using a treadmill or bicycle (Holmér, 1974), but during events of 800 and 1,500 m, the anaerobic metabolism provides between 5 and 10% of the energy (Åstrand and Rodahl, 1977, p. 317).

Table 3

Food Intake, Energy Expenditure
(Estimated from Relative Swimming Power and $\dot{V}O_2$max)
and Weight Loss during the Trial with Food Given in Fluid Form

	Food intake		Water	Estimated energy expenditure		Weight loss
Swimmer	(MJ)	(kJ•kg^{-1})	(L)	(MJ)	(kJ•kg^{-1})	(kg)
BM	43	630	6.5	53	780	−3.9
MF	30	545	3.7	23	420	−0.750
AM	16.5	275	2.3	22	360	−2
PB	37	380	8.6	37	380	0

Table 4
Blood Variables Measured on the Four Swimmers

	BM		MF		AM		PB	
	D_1	D_2	D_1	D_2	D_1	D_2	D_1	D_2
Albumin (g·L^{-1})	43	52	39.9	42.7	38.5	42.7	42.7	44.1
Hematocrit (%)	0.475	0.490	0.435	0.447	0.465	0.480	0.475	0.485
Hemoglobin (mM)	9.9	10.5	9.32	9.9	10.2	11.1	9.7	10.6
MCV	93.3	92.6	89.3	85.1	80.7	75.4	88.3	82.6
Indication of filterability	17	106	8.7	11.8	8.8	10.4	7.2	8.3
Haptoglobin (g·L^{-1})	–	–	0.31	0.45	0.10	0.17	2.96	3.57
ATP (mM)	1.33	1.30	–	–	–	–	–	–

Three of the swimmers experienced weight loss during the trial (Table 3); this follows the observations of Rooze and Hinsenkamp (1979) who reported a loss of 4 kg in weight after a distance of 65 km covered with flippers in 18 hr 30 min. That swimmer probably experienced an energy deficit as his food only supplied him with 5.3 MJ. However, Table 3 shows there is no relationship between energy deficit and weight loss; moreover, we have observed (unpublished data) a loss of 3 kg in a swimmer who covered 40 km using four styles of swimming in 13 hr 30 min when he was maintained in energy balance. The loss of weight could be attributed to fluid imbalances connected with immersion which might inhibit ADH secretion, as reviewed by Epstein (1978). Subject BM differed from the other three by a more important reduction in plasma volume (see later) and weight loss. This reduced plasma volume was manifested by an orthostatic hypotension accompanied by fainting as he came out of the water. It is impossible to determine if this difference resulted because he did not take breaks out of the water, whereas the other three swimmers' efforts were interrupted regularly by periods of 10-15 min out of the water. It is also unknown whether his difference was related to the greater relative power produced during the trial. Convertino et al. (1981) have in fact shown that disturbances in fluid balance during exercises out of the water occur only for a relative power value equal to at least 40% of MAP.

Too many unknown factors make it difficult to interpret the changes observed in blood variables. In three of the swimmers (MF, AM and PB) no sign of hemolysis was apparent at the end of the trial: The serum was clear and the level of haptoglobin was high in the plasma. This enabled us to calculate the variations in plasma volume (PV) using the equations worked out by Dill and Costill (1974), especially because the trial was accompanied by a variation in MCV. In these three swimmers, PV decreased by 8, 11 and 10%, respectively.

BM's serum was red so it is assumed that hemolysis occurred, thus prohibiting the use of hemoglobin as a reference. The decrease in PV calculated from increased plasma albumin was 21%, or even more if albumin had escaped from the blood vessels. Under these conditions the comparison between the hematocrit measured at the end of the trial and the theoretical hematocrit which can be calculated, taking into account the initial hematocrit and the decrease in PV and MCV, yields the percentage of red cell destruction. The percentage for BM was 14%, meaning that for an individual of his weight, at least 450 ml of red cells had been hemolyzed. A hemolysis of this proportion associated with the decreased plasma volume put this particular swimmer in real danger of renal damage. Rooze and Hinsenkamp (1979) observed red serum at the end of a long swimming test but they attributed this to the way the blood was taken. Hemolysis at the end of prolonged exercise is attributed to injuries such as feet impacting the floor during a run or a walk. In this particular case, however, hemolysis seems to be due to a considerable lowering of the red cell deformation which was not associated with a decrease in the level of erythrocytes in ATP (Table 4).

Conclusion

Uninterrupted swimming at a high relative power during 24 hr caused, in one swimmer, hemolysis to an extent provoking the risk of renal damage. As this type of endurance test in water tends to be increasing, it seems sensible to carefully check the swimmers' blood or urine during each trial. If other observations confirm the risk of hemolysis, the danger could be limited by ordering swimmers to come out of the water at regular intervals.

References

ÅSTRAND, P.-O., and Rodahl, K. 1977. *Textbook of Work Physiology.* McGraw-Hill.

CONVERTINO, V.A., Keil, L.C., Bernauer, E.M., and Greenleaf, J.E. 1981. Plasma volume, osmolality, vasopressin, and renin activity during graded exercise in man. *J. Appl. Physiol. Respirat. Environ. Exercise Physiol.* **50**:123-128.

DILL, D.B., and Costill, D.L. 1974. Calculation of percentage changes in volumes of blood, plasma and red cells in dehydration. *J. Appl. Physiol.* **37**:247-248.

EPSTEIN, M. 1978. Renal effects of head out water immersion in man: Implications for an understanding of volume homeostasis. *Physiol. Rev.* **58**:529-581.

HANSS, M. 1979. Etude de la déformabilité érythrocytaire par mesure du débit initial de filtration. 4ème séminaire sur la filtrabilité érythrocytaire. Ed. Hoechst-lab. 137-153.

HOLMÉR, I. 1974. Physiology of swimming man. *Acta. Physiol. Scand.* (Suppl.)407.

ROOZE, M., and Hinsenkamp, M. 1979. Traversée de la manche par un nageur de fond. Etude des modifications biologiques et comportementales. *Méd. Sport* **53**:317-327.

Fluid Shifts and Heart Rate Responses
During Prolonged Swimming

Bodil Nielsen
University of Copenhagen, Denmark

During exercise, heart rate and cardiac output increase within the first few minutes after the start in proportion to the exercise intensity. The distribution of blood flow is changed through dilation in the working muscles and a vasoconstriction in the inactive regions. Later a vasodilation in the skin occurs, probably as a result of the increasing core temperature. With prolonged exercise of moderate intensity, such as bicycling or running, a further gradual increase in heart rate takes place as the work continues. This rise may amount to 20-30 beats per min (bpm) during 2 hr of strenuous work. The "secondary" increase in heart rate could have various causes; for example, it has been attributed to the dehydration from sweating which leads to decreased blood volume and stroke volume. It could also be an effect of the vasodilation and increase in skin blood flow which produce a decrease in central blood volume and stroke volume; or, the contractility of the heart may have decreased as a sign of fatigue. In all these situations, compensatory reflexes would lead to an increased heart rate.

During swimming, the heart rate is lower than that for exercise at the same metabolic rate in air. The reason may be that the horizontal position and hydrostatic pressure favor the filling of the heart, and that heat dissipation causes no problem in cool water due to the high heat conductivity and heat capacity of water.

The effect of prolonged swimming on the secondary rise in heart rate was investigated. Both the breast stroke (predominantly arm work) and the isolated leg-kick of freestyle swimming were investigated and compared to bicycle exercise at the same metabolic rate.

Methods and Procedures

The swimming experiments took place in a swimming flume (Åstrand and Englesson, 1972). The subjects swam at a fixed speed which after 10 min of swimming produced a heart rate of 120-130 bpm. This speed was determined in preliminary experiments, where the rate of oxygen uptake also was measured. Water temperature was maintained at 29°C. The bicycle experiments were performed in a climatic chamber with the air temperature manipulated so that the average skin temperature became 29°C, equal to the water temperature.

Work was performed on a Krogh bicycle ergometer in which the saddle was replaced by a chair (Nielsen, 1938). The load was adjusted so that O_2 uptake was equal to that obtained by the subject during swimming.

The heart rates (HR) were measured from electrocardiograms. Signals were picked up from three electrodes, placed on the chest, through a radiotelemetric system (Danica) and transmitted to a recorder that was switched on for 30 sec every 5 min. Oxygen uptake was measured by the Douglas bag method. Gas analyses were made on a Servomex 0A180 paramagnetic 0_2 analyzer and a Beckman LB2 infrared CO_2 analyzer.

Blood samples were obtained from a superficial brachial vein. In the first series, the vein was punctured with minimal or no stasis during a short pause in swimming with the subject standing in the water. In the later experiments, blood was drawn during undisturbed work through an indwelling catheter with the tip placed at the v. subclavia level. It was inserted before the experiment and left in place for the duration of the work. Blood samples were taken before, after 15, 30, 60 and 90 min in the first series, and just before the start and at 5-10, 20, 30, 40, 60 and 90 min in the later experiments.

Blood samples (5-7 ml) were analyzed: Hematocrit (Hct) was measured in triplicate with a micro Hct centrifuge and was corrected for trapped plasma (factor 0.96) and for the venous-to-total body Hct ratio (factor 0.93). The hemoglobin (Hb) concentration was obtained with Drabkin's cyanomethemoglobin method. The relative changes in plasma volume (%ΔPV) were calculated from the Hct and Hb measurements as (Costill and Fink, 1974; Dill and Costill, 1974):

$$\%\Delta PV = [(100 - HctA/100 - HctB) \cdot (HbB/HbA) - 1] \cdot 100$$

where B = before and A = after.

Plasma osmolarity (Osmol) was determined by the freezing point depression method (advanced L3 osmometer), and plasma concentration of sodium (Na) and potassium (K) were determined by atomic absorption spectrophotometry. Plasma proteins were measured spectrophotometrically (Zeiss) by the Biuret reaction method (Boehringer reagents). The subjects' water balance during the experiment was obtained by weighing them on a Krogh balance (± 5 g) (Krogh and Trolle, 1936) before and after the work and by measuring the urine volume produced during the work. Metabolic water gains were calculated from the measured oxygen uptake and RQ. Combustion of carbohydrates (glycogen) was assumed to produce 0.6 g H_2O/g plus 2.7 g/g crystal water, and fats to deliver 1 g H_2O/g.

Rectal temperature and average skin temperature were measured during bicycling with thermocouples as described earlier (Nielsen and Nielsen, 1965). The rectal temperature during swimming was measured using a thermistor probe (Nielsen and Davies, 1976) in 10 experiments with two subjects.

Data on the subjects are shown in Table 1.

Results

A "secondary rise" in heart rate was observed during swimming. HR increased about 11% between the 10th and 90th min (from initial values of 122-155 bpm) during prolonged swimming (Figure 1). The %$\triangle$HR is the percentage difference from the HR values obtained after 10 min of exercise. This increase occurred even though the rate of oxygen uptake was unchanged (Table 2).

Hematocrit and Hb concentrations in the blood increased with prolonged swimming as well as with bicycling, which indicated water loss from the vascular bed. The relative changes in plasma volume (%$\triangle$PV) calculated from the Hct and Hb values are shown in Figure 2. The

Table 1

Subject Characteristics[a]

	Subject	(sex)	Age (yr)	Weight (kg)	Height (cm)	No. of experiments	
						Swim	Bicycle
	AM	(M)				1	
	KJ	(M)				1	
Breast	OS	(M)				2	
stroke	SG	(M)				2	
	AR	(M)	21.	71.5	190	5	1
	JD	(M)	20	67.5	180	5	1
Free	LHL	(M)	20	73.5	179	1	1
style	KAJ	(M)	20	71.0	172	1	1
leg-	TWC	(M)	22	80.0	196	1	1
kick	BEL	(M)	30	73.5	181	1	1
Free style	LSP	(F)				1	

[a]Seven young male subjects, students of biology or physical education, swam the breast stroke. One female student swam freestyle. Four swimmers took part in the freestyle leg kick/bicycling experiments. Their data, when obtained, are presented.

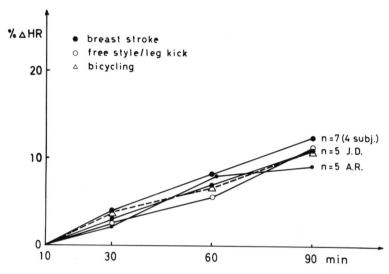

Figure 1 — Relative increase in heart rate (i.e., the heart rate expressed as a percentage of the heart rate at 10 min work) plotted against time. Breast stroke: • 7 experiments with 4 subjects; × 5 experiments with subject JD; + 5 experiments with subject AR. Freestyle leg-kick: ○ 4 experiments with 4 swimmers. Bicycling: △ 4 experiments with 4 swimmers.

plasma volume decreased during swimming on an average by about 7%. Both the leg-kick and the breast stroke (arm exercise) resulted in a rapid decline in PV within the first 5-10 min (Figure 2). The plasma volume remained low throughout the 90-min experiment, sometimes increasing, sometimes decreasing slightly. With bicycling, there was an immediate decrease and not much further change in PV for the 90-min prolonged exercise. The osmolality was already increased about 2% in the first blood sample (5-10 min) and remained at this level throughout the experiment. The same tendency was seen in the plasma Na and protein concentrations. These measurements offer no explanation for the plasma volume changes.

Table 2

Oxygen Uptake (L/min) Measured Between 20-30 min and 80-90 min of Exercise

	Subject	$\dot{V}O_2$ (20-30 min)	$\dot{V}O_2$ (80-90 min)
Breast stroke	JD ($n = 5$)	2.29	2.35
	AR ($n = 5$)	2.65	2.75
Freestyle	4 subj. ($n = 4$)	2.27	2.23
Bicycling	4 subj. ($n = 4$)	2.16	2.19

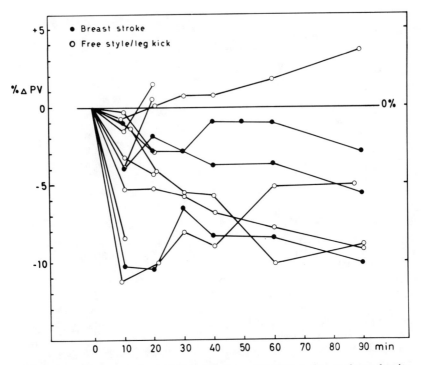

Figure 2 — Calculated changes in plasma volume, %△PV during prolonged swimming. • Breast stroke; ○ freestyle leg-kick.

In Figure 3, the relative change in heart rate (%△HR) is plotted against %△PV. This figure demonstrates that the secondary rise in HR is only weakly correlated with the changes in plasma volume, and therefore can hardly be explained by cardiovascular reflexes reacting to the fullness of the bloodstream.

Discussion

A study of circulatory adaptation to swimming may provide new information on some of the problems concerning the "fatigue" associated with prolonged exercise. In swimming, the exercise is performed in a horizontal position, in an environment which counteracts the gravitational force on circulation, and in conditions favoring heat loss without sweating due to the high conductivity and heat capacity of water compared to air.

Immersion of resting subjects leads to increased diuresis (e.g., Bazett et al., 1924; Henry et al., 1956). This is ascribed to a reflex suppression of the antidiuretic hormone via the atrial stretch receptors, caused by a redistribution of blood toward the central veins, and a shift of ex-

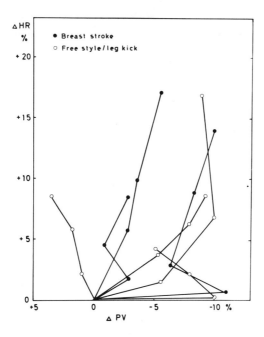

Figure 3—Relative change in heart rate, %ΔHR plotted against the change in plasma volume. • Breast stroke; ○ free style leg-kick.

travascular fluid into the blood during the early phase of immersion (Khosla and DuBois, 1979, 1981). Also during swimming, the heart apparently fills better, since the heart rate with swimming is lower than with bicycling or running for a given rate of oxygen consumption (Holmér et al., 1974).

In spite of these seemingly favorable circumstances during water immersion, the heart rate during prolonged swimming showed a secondary, gradual rise, just as large as with bicycling (Figure 1) and as described for exercise in air (Ekelund, 1967). The rise in HR occurred in the same general manner during the breast stroke, predominantly arm work, as during the leg kick of freestyle swimming.

The reason for the secondary rise in heart rate can hardly be the fluid shifts from the blood, because no close relationship was observed between %ΔHR and %ΔPV. Decreased plasma volume with swimming is contrary to the findings in resting subjects immersed in water (McCally, 1964; Khosla and DuBois, 1979, 1981).

The rate of oxygen consumption during prolonged swimming (and bicycling) remained constant. It varied less than 4%, that is, less than 100 ml/min between values measured in ca. 20 and 85 min (Table 2). In spite of this constant oxygen usage by the working muscles and the small and varying changes in PV, the HR rose continuously throughout the 90-min

Table 3

Rectal Temperature at 30 and 90 min Swimming Breast Stroke in 29°C water: Change in HR after 90 min (%$\triangle$HR) Compared to Core Temperature Changes

Subject	30 min	90 min	Change (°C)	%$\triangle$HR 90 min
JD	37.55	37.55	0.0	17.1
	37.45	37.40	− 0.05	9.0
	38.00	38.50	+ 0.5	13.9
	37.60	37.60	0.0	8.5
	37.40	37.30	− 0.1	7.2
AR	37.85	38.00	− 0.05	10.3
	37.35	37.10	− 0.25	3.5
	37.65	37.55	− 0.10	11.5
	37.70	36.60	− 0.10	12.0
	37.95	38.00	+ 0.05	8.4

exercise. Therefore, this sign of "fatigue" appears to be related to the function of the myocardium itself. Ekelund (1967) points to the effect of body temperature on the heart. In his study of a 60-min bicycle exercise in sitting and supine positions the secondary HR rise and body temperature had a highly significant correlation. Cornet et al. (1978) used a β-blocker (Pindolole), and found that the slow increase in heart rate during exercise was diminished, but not abolished by the blockade. Here also, the rise in core temperature was thought to produce the remaining half of the effect. In the present swimming study, on the other hand, body temperature did not rise (Table 3). The rectal temperature was constant from 30-90 min of swimming the breast stroke, whereas HR increased 4-17%, or 10% on the average. These results may indicate that the intrinsic contractility of the heart is decreased during prolonged exercise, and that a pressure-regulating mechanism is involved in order to maintain adequate cardiac output. Since β-blockade only partially abolished the HR drift, the possibility still remains that circulating adrenalin is the necessary stimulus.

Acknowledgments

These experiments were partly financed through a grant from the Danish Sports Research Council. The experiments with the swimmers were part of a more extensive study, performed in collaboration with Drs. G. Sjögaard and F. Bonde-Petersen, The August Krogh Institute, Copenhagen University.

References

ÅSTRAND, P.-O., and Englesson, S. 1972. A swimming flume. *J. Appl. Physiol.* **33**:514.

BAZETT, H.C., Thurlow, S., Crowell, C., and Stewart, W. 1924. Studies on the effects of baths on man II. The diuresis caused by warm baths, together with some observations on urinary tides. *Am. J. Physiol.* **70**:430-452.

CORNET, F., Scheen, A., Juchmes, J., and Cession-Fossion, A. 1978. Determinisme de la déquence cardiaque pendent l'exercise musculaire. *C.R. Soc. Biol.* **172**:569-574.

COSTILL, D.L., and Fink, W.J. 1974. Plasma volume changes following exercise and thermal dehydration. *J. Appl. Physiol.* **37**:521-525.

DILL, D.B., and Costill, D.L. 1974. Calculation of percentage changes in volumes of blood, plasma and red cells in dehydration. *J. Appl. Physiol.* **37**:247-248.

EKELUND, L.-G. 1967. Circulatory and respiratory adaptation during prolonged exercise. *Acta Physiol. Scand.* **70** (suppl.):292.

HENRY. J.P., Gauer, O.H., and Reeves, J.L. 1956. Evidence of atrial location of receptors influencing urine flow. *Circulation Res.* **4**:85-90.

HOLMÉR, I., Stein, E.M., Saltin, B., Ekblom, B., and Åstrand, P.-O. 1974. Hemodynamic and respiratory responses compared in swimming and running. *J. Appl. Physiol.* **37**:49-54.

KHOSLA, S.S., and DuBois, A.B. 1979. Fluid shifts during initial phase of immersion diuresis in man. *J. Appl. Physiol. Respirat. Environ. Exercise Physiol.* **46**:703-708.

KHOSLA, S.S., and DuBois, A.B. 1981. Osmoregulation and interstitial fluid pressure changes in humans during water immersion. *J. Appl. Physiol. Respirat. Environ. Exercise Physiol.* **51**:686-692.

KROGH, A., and Trolle, C. 1936. A balance for the determination of insensible perspiration in man and its use. *Skand. Arch. Physiol.* **73**:159-162.

MCCALLY, M. 1964. Plasma volume response to water immersion: Implications for space flight. *Aerosp. Med.* **35**:130-132.

NIELSEN, B., and Davies, C.T.M. 1976. Temperature regulation during exercise in water and air. *Acta Physiol. Scand.* **98**:500-508.

NIELSEN, B., and Nielsen, M. 1965. On the regulation of sweat secretion in exercise. *Acta Physiol Scand.* **64**:314-322.

NIELSEN, M. 1938. Die Regulation der Körpertemperatur bei Muskelarbeit. *Skand. Arch. Physiol.* **79**:193-230.

WILKERSON, J.E., Gutin, B., and Horvath, S.M. 1977. Exercise-induced changes in blood, red cell and plasma volume in man. *Med. Sci. Sports Exercise* **9**:155-58.

The Effects of Leg Action on Performance in the Sprint Front Crawl Stroke

James Watkins and Andrew T. Gordon
Scottish School of Physical Education, Glasgow

It is well known that using a flutter kick in the sprint front crawl stroke enables the swimmer to achieve a greater speed than can be achieved using the arm action alone. However, it is unclear how the flutter kick causes an increase in swimming speed. There seems to be at least three ways in which the flutter kick can positively affect swimming speed: (a) propulsion directly from the legs — a flutter kick can create propulsion directly as can be demonstrated in legs-only practice with the arms supported by a kick board. However, with regard to the full stroke, Counsilman (1968) and Onusseit (1972) both maintain that the leg action in front crawl does not aid propulsion directly; (b) streamlining the body — Counsilman (1977) suggests that the main function of the leg action in front crawl is to keep the body in a streamlined position and thereby reduce drag; and (c) stabilization of the trunk — Counsilman (1968) and Lawrence (1969) suggest that the kick in front crawl is used as a stabilizer and neutralizer, the implication being that leg action neutralizes the reaction of the rest of the body to the arm action and as a result, keeps the position of the trunk fairly stable. A fairly stable trunk position may reduce drag and/or produce more effective arm action. The purpose of this investigation was to assess the contribution of streamlining and trunk stabilization to swimming speed in the front crawl stroke.

Methods

The subjects consisted of 33 trained swimmers — 19 males (aged 17.0 ± 1.7 yr; wt 66.4 ± 6.2 kg; ht 177.5 ± 5.4 cm) and 14 females (aged 14.8 ± 1.6 yr; wt 52.3 ± 8.0 kg; ht 161.2 ± 5.1 cm). The mean best times for the subjects in the 100-m front crawl, short course, was 57.4 ± 1.86 sec and

64.2 ± 3.57 sec for the males and females, respectively. The subjects swam front crawl under three conditions: (a) full stroke, (b) arms only with ankles bound together and a pull-buoy held between the thighs and (c) arms only with the ankles and knees bound together.

Each trial consisted of swimming two lengths of a 25-m pool following a 10-m rolling start and using tumble turns. One set of trials consisted of all three conditions and each subject performed three sets of trials. Subjects were instructed to swim as quickly as possible throughout each trial. In order to minimize effects of the order in which the different conditions were performed, subjects were tested in groups of three using a 3 × 3 Latin square design (Edwards, 1968). Each subject rested for ca. 15 min between successive trials.

During each trial, the time was recorded using a stopwatch from the point at which the feet touched the wall during the first turn to hand touch at the end of the trial. The times for both turns were also recorded, from the point at which the feet touched the wall to the point of hand separation at the start of stroking. In addition to the three recorded times, a count was made of the total number of arm strokes taken by each subject in each trial.

In order to assess the distance covered by each subject during stroking, the distance covered in the turns was assessed. The first turn of each trial was recorded on videotape with a camera in an elevated position at the side of the pool. The bottom of the pool and the side of the pool opposite the camera were marked along its length in half-meter intervals up to a distance of 5 m from the end of the pool involved in the first turn. When the videotape was viewed in slow motion, it was possible, using the pool markings, to measure the distance covered by each subject during the first turn from push-off to the point of hand separation. The distance covered in the second turn was estimated from the average speed achieved in the first turn and the time of the second turn. The stroking distance in each trial was calculated by subtracting the distance covered in both turns from 50 m.

Results

In the first three columns of Table 1 the speeds achieved by the subjects in the three swimming conditions are presented. In column 4 of Table 1 the velocity achieved in the arms only with leg support condition, VS, is expressed as a percentage of the speed achieved in the full stroke condition, VF. These figures, 90.9% for males and 90.8% for females, are similar to those obtained by Watkins and Dukes (1981) (91.9% for males and 92.6% for females) in a study involving 26 trained swimmers.

In column 5 of Table 1, the speed achieved in the arms only condition, VA, is expressed as a percentage of the full stroke speed. These figures,

79.6% for males and 84.8% for females, suggest that in terms of relative
swimming speed, the absence of a flutter kick is more detrimental to the
male swimmers than to the female swimmers. This observation is
reflected in the absolute mean swimming velocities which show a significant difference ($p < 0.05$) between the males and females with regard to
the full stroke and arms only with support conditions, but no significant
difference between the groups with regard to the arms only condition (see
Table 1).

In the first column of Table 2 the velocity achieved in the arms only
condition (A) is expressed as a percentage of the speed achieved in the
arms only with leg support condition (S). Since it is reasonable to assume
that no propulsion was created directly by the legs in the A and S conditions and that the movement of the trunk would be similar in both conditions, it follows that the differences in velocities achieved under these
conditions by both groups must be due to changes in streamlining which
result from changes in leg position.

In column 2 of Table 2 the stroke length achieved in the A condition is
expressed as a percentage of the stroke length achieved in the S condition. A similar comparison of stroke rates is presented in column 3 of
Table 2. These figures show that the lower relative velocity achieved by
the males (compared to the females) in the A condition (compared to the
S condition) was mainly a result of lower relative stroke length.

Discussion

It is reasonable to assume that in the S condition no propulsion was
created by the legs and that, due to the leg support, the body would be in
a fairly streamlined position. Consequently, the decrease in speed which

Table 1

**Means ($\overline{X}$) and Standard Deviations (SD) of Velocities of Subjects in the Full
Stroke (VF) Arms Only with Support (VS) and Arms Only (VA) Conditions**

		VF (m/sec)	VS m/sec)	VA (m/sec)	VS/VF (%)	VA/VF (%)
Males	$\overline{X}$	1.56	1.42	1.24	90.9	79.6
($n = 19$)	SD	0.13	0.16	0.14		
Females	$\overline{X}$	1.44	1.31	1.22	90.8	84.8
($n = 14$)	SD	0.84	0.09	0.12		
Difference		*	*	—		

*Significant at .05 level.

Table 2

**Comparison of Velocity Stroke Length and Stroke Rate
in the Arms Only and Arms Only with Support Conditions[a]**

	VA/VS (%)	LA/LS (%)	RA/RS (%)
Males (n = 19)	86.8	89.6	96.6
Females (n = 14)	93.5	97.8	97.2

[a]VA, LA, RA = velocity, stroke length and stroke rate in condition A; VS, LS, RS = velocity, stroke length and stroke rate in condition S.

occurred in the S condition compared to the full stroke condition (F), that is, a decrease of ca. 9% for both males and females, must have been due to a combination of: (a) the absence of direct propulsion from the legs and (b) an unstable trunk position resulting in greater drag and/or a less effective arm action. If, as suggested by Onusseit (1972) and Counsilman (1968), the leg action in the full stroke does not aid propulsion directly, it follows from the present results that the effect of the leg action in stabilizing the trunk in the full stroke may account for ca. 9% of the full stroke speed for both males and females. The view that trunk stabilization is an important aspect of full stroke front crawl swimming is supported by the work of Clarys (1978). In a study involving 44 P.E. students and nine international swimmers, Clarys found that the active drag while swimming the front crawl was 30-40% greater in the untrained compared to the trained swimmers. Clarys concluded that in the full stroke, drag is created largely as a result of changes in the position of the various body segments, which implies that the speed and extent of changes in the positions of body segments should be kept to a minimum in order to minimize drag. Since the trunk comprises ca. 56% of the total body mass, it may be that the movement of such a large body segment has a considerable effect on drag, even though no relationship was found in the Clarys study between the size of the trunk, in terms of its cross sectional area, and drag. Alternatively, or in addition, it may be that a fairly stable trunk position results in more effective arm action. Presumably top swimmers achieve a compromise between body roll and arm action that maximizes net propulsion.

A decrease in speed of ca. 9% occurred between the F and S conditions for both groups. Between the S and A conditions, further decreases in speed occurred of ca. 11 and 6% (of full stroke speed) for the males and females, respectively. A decrease in speed between the S and A conditions was expected since the legs tended to sink in the A condition, and thereby producing a less streamlined body position which results in greater drag (Alley, 1952; Clarys et al., 1974). The decrease in speed between the S and C conditions was much greater for the males (11% of full stroke speed) than for the females (6% of full stroke speed). This difference between the two groups is consistent with the findings of Pendergast et al. (1977) who showed that the underwater body torque, that is, the tendency of the legs to sink when unsupported, was much greater in males than in females.

In summary, if it is assumed that the leg action in sprint front crawl does not contribute directly to propulsion, the results of this investigation suggest that leg action contributes indirectly to propulsion by: (a) stabilizing the trunk which accounts for ca. 9% of the full stroke speed in both males and females, and (b) streamlining the body which accounts for ca. 11 and 6% of full stroke speed in males and females, respectively.

References

ALLEY, L.E. 1952. An analysis of water resistance and propulsion in swimming the crawl stroke. *Res. Q.*, **23**:253-270.

CLARYS, J.P., Jiskoot, J., Rijken, H., and Brouwer, P.J. 1974. Total resistance in water and its relation to body form. In: R.C. Nelson and C.A. Morehouse (eds.), *Biomechanics IV*, pp. 187-196. University Park Press, Baltimore.

CLARYS, J.P. 1978. Relationship of human body form to passive and active hydrodynamic drag. In: E. Asmussen and K. Jørgensen (eds.), *Biomechanics VIB*, pp. 120-125. University Park Press, Baltimore.

COUNSILMAN, J.E. 1968. *The Science of Swimming*. Prentice-Hall, Englewood Cliffs, NJ.

COUNSILMAN, J.E. 1977. *Doc Counsilman on Swimming*. Pelham, London.

EDWARDS, A.L. 1968. *Experimental Design in Psychological Research*. Holt, Rinehart and Winston, London.

LAWRENCE, L. 1969. The importance of the freestyle leg kick. *Int. Swimmer*, **5**:11-12.

ONUSSEIT, H.F. 1972. Two-beat versus six-beat; which kick is best. *Swim. Tech.* **9**:41-43.

PENDERGAST, D.R., diPrampero, P.E., Craig, A.B., Wilson, D.R., and Rennie, D.W. 1977. Quantitative analysis of the front crawl in men and women. *J. Appl. Physiol.* **43**:475-479.

WATKINS, J., and Dukes, W. Sept. 1981. *The Contribution of the Arms and Legs to Swimming Speed in the Front Crawl Stroke*. Proceedings of the Society of Sport Sciences (U.K.).

Stroke Length and Stroke Frequency Variations in Men's and Women's 100-m Freestyle Swimming

Helga Letzelter and Werner Freitag

Johannes Gutenberg Universität, Mainz, West Germany

In swimming, the time needed to complete a 100-m race can be regarded as a function of stroke length (l_{100}) and stroke frequency (f_{100}). Moreover, the total time is a result of the time per lap (t_i), which also can be regarded as function of stroke length (l_i) and frequency (f_i).

From a practical point of view two questions arise:

- On which laps do the stronger swimmers mainly secure their lead, or are all laps equally responsible for the advantage?
- Is it preferable to swim with longer strokes or with a higher stroke frequency, or are better swimmers superior in both variables?

Methods and Procedures

This study was based on the performance of 34 male and 34 female participants in the German National Team Championships in 1980. The following time limits were set: t_{100} (male) = 60.0 sec; and t_{100} (female) = 67.5 sec.

For the analysis, the two groups M (male) and F (female) were divided into two performance-oriented subgroups ($n = 17$) M1 and M2 as well as F1 and F2. The analysis was based on videotapes. From the four 25-m laps (B_1 to B_4), four intermediate times, four section velocities (v_i), four section stroke lengths (l_i) and four section stroke frequencies (f_i) were calculated. Three-way analysis of variance, bivariate and multiple correlation, regression and trend analysis were performed.

Results and Discussion

The total 100-m times for all groups are presented in Table 1.

Velocity Characteristics

Velocity graphs for the entire sample and for the four subgroups are shown in Figure 1. In all cases, a velocity reduction from lap to lap was

Table 1

**Freestyle Times of 34 Male and 34 Female Swimmers for 100 m
(Range, Mean and Standard Deviation in sec)**

Group	Range	$\overline{X}$	SD
M	51.6-59.1	55.42	2.15
M1	51.6-54.5	53.53	0.74
M2	54.9-59.1	57.31	1.19
F	56.9-67.3	63.13	2.78
F1	56.9-62.9	60.88	1.90
F2	63.4-67.3	65.39	1.26

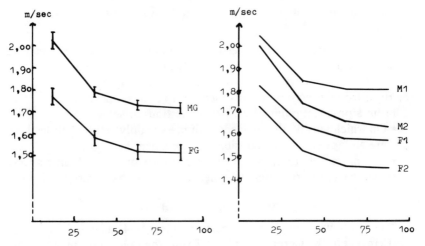

Figure 1—Velocity graphs, groups (MG-males; FG-females) left, subgroups (M1, M2, F1 and F2) right. (Distance on the abscissa and velocity on the ordinate.)

observed. This was most obvious from B_1 to B_2 as a result of the start. The decrease in velocity from B_3 to B_4 was small. Trend analysis demonstrated quadratic trends in all velocity graphs; whether this quadratic trend still existed after correction for the start was not investigated.

The velocity patterns for male and female swimmers (left part of Figure 1) were similar; difference varied between .25 and .21 m/sec. Consequently, there was no intercorrelation of laps and sex, which means the women did not decrease their velocity throughout the race more than the men. They were slower because from the beginning they swam about 12% slower throughout the race.

The velocity of both less highly skilled groups, M2 as well as F2, decreased more than the velocity of the better swimmers. All four laps con-

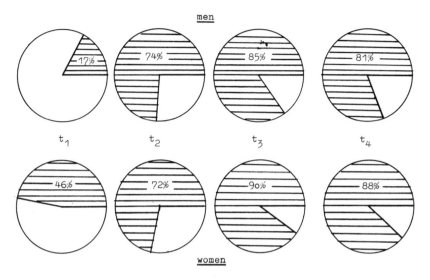

Figure 2 — Common variances of intermediate and final times.

tributed to the lead of the faster swimmers although not to the same extent. It was evident that the lead progressively increased. The first lap contributed least, the final lap most to the predominance of male over female and faster over slower swimmers. From the correlation between intermediate times and final time it was clear that the first lap influenced the total time less than the three following ones. The common variances were in the range from 17% (B_1) to 85% (B_3) for men and 46% (B_1) to 90% (B_3) for women (see Figure 2).

Multiple regression analyses quantified the specific contribution of each intermediate time. The proportional influences were as follows:

Time Intervals

t_1	:	t_2	:	t_3	:	t_4
1	:	1.3	:	1.6	:	1.4 for males
1	:	1.2	:	1.6	:	1.4 for females.

This confirmed the results of the computed correlations. For men and women the sequence of laps according to their influence on the total time was identical.

The intercorrelation of the four intermediate times varied considerably in some cases, especially with respect to the initial lap. Although in the case of female swimmers all intercorrelations were significant, the men who were faster on the first lap were not faster on the third and fourth laps. The relationship of the time for the first lap to the others were significantly lower than the intercorrelations between other intermediate times for women, too (Table 2). The exceptional role of the starting lap was demonstrated again. Women in general were more consistent in their

Table 2

Intercorrelations of Intermediate Times

	Males				Females			
	t_1	t_2	t_3	t_4	t_1	t_2	t_3	t_4
t_1	x	.40[a]	.18	.06	x	.46[a]	.56[a]	.50[a]
t_2		x	.70[a]	.68[a]		x	.73[a]	.75[a]
t_3			x	.86			x	.91[a]

[a]$p < 0.01$.

velocity patterns which can be seen from the mean intercorrelations $\bar{r} = .54$ (men) and $\bar{r} = .69$ (women).

Mean Stroke Length and Mean Stroke Frequency

The 34 male swimmers needed, on the average, 78.1 strokes to cover the 100 m. The women needed 17% more (91.2 strokes). Per stroke, men progressed 18 cm more than women. This advantage resulted in a total gain of 14.1 m, which corresponds, assuming a mean velocity of 1.8 m/sec, to a time gain of 7.8 sec. Whereas women were obviously inferior in stroke length, they swam with practically identical stroke frequencies (see Table 2). Stroke length was the only difference between male and female swimmers.

The performance difference between the subgroups could not always be explained by a single variable. The faster males were superior in stroke length as well as in frequency to the slower males. For women, stroke length was the only difference between F1 and F2. The advantage of F1 over F2 was 11 cm or 10.5%. Stroke length was the relevant performance variable for women; it was the only variable responsible for the better times since F1 was actually inferior by 0.9 strokes/min or 0.9% compared to F2 in stroke frequency. This also held true for the males although M1 swam with a 4.2-strokes/min or 5% higher frequency. Because of the enormous variation in both groups, this difference was not statistically significant.

It can be stated that in the male group, the overall advantage of M1 over M2 was a result of higher stroke frequency as well as greater stroke length. The difference in time of the swim caused by frequency was twice as large as the one resulting from the difference in stroke length. In contrast, the faster women achieved a better performance only through longer strokes, not through a higher stroke frequency.

The correlations between 100-m times and stroke length or frequency were rather low (Table 4). Because of the numerical dependence between stroke frequency and 100-m times η-coefficients of analysis of variance were computed. Correlation- and η-coefficients confirmed results of the

Table 3

Stroke Length in m (Upper Part) and Stroke Frequency in Strokes/min (Lower Part) for the Whole Sample and the Performance Subgroups (Range, Mean and Standard Deviation)

	Male		
Group	Range	$\overline{X}$	SD
M	1.00- 1.52	1.28	0.10
M1	1.05- 1.43	1.30	0.14
M2	1.05- 1.46	1.27	0.12
M	71.0 -110.5	85.4	8.3
M1	74.5 -110.5	87.5	10.1
M2	71.5 - 98.0	83.3	8.1
	Female		
Group	Range	$\overline{X}$	SD
F	0.86- 1.38	1.10	0.13
F1	0.98- 1.35	1.16	0.11
F2	0.86- 1.38	1.05	0.13
F	69.5 -109.0	86.5	8.9
F1	74.0 - 99.5	86.1	7.1
F2	69.5 -109.0	87.0	10.5

Table 4

Correlation and η-Coefficients as Indicators of the Relationship between 100-m Stroke Length, Stroke Frequency and 100-m Times

	Male		Female	
	r	η	r	η
Length/time	.08	.14	− .41[a]	− .47[a]
Frequency/time	− .30	.33	.05	.13

[a]Significant, $p < 0.01$.

comparison between groups. Only the relationship between stroke length and performance for the female subjects was statistically significant.

Stroke Length on the Four Laps

As a result of the start, fewer strokes were counted on the first lap; toward the finish, the stroke length decreased again. The variation in stroke length can be described in three phases: (a) maximal stroke length

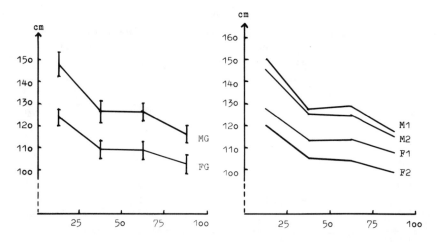

Figure 3 — Stroke length diagrams for the entire sample (left) and for the subgroups (right). (Distance on the abscissa and length at stroke on the ordinate.)

on the first lap and significant stroke length reduction on the second lap; (b) constant stroke lengths on B2 and B3; and (c) stroke length was at a minimum because of a second significant decrease on the last lap. This tendency was apparent for the total group of males and females as well as for the subgroups (Figure 3).

As men had a considerably longer pull, the factor "sex" was systematic. This held true for all four laps, with the difference in favor of the men varying from 13 to 23 cm/stroke. Figure 3 shows that for males as well as females, stroke length was greater for the faster swimmers. This tendency was more pronounced in females. The analysis of variance confirmed, in general, the influence of qualification as being significant. Thus, the stroke length for the individual laps must be considered relevant to performance.

Precise statements about the performance relevance of stroke length on the different laps for males and females were possible, however. The comparatively small differences in means (2-4 cm) cannot be considered significant for the males. For women, however, differences in means of 8-10 cm were observed.

The mean stroke length (l_{100}) as well as the stroke length on the four laps (l_1 to l_4) did not correlate with the final times (Table 5). The internal structure of stroke length was extremely homogeneous. This was also reflected in the mean intercorrelations: $\bar{r} = .88$ (men) and $\bar{r} = .91$ (women). Compared to velocity variations, one basic difference was observed. Swimmers who were faster on the initial lap were not faster on the final lap. But competitors who swam with longer strokes on the first lap were also superior in this variable on the last lap.

Table 5

**Correlations among Stroke Lengths on the Four Laps
and with the Final Time**

	Male						Female				
	l_1	l_2	l_3	l_4	t_{100}	l_1	l_1	l_2	l_3	l_4	t_{100}
l_1	x	.85[a]	.89[a]	.81[a]	−.11	x		.88[a]	.90[a]	.90[a]	−.33[b]
l_2		x	.88[a]	.91[a]	.00		x		.94[a]	.89[a]	−.36[b]
l_3			x	.90[a]	−.12			x		.92[a]	−.46[b]
l_4				x	.01				x		−.47[b]

[a]$p < 0.01$.
[b]$p < 0.05$.

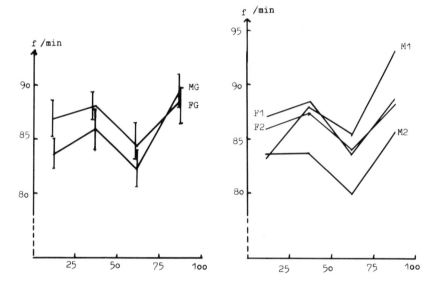

Figure 4 — Stroke frequency diagrams for the entire sample (left) and for the subgroups (right). (Distance on the abscissa and frequency in strokes/min on the ordinate.)

Stroke Frequency on the Four Laps

Men and women demonstrated a "zig-zag" pattern in stroke frequency which was just slightly more pronounced in male subjects. For both groups, the frequencies reach a maximum on the last lap (Figure 4).

The interaction of sex and lap was systematic. Thus, one cannot assume an identical stroke frequency behavior for men and women. This was a result of the men's rapidly increasing stroke frequency toward the finish. Besides the sex factor, the factor "qualification," based on the comparison of males and females, did not influence the stroke frequen-

Table 6

Correlations among Stroke Frequencies on the Four Laps and with the 100-m Time

	Male					Female				
	f_1	f_2	f_3	f_4	t_{100}	f_1	f_2	f_3	f_4	t_{100}
f_1	x	.78[a]	.73[a]	.69[a]	−.09[b]	x	.81[a]	.80[a]	.84[a]	.11
f_2		x	.87[a]	.85[a]	−.29[b]		x	.89[a]	.85[a]	−.01
f_3			x	.91[a]	−.32[b]			x	.90[a]	.05
f_4				x	−.46[b]				x	.01

[a]$p < 0.01$.
[b]$p < 0.05$.

cies on the four laps to any significant extent. This finding was also evident from the diagrams (Figure 4) for F1 and F2. However, the male swimmers had a difference in frequency on laps B2, B3 and B4.

For women, the impression gained from stroke frequency diagrams was fully confirmed: There was no systematic advantage (higher stroke frequency) for the better swimmers. The qualification factor does have a systematic influence for the male subjects. The better swimmers were, among the other factors, faster because they are able to swim with higher frequencies. Since the difference between M1 and M2 increased, mainly because of B2 and B4, throughout the race, the interdependence between qualification and laps was nonrandom. Stroke frequency behavior was thus dependent on the performance.

These results which were based on a comparison of groups were confirmed by computed correlations. For female groups, there was an almost perfect independence of the total time from the difference in stroke frequency behavior. For the male swimmers, only three out of four stroke frequency values (f_2, f_3, and f_4) were performance-relevant. The faster swimmers swam with a higher frequency, especially toward the finish. This tendency was not observed on the starting lap and was only slightly present in B2 and B3 (Table 6). However, the correlation coefficients were rather small. In no phase of the race did faster women swim with higher frequencies than the slower group of women. Stroke frequencies on four laps were strongly interrelated. A similar result was previously stated for stroke length. The competitors using higher frequencies at the starting lap also swam with higher frequencies throughout the remaining laps. Thus, a structural similarity to stroke length behavior was observed, but not so for the changes in the intermediate times. Intercorrelations among stroke frequencies were similar. As observed in the case of intermediate times and stroke length, the mean intercorrelation of stroke frequency was higher for females, $\bar{r} = .87$ compared to $\bar{r} = .82$ for males.

Profiles of Competitors Using Different Patterns in Front Crawl Events

Ulrik Persyn, Daniel Daly, Harold Vervaecke,
Luc Van Tilborgh, and Dirk Verhetsel
Catholic University of Leuven, Heverlee, Belgium

In top level crawl swimming, competitors use various patterns. The most common patterns in the sprint events are the 6-beat, typified by continuous kicking and lengthened pulling, and the 2-beat crossover, typified by interrupted kicking and shortened pulling. In the longer events, 2-beat and 4-beat patterns are frequently seen in addition to the 2-beat cross over. Nevertheless, all four patterns appear in each distance.

It can be expected that top level competitors use their optimal pattern at their best distance and that they possess an optimal combination of physical characteristics (somatic, strength, flexibility, etc.) required for the specific event. However, the optimal pattern can vary for each swimmer at each distance. These patterns are then assumed to be, at each distance, the best compromise between propulsion and balance on the one hand and endurance on the other. Lower level competitors do not always find an optimal pattern on their own (Persyn et al., 1979), although it has been shown that most swimmers can learn different patterns if specific skill training is stressed (Daly et al., 1980). Nevertheless, coaches rarely attempt to change the original pattern.

When morphologists and physiologists have studied physical characteristics in the crawl stroke, the existence of various patterns has not been taken into account (Bulgakova, 1978; Holmer, 1974; Mader, 1978). In order to orient swimmers toward their best pattern at each distance, then, it might be interesting to examine the characteristics per pattern group for sprint and for distance freestyle swimming, and that was the purpose of this study.

Procedure

In order to define physical characteristics that determine success in the various patterns and distances, the observation and investigation of the most outstanding swimmers is indicated. However, our coaching courses and the evaluation and selection of swimmers deal mainly with national level Belgian and Dutch swimmers.

For the purpose of this study, from 105 evaluated male competitors at this national level (10.2-22.6 yr) a sample of 62, specifically trained to use different crawl patterns, was selected. This sample included two groups: (a) 2-beat crossover specialists using the same (best) pattern at each distance ($n = 27$), and (b) 6-beat specialists in sprint using the 4- or 2-beat patterns at longer events ($n = 35$).

In the two groups, age and swimming performances in the different events (sprint, 50 or 100 m; distance, 400 or 1,500 m) did not differ significantly (t-test, $p > 0.05$). In order to make this assertion, the individual competitive times had first been transformed to European performance scores (Coen, 1978). To further compare the performances between the various age groups, the mean scores of the 10 best West Germans in each age group and at each distance were used as references. Individual performances were then expressed as a percentage of these obtained mean scores. The average levels of the two experimental groups were 90% of these German mean scores which represents, for example, a 100-m performance of 58.3 sec for an 18-yr-old competitor.

In order to develop profiles, including specifications for each pattern in each event, in addition to the data from film analyses (Persyn et al., 1975) and the knowledge of the swimming performances (50-1,500 m), the following information was collected for each individual (see Figure 1): (a) chronological age and biological age, determined from X-rays of the wrist and hand (Tanner et al., 1962); (b) physical characteristics: somatic, isometric strength and flexibility data (Vervaecke and Persyn, 1981), buoyancy and "leg weight," relationship between gravity and upward pressure forces (Van Tilborgh et al., 1983, this volume), peak $\dot{V}O_2$ and lactate concentration in a 2-min all-out pulling effort in tethered swimming (Daly et al., 1981); and (c) training background, dryland and water, obtained from a questionnaire and an interview.

In each pattern group the significance of the differences in means of the various data was determined by t-test and Pearson correlations were calculated between training background, physical characteristics and swimming performance. All statistical work was done using BMDP computer programs (Dixon, 1981).

In order to eliminate the effect of growth on statistical analyses, specific corrections of the data were necessary. Somatic and isometric strength data were transformed using the allometric equation of Huxley (power function $y = ax^b$) (1932). For the somatic variables, height was used in the equation and for isometric strength, weight was used. It has been shown previously that flexibility does not change with increasing age; thus, these data did not need to be corrected (Vervaecke and Persyn,

1981). Buoyancy and peak $\dot{V}O_2$ were corrected by dividing by weight, whereas training was considered in the respective biological age groups. The correction of the calculated swimming performance scores was made for percentage adult height (linear regression), derived from present height and biological age (Tanner et al. 1975; Walker, 1974).

Results

In column A of Figure 1, some significant differences in means of the data for the two pattern groups are specified. The 2-beat crossover specialists had relatively longer legs than the 6-beat specialists (see no. 9). A 6-beat executed by long legs could slow the stroke rate excessively. Six-beat specialists had a larger vital capacity (no. 10) and experienced greater sinking force of the lower limbs (no. 29) (being supported by the continuous kick). In the 6-beat group, the inward rotation of the hips was greater (no. 23), allowing a propulsive lift force with the outside of the foot in the downward kick. In this context it is worth mentioning that the kicking sprint velocity was significantly higher within the 6-beat specialists ($p \leq 0.05$) (not shown in Figure 1).

On the horizontal scales of the figure, the individual scores can be printed in relation to the data of the 105 evaluated competitors, including specialists in the four strokes. A score of 75, for example, is obtained when 25% of the evaluated population reaches a higher score than the individual in question. The mean scores obtained for the two experimental groups are presented as an illustration (broken lines). They illustrate differences between 6-beaters and 2-beat crossover swimmers for this national level.

In columns C-F, the correlations between physical characteristics as well as dryland and water training background and the swimming performances (sprint and distance) are given for the two different pattern groups, and, as supplementary information, for the total evaluated group in crawl sprint swimming ($n = 105$) (see column B).

Primarily, the isometric strength variables were important characteristics for performance in this total group (which generally lacked power training). If the two pattern groups are considered separately one can further state, first in the 2-beat crossover group, that particular isometric strength variables were relevant for sprint velocity—for example, the "pull push" and the "bringing together" data (nos. 11 and 14) of the arms (which correspond with the shortened arm action typical in this pattern). Hip flexion strength was only relevant in the 2-beat crossover pattern (no. 17), which corresponds with the explosive downward kick, notwithstanding significantly longer legs (no. 9).

Next, in the 6-beat pattern group the "push" and "upward lift" of the arms were most relevant (nos. 12 and 13). These specific strength

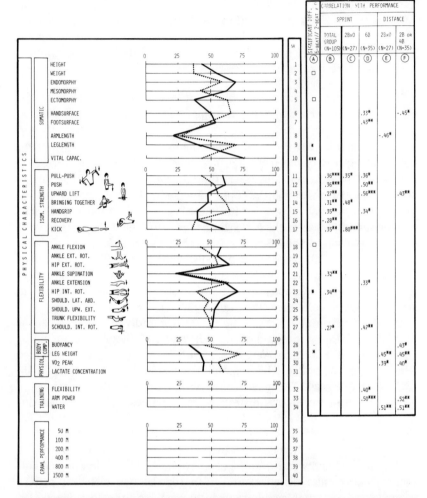

Figure 1—Profile card used to rank physical characteristics, training background and swimming performance data (sprint, 50-100 m and distance, 400-1,500 m) in competitive male front crawl swimmers using various patterns. 2B = 2-beat pattern; 4B = 4-beat pattern; 6B = 6-beat pattern; and 2B×0 = 2-beat crossover pattern. —: averages of experimental 6-beat group (n = 35) (columns D and F); ⋯: averages of experimental 2-beat crossover group (n = 27) (columns C and E); and 0-100: percentile scores based on whole evaluated group (n = 105). Significance levels: □ = $p \leq .10$; * = $p \leq .05$; ** = $p \leq .01$; *** = $p \leq .001$.

variables (nos. 12 and 13), in combination with hand grip strength (no. 15) and also with hand surface (no. 6), supported the typical lengthened pulling action. Further, arm power training, as well as flexibility training influenced the sprint performance in this group (nos. 32 and 33). Finally, as expected, the quantity of water training and peak $\dot{V}O_2$ as well as leg weight were important for distance swimming in each pattern group (nos. 29, 30 and 34).

Conclusion

Two experimental groups of competitive swimmers using different optimal patterns in the sprint and distance events were investigated. Significant differences between those groups were found with regard to some somatic, flexibility and buoyancy data. Some of these differences helped to explain the use of different optimal patterns. These findings suggest that in studying physical characteristics of competitive crawl swimmers, pattern groups should be treated separately if possible. Realistic reference data, used for detecting weaknesses in physical characteristics and for the orientation of competitors toward optimal patterns at each distance, should be obtained from the mean scores of better pattern groups than the ones used in the present study.

References

BULGAKOVA, N. 1978. [The selection of young swimmers.] Moscow.

COEN, G. 1978. *Schwimmsportliche Leistungstabelle.* (Comparative swimming performance tables.) Gödicke.

DALY, D., Thewissen, M., and Persyn, U. 1980. The influence of swimming aids on the progress of speed in the four swimming strokes with first year P.E. students. In: H. Haag, J. Bielefeld, J. Falke, D. Kayser, W. Kneyer and A. Morawietz (eds.), *Proceedings of the XXII. ICHPER World Congress*, pp. 217-225. Christain Albrechts Universität, Kiel.

DALY, D., Thevelein, X., and Persyn, U. 1981. The effectiveness of crawl stroke swimming: A case study. In: J. Ghesquiere and D. Van Gerven (eds.), *Proceedings of the International Meeting of Physical Fitness Research*, pp. 427-434. Hermes, Leuven.

DIXON, W.J. (ed.). 1981. *BMDP Statistical Software.* University of California Press, Berkeley.

HOLMER, I. 1974. Propulsive efficiency of breaststroke and free-style swimming. *Eur. J. Appl. Physiol.* 33:95-103.

HUXLEY, J.S. 1932. *Problems of Relative Growth.* Methuen, London.

MADER, A., Heck, H., and Holmann, W. 1978. Evaluation of lactic acid anaerobic energy contribution by determination of post exercise lactic acid concentration of ear capillary blood in middle distance runners and swimmers. In: F. Landry and W. Orban (eds.), *Exercise Physiology*, pp. 187-200. Symposia Specialists, Miami.

PERSYN, U., De Maeyer, J., and Vervaecke, H. 1975. Investigation of hydro-dynamic determinants of competitive swimming strokes. In: J. Clarys and L. Lewillie (eds.), *Swimming II*, pp. 214-222. University Park Press, Baltimore.

PERSYN, U., Hoeven, R., and Daly, D. 1979. An evaluation center for competitive swimmers. In: J. Terauds and W. Bedingfield (eds.), *Swimming III*, pp. 182-195. University Park Press, Baltimore.

TANNER, J.M., Whitehouse, R.H., and Healy, M.J.R. 1962. *A New System for Estimating Skeletal Maturity from Hand and Wrist, with Standards Derived from a Study of 2600 British Children: Vol. II. The Scoring System.* International Children's Center, Paris.

TANNER, J.M., Whitehouse, R.H., and Healy, M.J.R. 1975. *Assessment of Skeletal Maturity and Prediction of Adult Height.* Academic Press, London.

VAN TILBORGH, L., Daly, D., and Persyn, U. 1983. The influence of some somatic factors on passive drag: gravity and buoyancy forces in competitive swimmers. In: *Biomechanics and Medicine in Swimming*, pp. 207-214. Human Kinetics, Champaign.

VERVAECKE, H., and Persyn, U. 1981. Some differences between men and women in various factors which determine swimming performances. In: J. Borms, M. Hebbelinck and A. Vernerando (eds.), *The Women Athlete, Medicine and Sport* (Vol. XV), pp. 150-156. Karger, Basel.

WALKER, R.H. 1974. Standards for somatotyping children: I: The prediction of youth adult height from children's growth data. *Ann. Human Biol.* 1:149-158.

Effects of Isokinetic, Isotonic and Swim Training on Swimming Performance

Mitsumasa Miyashita and Hiroaki Kanehisa
University of Tokyo, Japan

Strength training has become one of the major components of programs to improve athletic performance. Previous studies have shown that isotonic training was effective for improving motor performance (Berger, 1963; Capen, 1959; Chui, 1959). More recently, Pipes and Wilmore (1975) demonstrated a clear superiority of the isokinetic training procedures over the isotonic procedures relative to strength, anthropometric measures and motor performance tasks. Later they qualified this statement because of the specificity of training at a given velocity. However, very few studies have dealt with the question of whether the gain in muscular output after strength training results in the improvement of athletic performance, especially in swimming (Sharp et al., 1982). This study was designed to investigate the effects of muscular strength training on swimming performance.

Methods

Subjects

Eight male swimmers, members of a high school swimming team, aged 15-17 years, participated in this study. All subjects were fully informed of all risks and stresses associated with the project and consented to participate.

Testing Procedures

Measurements of muscular power output, anthropometric characteristics and swimming performance were conducted on seven occasions before, during (ca. every 2 months) and after 10 months from October 1980

329

to July 1981. Cybex II (Lumex, New York) was used to determine the peak torque during isokinetic contractions. The subjects performed maximal shoulder rotation with the lever arm grasped in the right hand. The machine's axis of rotation was aligned with an anatomical axis of rotation in the shoulder joint. The range of rotation was 180°, from 0 to 180° (0° = horizontal). The subjects assumed a prone position on a bench and grasped the lever arm with the right hand with the elbow joint flexed at 120°. The subjects were asked to perform this arm-pull movement in a manner similar to the upper-arm movement used when swimming the crawl stroke. After familiarization with the apparatus, the subjects performed two maximal contractions at selected velocities of 0, 30, 120 and 210°/sec. The best of the two scores was used as the subject's score.

In order to determine muscular endurance, the subjects performed continuously a similar arm-pulling movement 100 times at a speed of 210°/sec. The average peak torque for the 100 repetitions was used as a measure of muscular endurance. The anthropometric measures included body weight, body height, girth of the right upper arm and three skinfold thicknesses, from triceps, chest and scapula. In order to evaluate swimming performances, the subjects performed a 50-m maximal swim with their customary stroke in a 25-m swimming pool. They were timed from the sound of the starting pistol until their hand touched at the finish.

The Training Program

The training program of isokinetic, isotonic and swim training was conducted 6 days/week throughout the 10-month training program. In the isokinetic training, the subjects performed a 20-sec bout of double-arm pulls with their best efforts at a velocity of ca. 180°/sec on a swim bench (Mini-Gym, USA). The double-arm pulls consisted of three different movement patterns (catch, pull and entire stroke).

In the isotonic training, the subjects performed the bench press, squat, two-hand curls, triceps extension and standing military press exercise. Each exercise was repeated for 20 sec with a resistance that could be lifted 20 times. In both the isokinetic and isotonic training, the subjects were instructed by the coach to perform each exercise as fast as possible, and to repeat each exercise twice a day.

The total distance per day in swim training varied roughly from 2,500 m (Oct. to Dec. 1980), 5,000 m (Jan. to Apr. 1981 and July 1981) to 10,000 m (May to June 1981).

Statistics

The differences in mean values of the variables before and after training were tested with Student's t-ratios. Significant level of differences was set at $p < .05$. A Pearson product-moment correlation coefficient

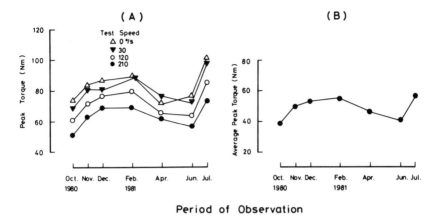

Period of Observation

Figure 1 — Seasonal changes of muscular output. (A) Changes in peak torque at each test speed. (B) Muscular endurance.

and regression equation were calculated between the increases in mean maximal velocity of the 50-m swim and the mean improvements in muscular endurance.

Results

Through the training period, the mean value of body height increased significantly from 172.6 to 173.5 cm, but the body weight remained unchanged at 67.0 kg. The mean value of the skinfold thicknesses decreased significantly by 3.9 mm at the chest site, but girth of the upper arm increased significantly on the average of 1.9 cm.

The seasonal changes in peak torque and muscular endurances are presented in Figure 1. Peak torques at different speeds and the muscular endurance expressed as average peak torque during 100 repetitions tended to change in a similar way, that is, increasing from October 1980 to February 1981; thereafter, decreasing until June 1981 and increasing again in July. However, none of these changes was statistically significant.

All subjects improved their mean speed of 50-m maximal swimming and exceeded their previous best times in competition (Table 1). Improvement in mean times were 2.3% for the 50-m dash and 2.0% for the swimming races. A significant correlation was found between the gain in speed of 50-m swimming and in muscular endurance (Figure 2).

Discussion

In order for a training program to have the most beneficial effects, it must be constructed in a manner such that the specific physiological

Table 1

Physical Characteristics, Mean Speeds in 50-m Maximal Swimming and Personal Records of Subjects[a]

Subject	Age (yr) Oct. 1980	Body weight (kg)		Body height (cm)		Event	Average speed for 50-m swim (m/sec)		Event	Personal record	
		Oct. 1980	July 1981	Oct. 1980	July 1981		Oct. 1980	July 1981		Oct. 1980	July 1981
ST	17.8	176.1	176.4	70.5	72.3	Fr	1.93	1.97	200IM	2'12"73	2'10"12
									400IM	4'40"73	4'33"89
									100Fr	55"71	53"76
									200Fr	1'58"43	1'55"61
									100Bu	1'00"89	58"85
									200Bu	2'10"54	2'03"91
FH	15.9	164.4	165.3	67.4	60.2	Fr	1.90	1.93	200Fr	2'01"08	2'00"83
WH	16.1	178.5	179.3	67.4	68.8	Br	1.39	1.46	200Br	2'40"79	2'37"77
YH	15.5	167.0	168.6	55.7	58.0	Fr	1.86	1.88	200Fr	2'11"40	2'05"51
HH	17.2	176.5	177.0	72.4	69.5	Fr	1.87	1.89	100Fr	57"24	56"84
KN	16.0	176.4	177.5	65.4	67.9	Bu	1.78	1.82	100Bu	1'00"24	58"72
									200Bu	2'10"72	2'07"97
NB	15.5	172.4	173.8	74.1	75.0	Ba	1.57	1.62	100Ba	1'04"39	1'03"67
									200Ba	2'17"43	2'14"81
SM	16.0	169.8	170.4	67.9	64.1	Fr	1.83	1.87	200IM	2'23"30	2'21"48

[a]IM = individual medley, Fr = freestyle, Bu = butterfly, Ba = backstroke, Br = breaststroke

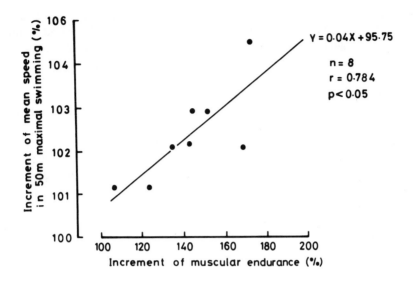

Figure 2— Relationship between percentage increment of muscular endurance and that of mean speed in 50-m maximal swimming.

capabilities required to perform a given sports skill or activity will be developed (Fox, 1979). The performance times for competitive swimming are very different, ranging from 50 sec for 100-m freestyle to 15 min for the 1,500-m freestyle. Therefore, the energy to the working muscles used in competitive swimming must be supplied by both anaerobic and aerobic energy systems. In other words, training for competitive swimmers should be aimed at improving these two systems.

Lesmes et al. (1978) reported that isokinetic training at 180°/sec for 30 sec stressed the anaerobic energy system. Sharp et al. (1982) reported that untrained subjects improved their torque 19% and their sprint swim performance 4% during a 4-week isokinetic strength training program. In the present study, the short training bout (20 sec) with high speed (180°/sec) was selected for isokinetic training and light resistance with high repetitions for isotonic training in order to increase swimming speed.

Previous studies of isokinetic training have shown that although low-speed training resulted in significant gains in muscular output, this occurred only at slow test speeds. High-speed training brought about a significant gain both at slow and fast test speeds (Moffroid and Whipple, 1970; Pipes and Wilmore, 1975). The present study resulted in significant gains in peak torque after training at all speeds tested. This implies that the speed of 180°/sec used in this study for training is optimal to improve the muscular torque at both slow and fast movement speeds.

Although the strength training protocols were unchanged throughout a period of observation, muscular output gradually decreased from February 1980 to June 1981. It seems there are only two plausible reasons for this. One was a psychological factor, for example, monotony of relatively intense on-land training during the first 3 months. The other was that the amount of work done in swimming increased beginning in January 1981. Such a change from sprint type of swimming training to long-distance training generally induces aerobic adaptation within the muscles. As a result, performance of 50-m maximal swimming decreased slightly in February 1981. On the other hand, the increase in muscular torque from June to July 1981 was probably due to the specialized training program used during this time for competition, that is, short distance and/or sprint swimming.

An interesting finding of this study was that there was a significant correlation between the final increases in swimming performance and in muscular endurance, whereas no significant correlation was found in swimming performance and the muscular torque during a single isokinetic contraction. Considering the modes of competitive swimming, it seems that the muscular endurance exercise used in the present study is more useful than a program of single, maximal contractions.

References

BERGER, R.A. 1963. Effect of dynamic and static training on vertical jump ability. *Res. Q.* **34**:419-424.

CAPEN, E.K. 1950. The effect of systematic weight training on power, strength, and endurance. *Res. Q.* **21**:83-93.

CHUI, E.F. 1950. The effect of systematic weight training on athletic power. *Res. Q.* **21**:188-194.

LEE, W., and Wilmore, J.H. 1981. Specificity of power improvements through slow and fast isokinetic training. *J. Appl. Physiol. Respirat. Environ. Exercise Physiol.* **51**:1437-1442.

FOX, E.L. 1979. *Sport Physiology.* W.B. Saunders, Philadelphia.

LESMES, G.R., Costill, D.L., Coyle, E.F., and Fink, W.J. 1978. Muscle strength and power changes during maximal isokinetic training. *Med. Sci. Sports* **10**:266-269.

MOFFROID, M.T., and Whipple, R.H. 1970. Specificity of speed of exercise. *Physical Ther.* **50**:1692-1699.

PIPES, T.V., and Wilmore, J.H. 1975. Isokinetic vs isotonic strength training in adult men. *Med. Sci. Sports* **7**:262-274.

SHARP, R.L., Troup, J.P., and Costill, D.L. 1982. Relationship between power and sprint freestyle swimming. *Med. Sci. Sports* **14**:53-56.

Estimation of the Peak Performance in the 100-Meter Breast Stroke on the Basis of Serum Lactate Measurement during Two Submaximal Test Heats at Different Velocities

Michael Elliott and Paul Haber

Medical University Clinic of Vienna, Austria

Medical supervision of training is becoming more and more important. The methods used should be practical not only in the laboratory but also at the training place and they should be adjusted to the particular form of sport.

Forms of competitive sports favoring short-time endurance require reliable methods for judging special endurances, which can be defined as the optimal combination of special strength and techniques as well as aerobic and anaerobic capacity required for the length of the competition. Provided the competition does not last significantly longer than 2 min, the necessary energy is provided mainly through the lactacid anaerobic system. Serum lactate is a measure of the rate of glycolytically formed energy and thus constitutes an objective measure of work intensity in short-time endurance activities. The individual's special endurance determines the relationship between serum lactate and speed. Consequently, it must be possible to estimate velocity at maximal lactate after having determined the individual relationship between lactate and velocity during submaximal work. This assumption was substantiated by comparing the actual measured maximal velocity with the estimated maximal velocity, based on this individual relationship.

Methods

Mader et al. (1976) have shown that for short-time endurance, an exponential relationship exists between velocity and serum lactate when serum lactate exceeds 4 mmol/L and energy required is provided mainly

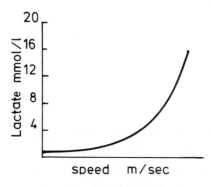

Figure 1—Schematic drawing of the exponential relationship between speed and serum lactate.

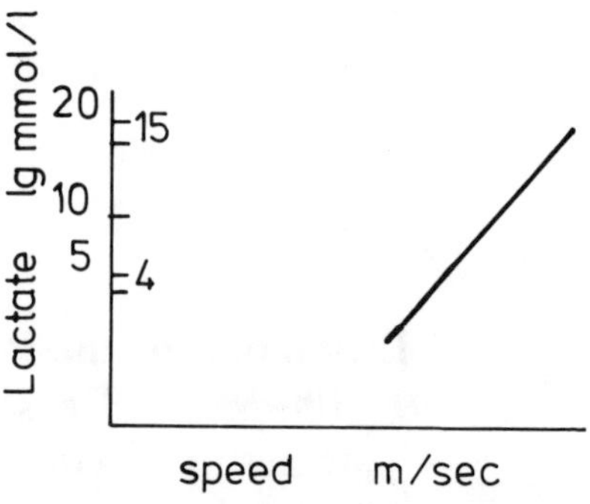

Figure 2—Linear relationship between speed and serum lactate drawn on a graph with a semilogarithmic system of coordinates.

by the lactacid anaerobic system, as shown schematically in Figure 1. Different curves are observed for different subjects and the appearance of the curve depends on the momentary individual special endurance.

The logarithm of the Δ lactate figures (that is, lactate of performance minus lactate during rest), marked on the ordinate, changes the exponential relationship into a linear one (Haber and Pont, 1977), as Figure 2 shows schematically. This is only true for a limited range at higher velocities. Therefore, from the data gained by two submaximal test-runs at different velocities, assuming a linear relationship between the logarithm of lactate concentration and velocity, the maximal velocity can be estimated if maximal lactate concentration is known.

In the present test series, velocity was calculated from swimming time over 100 m and lactate was measured with a lactate analyzer (Roche 640). Blood was taken from the earlobe hyperemized with finalgon with heparinized glass capillaries. Immediately afterwards, the blood was placed into small plastic containers which had been prepared for hemolyzing all erythrocytes to stop glycolysis.

The swimmers had to undergo three test-runs of 100-m each using the breast stroke at the following velocities. The first run was at long-distance velocity with a production of less than 4 mmol serum lactate/L. The second run was at medium-distance velocity with less than 5 mmol serum lactate/L. The third run was at competitive speed and maximal effort. Lactate was first measured with subjects at rest. In the first run, blood was taken immediately after touch, in the second run during the third min after touch and in the third run during the fifth min after touch because when serum lactate levels are more than 5 mmol/L, the lactate increases for up to 5 min after performance. The swimmers were given 45-min rest periods between each of the three swims in order to ensure the serum lactate returned to its initial level. The third run was done to verify the estimated maximal speed by regression equations of the first two runs.

Subjects

Well trained male swimmers ($n = 11$) took part in the test series. Not all of them specialized in breast stroke so that different individual special endurances for the chosen distance were expected. Their average age was 17 ± 1.6 yr. The swimmers were informed about the purpose of the test at the time they volunteered to participate.

Results

During rest, serum lactate was 0.71 ± 0.1 mmol/L. Table 1 shows the average time and serum lactate levels after the three test runs. Figure 3 shows the relationship between actual measured and estimated maximal velocities, with a resulting correlation coefficient of $r = 0.86$ ($p < 0.001$) and a standard deviation of the estimated linear value of $S_{y \cdot x} = \pm 0.06$ m/sec.

Discussion

This estimation is precise enough to apply the method in training supervision. It has the advantage of not requiring a laboratory and can be carried out during actual training. The maximal serum lactate necessary for the estimation of peak performance can be obtained from values in competition or from empirical values. Differences between estimated and actual peak performances suggest faults in individual com-

Table 1

**Average Time and Average Serum Lactate
of 11 Swimmers in Three Test Runs of the 100-m Breast Stroke**

Run	Time (sec)	Δ Lactate (mmol/L)
1	98 ± 6	1.65 ± 1.05
2	89 ± 5	3.53 ± 1.25
3	83 ± 5	7.74 ± 2.55

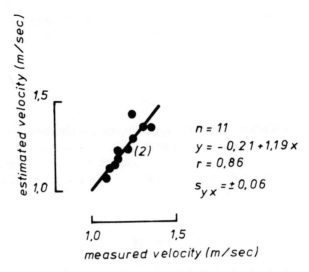

Figure 3—Linear regression and correlation between actual measured velocity on the abscissa and estimated velocity on the ordinate derived from two submaximal test runs of the 100-m breast stroke.

petitive techniques. On the basis of only two measurements, the method presented makes an exact determination of the momentary special endurance possible and also can be the basis for intraindividual control over a longer period of time.

References

HABER, P., and Pont, J. 1977. Objektivierung der speziellen Ausdauer für zyklische Sportarten im Kurzzeitausdauer-bereich mittels Mikroblutgasanalyse. (Objectivity of special endurance for cyclic sports performances in short time endurance by means of micro-blood gas analysis.) *Sportarzt Sportmed.* 12:357-362.

MADER, A., Liesen, H., Heck, H., Philippi, H., Rost, R., Schürch, P., and Hollmann, W. 1976. Zur Beurteilung der sportartspezifischen Ausdauerleistungsfähigkeit im Labor. (Estimation of specific sport performance endurance capability in the laboratory.) *Sportarzt Sportmed.* 27:80-89, 109-112.

Heart Rate Measurement Technique in Swimming Performance Prediction

Robert J. Treffene

Queensland Institute of Technology, Brisbane, Australia

Treffene (1975, 1978a, 1978b) and Treffene et al. (1979) have described a protocol using heart rates measured immediately after constant pace swims to calculate the minimal constant velocity (V_{cr}) at which a swimmer's heart rate achieves its maximum. Maximal oxygen uptake should also first occur at this speed (Andersen et al., 1971; Charbonnier et al., 1975; Simonsen, 1971). The protocol used was similar to the recommended World Health Organization multistage extrapolation method (Andersen et al., 1971). Extrapolation to each subject's measured maximal heart rate was used, however, to determine V_{cr}.

It has been assumed (Treffene, 1978a, 1978b) that the total anaerobic energy used for 100-m swimming events is about the same as that available for the 200-m events. A rapid increase in muscle lactic acid accumulation rate ($\dot{L}a_m$), as indicated by blood lactate measurements, occurs when V_{cr} or $\dot{V}O_2$max is reached (Piiper et al., 1966; Treffene et al., 1980). The $\dot{L}a_m$ for the 200-m swimming velocity was assumed to be half of the $\dot{L}a_m$ for the 100-m velocity so that the total anaerobic energy used could be equated.

If the average velocity for the 100-m is Y m·sec^{-1} and writing V_{cr} as X m·sec^{-1}, Treffene (1980) deduced that V_{cr} for the 200- and the 400-m events would be seen at velocities of $(X + Y/2)$ m·sec^{-1} and $(3X + Y/4)$ m·sec^{-1}, respectively. The model also predicts that the 800- and 1,500-m events will be swum at velocities close to V_{cr}.

The purpose of this study was to investigate the correlation between individual V_{cr} values and competition swimming speeds over 200- and 400-m distances and to determine whether the prediction formula of Treffene (1978a, 1978b, 1980) already mentioned agree with competitive performance results.

Methods

Tests were conducted in pools with water temperatures of 23-26°C and 50-m length, similar to competitive pools. All swimmers tested ($N = 88$: 51 males, 37 females) were elite competitive swimmers and qualified for competition in the Queensland Age titles. Informed consent was obtained. The tests were conducted immediately prior to major State, Australian, National or International meets. (Data are shown in Table 1.)

Each subject performed at least three 300- to 200-m swims (duration of 3 min or more) in their chosen stroke at different constant submaximal speeds with only small rests in between. Instantaneous heart rate was recorded within 3 sec after completion of each swim using an accurately calibrated Heart Rate Industries HRM 3 heart rate monitor. Maximal heart rate was determined for each subject as described by Treffene (1978a, 1980) after a maximal 200-m effort. For each swimmer, a V_{cr} value was determined by using extrapolation of heart rate-velocity relationships to maximal heart rate.

The best official results for each swimmer in the swimming meet for 100, 200, 400, 800 and 1,500 m were obtained from the official records of the Queensland Amateur Swimming Association. Not all subjects swam each competition distance.

Results

One hundred 200-m competition swims were recorded for the 88 subjects. The mean of the difference between the predicted speed (X + Y/2) m•sec^{-1} and the actual average velocity recorded for the 200-m event expressed as a percentage was 0.5%. The average competitive velocity was slower than the average predicted velocity.

The correlation coefficient ($n = 100$) indicates a close correlation between predicted velocities and competition velocities ($r = 0.99$). The results were highly significant ($p < 0.001$) (see Table 2). The predicted

Table 1

Mean Data for Subjects

	N	V_{cr} (m•sec^{-1})	Age (yr)	Mean 100-m speed (m•sec^{-1})	Maximal heart rate (bpm)
$\overline{X} \pm SD$ overall	88	1.44 ± 0.15	14.7 ± 2.2	1.61 ± 0.15	190.8 ± 8.7

Table 2

**Mean V_{cr}, 100-m Swimming Speed,
200-m Swimming Speed, 200-m Predicted Speed,
400-m Swimming Speed and 400-m Predicted Speed**

	Distance (m)	n	V_{cr} (m·sec^{-1})	Swimming speed (m·sec^{-1})	Predicted speed (m·sec^{-1})
$\overline{X} \pm SD$	100	100	1.44 ± 0.14	1.61 ± 0.15	
$\overline{X} \pm SD$	200	100	1.44 ± 0.14	1.52 ± 0.14	1.52 ± 0.15
$\overline{X} \pm SD$	400	67	1.47 ± 0.12	1.50 ± 0.11	1.52 ± 0.11

velocities $(3X + Y/4)$ m·sec^{-1} compared to actual recorded average velocities ($n = 67$, $N = 59$) for the 400-m swim agree within 0.7% and a high degree of correlation ($r = 0.98$) existed between the two velocities ($p < 0.001$). The average 400-m competitive velocity was slower than the average predicted velocity.

Data also were collected for 800- and 1,500-m events. Of the recorded 45 swims of 800 m, only four swimmers swam faster than V_{cr} and then only marginally. In 31 swims of 1,500 m, no swimmer swam faster than V_{cr}. The average speed for the 800-m event was 99 (± 2 SD)% V_{cr} and for the 1,500 swim was 98 (± 2 SD)% V_{cr}.

Discussion

This study has shown that a very good relationship ($r > 0.98$) exists between a predicted swimming velocity and an actual competitive velocity for 200 and 400 m. The model from which these predicted velocities were formulated assumes that the rate of muscle $\dot{L}a_m$ is only slightly below V_{cr}, but increases significantly at velocities above V_{cr}. This increase in $\dot{L}a_m$ is assumed to be proportional to velocity above V_{cr}. The significant change in $\dot{L}a_m$ at V_{cr} and $\dot{V}O_2$max onset has been reported for swimmers (Treffene et al., 1980) and dogs (Piiper et al., 1966).

The 200-m velocities are so well predicted by this formula that the assumptions involved in the model must have reasonable validity. The averages of the 100-, 200- and 400-m velocities were 112, 106 and 102% of V_{cr}, respectively.

Every 400-m event was swum at speeds slightly greater than V_{cr} and every 800- and 1,500-m event was swum at speeds slightly below V_{cr}. This

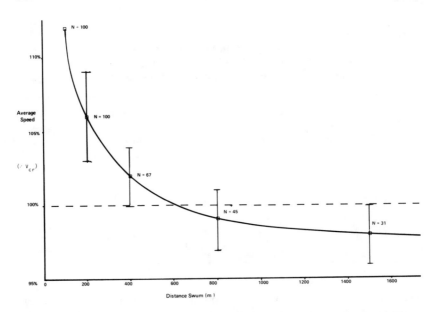

Figure 1 – Average velocity (*n* = 100-31) of the competitive speeds for distances of 100, 200, 400, 800 and 1,500 m compared to the distance swum. The velocity is determined as a percentage of the V_{cr} for each subject measured in the week prior to competition and then averaged for each sample group. Vertical bars indicate a range of ± 1 *SD* for the mean of $\%V_{cr}$. Competitive speeds were recorded for the 88 competitors, some of whom over several years competed more than once having different measured V_{cr} values. Not all swimmers in the sample competed in all events. Thus, *n* for each event was different.

suggests an asymptotic approach to a speed slightly below V_{cr} as the competitive times approach 18-20 min. The predictive model assumed an asymptotic approach to V_{cr}. The asymptotic approach to a speed slightly below V_{cr} (Figure 1) could indicate that V_{cr} has been overestimated or that other factors not considered in the model are important.

The heart rate-velocity curves were determined by steady-state, 3-min swims. The swimming time of 3 min may not have been sufficient to allow the heart rate to plateau. Treffene (1975) and others using radio-telemetry have shown that a heart rate plateau is reached for fit swimmers within 90 sec from commencement of a swim. Any increase in heart rate after 3 min would be small and probably dependent on the slight gradient in muscle lactic acid level with the increase in exercise time when at submaximal effort (Treffene et al., 1980; Wasserman, 1967). If this is the case, it would lead to a small overestimate of V_{cr}. Therefore, if V_{cr} was overestimated, the speed to which the longer distance events asymptotically approach could still be that at which maximal heart rate is first reached in steady-state exercise.

Incorrect race pace could also explain this discrepancy. It is difficult to swim at an exactly constant speed to a predetermined schedule. Swimming at speeds higher than V_{cr} would cause the rapid increase in $\dot{L}a_m$ as reported by Piiper et al. (1966) and Treffene et al. (1980). In order to avoid this possibility most competitors seemed to adopt a speed marginally below V_{cr} in the early stages of a distance race. Swimming below maximal oxygen uptake speeds would waste aerobic energy resources which cannot be recovered at later stages in the race. For this reason, it is to be expected that swimmers without prior training exactly at V_{cr} would probably swim in competition at speeds just below V_{cr}.

Improvement in performance for competitors is paralleled by an improvement in V_{cr} (Treffene, 1980). This enables one to anticipate improved times in competition relative to past recorded times by comparing corresponding heart rate-velocity curves. This has been used successfully to plan national, international and world record performances.

This study has indicated that a very high correlation between competitive times and predicted times existed. The predictions assume an exact relationship between V_{cr} and the speed at which maximal oxygen uptake was first achieved. Events for 100, 200 and 400 m were all swum at speeds exceeding V_{cr}. It would therefore be expected that these events would also be swum at speeds above the point at which maximal oxygen uptake would be achieved. Verification of this could perhaps be made by research groups with swimming flumes.

Acknowledgment

This study was funded by the Australian Department of Home Affairs, Speedo Knitting Mills, the Australian Swimming Coaches' Association and the Queensland Institute of Technology.

References

ANDERSEN, K.L., Shephard, R.J., Denolin, H., Vam Aushaus, E., and Mastroni, R. 1971. *Fundamentals of Exercise Testing*. World Health Organization, Geneva.

BRIGGS, C.A. 1977. Maximum aerobic power and endurance as predictors of middle distance running success. *Aust. J. Sports Med.* 9:28-31.

CHARBONNIER, J.P., Lacour, J.R., Riffat, J., and Flandrois, R. 1975. Experimental study of the performance of competitive swimmers. *Eur. J. Appl. Physiol.* 34:157-167.

COSTILL, D.L., and Fox, E.L. 1969. Energetics of marathon running. *Med. Sci. Sports* 1:81-86.

PIIPER, J., Cerretelli, F., Cuttica, F., and Mangill, F. 1966. Energy metabolism and circulation in dogs exercising in hypoxia. *J. Appl. Physiol.* **21**:1143-1149.

SIMONSEN, E. 1971. *Physiology of Work Capacity and Fatigue.* Charles C. Thomas, Springfield, IL.

TREFFENE, R.J. 1975. *An Investigation of the E.C.G. in Sports and Sports Medicine Using Radiotelemetry.* Unpublished masters thesis, University of London.

TREFFENE, R.J. 1978a. Swimming performance test. A method of training and performance time selection. *Aust. J. Sports Med.* **10**:33-38.

TREFFENE, R.J. 1978b. Predict performance by heart rate measurements. *Int. Swimmer* **14**:15-17.

TREFFENE, R.J. 1980. Swim training and race control utilising physiological measurements. *Int. Swimmer* **17**:13-16.

TREFFENE, R.J., Alloway, J., and Jull, J. 1979. Use of a heart rate meter in swimming and athletic performance measurement. In: J. Terauds and B.W. Bedingfield (eds.), *Swimming III*, pp. 275-280. University Park Press, Baltimore.

TREFFENE, R.J., Dickson, R., Craven, C., Osborne, C., Woodhead, K., and Hobbs, K. 1980. Lactic acid accumulation during constant speed swimming at controlled relative intensities. *J. Sports Med.* **20**:244-254.

TREFFENE, R.J., Frampton, D., Tunstall Pedoe, D., and Idle, M. 1978. Swimming proficiency measurement using heart rate telemetry. *Aust. J. Sports Med.* **10**:30-32.

VOLKOV, N.I., Shirkovets, E.A., and Boril Kevich, V.E. 1975. Assessment of aerobic and anaerobic capacity of athletes in treadmill running tests. *Eur. J. Appl. Physiol.* **34**:121-130.

WASSERMAN, K. 1967. Lactate and related acid base and blood gas changes during constant load and graded exercise. *Can. Med. Assoc. J.* **96**:775-779.

Swimming Direction and Visual Control

Jaroslav Novák
Research Institute of Physical Culture,
Prague, Czechoslovakia

Maintaining a straight course during competitive swimming is undoubtedly one of the prerequisites for achieving maximal performance. This is no problem in swimming pools where hygienic requirements for water quality are maintained and aids are available for visual control of the desired direction over the water surface (such as lanes and lateral and opposite walls of the pool). The lanes are marked by dark lines of 0.20-0.31 m thickness at the bottom of the pool according to the FINA rules so that the swimmers can use them for orientation.

A completely different situation exists in long distance swimming competition in open water. Judgment of the distance from the control buoy, which marks the course of competition, or orientation to the other participants of the race, presuming they swim straight, are used for visual control of the desired direction. Crews in accompanying boats should be careful to hold a straight course when boats are available to the swimmers. In spite of that, most long-distance swimmers have serious problems in holding a straight course. The purpose of this study was to determine to the degree of deviation from a straight course which would result in a pool of 50 × 25 m size when no aids to visual control were available.

Subjects and Methods

Fifty swimmers, males and females aged 12-17 yr with 2-5 yr competitive swimming experience participated in the investigation, which was conducted during a summer training camp. Their goal was to swim as straight as possible to the opposite side of a 50-m pool from a start in the middle of the 25-m side. Goggles covered with nontransparent material were used in each attempt. The subjects used the breaststroke the first day and the front crawl on the next day of the experiment. Motivation was insured by including this procedure in the summer camp Olympiad program, and the winners were rewarded in the same way as in the other events.

A graphical record of the course was recorded for each swimmer. An observer stood on the poolside behind the swimmer's starting point, and drew the course of each attempt on a prepared squared recording sheet. In order to simplify the data for the statistical evaluation, one of three possibilities was classified:

- Swimmers held a straight swimming course if they did not deviate by more than 12.5 m left or right from a straight course in swimming to the opposite side of the pool.
- Swimmers deviated to the right if they finished their attempt by touching the opposite wall to the right of the straight course.
- Swimmers deviated to the left if they finished their attempt by touching the opposite wall to the left of the straight course.

A moment before touching the wall, swimmers were given a signal by a whistle or were restrained physically to prevent them from injury as a result of swimming into the opposite side of the pool. No individuals were present in the pool at the time of the measurements except the subjects actually swimming. The results were evaluated using a frequency chi-square analysis and $p < 0.05$ was considered statistically significant.

Results

Figure 1 presents a sample of some individual swimmers' records. The ability to hold a straight swimming course was very different in individual swimmers. Some were able to hold a straight direction with no visual feedback while swimming both front crawl and breaststroke, whereas others could maintain the desired course using one stroke only or couldn't hold it at all. In some cases, swimmers deviated from the straight direction to the point that they swam back before having touched the *side* wall.

Statistical analysis showed that:

- The majority of the swimmers could not hold a straight course (Table 1). When swimming the breaststroke, 73% of the swimmers and 57% in the crawl deviated by more than 12.5 m from the desired course.
- Swimmers who could not maintain a straight course in the breaststroke deviated significantly more often from the straight direction in the front crawl (Tables 2 and 3).
- There was no relationship between the side of inspiration and the side to which the swimmer turned (Table 4).

Discussion

No similar report has yet been found in literature using swimmers although there are well known experiments by Krestovnikov (1954) with

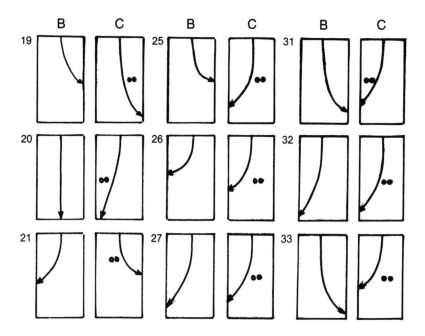

Figure 1—Selected records of swimming direction in 9 swimmers. B = breaststroke, C = front crawl, oo = side of inspiration in crawl.

different sports groups. With complete exclusion of visual control in gymnasts, Krestovnikov found complete loss of space orientation and difficulties with determination of the exact body position. Walking without sight control led to an obvious detour of movement to the right. Formation of figures on an ice surface was considerably altered in figure skating. The range of throw increased by 6 m in hammer throwing, whereas discus throwers tended to lose their balance after releasing the discus.

Deviations from the straight course in swimming are evoked by reasons other than the side of inspiration in the front crawl, as movement asymmetry or unequal propulsive force during strokes were observed in both strokes. The question of why needs further study.

Conclusions

Swimming without visual control leads to significant alterations in holding a straight swimming course. If deviations occur in the case of the breaststroke, they usually also occur in the front crawl. There was no correlation between the side of inspiration and the side to which swimmers deviated. For long-distance swimming it may be concluded that

Table 1

Holding a Straight Course during Swimming

Variable[a]	n	Significance
CD	33	$p < 0.05$
CS	12	NS
BD	28	$p < 0.05$
BS	21	NS

[a]CD—deviation in crawl; CS—straight direction in crawl; BD—deviation using breast-stroke; BS—straight direction with breaststroke.
NS = not significant.

Table 2

Mutual Relationship of the Deviation from a Straight Direction While Swimming the Crawl and Breaststroke

Relationship of variables[a]	n	Significance
CD-BD	22	$p < 0.01$
CD-BS	11	NS
CS-BD	2	NS
CS-BS	9	NS

Abbreviations as in Table 1.

Table 3

Mutual Relationship of the Deviation from a Straight Direction in the Crawl and Breaststroke

Relationship of Variables[a]	n	Significance
CL-BL	4	NS
CL-BR	6	NS
CL-BS	7	NS
CR-BL	7	NS
CR-BR	5	NS
CR-BS	4	NS
CS-BL	1	NS
CS-BR	1	NS
CS-BS	9	NS

[a]CL—deviation to the left in crawl; CR—deviation to the right in crawl; CS—straight direction in crawl; BL—deviation to the left in breaststroke; BR—deviation to the right in breaststroke; BS—straight direction in breaststroke.

Table 4

Relationship between the Direction of the Deviation and the Side of Inspiration in the Crawl

Relationship of variables[a]	n	Significance
CL-L	7	NS
CR-L	8	NS
CS-L	3	NS
CL-R	8	NS
CR-R	7	NS
CS-R	7	NS

[a]L—inspiration on the left side; R—inspiration on the right side. For other symbols, see Table 3.

continuous visual control during swimming is necessary if swimmers desire to maintain the correct course.

Reference

KRESTOVNIKOV, A.N. 1954. An outline of physiology and exercise (in Czech). Praha, STN.

Factor Analysis of a Swimming Performance Test

Jean Nowlan
Université de Moncton, Canada

Paul Godbout
Université Laval, Québec, Canada

Many studies of swimming performance tests have been reported in the literature (Burris, 1964; Fox, 1959; Jackson et al., 1979; Nowlan, 1979; Rosentswieg, 1968; Santeusanio, 1980). Swim literature also abounds with utilitarian swimming tests (Cureton, 1943; Guilbert, 1973; Lanoue, 1963; Reece, 1980; Silvia, 1966). Lifesaving and survival swimming skills are defined in an array of swimming test items with many similarities from one lifesaving society to another. These swimming tests have face validity and to some extent logical validity. The purpose of this study was to establish the construct validity of the Université de Moncton swimming performance test.

Methods

A total of 132 subjects, 87 males and 45 females, participated in this study. Their mean age was 12.4 yr with a standard deviation of 2.2 yr and a range of 8 yr. A wide range of swimming ability was represented by this group. The subjects were tested once with the swimming performance test; then 56 of the subjects were retested in a reliability study. An informational session and a warm-up preceded testing in a 25-m pool. The Université de Moncton swimming performance test is composed of four test items. *Underwater swim:* From an in-the-water start, the subject swims underwater nonstop a maximal distance of up to 25 m while passing under four underwater obstacles. These obstacles are light metal tubing suspended across the swimming lane on the lane markers at depths of

This paper summarizes part of a M.Sc. thesis, Université Laval, 1981.

25 cm at the 5-m mark and 50 cm at the 10-, 15- and 20-m marks. *Speed swim:* From a diving start, the subject swims freestyle 50 m as fast as possible. *Transport swim:* From an in-the-water start, the subject pushes a weighted block 25 m and returns to the point of departure towing the block as fast as possible. The block weighs 75 kg and measures 20 × 50 × 120 cm. *Distance swim:* From a diving start, the subject swims freestyle nonstop a maximal distance of up to 1,000 m as fast as possible. Time was recorded for every 5 m of the underwater swim and for every 50 m of the distance swim. The maximal distance swum recorded to the last 5 m or 50 m was multiplied by the velocity for this same distance ($d \times v$). This composite score constituted the performance score for the underwater swim and the distance swim. The swimming velocity (v) constituted the performance scores for the speed swim and the transport swim. Data were analyzed using SPSS programs.

Results and Interpretations

Intraclass correlation coefficients were calculated with the test-retest data. Reliability coefficients of .83, .98, .96, .97 and .97, respectively, were calculated ($p < .01$) for the underwater swim, speed swim, transport swim, distance swim and four test items combined; 90% confidence intervals of .74-.89, .97-.99, .94-.98, .94-.98 and .95-.98 were also calculated. The total test score was obtained by adding the standardized scores of the four test items. The total swimming performance test score and test items were thus found to be very stable.

A review of the descriptive statistics (Table 1) reveals that the distribution curves of the speed swim, the transport swim and the distance swim were platykurtic and present a positive skew. This departure from the normal curve was attributed to the relatively small sample of swimmers and to the fact that poorer swimmers did not participate in the study whereas the range of skilled swimmers was unlimited. It was also felt that the high positive skew of 1.10 on the underwater swim reflects the fact that the swimmers seldom practiced underwater swimming.

Four factors were generated in a principal-components factor analysis (Table 2). The first general factor was identified as relative swimming performance. The subsequent factors were interpreted as being related to body density, drag and propulsive force components. Factor loadings of .56 and − .30 on factor 2 for the underwater swim and the distance swim were consistent with the relationship of body density to swimming efficiency. Body density has a positive relationship with high performance in the underwater swim, whereas it has a negative contribution to performance in the distance swim (Hemmingsen, 1958, Pugh et al., 1960). The speed swim and the transport swim with factor loadings close to zero, − .13 and − .08, respectively, show that body density does not affect per-

Table 1

**Descriptive Statistics for the Four Test Items of
the Université de Moncton Swimming Performance Test[a]**

	Underwater swim ($d \times v$)	Speed swim (v)	Transport swim (v)	Distance swim ($d \times v$)
Mean	12.13	1.10	.59	689.99
Std. error	.67	.02	.01	18.35
Median	9.02	1.06	.58	665.07
Mode	4.10	1.10	.55	775.19
Std. dev.	7.68	.26	.11	209.17
Variance	58.99	.07	.01	43,753.61
Kurtosis	.21	−0.50	−.32	−0.52
Skew	1.10	.34	.07	.44
Range	32.38	1.28	.60	938.60
Minimum	0.00	.52	.27	262.60
Maximum	32.38	1.80	.87	1,201.20

[a]n = 132.

Table 2

**Summary of the Université de Moncton Swimming Performance Test
Principal-Components Factors Analysis[a]**

	Factors before rotation				Factors after varimax rotation			
	F1	F2	F3	F4	F1	F2	F3	F4
1. Underwater swim	.82	.56	.10	.05	.24	.91	.27	.23
2. Speed swim	.94	−.13	.06	−.32	.45	.35	.39	.72
3. Transport swim	.90	−.08	−.42	.09	.34	.32	.84	.29
4. Distance swim	.89	−.30	.27	.20	.86	.26	.32	.31
Eigen value	3.15	.43	.27	.15				
% variance	78.9	10.7	6.6	3.8				
Cumulative %	78.9	89.6	96.2	100.				

[a]n = 132.

formance in speed swimming (Bloomfield and Sigerseth, 1965). It was hypothesized that nonswimmers and poor swimmers with high body density, because of difficulties in surface swimming, drop out of swimming whereas swimmers with lower body density pursue swimming activities. This could further explain the high positive skew in the underwater swim.

A factor loading of $-.42$ for the transport swim on factor 3 and a loading of .27 for the distance swim are attributed to two extremes of a drag intensity continuum. In the transport swim, swimmers not only have to overcome drag created by their own bodies but also have to overcome the added drag of the block — hence the high negative factor loading. A coefficient of .27 for the distance swim indicates that this swim offers the least drag because of a relatively slow swimming speed and an over-the-water arm stroke recovery. High swimming speed explains the .06 factor loading on the speed swim (Clarys and Jiskoot, 1975; Counsilman, 1968). A coefficient of .10 for the underwater swim demonstrates that this test item offers considerable drag; but in this case, complete immersion of the body and underwater recovery of the arms and legs movement are additional factors creating drag (Jiskoot and Clarys, 1975; Miyashita and Tsunoda, 1978).

The fourth factor, despite its relatively lower importance — 3.8% of the total variance — we believe represents propulsive force. There is a constant relationship between drag and propulsive force when comparing factors 3 and 4 with the exception of the transport swim. The irregularity in this two-factor structure is explained by the added drag created by the block while no additional propulsive force is available. With factor loadings of .45, .35, .39 and .72 on factors 1-4 after a varimax rotation, it is evident that the speed swim does not contribute substantially to the test construct (Table 2). This is further evident when considering that the correlations between test items ranged from .60 to .73 with the exception of the speed swim, which had correlations of .80 and .82 with the transport and distance swims.

Recommendations

In light of these interpretations, it is recommended that the speed swim be eliminated from the swimming performance test; that the underwater swim be segmented by a right and a left 90° turn and that a 25-m weight-carrying swim be added to the swimming performance test. It is assumed that these changes in test structure and composition will reduce the percentage of total variance in the first general factor and increase the percentage of total variance in factors 2, 3 and 4, thus increasing the test construct validity.

The assumptions made in this study suggest the possible validation of factor scores as indirect measures of the components identified. Further studies are now being conducted to validate the factor loadings.

References

BLOOMFIELD, J., and Sigerseth, P.O. 1965. Anatomical and physiological differences between sprint and middle distance swimmers at the university level. *J. Sports Med. Phys. Fitness* **5**:76-81.

BURRIS, B.J. 1964. *A Study of the Speed-Stroke Test of Crawl Stroking Ability and Its Relationship to Other Tests of Crawl Stroking Ability.* Unpublished master's thesis, Temple University, Philadelphia, PA.

CLARYS, J.P., and Jiskoot, J. 1975. Total resistance of selected body positions in the front crawl. In: L. Lewillie and J.P. Clarys (eds.), *Swimming II*, pp. 110-117. University Park Press, Baltimore.

COUNSILMAN, J.E. 1968. *The Science of Swimming.* Prentice-Hall, Englewood Cliffs, NJ.

CURETON, T.K. 1943. *Warfare Aquatics.* Stipes, Chicago.

FOX, M.G. 1964. Swimming power test. *Res. Q.* **35**:126-134.

GUILBERT, P.R. 1973. *La Natation d'Aujourd'hui.* Editions Bornemann, Paris.

HEMMINGSEN, I. 1958. The consumption of energy by females and males during swimming. *Fed. Int. Educ. Physique Bull.* **28**:21-27.

JACKSON, A., Jackson, A.S., and Frankiewiez, R.G. 1979. The construct and concurrent validity of a 12-minute crawl stroke swim as a field test of swimming endurance. *Res. Q.* **50**:641-648.

JISKOOT, J., and Clarys, J.P. 1975. Body resistance on and under the water surface. In: L. Lewillie and J.P. Clarys (eds.), *Swimming II*, pp. 105-109. University Park Press, Baltimore.

LANOUE, F. 1963. *Drownproofing.* Prentice-Hall, Englewood Cliffs, NJ.

MIYASHITA, M., and Tsunoda, T. 1978. Water resistance in relation to body size. In: B. Eriksson and B. Furberg (eds.), *Swimming Medicine IV*, pp. 395-401. University Park Press, Baltimore.

NOWLAN, J. 1979. Développement de tests d'efficience physique en sauvetage riverain et en sauvetage nagé. *CAHPER J.* **46**:6-13.

PUGH, L.G.C.E., Edholm, O.G., Fox, R.H., Wolff, H.S., Hervey, G.R., Hammond, W.H., Tanner, J.M., and Witehouse, R.H. 1960. A physiological study of channel swimming. *Clin. Sci.* **19**:257-273.

REECE, A.M. 1980. University of Kentucky swimming proficiency test. In: D.R. Kirkendall, J.J. Gruber and R.E. Johnson (eds.), *Measurement and Evaluation for Physical Education.* W.C. Brown, Iowa.

ROSENTSWIEG, J. 1968. A revision of the power swimming test. *Res. Q.* **39**:818-819.

SANTEUSANIO, D.B. 1980. A swimming test for prediction of maximum oxygen consumption. *Med. Sci. Sport Exercise* **12**:118.

SILVIA, C.E. 1966. *Lifesaving and Water Safety Today.* Association Press, New York.

Endurance in Swimming, Analyzed from the Standpoint of Automatic Regulation Theory

**Vladimir Schor, I. Stupineanu, P. Hillerin,
and D. Constantinescu**
The Research Centre for Physical Education and Sport,
Bucharest, Rumania

Studies on energy production distinguish three sources of energy (aerobic, anaerobic and anaerobic lactacid). The ability to supply energy through these mechanisms continuously over a period of time is the basis for endurance (Liesen et al., 1977; Mader and Hollmann, 1977). Yet, in competitive sports one way to define endurance is the capacity to achieve and maintain a high average speed over distance during a race (Schmidt, 1977; Tschiene, 1977).

It is very difficult to keep variations in speed as low as possible because of the influence of many disturbing factors which interfere with the athlete's regulatory and control systems. Residual products of effort have a negative influence on the quality of the regulatory systems. This deterioration in function leads to blocking or uneconomical use of energy.

The purpose of this study was to investigate the arm propulsive force-velocity curves and force-displacement curves, obtained from a swimmer using a modular ergometer (Schor, 1983, this volume). The specific objectives were to determine: (a) the two-variable function $F(v,s)$; (b) whether the shapes of the curves had a relative stability from one cycle to another; (c) whether the shapes of curves were influenced by fatigue; and (d) whether an endurance factor could be described using the function $F(v,s)$.

Methods

Two subjects were tested on the modular ergometer (see Figure 1 and Schor, 1983, this volume). Both subjects performed arm strokes, one a "simulated front crawl" (40 strokes/min), and another one of a "simulated butterfly" (48 strokes/min), during two trials of 1-min duration each at maximal effort.

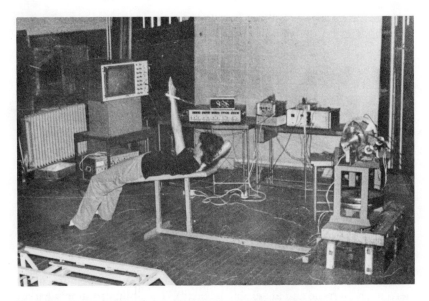

Figure 1—General view of simulation and control equipment.

The first trial was performed "blind," that is, without visual feedback. During the second trial, subjects were provided with instantaneous visual feedback of their efforts. This feedback was superimposed upon a model force-displacement curve (Hillerin et al., Note 1; Schor et al., Notes 2 and 3). Subjects were told to reproduce this curve for each cycle of the right arm during the trial. The modular ergometer was connected to an electronic analog measurement system, a four-channel analog tape recorder ("Orion" model 4676) and visual display monitor (RFT, model USC-101). In order to produce graphic representations, the analog tape recorder was connected to an X-Y recorder (EMG type Endine model 620.02).

It has been shown (Schor, 1983, this volume) that the displacements of the center of mass during swimming, modeled on the modular ergometer, follows the differential equation:

$$M \frac{d^2s}{dt^2} + K \frac{ds}{dt} = F(t),$$

where M = the athlete's body mass; K = the coefficient of passive drag resistance; s = length of the radial vector of the propelling force at its point of application; and $F(t)$ = propelling force translated in the weight center of mass.

For the experimental conditions an $M = 60$ kg was chosen which was approximately equal to each swimmers' body mass. The passive drag coefficient was adapted so that the "simulated drag" was the same for both subjects and the resulting "simulated speed" equaled the individual's swimming speed. Its value was 29.5 N • sec/m.

Results and Discussion

Using a curve with arm propulsive force represented on the ordinate and arm displacement on the abscissa, the area under the curve was the amount of mechanical work per cycle. Many curves may yield the same area, that is, the same amount of work. This means that the same mechanical work can be done in many different ways. According to dynamic control system theory, an evolution of the system dynamics is obtained only from the shape of the force curve and therefore can change even if the work of the propulsive forces during one cycle remains constant. This evolution depends on the horizontal projection of the speed at the very beginning of a new cycle and on the horizontal projection of the arm position. According to Kalman et al. (1969), the two-variable function $F(v,s)$ (F = force, v = velocity, s = space) is the system control governing function (SCGF). This function completely determines the system evolution and the subjects' performances.

For the experiments without visual feedback the time dependence of the force and velocity are given in Figures 2A and B for simulated front crawl stroke and Figures 3A and B for simulated butterfly. Figures 2C and 3C show the relationship between force and velocity. In Figures 4A and B and 5A and B the force-displacement curves shown were obtained during the first and second halves of the subject's work period.

For the steady phase, the shape of the SCGF-projections $F(v)$ and $F(s)$ in "blind" experiments had fluctuations, but these were rather limited. This result indicated that the subject tried to follow a certain pattern with reference to an internal image of the movement.

Comparing the average curve during the first and second halves of the work period (4A with 4B and 5A with 5B), one can also observe an average curve alteration, possibly due to fatigue. The cause of this fatigue may have been due to the muscle groups involved or a decreased control capacity, or both.

The results obtained in feedback trials (Figures 4C and D and 5C and D) shed some light on these questions. These tests were made one day after the "blind" test, so no essential modifications in effort capacity can be assumed. One can observe both closer limits of SCGF fluctuations and less alteration in the average shape of the curve during the trial. Obviously, by using a feedback system, the control task of human movement control systems was made easier. Helping the human movement control system with a feedback system resulted in an important increase in constancy.

This finding emphasizes the idea that control capacity plays an important role in swimming endurance which should not be neglected when we

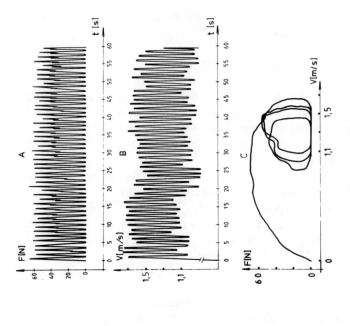

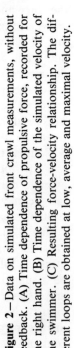

Figure 2 – Data on simulated front crawl measurements, without feedback. (A) Time dependence of propulsive force, recorded for the right hand. (B) Time dependence of the simulated velocity of the swimmer. (C) Resulting force-velocity relationship. The different loops are obtained at low, average and maximal velocity.

Figure 3 – Data on simulated butterfly measurements, without feedback. A, B and C as in Figure 2.

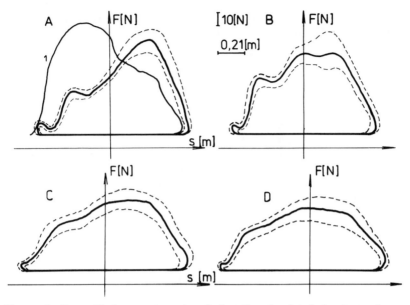

Figure 4—Force-displacement curves during the simulated front crawl arm stroke. The limits of force-fluctuation are shown by the interrupted lines. (A) Observation during the first half of the work period, without feedback; first stroke indicated by 1. (B) Observation during the second half of the work period, without feedback. (C) Same as A but with visual feedback. (D) Same as B but with visual feedback.

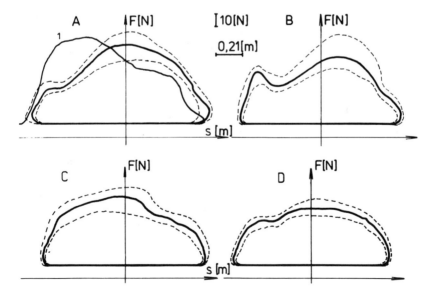

Figure 5—Force-displacement curves during a simulated butterfly arm stroke. For further explanation, see legend to Figure 4.

coach top swimmers. At the same time, the feedback system presented may be a useful tool for training endurance control capacity.

Notes

1. Hillerin, P., Stupineanu, I., and Schor, V. 1979. *Biomechanics Contributions to Improving Sports Performance in Female Rowing.* Paper presented at the VIIth Congress of Biomechanics, Warsaw.
2. Schor, V., Stupineanu, I., and Hillerin, P. 1980. *Modern Solutions for Objective Determination and Correction of Technical Shortcomings in Rowing.* Paper presented at the Pre-Olympic Sports Congress, Tbilisi.
3. Schor, V. 1981. *Vision on Problems Raised by Making Training Equipment in Romania.* Paper presented at the Conference on Training Equipment in Sport, Warsaw.

References

KALMAN, R.E., Falb, P.L., and Arbib, M.A. 1969. *Topics in Mathematical System Theory.* McGraw-Hill, New York.

LIESEN, H., Mader, A., Heck, H., and Hollmann, W. 1977. Die Ausdauerleistungsfahigkeit bei verschiedenen Sportarten unter Besonderer Berucksichtigung des Metabolismus: Zur Ermittlung der optimalen Belastungsintensitat in Training. (Endurance performance capability in different sports under special metabolic considerations: For determination of optimal intensity of stress in training.) In: S. Starischka (ed.), *Leistungssport — Informationen zum Training* (Beiheft 9), pp. 63-79. DSB Bundesausschuss Leistungssport, Berlin.

MADER, A., and Hollmann, W. 1977. Zur Bedeutung der Stofwechselleistungsfahigkeit des Eliteruderers im Training und Wettkampf. (Significance of metabolic performance capability of elite oarsmen in training and competition.) In: S. Starischka (ed.), *Leistungssport — Informationen zum Training* (Beiheft 9), pp. 8-62. DSB Bundesausschuss Leistungssport, Berlin.

SCHMIDT, P. 1977. Trainingsformen zur Erziehung einer hohen Ubersauerung. (The nature of conditioning for training at an elevated acidic level.) In: S. Starischka (ed.), *Leistungssport — Informationen zum Training* (Beiheft 9), pp. 104-111. DSB Bundesausschuss Leistungssport, Berlin.

SCHOR, V. 1983. Multifunctional modular ergometer for simulating the specific dynamics in swimming. In: A.P. Hollander, P.A. Huijing, and G. de Groot (eds.), *Biomechanics and Medicine in Swimming*, pp. 108-112. Human Kinetics, Champaign, IL.

TSCHIENE, P. 1977. Bemerkungen zum speziellen Ausdauertraining. (Remarks concerning special endurance training.) In: S. Starischka (ed.), *Leistungssport — Informationen zum Training* (Beiheft 9), pp. 112-120. DSB Bundesausschuss Leistungssport, Berlin.

Index of Contributors

Adrian, Marlene J. (142)*
Dept. of Physical Education
University of Illinois, Urbana-
 Champaign
Urbana, IL 61801
USA

Baldi, Lucia (33)
Inst. di Fisiologia Umana, Scuola de
 Medicina dello Sport
Universita di Siena
Via Laterina 8
53100 Siena
Italy

Bambauer, B.C.N. (113)
Occidental College
1600 Campus Road
Los Angeles, CA 90041
USA

Berger, Jiri (281)
Neurological Clinic, Faculty Hospital
Plzen
Czechoslovakia

Bernink, M.J.E. (41, 51)
Dept. of Physiology
State University of Utrecht
Vondelllaan 24
3521 GG Utrecht
The Netherlands

Bolger, M. (62)
Irish Amateur Swimming Association
Dublin
Ireland

Bonifazi, Marco (33)
Inst. de Fisiologia Umana, Scuola di
 Medicina dello Sport
Universita di Siena
Via Latarina 8
53100 Siena
Italy

Bourgeois, Marc (96)
Venelle aux Quatre Noeuds 100
Université Libre de Bruxelles
1150 Brussels
Belgium

Caldwell, Jay E. (235)
5324 Keuka Court
Anchorage, AK 99504
USA

Carli, Giancarlo (33)
Inst. di Fisiologia Umana, Scuola di
 Medicina dello Sport
Universita di Siena
Via Laterina 8
53100 Siena
Italy

Caspel, Jon van (28)
Netherlands Sports Federation, Sports
 Medicine Dept.
Papendal
Arnhem
The Netherlands

*Page number of article appears in parentheses.

Hollander A. Peter   (1, 165)
Workgroup of Exercise Physiology and
  Health, Faculty of Physical Education
Free University
Vondelstraat 48
Amsterdam
The Netherlands

Holmér, Ingvar   (154, 258)
Dept. of Work Physiology
National Board of Occuptational Safety
  and Health
S-171 84 Solna
Sweden

Hopper, Robert T.   (113)
Health Management Associates
99 South Raymond Ave. Suite 605
Pasadena, CA 91105
USA

Houben, Marielle   (66)
Labo. Jeco
Catholic University of Louvain
Place P. de Coubertin 1
1348 Louvain-LaNeuve
Belgium

Huijing, Peter A.   (1)
Dept of Anatomy, Faculty of Physical
  Education
Free University
V.D. Boechorststraat 7
Amsterdam
The Netherlands

Huisveld, I.A.   (41)
Dept. of Physiology
State University of Utrecht
Vondellaan 24
3521 GG Utrecht
The Netherlands

Ingen Schenau, G.J. van   (165)
Dept. of Anatomy, Faculty of Physical
  Education
Free University
V.D. Boechorststraat 7
Amsterdam
The Netherlands

Jiskoot, Jan   (199)
Academy of Physical Education
Willinklaan 5
1067 SL Amsterdam
The Netherlands

Kanehisa, Hiroaki   (329)
Lab for Exercise Physiology and Biome-
  chanics, Faculty of Education
University of Tokyo
Hongo 7-3-1 Bunkyo ku
Tokyo
Japan

Kemper, Hans C.G.   (199)
University of Amsterdam
1E Const. Huygensstraat 20
1054 BW Amsterdam
The Netherlands

Lacour, J.R.   (293)
Lab. de Physiologie
U.E.R. de Médicine
30 Rue Ferdinand Gambon
42023 Saint-Etienne Cedex
France

Lavoie, Jean-Marc   (222, 228)
Dept. d'Education Physique
Universite de Montreal
Case Postal 6128 Succ A
Montreal, Quebec H3C 3J7
Canada

Léger, L.A.   (222)
Dept. d'Education Physique
Université de Montreal
Case Postale 6128 Succ A
Montreal, Quebec H3C 1J7
Canada

Letzelter, Helga   (315)
Johannes Gutenberg Universität, Mainz
Fachbereich Sport
Postfach 3980-Saarstrasze 21
6500 Mainz
West Germany

Lewillie, Léon   (7)
Laboratoire de l'Effort
Université Libre de Bruxelles
28 Avenue Paul Heger
B-1050 Bruxelles
Belgium

Lupo di Prisco, Concetta   (33)
Inst. di Fisiologia Umana, Scuola di
  Medicina dello Sport
Universita di Siena
Via Laterina 8
53100 Siena
Italy